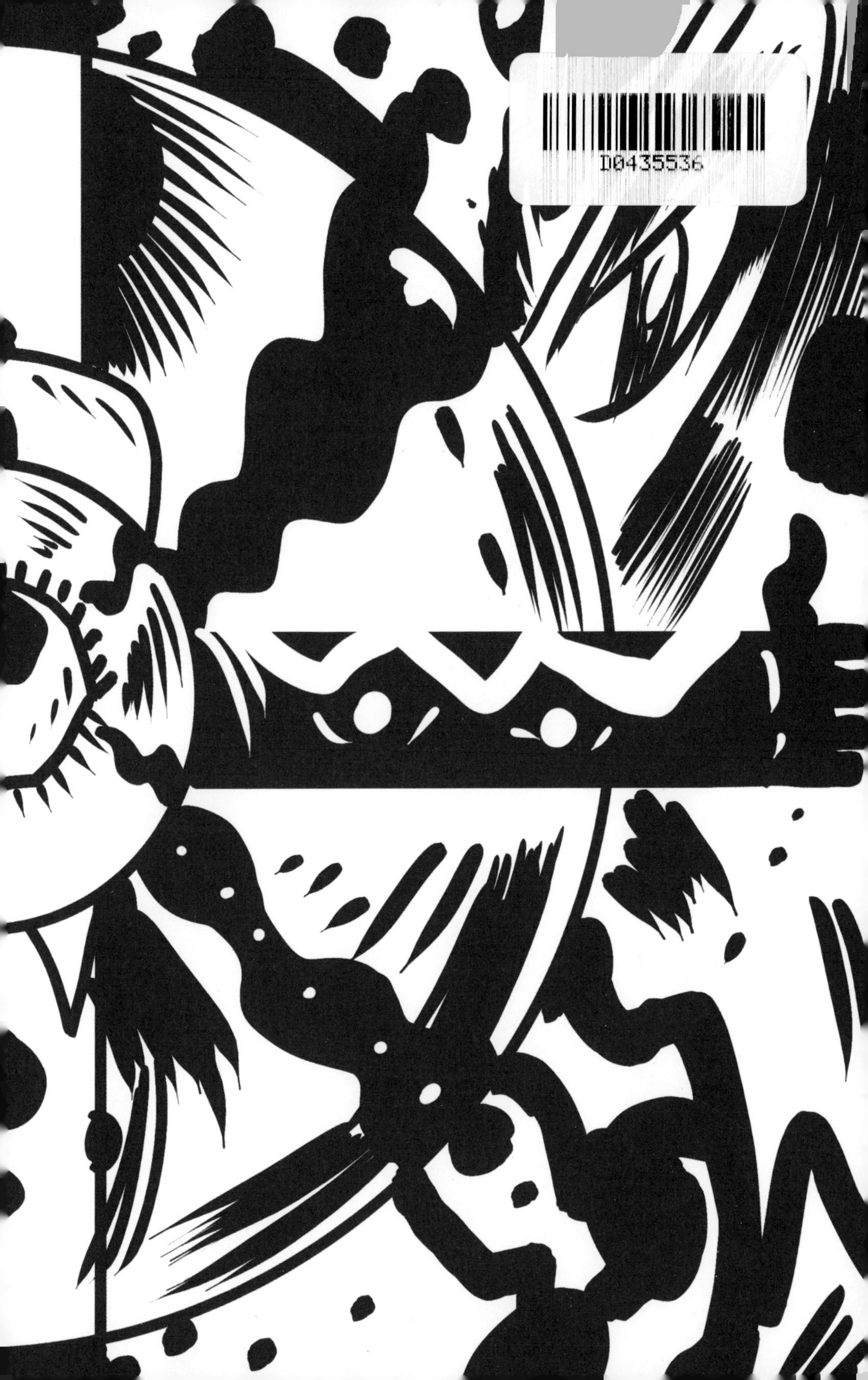

THE EIGHTFOLD PATH

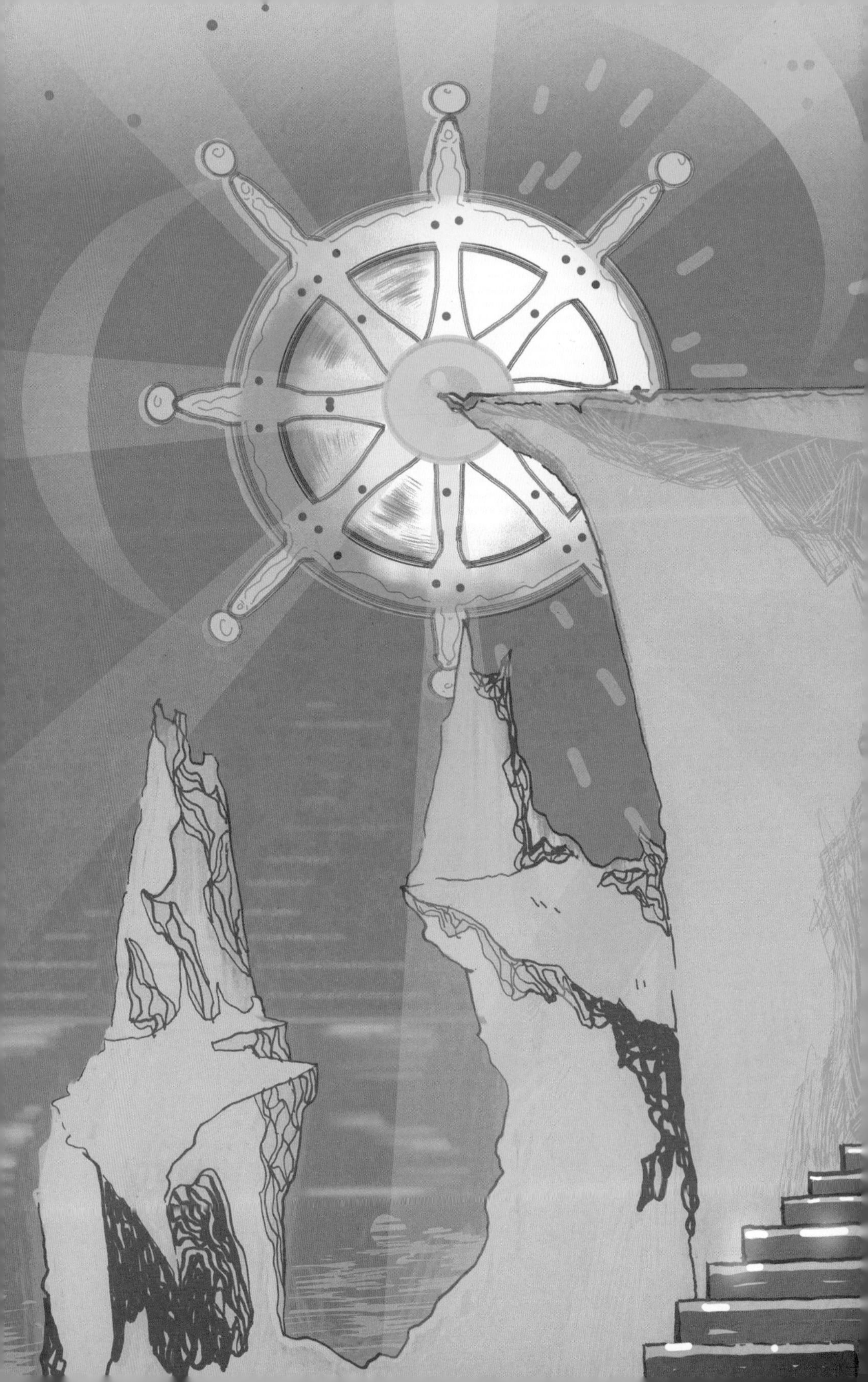

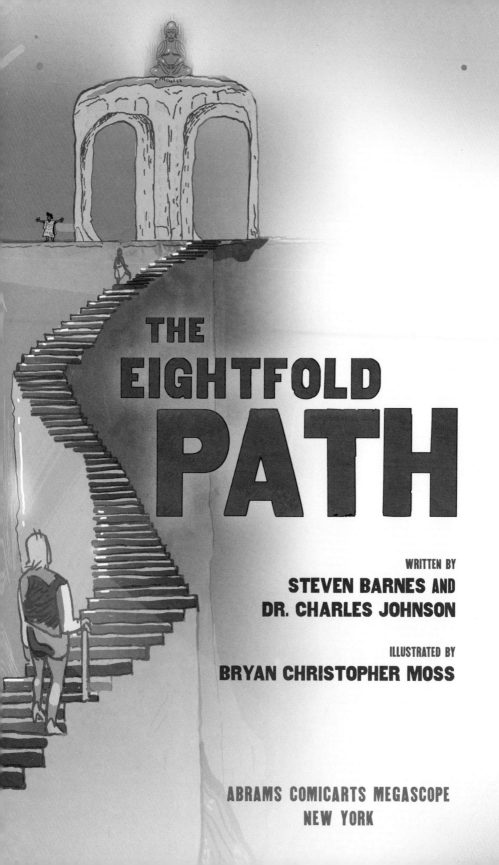

THE
EIGHTFOLD
PATH

WRITTEN BY
STEVEN BARNES AND
DR. CHARLES JOHNSON

ILLUSTRATED BY
BRYAN CHRISTOPHER MOSS

ABRAMS COMICARTS MEGASCOPE
NEW YORK

MEGASCOPE Curator: John Jennings
Editor: Charlotte Greenbaum
Assistant Editor: Jazmine Joyner
Designer: Charice Silverman
Production Manager: Alison Gervais
Lettering: Dave Sharpe

Library of Congress Cataloging Number 2021933728

ISBN 978-1-4197-4447-1

Printed and bound in China
10 9 8 7 6 5 4 3 2 1

Abrams ComicArts books are available at special
discounts when purchased in quantity
for premiums and promotions as well as fundraising
or educational use. Special editions can also be created
to specification. For details, contact specialsales@
abramsbooks.com or the address below.

Abrams ComicArts® is a registered
trademark of Harry N. Abrams, Inc.
MEGASCOPE® is a trademark of
John Jennings and Harry N. Abrams, Inc.

ABRAMS The Art of Books
195 Broadway, New York, NY 10007
abramsbooks.com

MEGASCOPE

MEGASCOPE is dedicated to show-
casing speculative works by and
about people of color, with a focus
on science fiction, fantasy, horror,
and stories of magical realism. The
megascope is a fictional device
imagined by W. E. B. Du Bois that
can peer through time and space
into other realities. This magical
invention represents the idea that so
much of our collective past has not
seen the light of day, and that there
is so much history that we have yet to
discover. MEGASCOPE will serve as a
lens through which we can broaden
our view of history, the present, and
the future, and as a method by which
previously unheard voices can find
their way to an ever-growing diverse
audience.

For **WILLIAM GAINES**,
publisher of Tales From the Crypt and Weird Science comics—
a man who, like Shakespeare, understood that the High and
the Low are necessary parts of the same continuum
—S.B. and C.J.

This book is dedicated to my parents, **LESLIE ANN MOSS**
and **FRANK BELL MOSS**, and the rest of the Moss family
—B.C.M.

"IT IS YOUR MIND THAT
CREATES THIS WORLD."

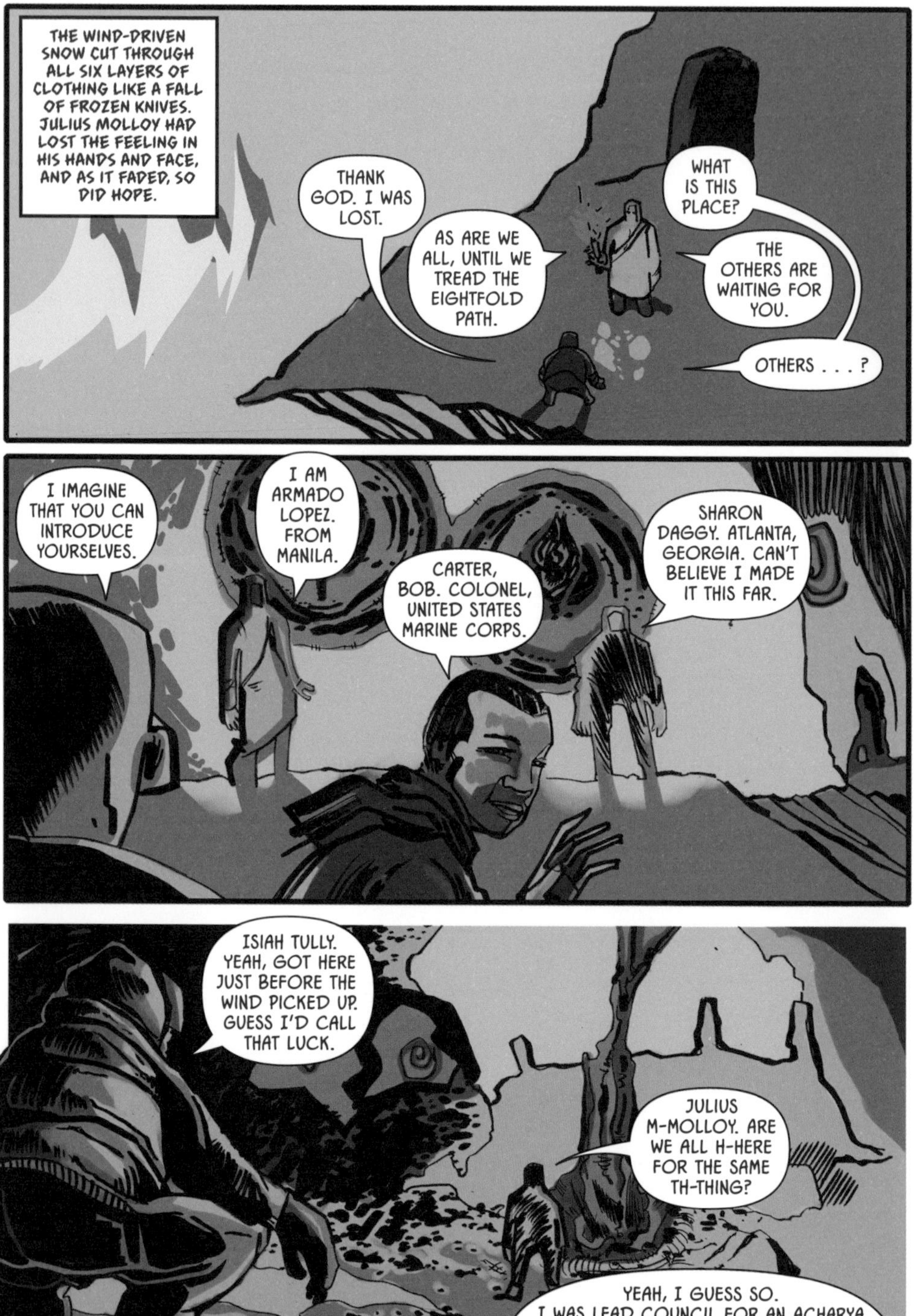
THE WIND-DRIVEN SNOW CUT THROUGH ALL SIX LAYERS OF CLOTHING LIKE A FALL OF FROZEN KNIVES. JULIUS MOLLOY HAD LOST THE FEELING IN HIS HANDS AND FACE, AND AS IT FADED, SO DID HOPE.
THANK GOD. I WAS LOST.
AS ARE WE ALL, UNTIL WE TREAD THE EIGHTFOLD PATH.
WHAT IS THIS PLACE?
THE OTHERS ARE WAITING FOR YOU.
OTHERS . . . ?
I IMAGINE THAT YOU CAN INTRODUCE YOURSELVES.
I AM ARMADO LOPEZ. FROM MANILA.
CARTER, BOB. COLONEL, UNITED STATES MARINE CORPS.
SHARON DAGGY. ATLANTA, GEORGIA. CAN'T BELIEVE I MADE IT THIS FAR.
ISIAH TULLY. YEAH, GOT HERE JUST BEFORE THE WIND PICKED UP. GUESS I'D CALL THAT LUCK.
JULIUS M-MOLLOY. ARE WE ALL H-HERE FOR THE SAME TH-THING?
YEAH, I GUESS SO. I WAS LEAD COUNCIL FOR AN ACHARYA BODHI MEDITATION CENTER IN THAILAND. I REMEMBER ACHARYA SAYIN' THAT WE'RE ALL ON THE PATH, WHETHER WE KNOW IT OR NOT. AND NO TWO PEOPLE WALK IT EXACTLY THE SAME WAY. SO . . . I'M HERE TO START WALKING.

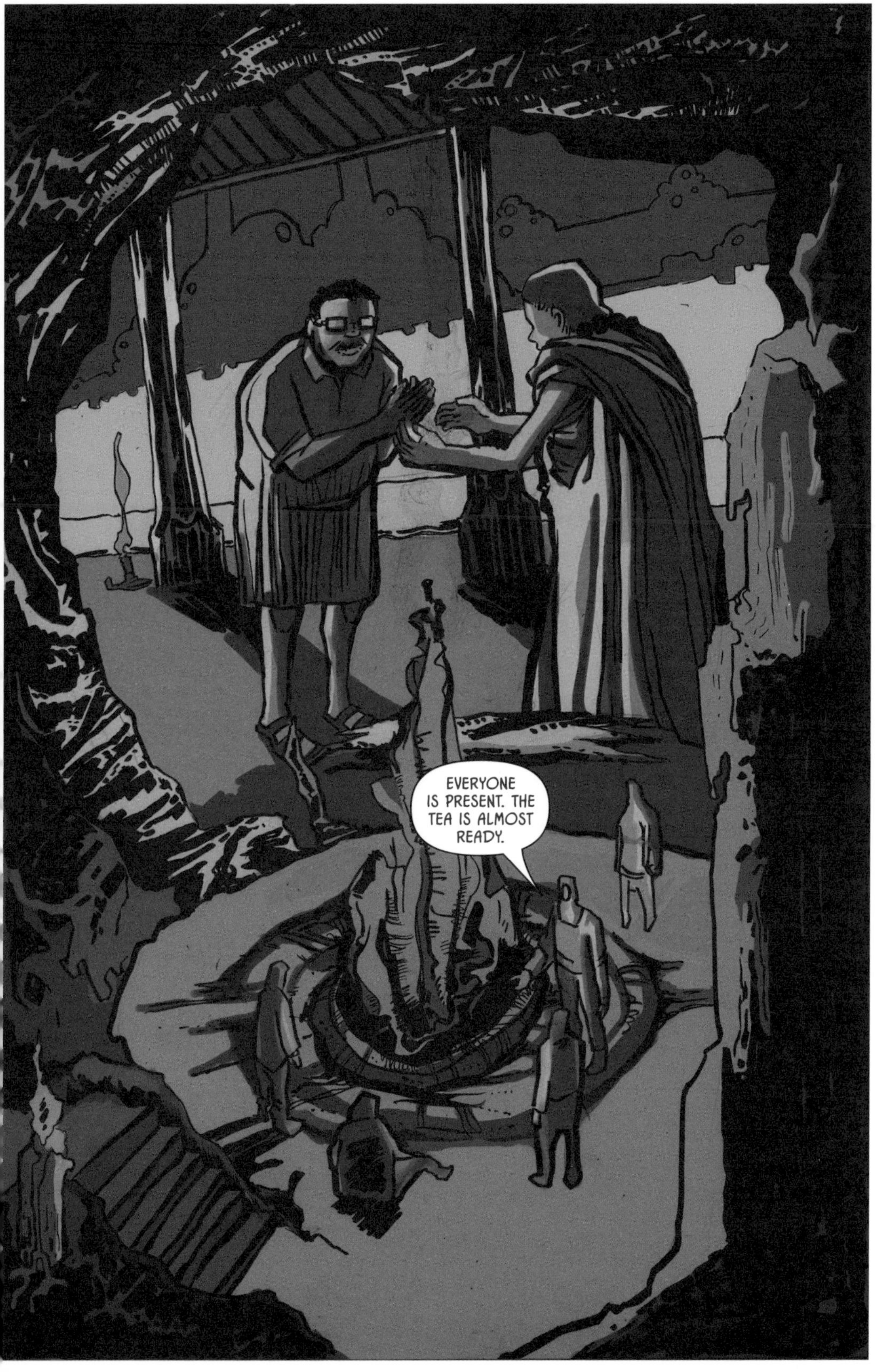
EVERYONE IS PRESENT. THE TEA IS ALMOST READY.

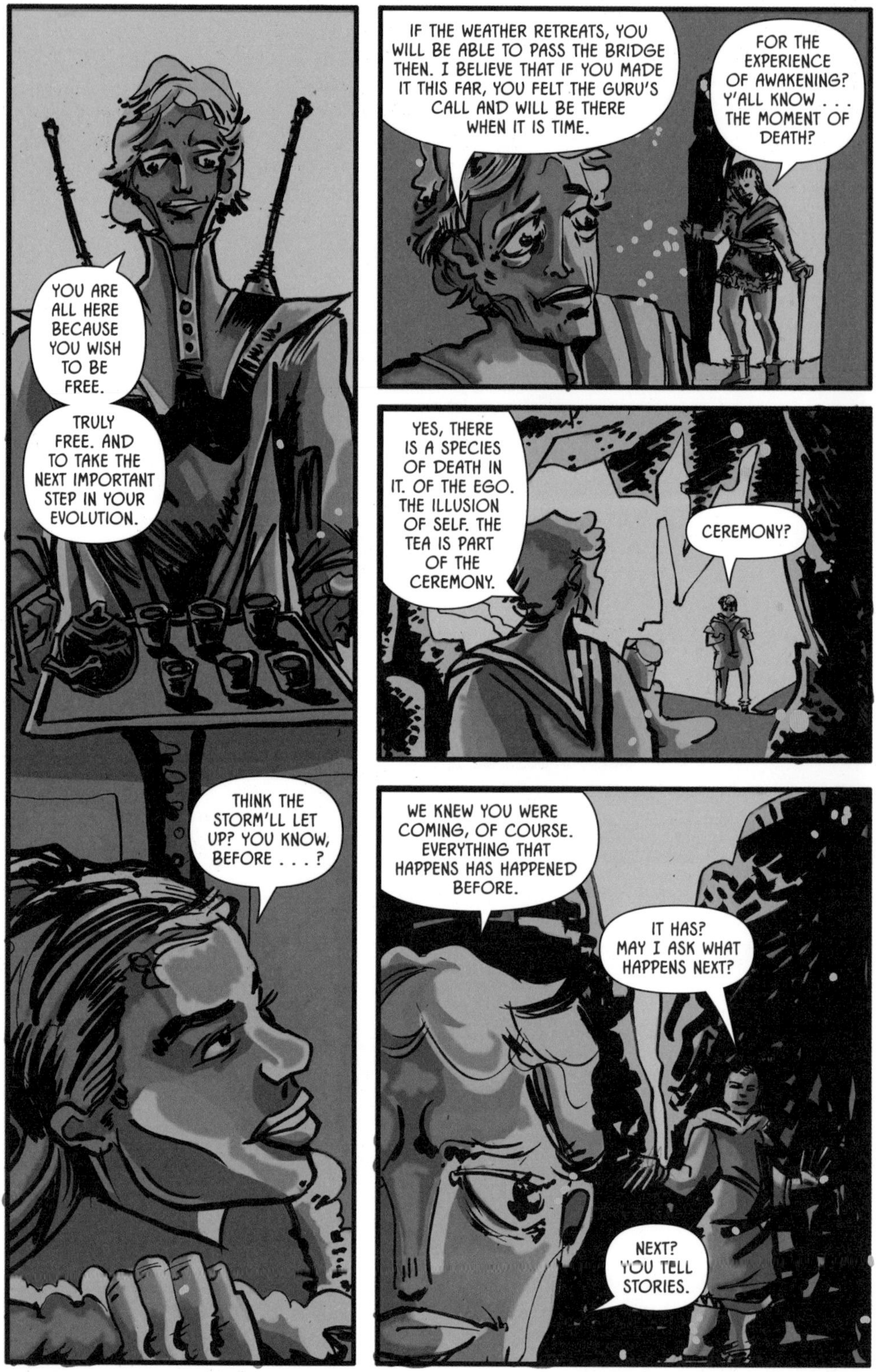
YOU ARE ALL HERE BECAUSE YOU WISH TO BE FREE.
TRULY FREE. AND TO TAKE THE NEXT IMPORTANT STEP IN YOUR EVOLUTION.
THINK THE STORM'LL LET UP? YOU KNOW, BEFORE . . . ?
IF THE WEATHER RETREATS, YOU WILL BE ABLE TO PASS THE BRIDGE THEN. I BELIEVE THAT IF YOU MADE IT THIS FAR, YOU FELT THE GURU'S CALL AND WILL BE THERE WHEN IT IS TIME.
FOR THE EXPERIENCE OF AWAKENING? Y'ALL KNOW . . . THE MOMENT OF DEATH?
YES, THERE IS A SPECIES OF DEATH IN IT. OF THE EGO. THE ILLUSION OF SELF. THE TEA IS PART OF THE CEREMONY.
CEREMONY?
WE KNEW YOU WERE COMING, OF COURSE. EVERYTHING THAT HAPPENS HAS HAPPENED BEFORE.
IT HAS? MAY I ASK WHAT HAPPENS NEXT?
NEXT? YOU TELL STORIES.

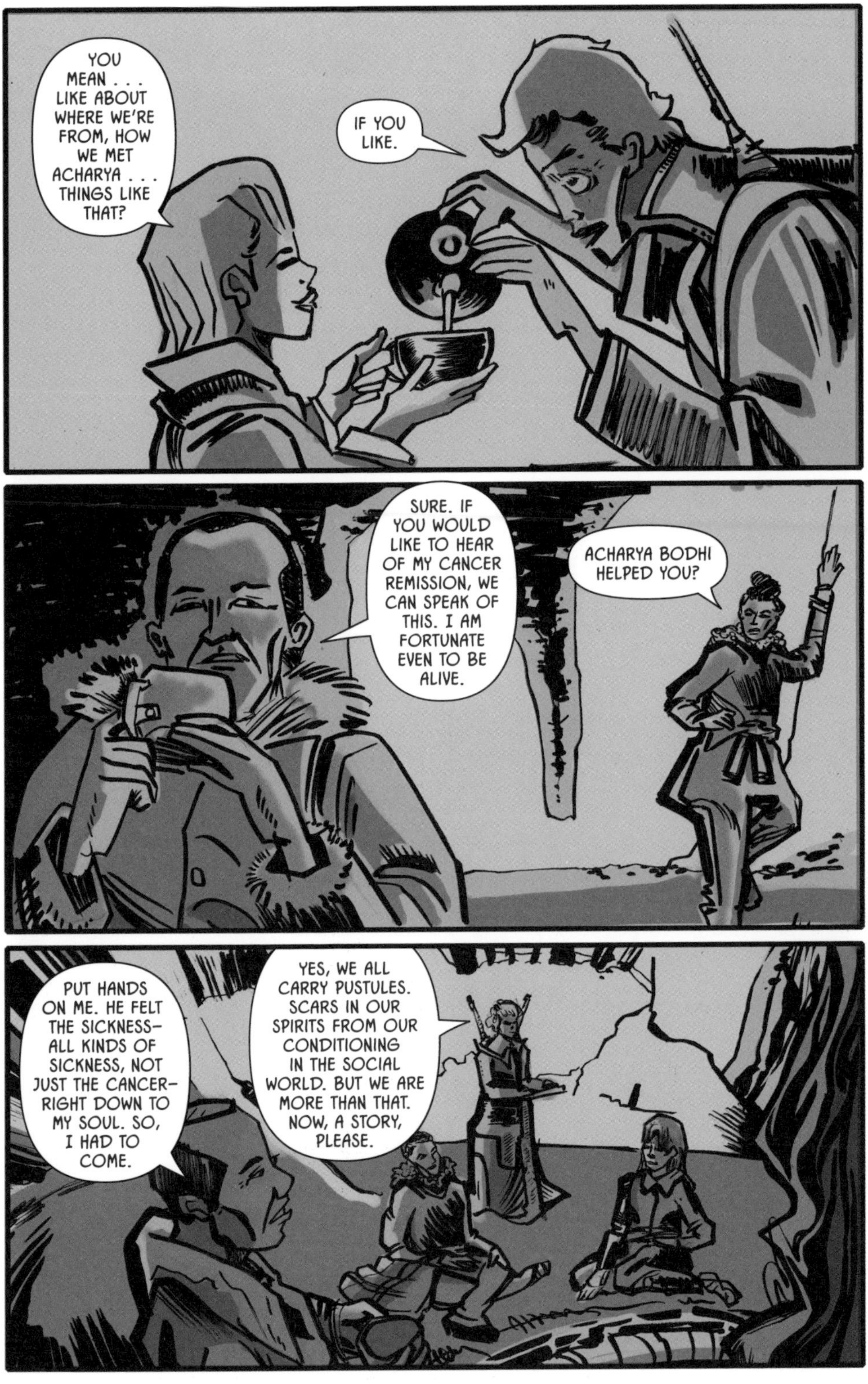
YOU MEAN . . . LIKE ABOUT WHERE WE'RE FROM, HOW WE MET ACHARYA . . . THINGS LIKE THAT?
IF YOU LIKE.
SURE. IF YOU WOULD LIKE TO HEAR OF MY CANCER REMISSION, WE CAN SPEAK OF THIS. I AM FORTUNATE EVEN TO BE ALIVE.
ACHARYA BODHI HELPED YOU?
PUT HANDS ON ME. HE FELT THE SICKNESS—ALL KINDS OF SICKNESS, NOT JUST THE CANCER—RIGHT DOWN TO MY SOUL. SO, I HAD TO COME.
YES, WE ALL CARRY PUSTULES. SCARS IN OUR SPIRITS FROM OUR CONDITIONING IN THE SOCIAL WORLD. BUT WE ARE MORE THAN THAT. NOW, A STORY, PLEASE.

BUT WHAT IF WE DO SOMETHING DIFFERENT?

DIFFERENT HOW?

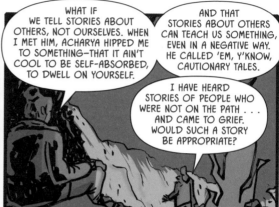

WHAT IF WE TELL STORIES ABOUT OTHERS, NOT OURSELVES. WHEN I MET HIM, ACHARYA HIPPED ME TO SOMETHING—THAT IT AIN'T COOL TO BE SELF-ABSORBED, TO DWELL ON YOURSELF.

AND THAT STORIES ABOUT OTHERS CAN TEACH US SOMETHING, EVEN IN A NEGATIVE WAY. HE CALLED 'EM, Y'KNOW, CAUTIONARY TALES.

I HAVE HEARD STORIES OF PEOPLE WHO WERE NOT ON THE PATH . . . AND CAME TO GRIEF. WOULD SUCH A STORY BE APPROPRIATE?

IF THEY CAN TEACH US SOMETHING, HELP US WALK THIS "PATH" BETTER, WHY NOT?

SO, WHO GOES FIRST?

I'M NOT SO GOOD AT STORYTELLING, BUT MY SON—HE'S TWELVE—SLIPPED THIS INTO MY BACKPACK TO GIVE ME SOMETHING TO READ WHILE I WAS TRAVELING.

I COULD READ YOU A STORY FROM THIS.

ALL THE STORIES ARE TOLD BY SOMEONE CALLED THE SWAMP WOMAN...

CREEP VAULT

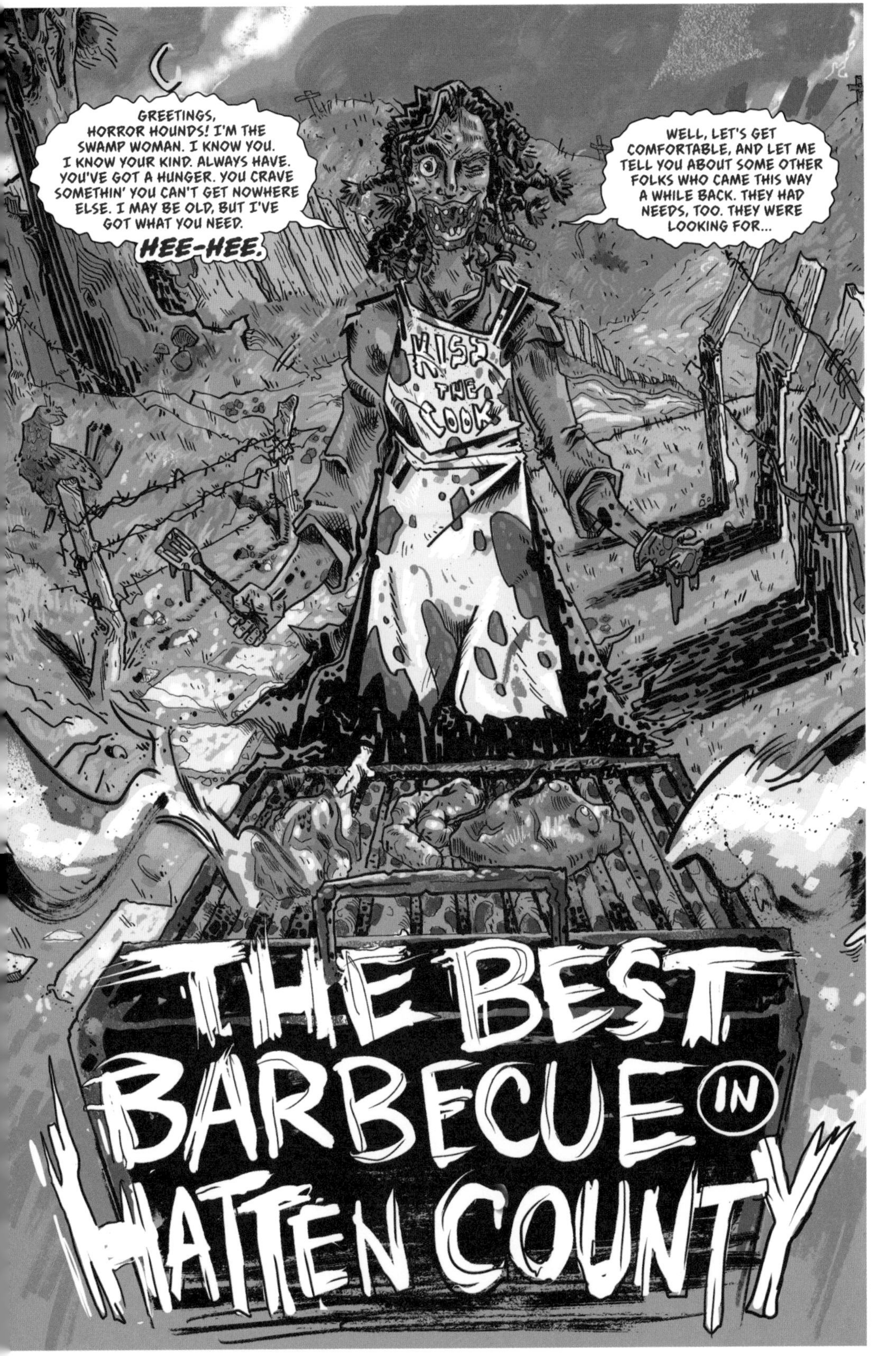
GREETINGS, HORROR HOUNDS! I'M THE SWAMP WOMAN. I KNOW YOU. I KNOW YOUR KIND. ALWAYS HAVE. YOU'VE GOT A HUNGER. YOU CRAVE SOMETHIN' YOU CAN'T GET NOWHERE ELSE. I MAY BE OLD, BUT I'VE GOT WHAT YOU NEED.
HEE-HEE.
WELL, LET'S GET COMFORTABLE, AND LET ME TELL YOU ABOUT SOME OTHER FOLKS WHO CAME THIS WAY A WHILE BACK. THEY HAD NEEDS, TOO. THEY WERE LOOKING FOR...
KISS THE COOK
THE BEST BARBECUE IN HATTEN COUNTY

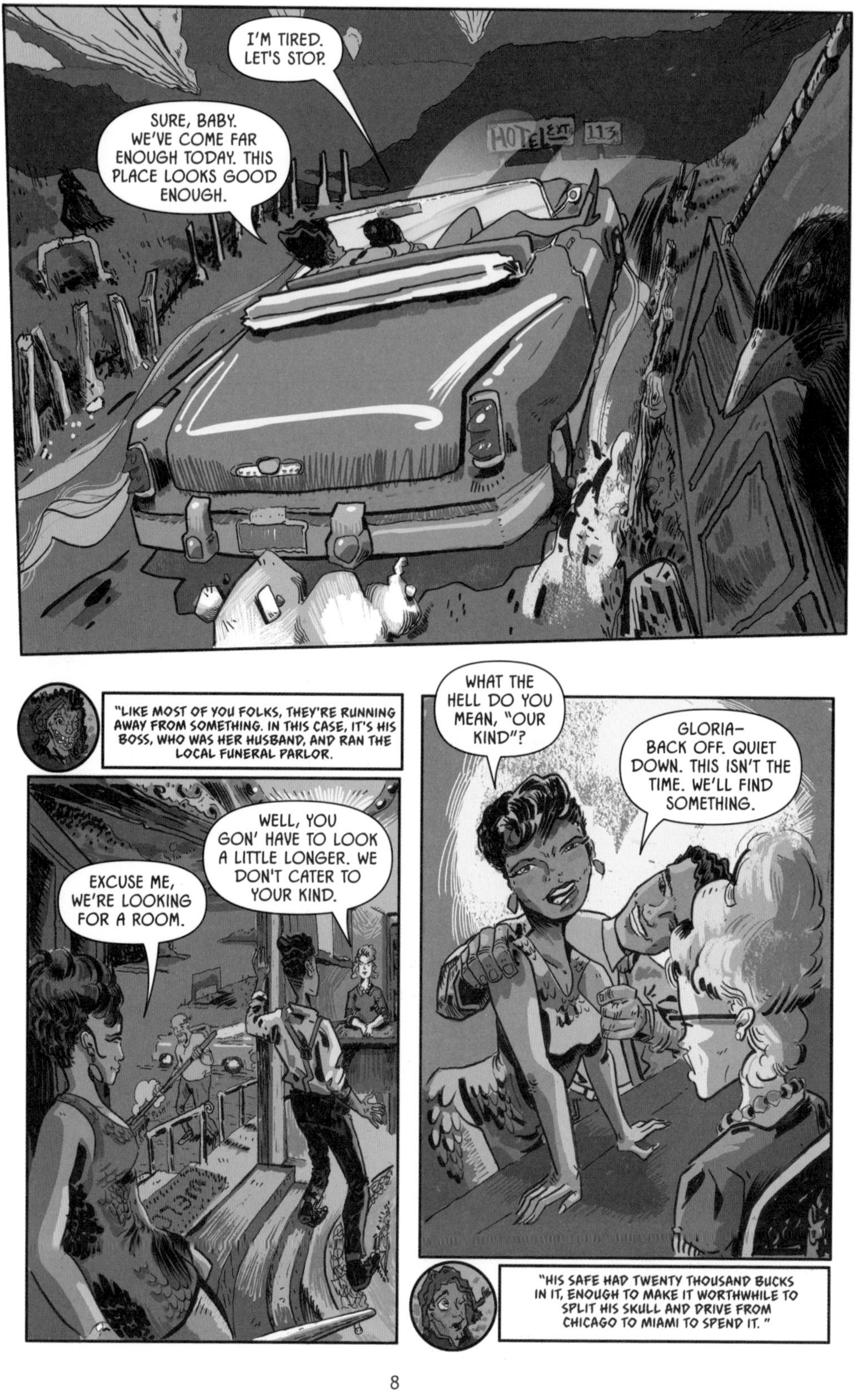
I'M TIRED. LET'S STOP.
SURE, BABY. WE'VE COME FAR ENOUGH TODAY. THIS PLACE LOOKS GOOD ENOUGH.
HOTEL
EXT 113
"LIKE MOST OF YOU FOLKS, THEY'RE RUNNING AWAY FROM SOMETHING. IN THIS CASE, IT'S HIS BOSS, WHO WAS HER HUSBAND, AND RAN THE LOCAL FUNERAL PARLOR.
EXCUSE ME, WE'RE LOOKING FOR A ROOM.
WELL, YOU GON' HAVE TO LOOK A LITTLE LONGER. WE DON'T CATER TO YOUR KIND.
WHAT THE HELL DO YOU MEAN, "OUR KIND"?
GLORIA— BACK OFF. QUIET DOWN. THIS ISN'T THE TIME. WE'LL FIND SOMETHING.
"HIS SAFE HAD TWENTY THOUSAND BUCKS IN IT, ENOUGH TO MAKE IT WORTHWHILE TO SPLIT HIS SKULL AND DRIVE FROM CHICAGO TO MIAMI TO SPEND IT."

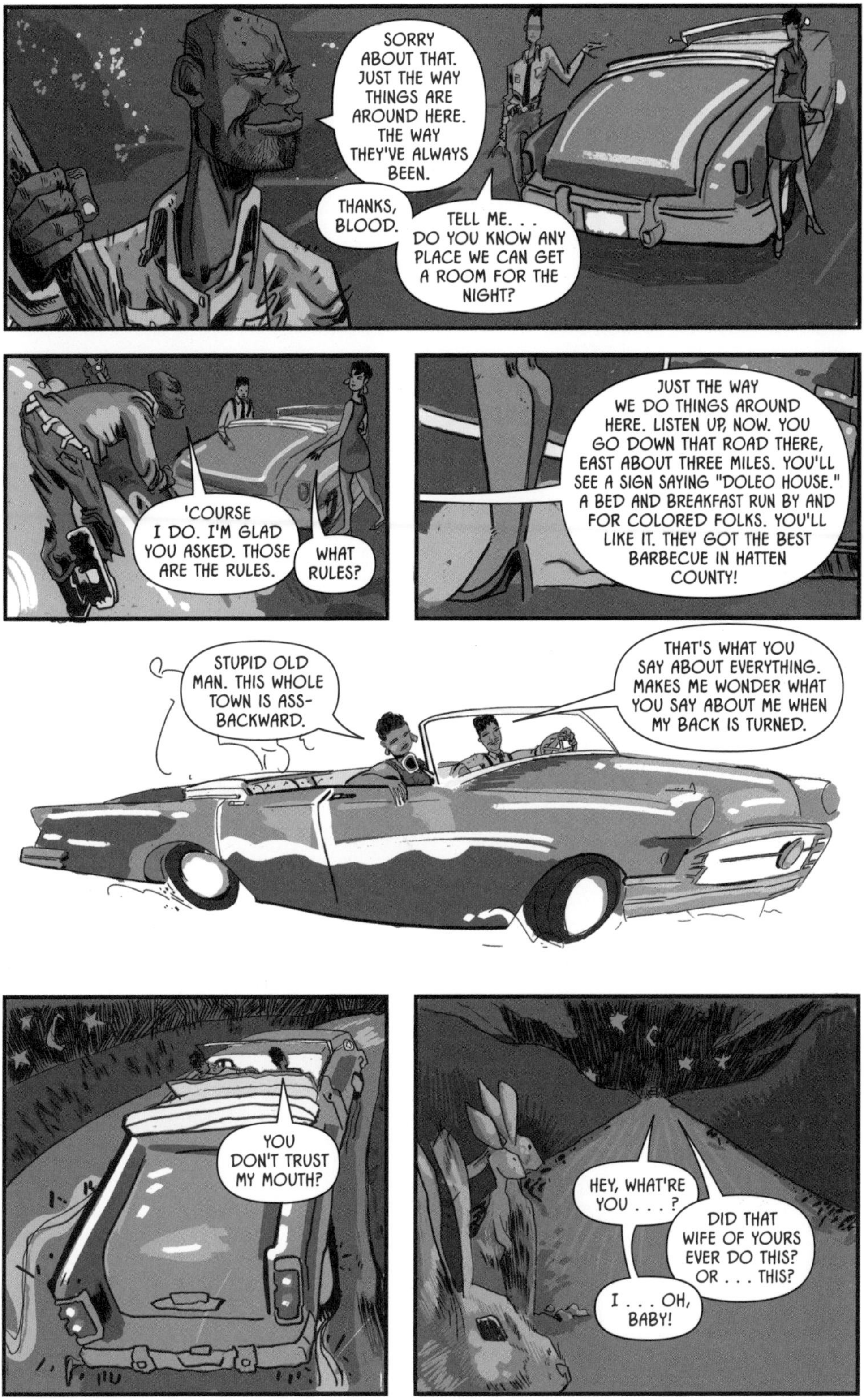
SORRY ABOUT THAT. JUST THE WAY THINGS ARE AROUND HERE. THE WAY THEY'VE ALWAYS BEEN.
THANKS, BLOOD.
TELL ME. . . DO YOU KNOW ANY PLACE WE CAN GET A ROOM FOR THE NIGHT?
'COURSE I DO. I'M GLAD YOU ASKED. THOSE ARE THE RULES.
WHAT RULES?
JUST THE WAY WE DO THINGS AROUND HERE. LISTEN UP, NOW. YOU GO DOWN THAT ROAD THERE, EAST ABOUT THREE MILES. YOU'LL SEE A SIGN SAYING "DOLEO HOUSE." A BED AND BREAKFAST RUN BY AND FOR COLORED FOLKS. YOU'LL LIKE IT. THEY GOT THE BEST BARBECUE IN HATTEN COUNTY!
STUPID OLD MAN. THIS WHOLE TOWN IS ASS-BACKWARD.
THAT'S WHAT YOU SAY ABOUT EVERYTHING. MAKES ME WONDER WHAT YOU SAY ABOUT ME WHEN MY BACK IS TURNED.
YOU DON'T TRUST MY MOUTH?
HEY, WHAT'RE YOU . . . ?
DID THAT WIFE OF YOURS EVER DO THIS? OR . . . THIS?
I . . . OH, BABY!

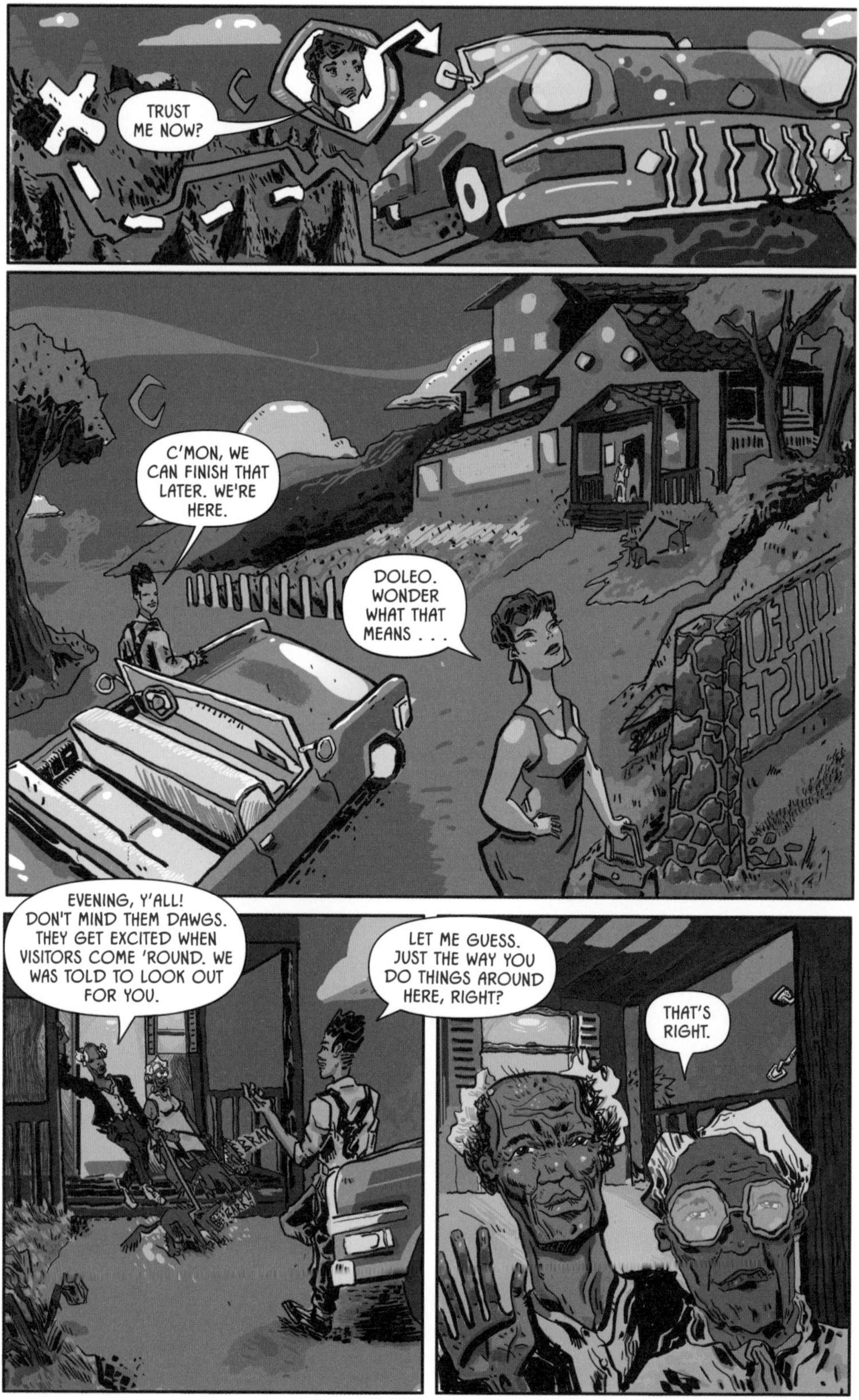
TRUST ME NOW?
C'MON, WE CAN FINISH THAT LATER. WE'RE HERE.
DOLEO. WONDER WHAT THAT MEANS . . .
EVENING, Y'ALL! DON'T MIND THEM DAWGS. THEY GET EXCITED WHEN VISITORS COME 'ROUND. WE WAS TOLD TO LOOK OUT FOR YOU.
LET ME GUESS. JUST THE WAY YOU DO THINGS AROUND HERE, RIGHT?
THAT'S RIGHT.

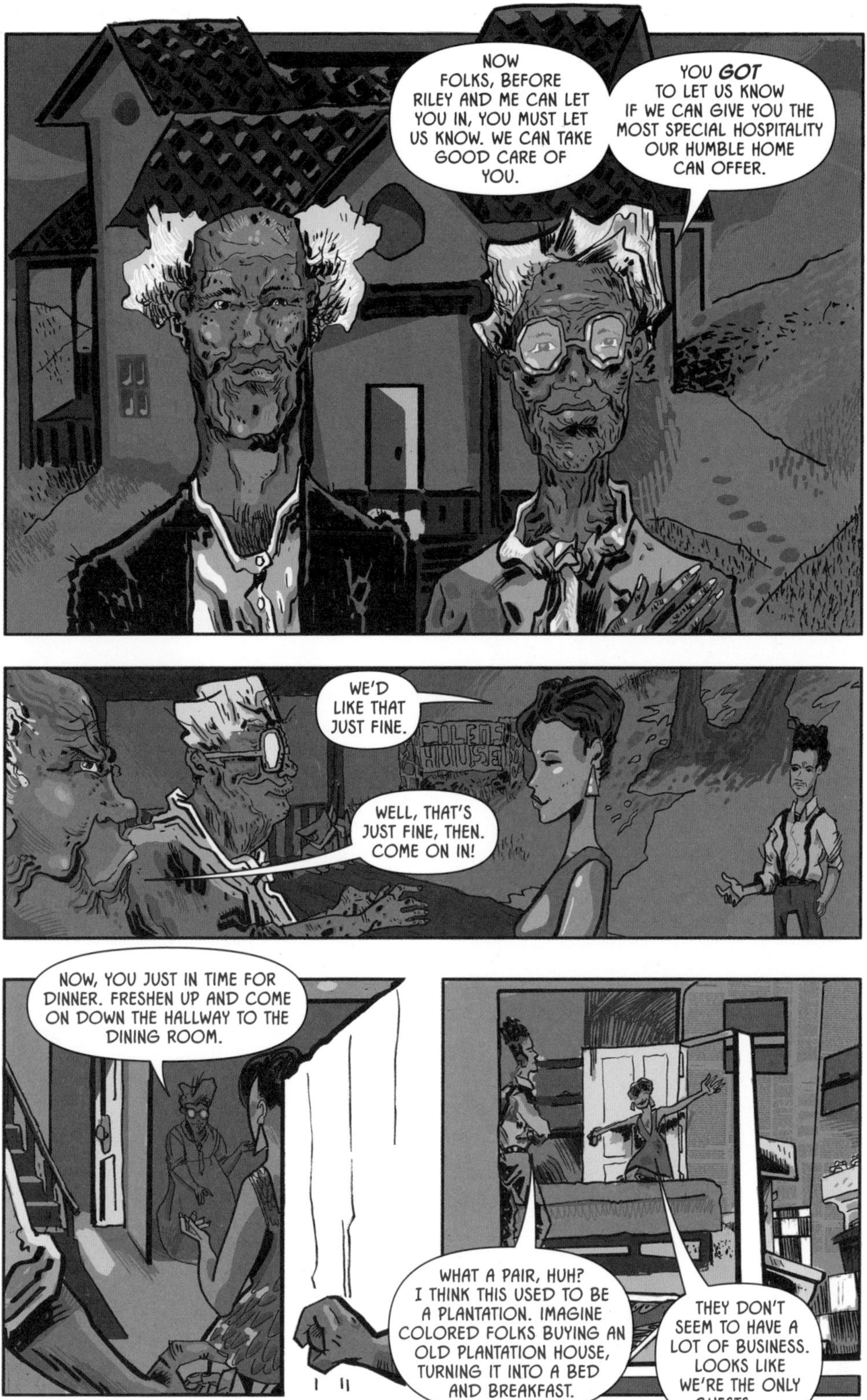
NOW FOLKS, BEFORE RILEY AND ME CAN LET YOU IN, YOU MUST LET US KNOW. WE CAN TAKE GOOD CARE OF YOU.
YOU ***GOT*** TO LET US KNOW IF WE CAN GIVE YOU THE MOST SPECIAL HOSPITALITY OUR HUMBLE HOME CAN OFFER.
WE'D LIKE THAT JUST FINE.
WELL, THAT'S JUST FINE, THEN. COME ON IN!
NOW, YOU JUST IN TIME FOR DINNER. FRESHEN UP AND COME ON DOWN THE HALLWAY TO THE DINING ROOM.
WHAT A PAIR, HUH? I THINK THIS USED TO BE A PLANTATION. IMAGINE COLORED FOLKS BUYING AN OLD PLANTATION HOUSE, TURNING IT INTO A BED AND BREAKFAST.
THEY DON'T SEEM TO HAVE A LOT OF BUSINESS. LOOKS LIKE WE'RE THE ONLY GUESTS . . .

PROBABLY WHY THEY'RE SO FRIENDLY. LOOK AT THIS! BIBLE VERSES ON THE WALLPAPER.

BIBLE BY THE BED.

YOU WILL *NOT* BELIEVE THIS! LOOK!

THERE'S SCRIPTURE PRINTED ON THE TOILET PAPER, TOO. GUESS THE IDEA IS THAT WE READ IT WHILE WE SQUAT?

WELL, LET'S GET DOWN TO DINNER!

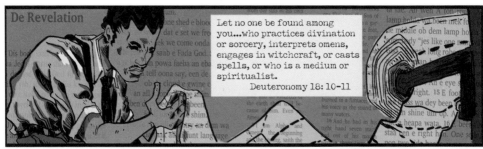

De Revelation

Let no one be found among you...who practices divination or sorcery, interprets omens, engages in witchcraft, or casts spells, or who is a medium or spiritualist.
Deuteronomy 18: 10-11

NOW, THAT *IS* DELICIOUS BARBECUE. THE SAUCE IS SO TANGY. I HATE TO ASK— BUT IS THAT BEEF OR PORK?

YOU JEWISH?

HELL NO!

THEN DON'T WORRY NONE.

BET THEY DON'T LIKE JEWS AROUND HERE MUCH. DON'T TAKE TO COLORED, NEITHER.

YES, THINGS ARE SLOW TO CHANGE AROUND HERE. SOME THINGS BARELY CHANGE AT ALL.

SO, WHAT'S THE STORY OF THIS PLACE?

BEEN IN THE FAMILY A LONG TIME. WE BEEN HERE, SEEMS FOREVER.

THERE'S A LITTLE BOOK BY THE SIDE OF YO' BED. IT'S A SILLY FANTASY THING, BUT I RECKON IT HAS JUST ENOUGH TRUTH IN IT TO GIVE YOU A LITTLE HISTORY. NOW, Y'ALL EAT UP, HEAR?

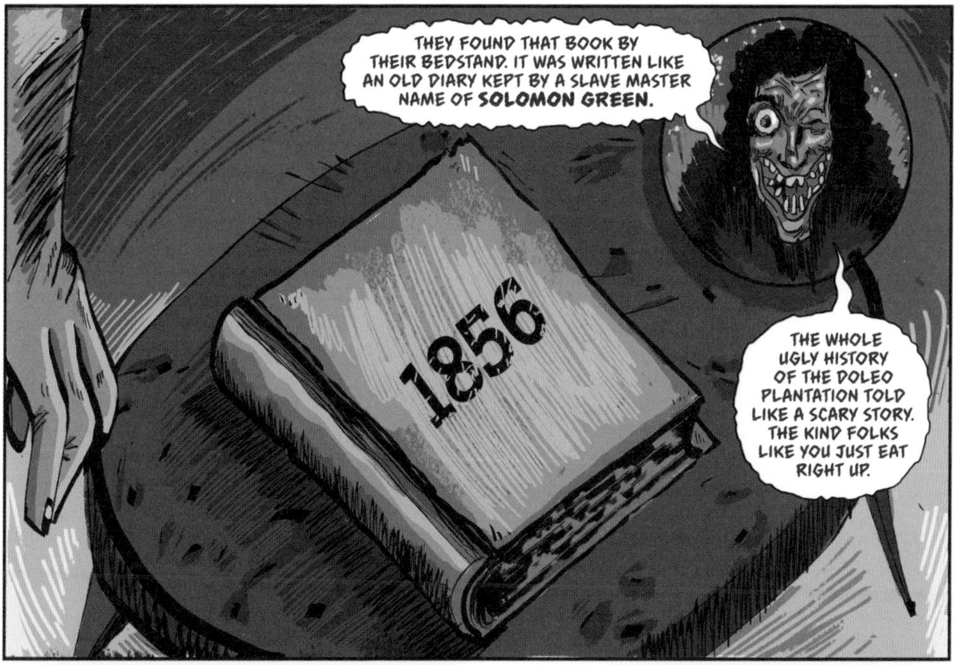
THEY FOUND THAT BOOK BY THEIR BEDSTAND. IT WAS WRITTEN LIKE AN OLD DIARY KEPT BY A SLAVE MASTER NAME OF **SOLOMON GREEN.**
1856
THE WHOLE UGLY HISTORY OF THE DOLEO PLANTATION TOLD LIKE A SCARY STORY. THE KIND FOLKS LIKE YOU JUST EAT RIGHT UP.

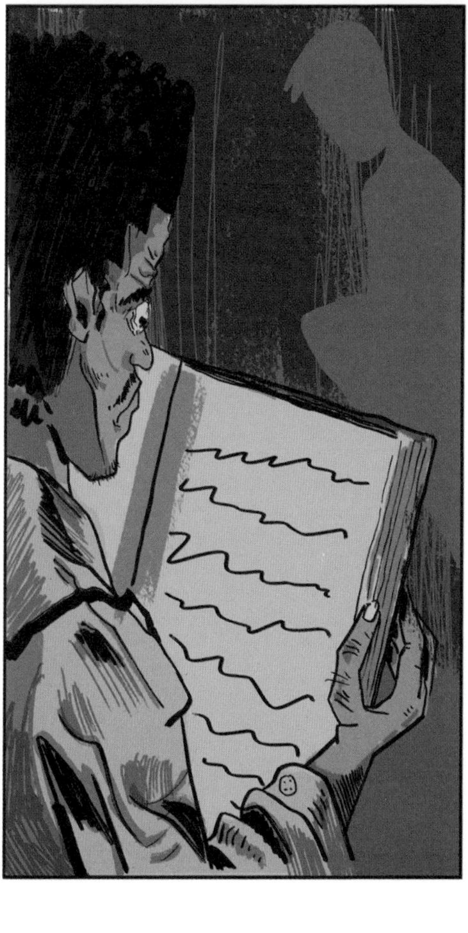

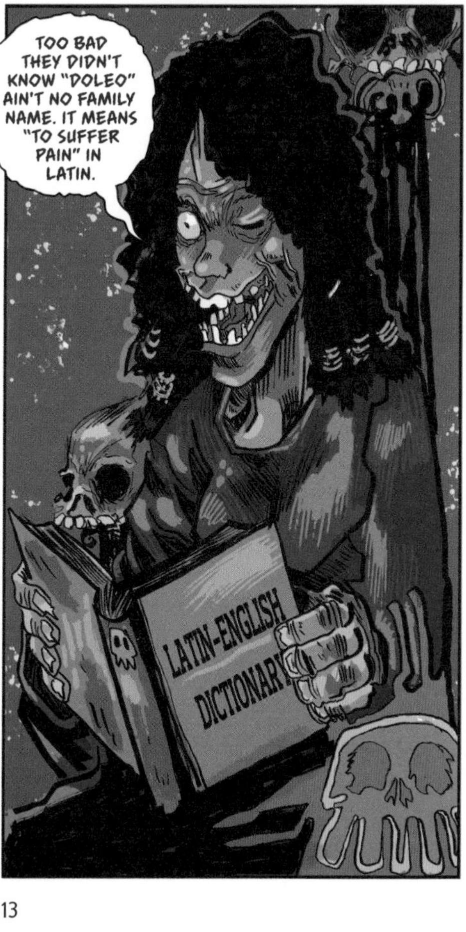
TOO BAD THEY DIDN'T KNOW "DOLEO" AIN'T NO FAMILY NAME. IT MEANS "TO SUFFER PAIN" IN LATIN.
LATIN-ENGLISH DICTIONARY

DOLEO PLANTATION, 1801

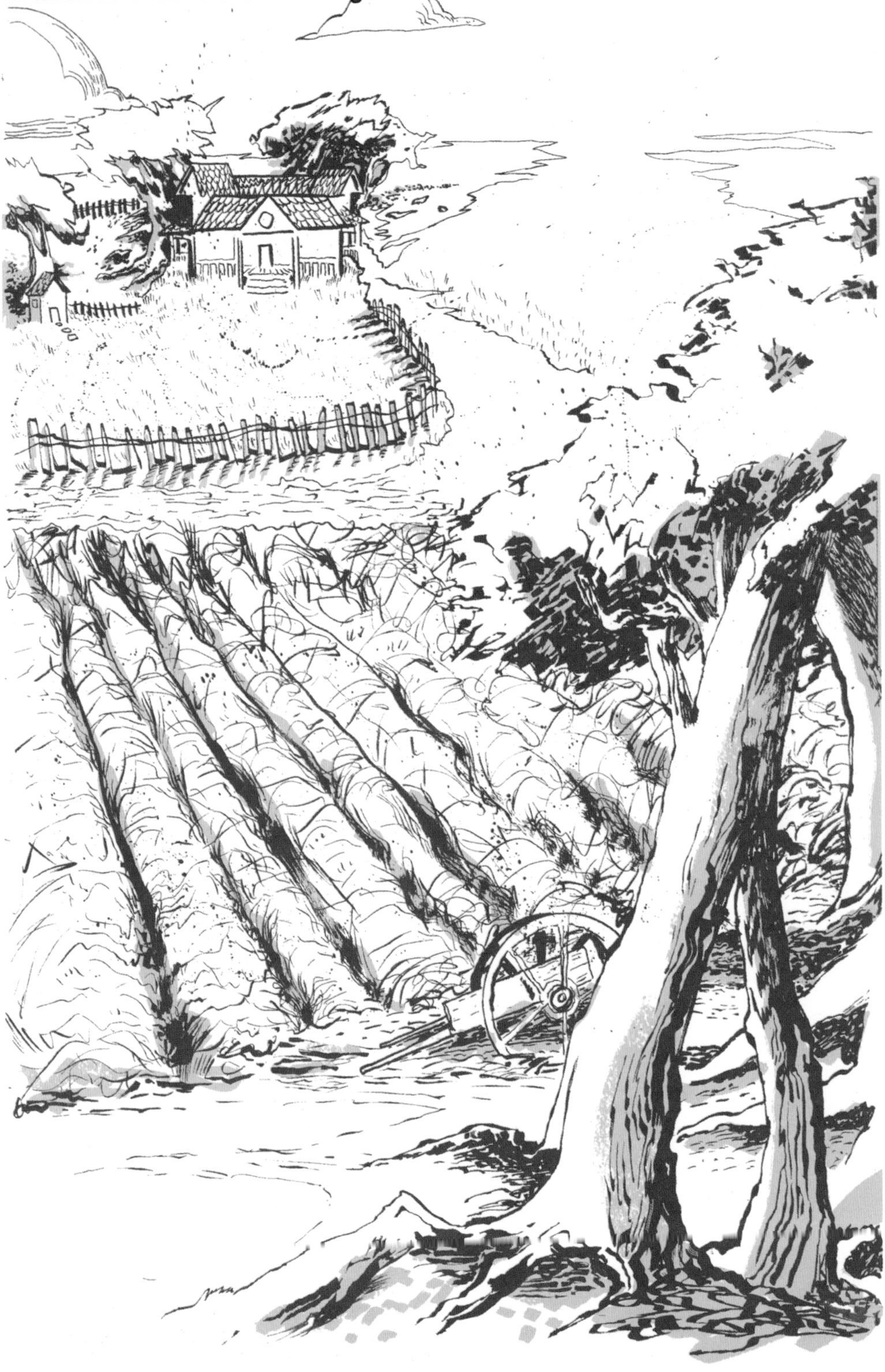

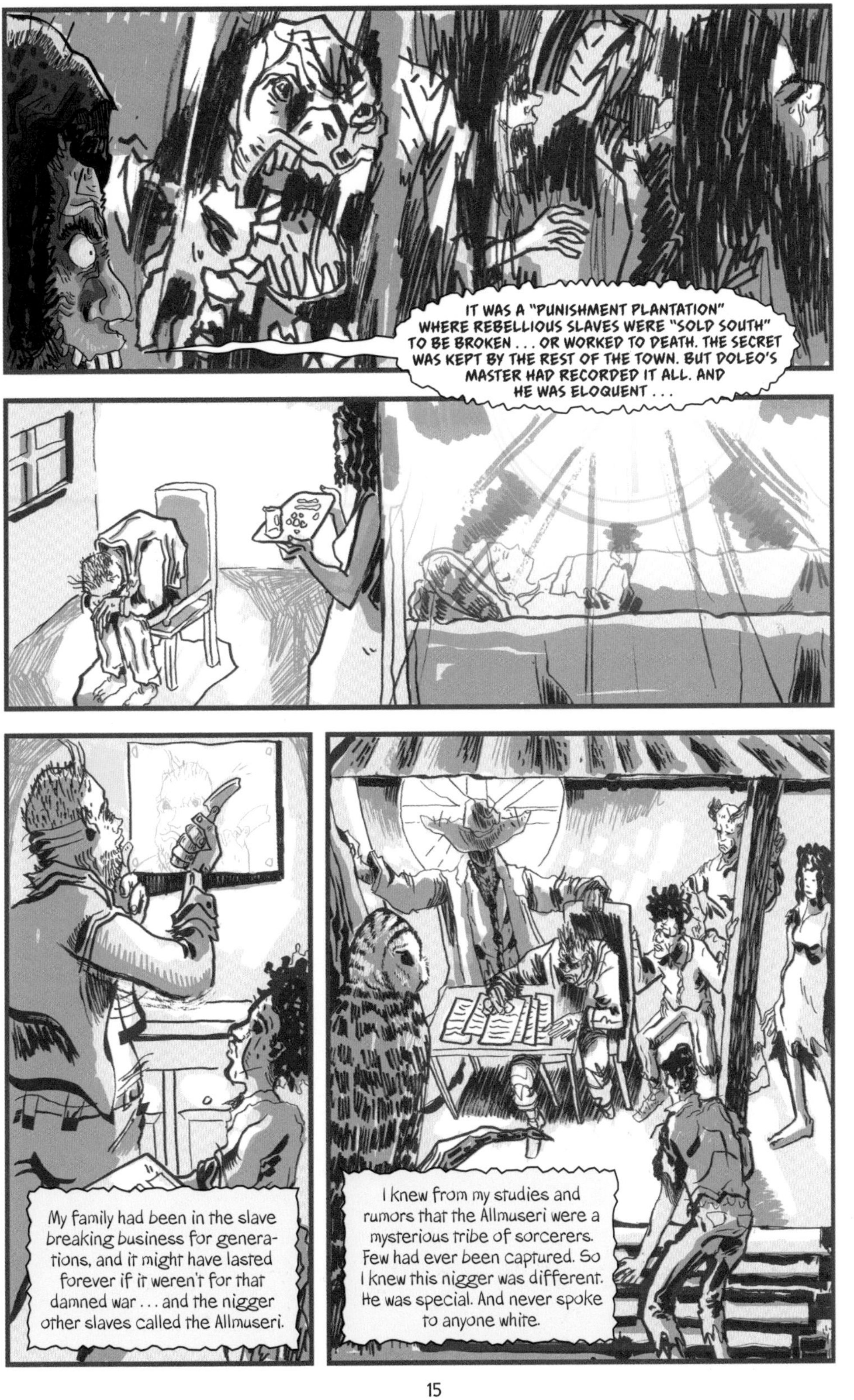

IT WAS A "PUNISHMENT PLANTATION" WHERE REBELLIOUS SLAVES WERE "SOLD SOUTH" TO BE BROKEN . . . OR WORKED TO DEATH. THE SECRET WAS KEPT BY THE REST OF THE TOWN. BUT DOLEO'S MASTER HAD RECORDED IT ALL. AND HE WAS ELOQUENT . . .
My family had been in the slave breaking business for generations, and it might have lasted forever if it weren't for that damned war . . . and the nigger other slaves called the Allmuseri.
I knew from my studies and rumors that the Allmuseri were a mysterious tribe of sorcerers. Few had ever been captured. So I knew this nigger was different. He was special. And never spoke to anyone white.

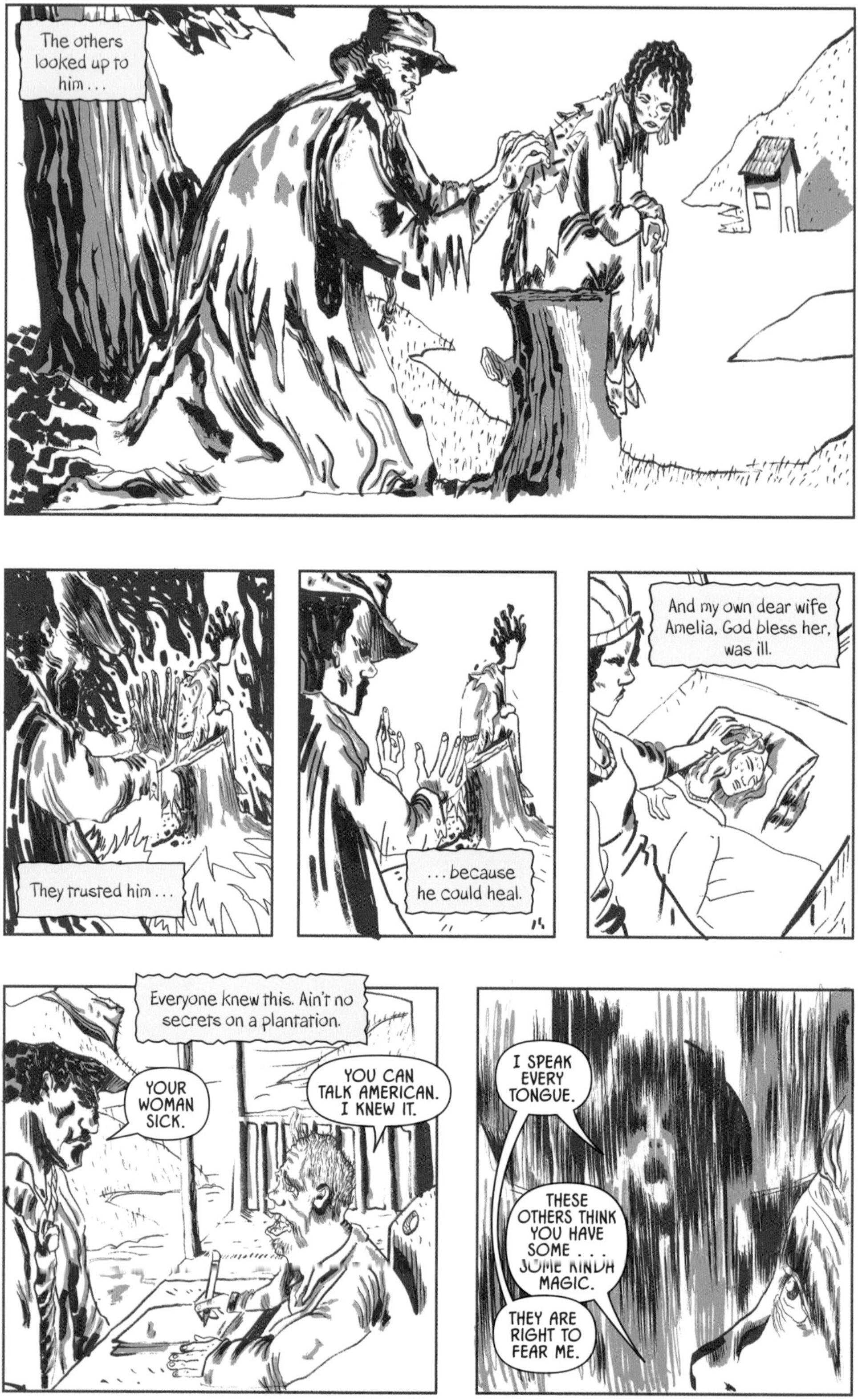
The others looked up to him . . .
They trusted him . . .
. . . because he could heal.
And my own dear wife Amelia, God bless her, was ill.
Everyone knew this. Ain't no secrets on a plantation.
YOUR WOMAN SICK.
YOU CAN TALK AMERICAN. I KNEW IT.
I SPEAK EVERY TONGUE.
THESE OTHERS THINK YOU HAVE SOME . . . SOME KINDA MAGIC.
THEY ARE RIGHT TO FEAR ME.

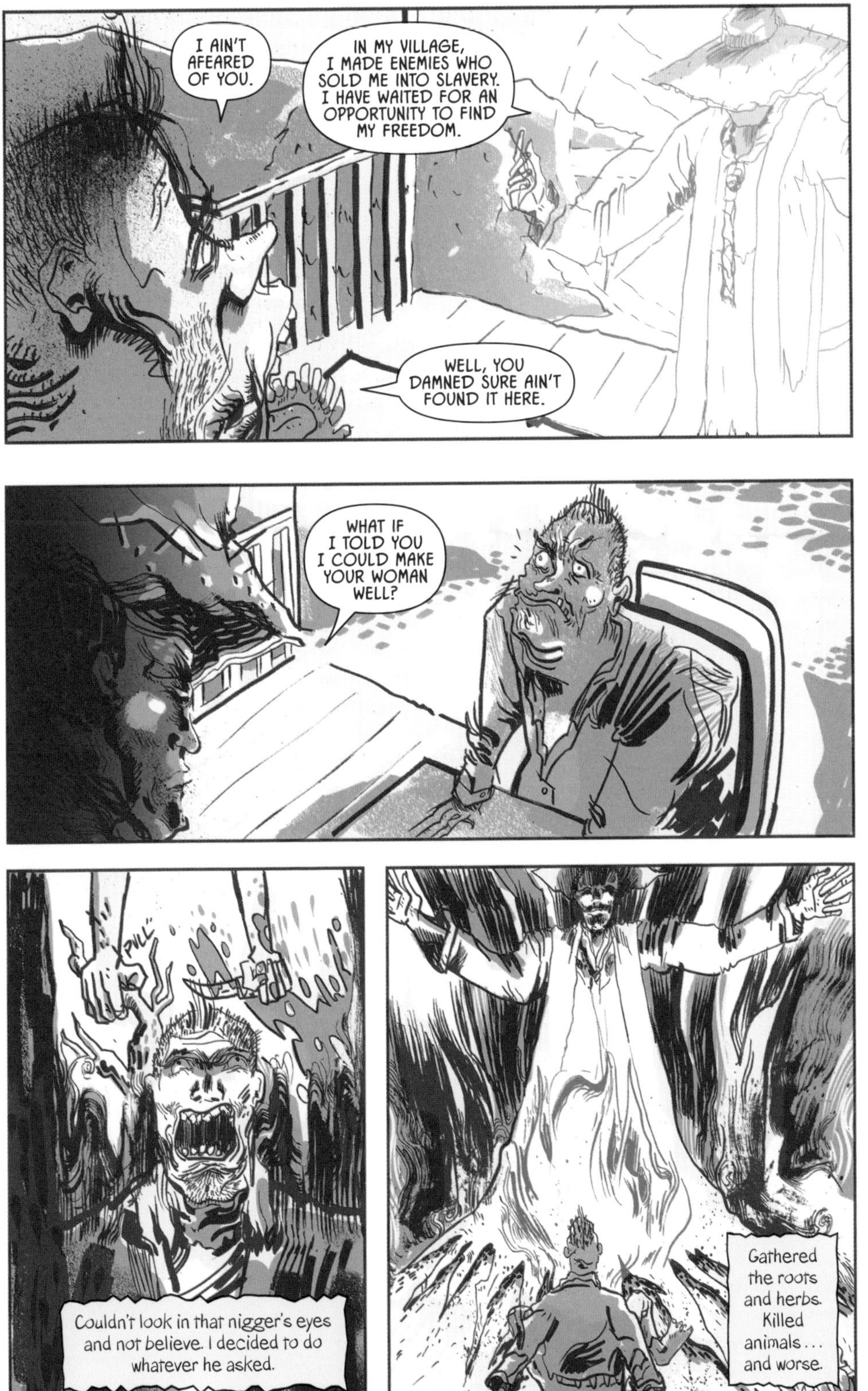
I AIN'T AFEARED OF YOU.
IN MY VILLAGE, I MADE ENEMIES WHO SOLD ME INTO SLAVERY. I HAVE WAITED FOR AN OPPORTUNITY TO FIND MY FREEDOM.
WELL, YOU DAMNED SURE AIN'T FOUND IT HERE.
WHAT IF I TOLD YOU I COULD MAKE YOUR WOMAN WELL?
PULL
Couldn't look in that nigger's eyes and not believe. I decided to do whatever he asked.
Gathered the roots and herbs. Killed animals . . . and worse.

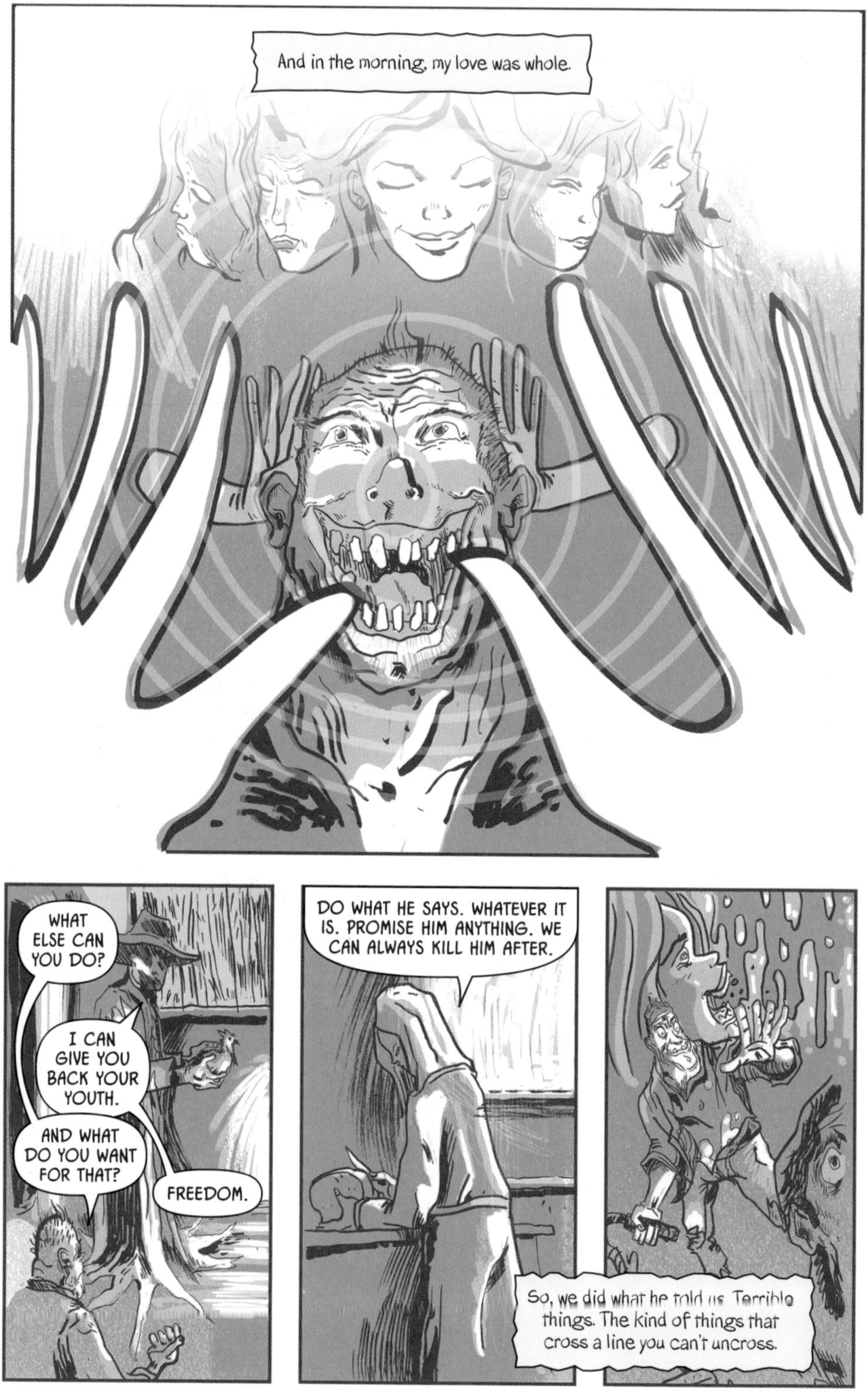
And in the morning, my love was whole.
WHAT ELSE CAN YOU DO?
I CAN GIVE YOU BACK YOUR YOUTH.
AND WHAT DO YOU WANT FOR THAT?
FREEDOM.
DO WHAT HE SAYS. WHATEVER IT IS. PROMISE HIM ANYTHING. WE CAN ALWAYS KILL HIM AFTER.
So, we did what he told us. Terrible things. The kind of things that cross a line you can't uncross.

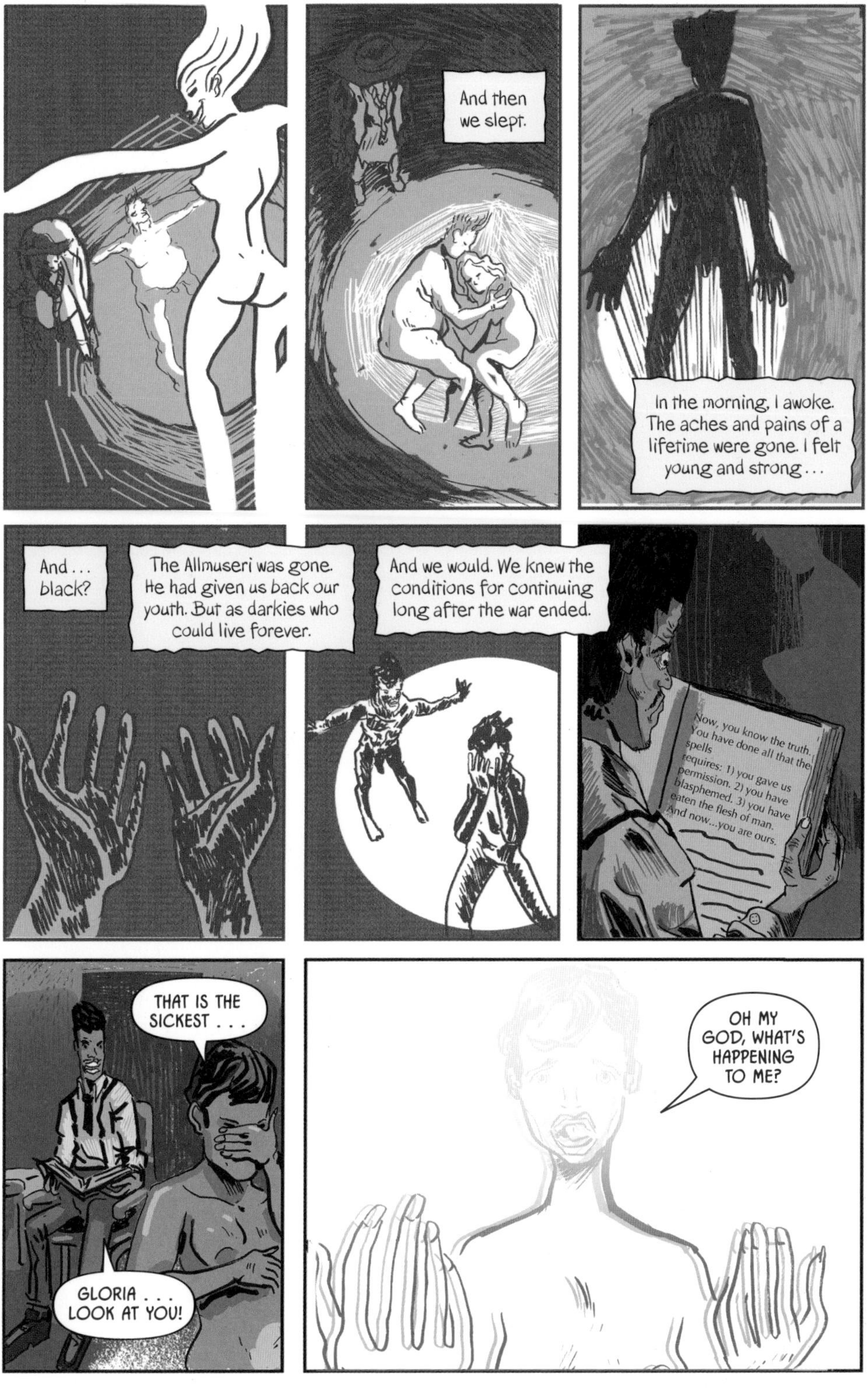
And then we slept.
In the morning, I awoke. The aches and pains of a lifetime were gone. I felt young and strong . . .
And . . . black?
The Allmuseri was gone. He had given us back our youth. But as darkies who could live forever.
And we would. We knew the conditions for continuing long after the war ended.
Now, you know the truth. You have done all that the spells requires: 1) you gave us permission. 2) you have blasphemed. 3) you have eaten the flesh of man. And now...you are ours.
THAT IS THE SICKEST . . .
GLORIA . . . LOOK AT YOU!
OH MY GOD, WHAT'S HAPPENING TO ME?

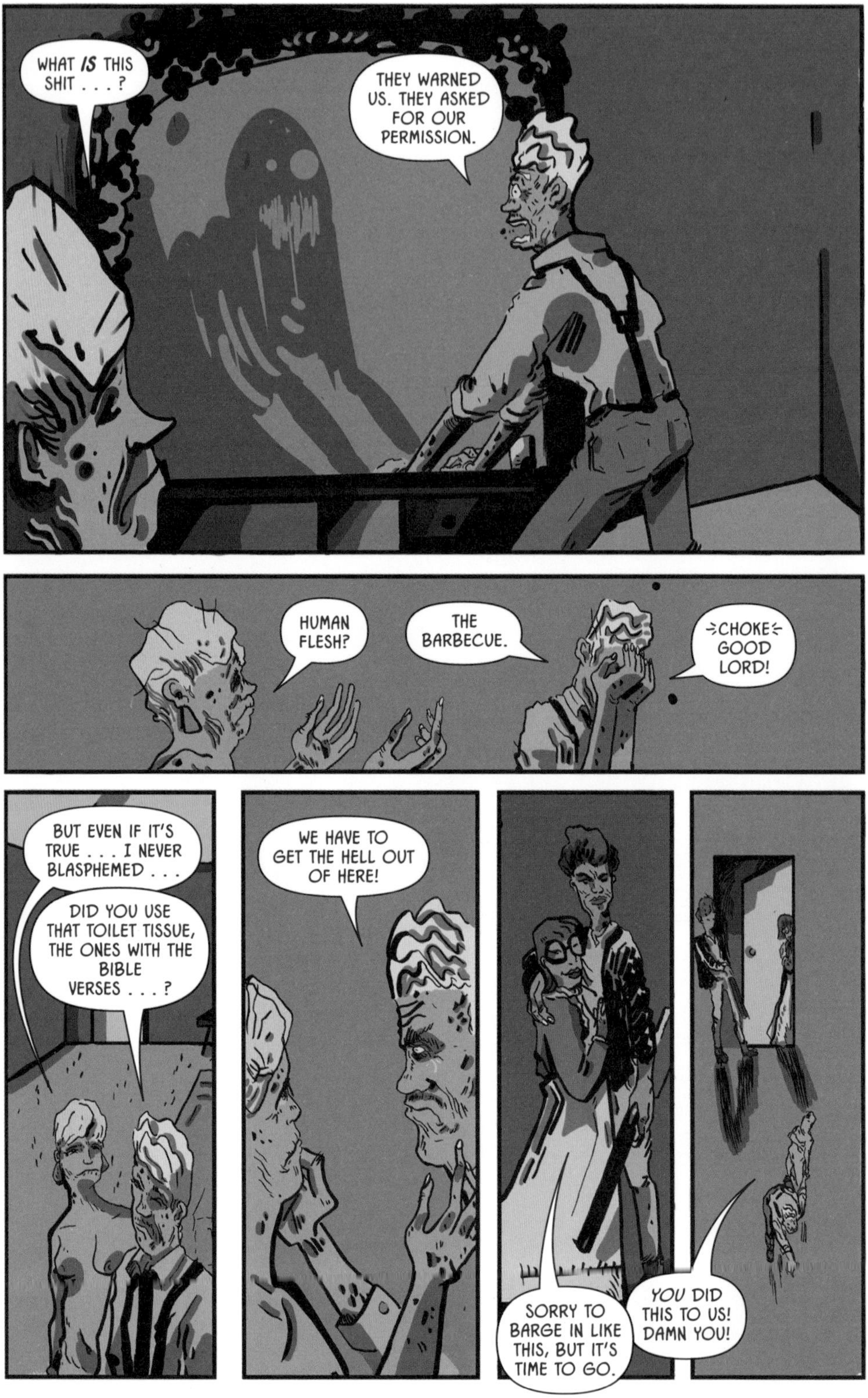
WHAT *IS* THIS SHIT . . . ?
THEY WARNED US. THEY ASKED FOR OUR PERMISSION.
HUMAN FLESH?
THE BARBECUE.
CHOKE GOOD LORD!
BUT EVEN IF IT'S TRUE . . . I NEVER BLASPHEMED . . .
DID YOU USE THAT TOILET TISSUE, THE ONES WITH THE BIBLE VERSES . . . ?
WE HAVE TO GET THE HELL OUT OF HERE!
SORRY TO BARGE IN LIKE THIS, BUT IT'S TIME TO GO.
YOU DID THIS TO US! DAMN YOU!

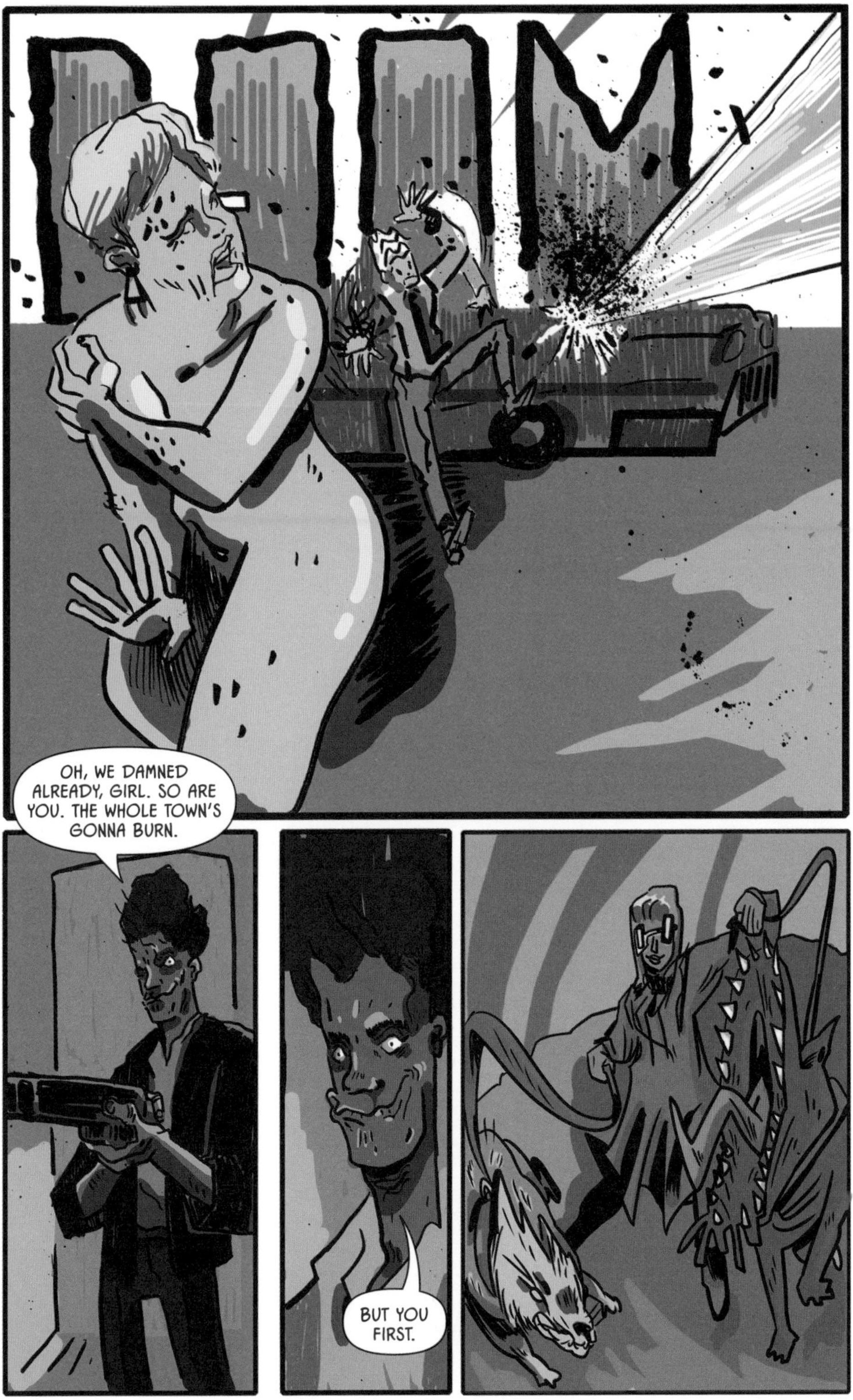
OH, WE DAMNED ALREADY, GIRL. SO ARE YOU. THE WHOLE TOWN'S GONNA BURN.
BUT YOU FIRST.

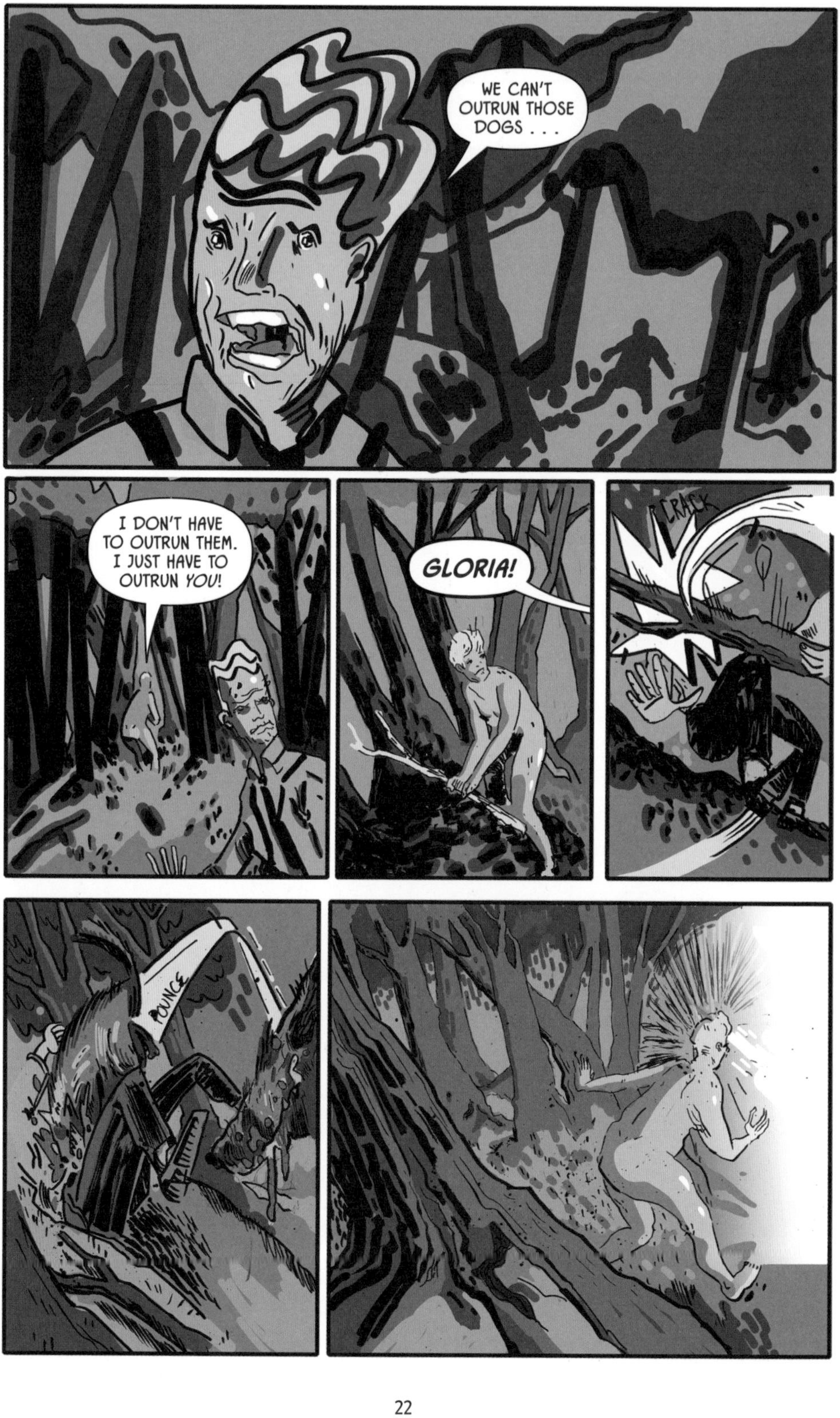
WE CAN'T OUTRUN THOSE DOGS . . .
I DON'T HAVE TO OUTRUN THEM. I JUST HAVE TO OUTRUN *YOU*!
GLORIA!
CRACK
POUNCE

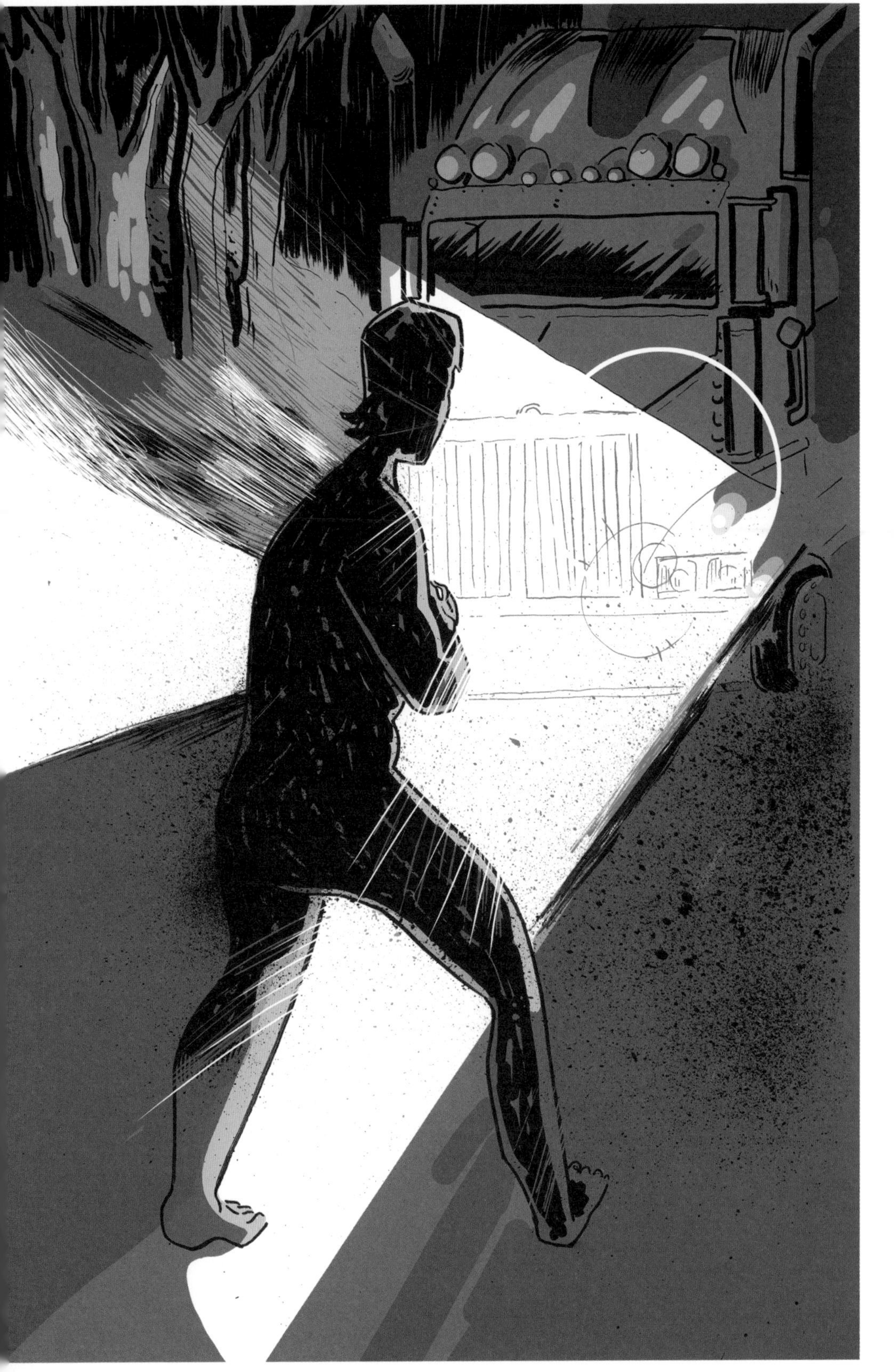

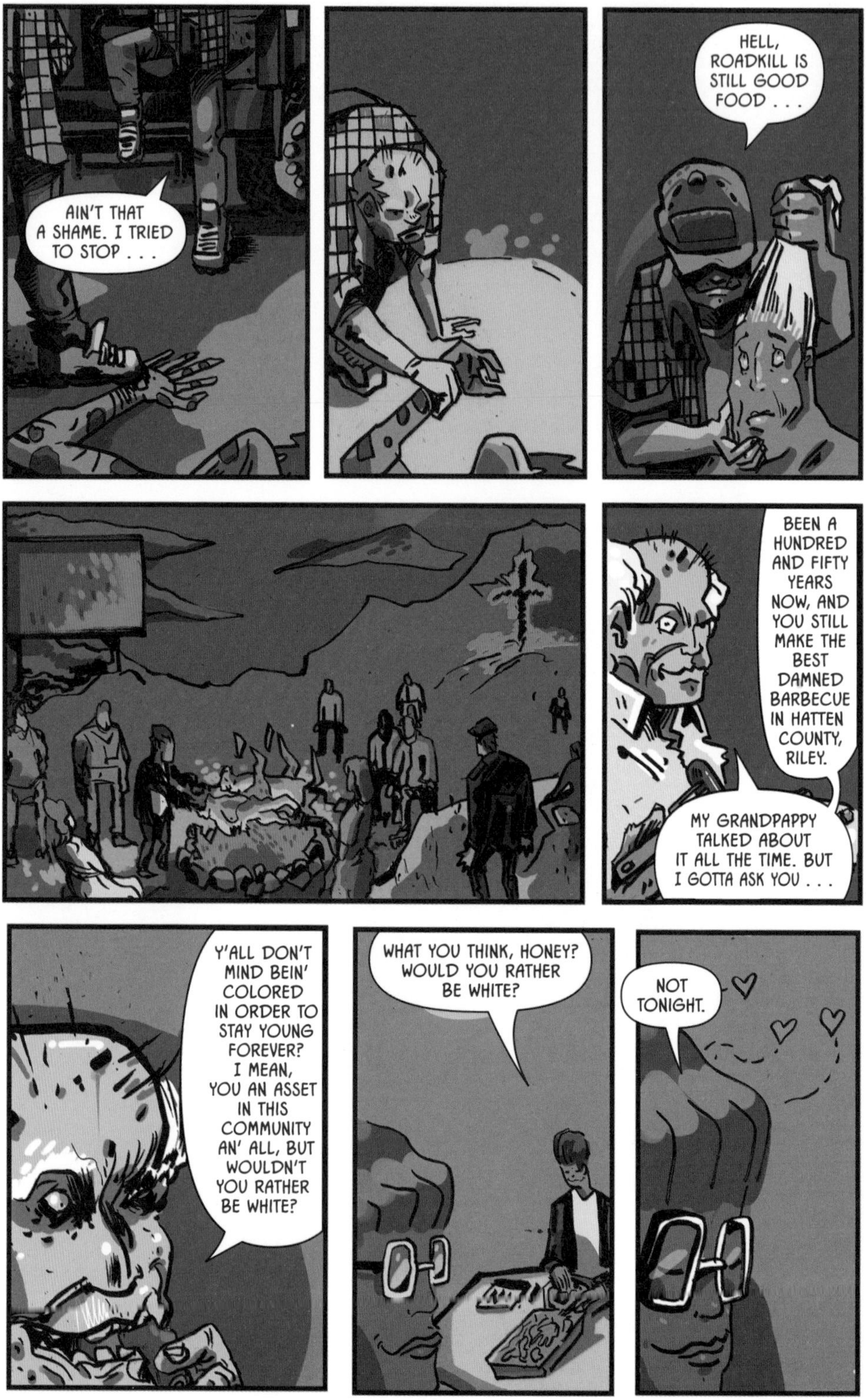
AIN'T THAT A SHAME. I TRIED TO STOP . . .
HELL, ROADKILL IS STILL GOOD FOOD . . .
BEEN A HUNDRED AND FIFTY YEARS NOW, AND YOU STILL MAKE THE BEST DAMNED BARBECUE IN HATTEN COUNTY, RILEY.
MY GRANDPAPPY TALKED ABOUT IT ALL THE TIME. BUT I GOTTA ASK YOU . . .
Y'ALL DON'T MIND BEIN' COLORED IN ORDER TO STAY YOUNG FOREVER? I MEAN, YOU AN ASSET IN THIS COMMUNITY AN' ALL, BUT WOULDN'T YOU RATHER BE WHITE?
WHAT YOU THINK, HONEY? WOULD YOU RATHER BE WHITE?
NOT TONIGHT.

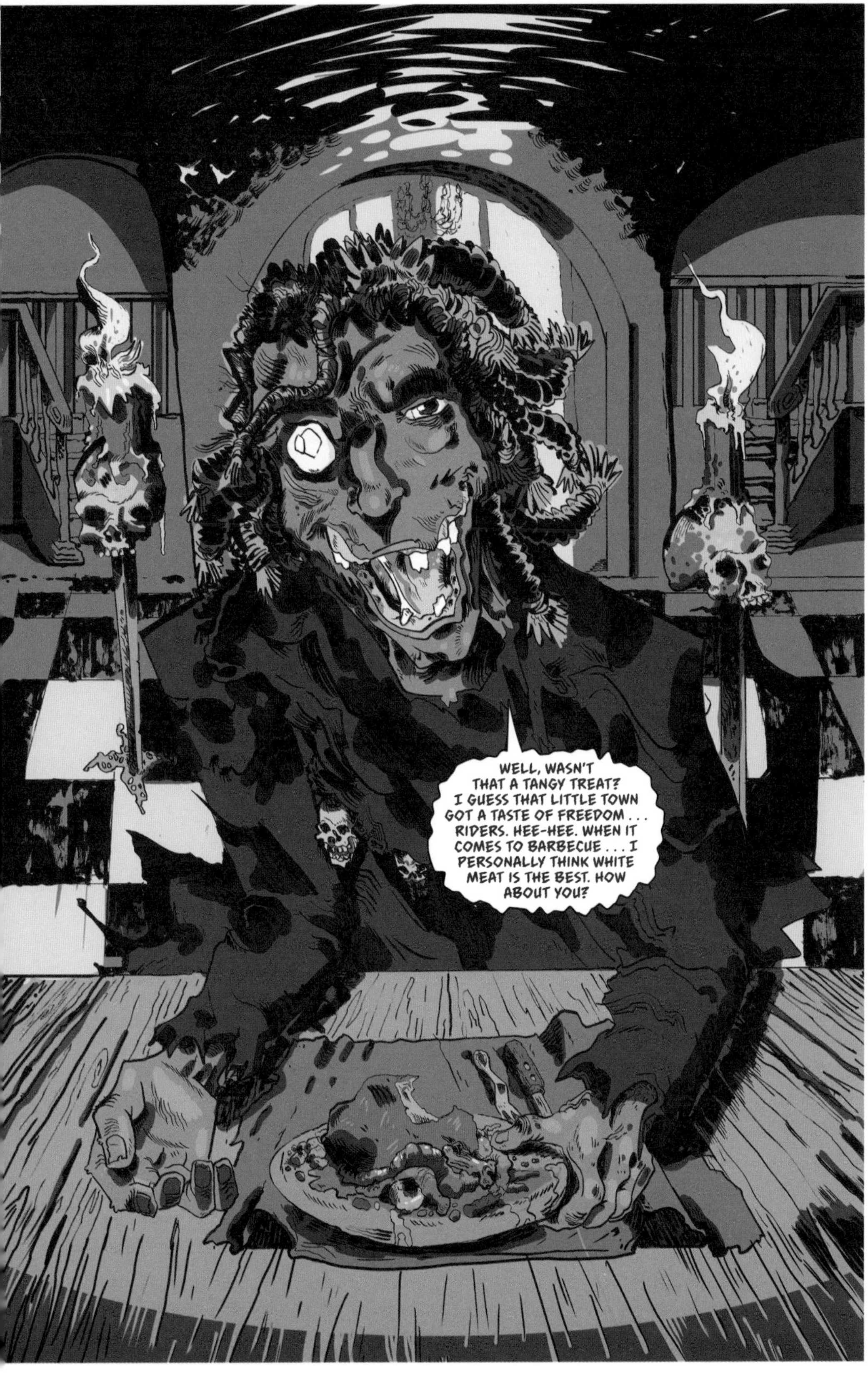
WELL, WASN'T THAT A TANGY TREAT? I GUESS THAT LITTLE TOWN GOT A TASTE OF FREEDOM . . . RIDERS. HEE-HEE. WHEN IT COMES TO BARBECUE . . . I PERSONALLY THINK WHITE MEAT IS THE BEST. HOW ABOUT YOU?

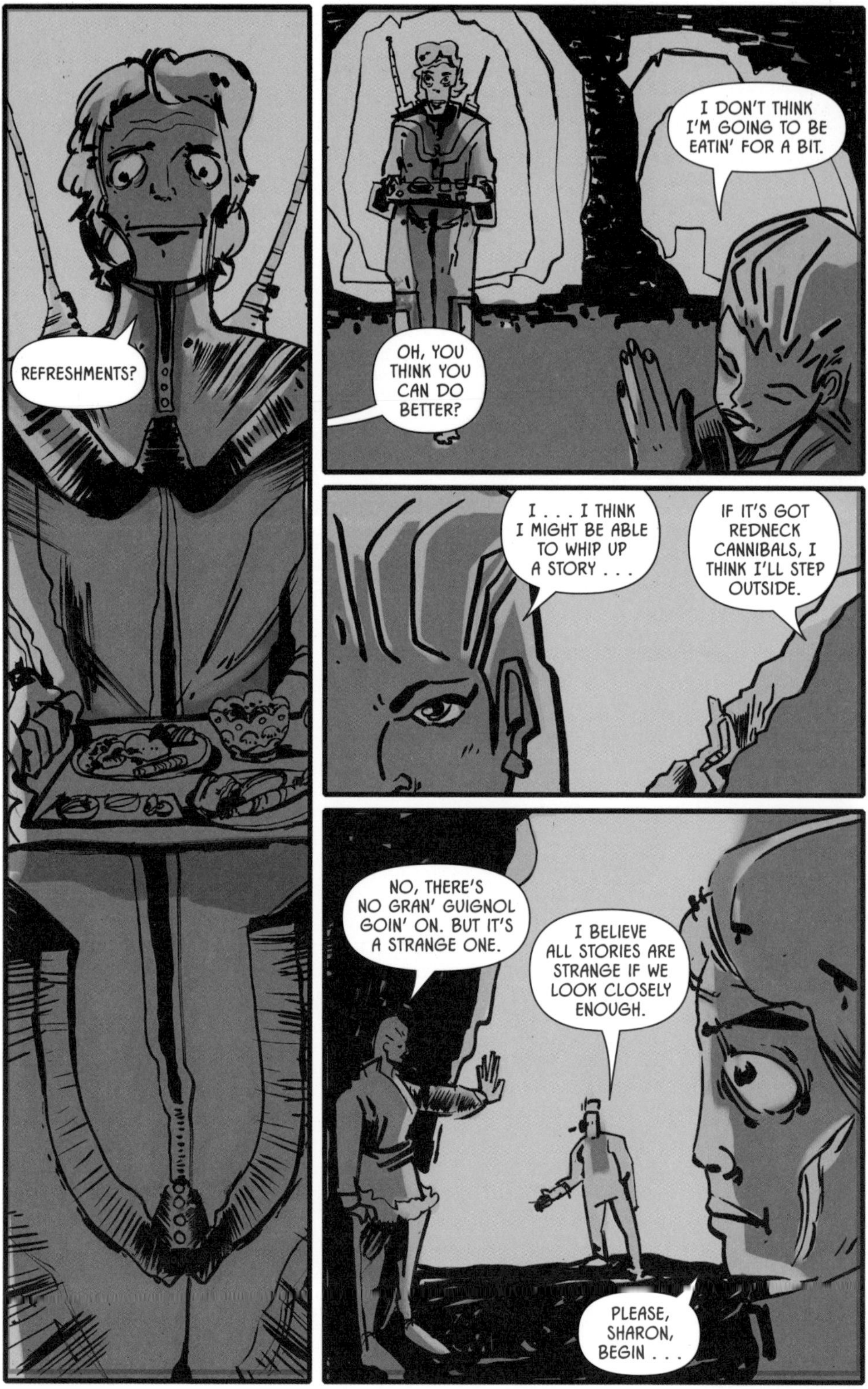
REFRESHMENTS?
I DON'T THINK I'M GOING TO BE EATIN' FOR A BIT.
OH, YOU THINK YOU CAN DO BETTER?
I . . . I THINK I MIGHT BE ABLE TO WHIP UP A STORY . . .
IF IT'S GOT REDNECK CANNIBALS, I THINK I'LL STEP OUTSIDE.
NO, THERE'S NO GRAN' GUIGNOL GOIN' ON. BUT IT'S A STRANGE ONE.
I BELIEVE ALL STORIES ARE STRANGE IF WE LOOK CLOSELY ENOUGH.
PLEASE, SHARON, BEGIN . . .

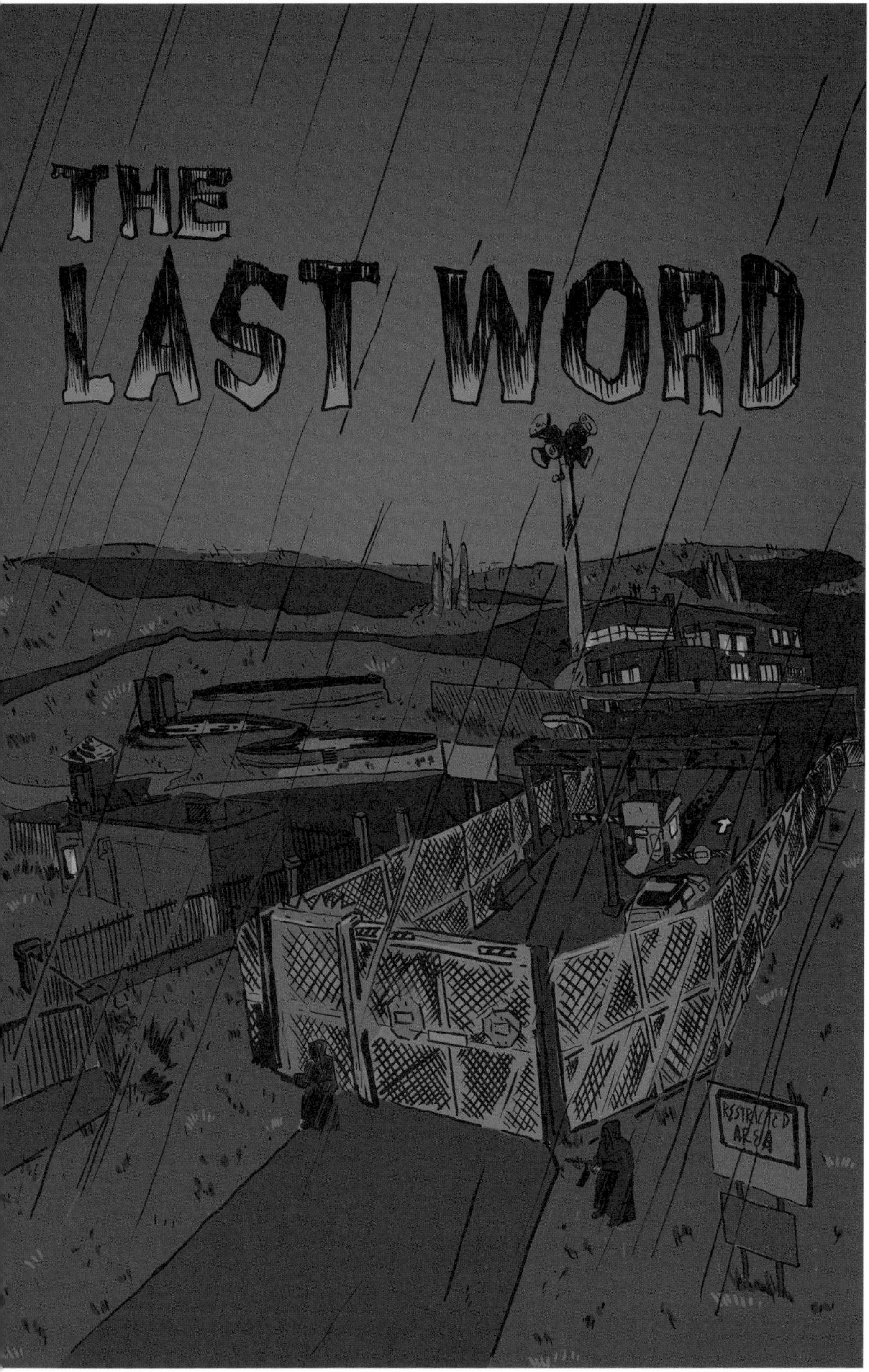
THE
LAST WORD
RESTRICTED
AREA

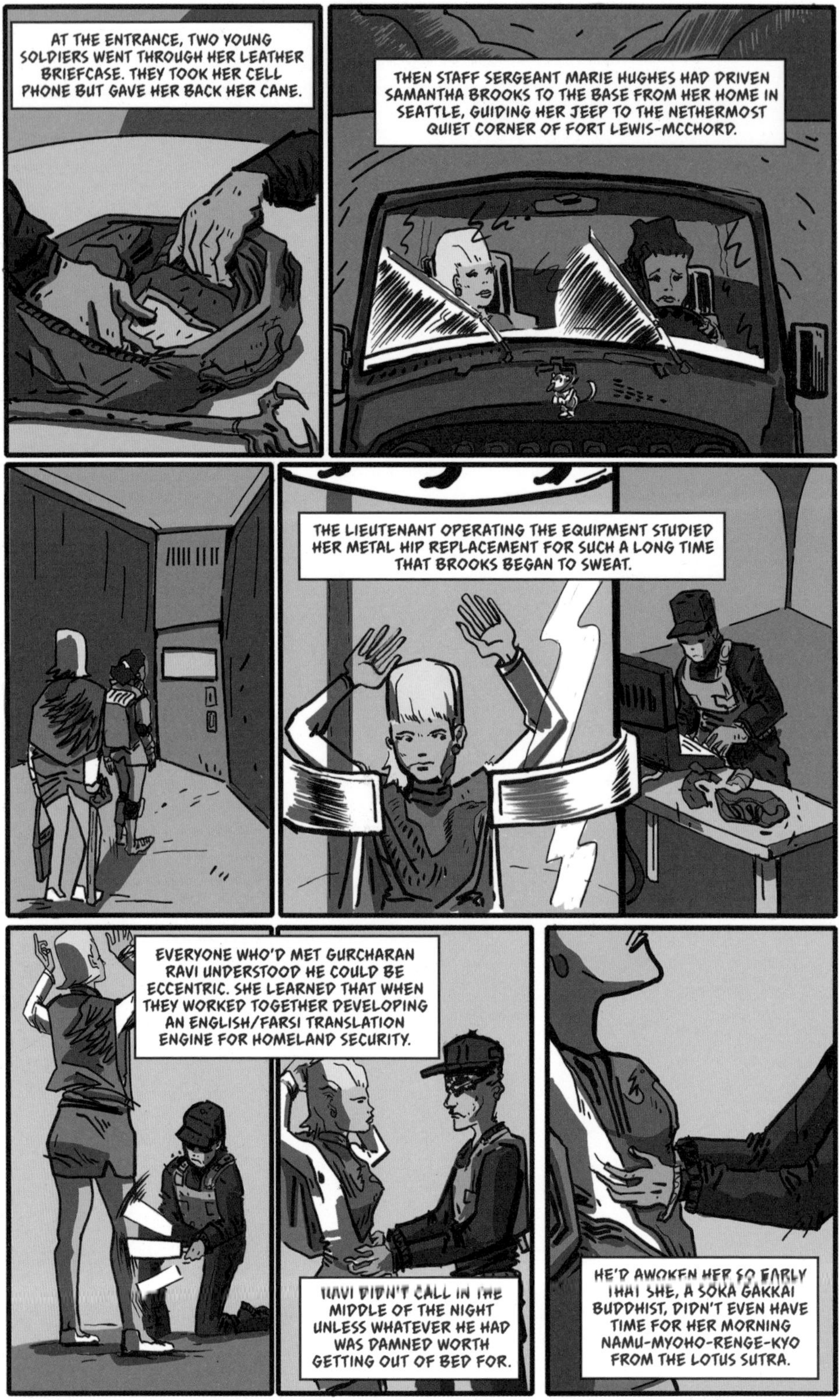
AT THE ENTRANCE, TWO YOUNG SOLDIERS WENT THROUGH HER LEATHER BRIEFCASE. THEY TOOK HER CELL PHONE BUT GAVE HER BACK HER CANE.
THEN STAFF SERGEANT MARIE HUGHES HAD DRIVEN SAMANTHA BROOKS TO THE BASE FROM HER HOME IN SEATTLE, GUIDING HER JEEP TO THE NETHERMOST QUIET CORNER OF FORT LEWIS-MCCHORD.
THE LIEUTENANT OPERATING THE EQUIPMENT STUDIED HER METAL HIP REPLACEMENT FOR SUCH A LONG TIME THAT BROOKS BEGAN TO SWEAT.
EVERYONE WHO'D MET GURCHARAN RAVI UNDERSTOOD HE COULD BE ECCENTRIC. SHE LEARNED THAT WHEN THEY WORKED TOGETHER DEVELOPING AN ENGLISH/FARSI TRANSLATION ENGINE FOR HOMELAND SECURITY.
RAVI DIDN'T CALL IN THE MIDDLE OF THE NIGHT UNLESS WHATEVER HE HAD WAS DAMNED WORTH GETTING OUT OF BED FOR.
HE'D AWOKEN HER SO EARLY THAT SHE, A SOKA GAKKAI BUDDHIST, DIDN'T EVEN HAVE TIME FOR HER MORNING NAMU-MYOHO-RENGE-KYO FROM THE LOTUS SUTRA.

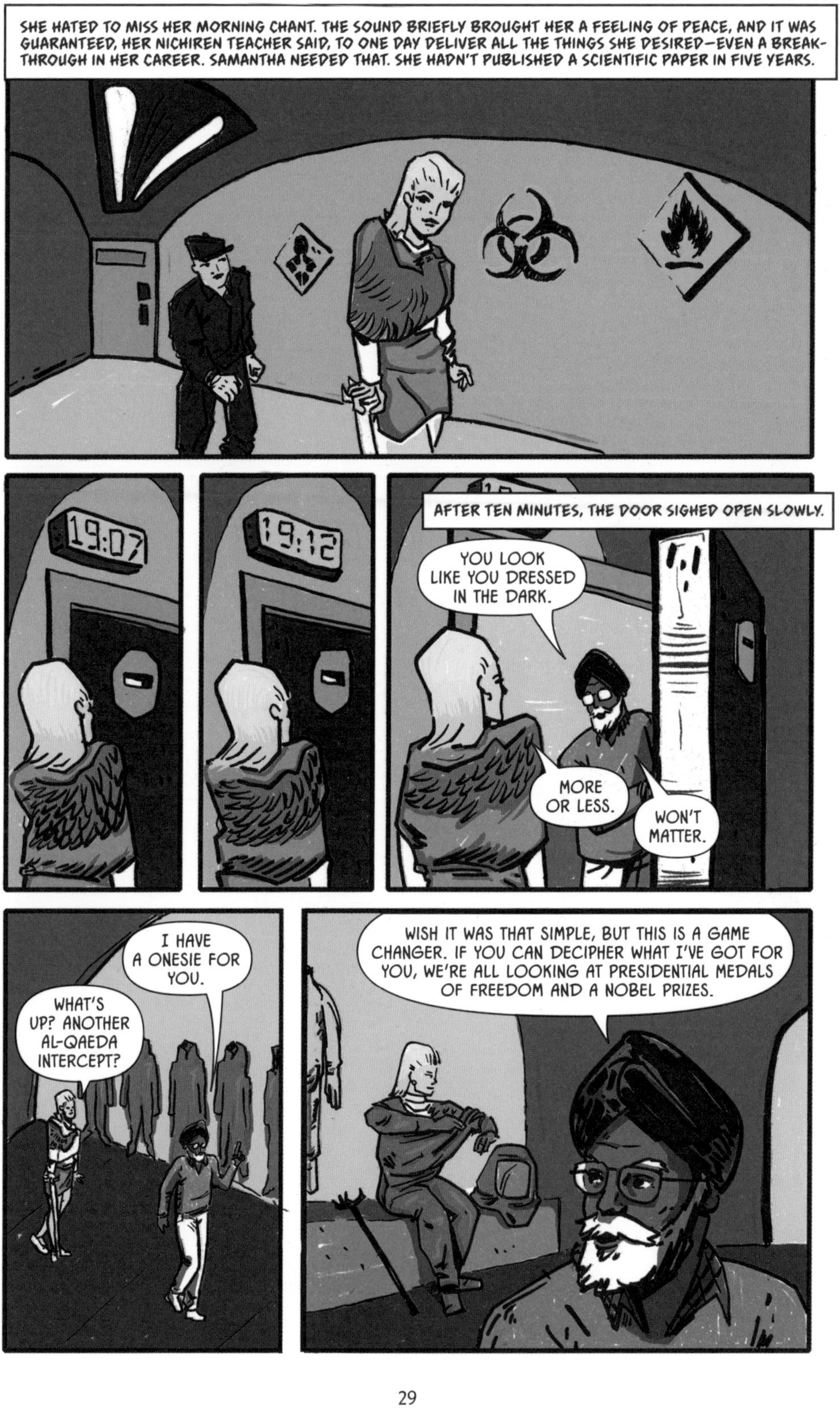
SHE HATED TO MISS HER MORNING CHANT. THE SOUND BRIEFLY BROUGHT HER A FEELING OF PEACE, AND IT WAS GUARANTEED, HER NICHIREN TEACHER SAID, TO ONE DAY DELIVER ALL THE THINGS SHE DESIRED—EVEN A BREAK-THROUGH IN HER CAREER. SAMANTHA NEEDED THAT. SHE HADN'T PUBLISHED A SCIENTIFIC PAPER IN FIVE YEARS.
19:07
19:12
AFTER TEN MINUTES, THE DOOR SIGHED OPEN SLOWLY.
YOU LOOK LIKE YOU DRESSED IN THE DARK.
MORE OR LESS.
WON'T MATTER.
WHAT'S UP? ANOTHER AL-QAEDA INTERCEPT?
I HAVE A ONESIE FOR YOU.
WISH IT WAS THAT SIMPLE, BUT THIS IS A GAME CHANGER. IF YOU CAN DECIPHER WHAT I'VE GOT FOR YOU, WE'RE ALL LOOKING AT PRESIDENTIAL MEDALS OF FREEDOM AND A NOBEL PRIZES.

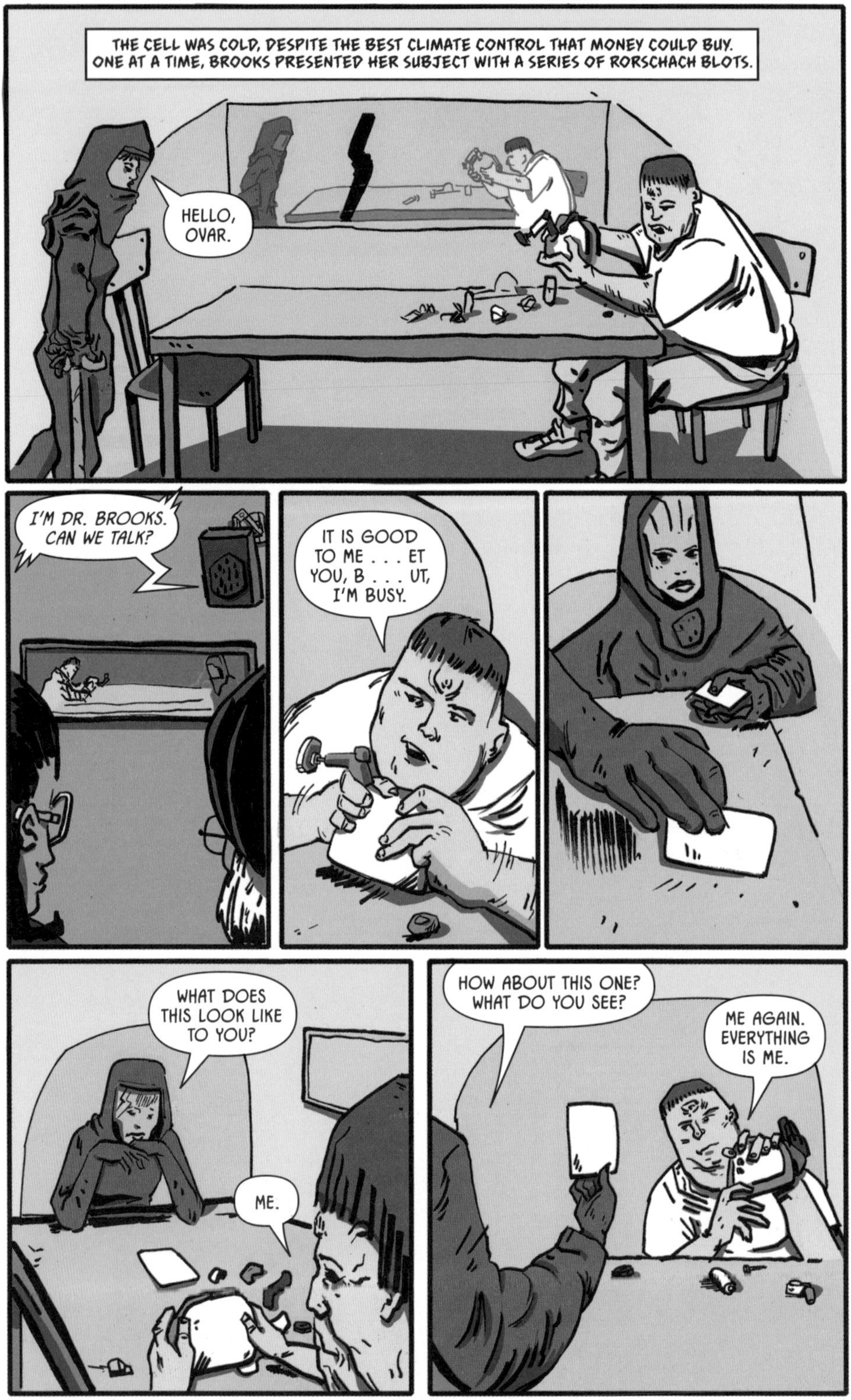
THE CELL WAS COLD, DESPITE THE BEST CLIMATE CONTROL THAT MONEY COULD BUY. ONE AT A TIME, BROOKS PRESENTED HER SUBJECT WITH A SERIES OF RORSCHACH BLOTS.
HELLO, OVAR.
I'M DR. BROOKS. CAN WE TALK?
IT IS GOOD TO ME . . . ET YOU, B . . . UT, I'M BUSY.
WHAT DOES THIS LOOK LIKE TO YOU?
ME.
HOW ABOUT THIS ONE? WHAT DO YOU SEE?
ME AGAIN. EVERYTHING IS ME.

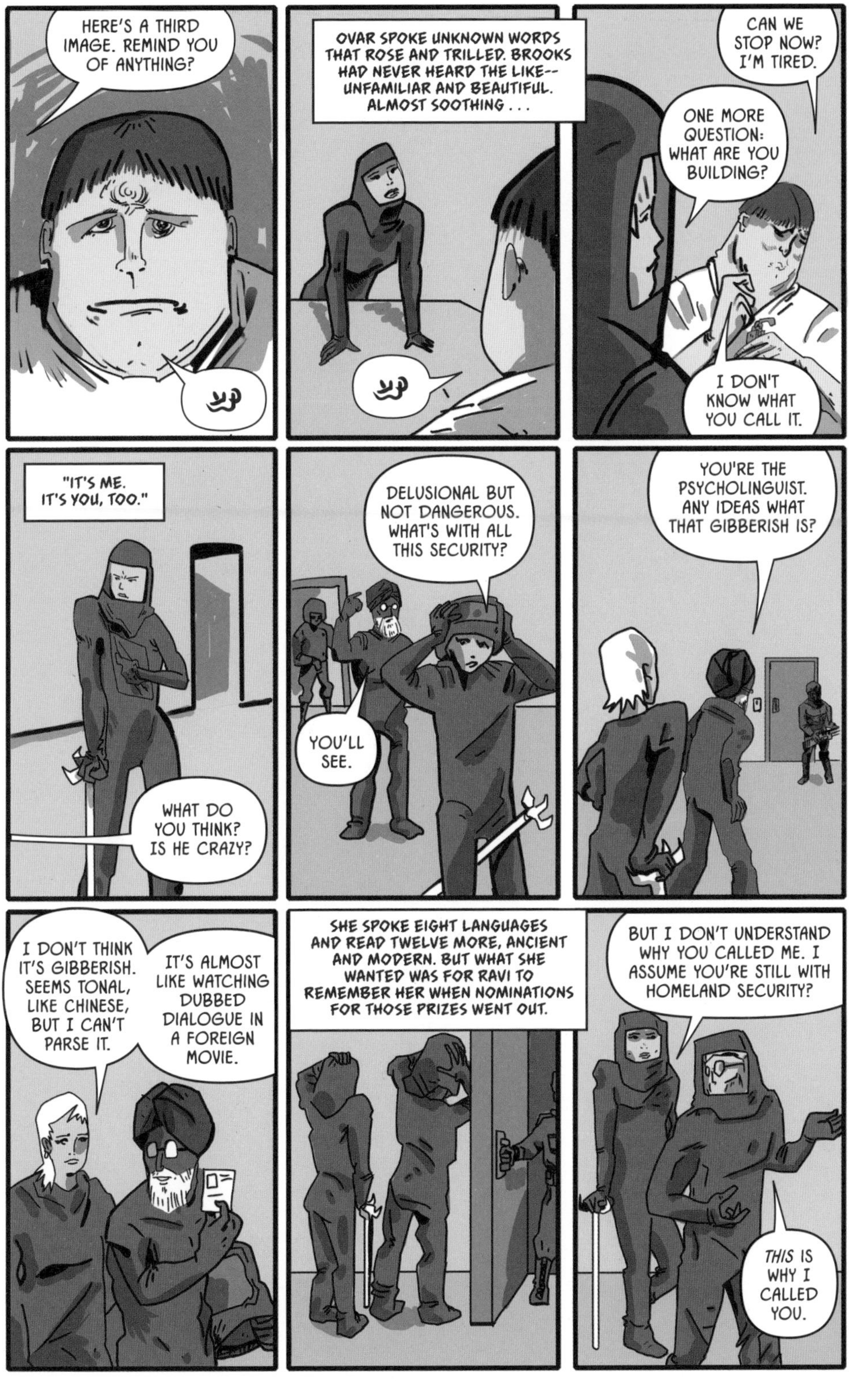
HERE'S A THIRD IMAGE. REMIND YOU OF ANYTHING?
OVAR SPOKE UNKNOWN WORDS THAT ROSE AND TRILLED. BROOKS HAD NEVER HEARD THE LIKE--UNFAMILIAR AND BEAUTIFUL. ALMOST SOOTHING . . .
CAN WE STOP NOW? I'M TIRED.
ONE MORE QUESTION: WHAT ARE YOU BUILDING?
I DON'T KNOW WHAT YOU CALL IT.
"IT'S ME. IT'S YOU, TOO."
WHAT DO YOU THINK? IS HE CRAZY?
DELUSIONAL BUT NOT DANGEROUS. WHAT'S WITH ALL THIS SECURITY?
YOU'LL SEE.
YOU'RE THE PSYCHOLINGUIST. ANY IDEAS WHAT THAT GIBBERISH IS?
I DON'T THINK IT'S GIBBERISH. SEEMS TONAL, LIKE CHINESE, BUT I CAN'T PARSE IT.
IT'S ALMOST LIKE WATCHING DUBBED DIALOGUE IN A FOREIGN MOVIE.
SHE SPOKE EIGHT LANGUAGES AND READ TWELVE MORE, ANCIENT AND MODERN. BUT WHAT SHE WANTED WAS FOR RAVI TO REMEMBER HER WHEN NOMINATIONS FOR THOSE PRIZES WENT OUT.
BUT I DON'T UNDERSTAND WHY YOU CALLED ME. I ASSUME YOU'RE STILL WITH HOMELAND SECURITY?
THIS IS WHY I CALLED YOU.

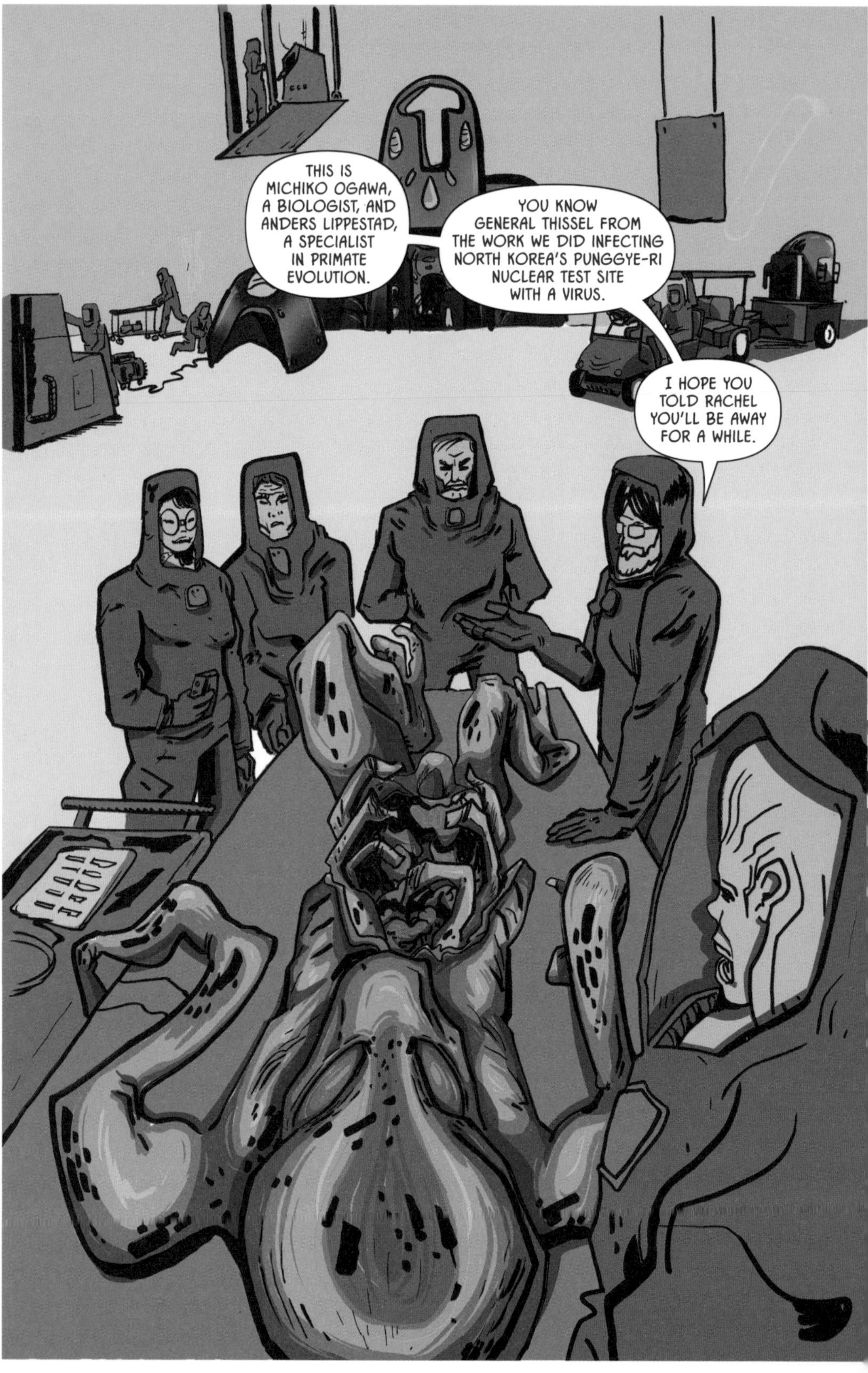
THIS IS MICHIKO OGAWA, A BIOLOGIST, AND ANDERS LIPPESTAD, A SPECIALIST IN PRIMATE EVOLUTION.
YOU KNOW GENERAL THISSEL FROM THE WORK WE DID INFECTING NORTH KOREA'S PUNGGYE-RI NUCLEAR TEST SITE WITH A VIRUS.
I HOPE YOU TOLD RACHEL YOU'LL BE AWAY FOR A WHILE.

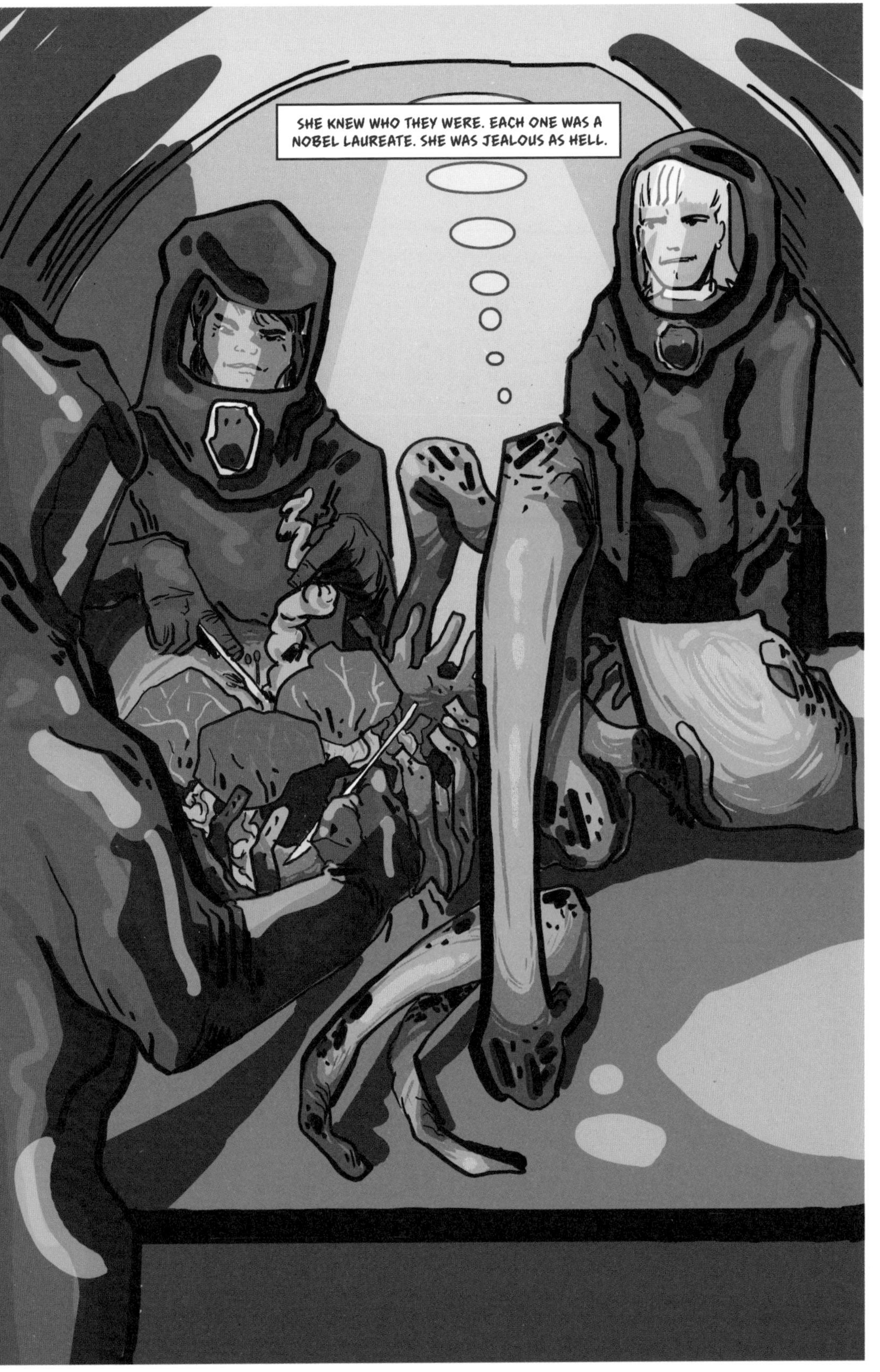
SHE KNEW WHO THEY WERE. EACH ONE WAS A NOBEL LAUREATE. SHE WAS JEALOUS AS HELL.

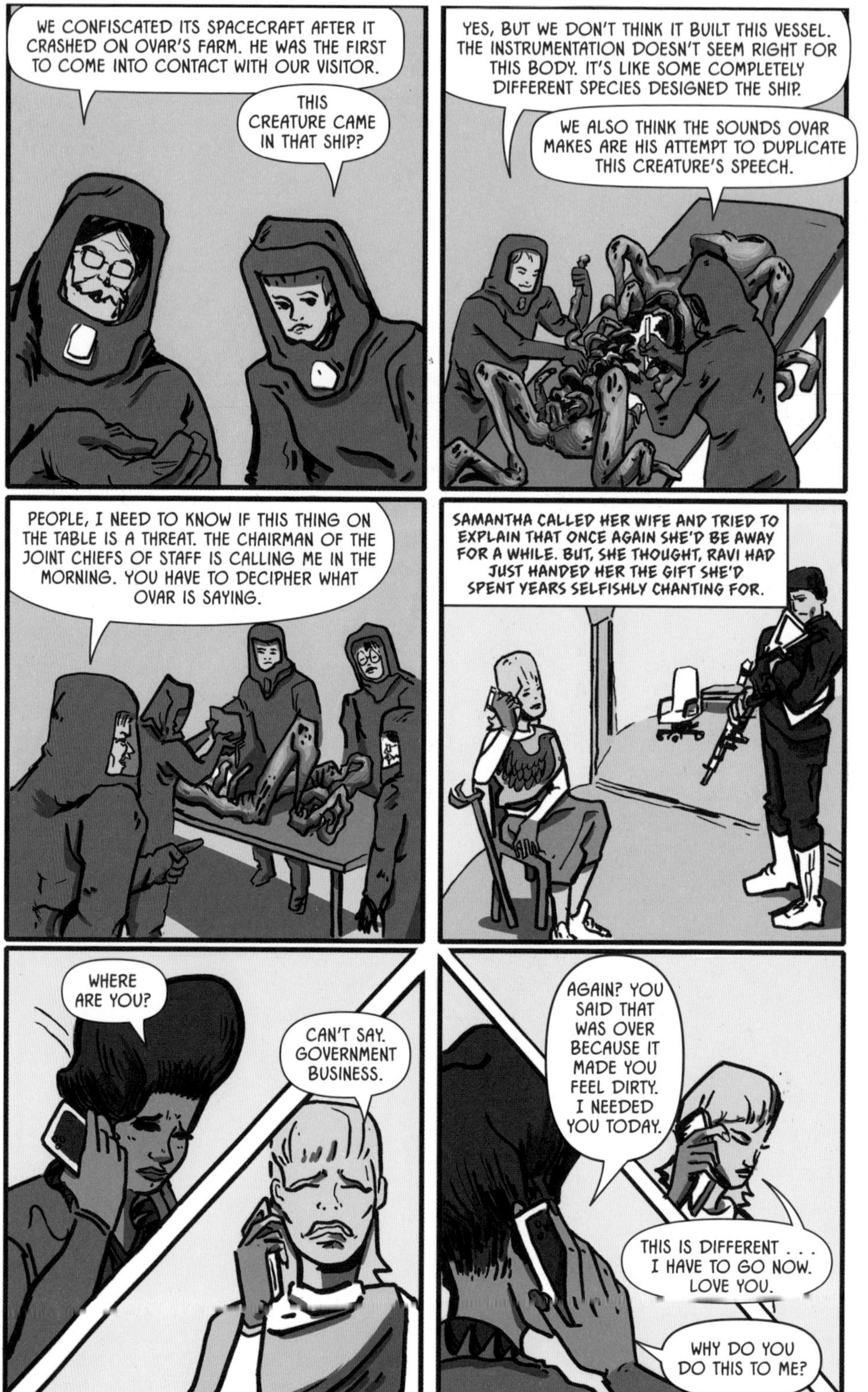
WE CONFISCATED ITS SPACECRAFT AFTER IT CRASHED ON OVAR'S FARM. HE WAS THE FIRST TO COME INTO CONTACT WITH OUR VISITOR.
THIS CREATURE CAME IN THAT SHIP?
YES, BUT WE DON'T THINK IT BUILT THIS VESSEL. THE INSTRUMENTATION DOESN'T SEEM RIGHT FOR THIS BODY. IT'S LIKE SOME COMPLETELY DIFFERENT SPECIES DESIGNED THE SHIP.
WE ALSO THINK THE SOUNDS OVAR MAKES ARE HIS ATTEMPT TO DUPLICATE THIS CREATURE'S SPEECH.
PEOPLE, I NEED TO KNOW IF THIS THING ON THE TABLE IS A THREAT. THE CHAIRMAN OF THE JOINT CHIEFS OF STAFF IS CALLING ME IN THE MORNING. YOU HAVE TO DECIPHER WHAT OVAR IS SAYING.
SAMANTHA CALLED HER WIFE AND TRIED TO EXPLAIN THAT ONCE AGAIN SHE'D BE AWAY FOR A WHILE. BUT, SHE THOUGHT, RAVI HAD JUST HANDED HER THE GIFT SHE'D SPENT YEARS SELFISHLY CHANTING FOR.
WHERE ARE YOU?
CAN'T SAY. GOVERNMENT BUSINESS.
AGAIN? YOU SAID THAT WAS OVER BECAUSE IT MADE YOU FEEL DIRTY. I NEEDED YOU TODAY.
THIS IS DIFFERENT . . . I HAVE TO GO NOW. LOVE YOU.
WHY DO YOU DO THIS TO ME?

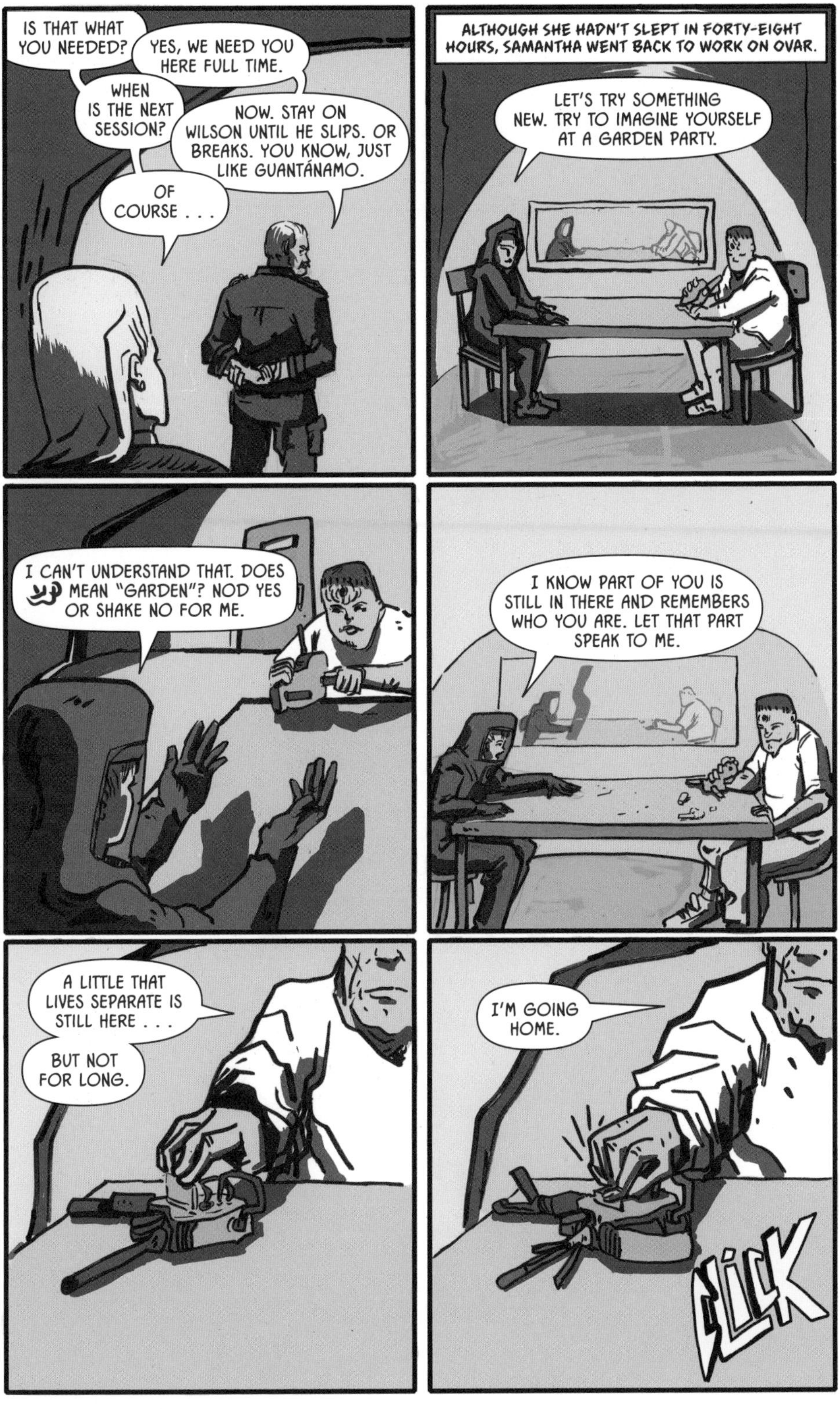
IS THAT WHAT YOU NEEDED?
YES, WE NEED YOU HERE FULL TIME.
WHEN IS THE NEXT SESSION?
NOW. STAY ON WILSON UNTIL HE SLIPS. OR BREAKS. YOU KNOW, JUST LIKE GUANTÁNAMO.
OF COURSE . . .
ALTHOUGH SHE HADN'T SLEPT IN FORTY-EIGHT HOURS, SAMANTHA WENT BACK TO WORK ON OVAR.
LET'S TRY SOMETHING NEW. TRY TO IMAGINE YOURSELF AT A GARDEN PARTY.
I CAN'T UNDERSTAND THAT. DOES MEAN "GARDEN"? NOD YES OR SHAKE NO FOR ME.
I KNOW PART OF YOU IS STILL IN THERE AND REMEMBERS WHO YOU ARE. LET THAT PART SPEAK TO ME.
A LITTLE THAT LIVES SEPARATE IS STILL HERE . . .
BUT NOT FOR LONG.
I'M GOING HOME.
CLICK

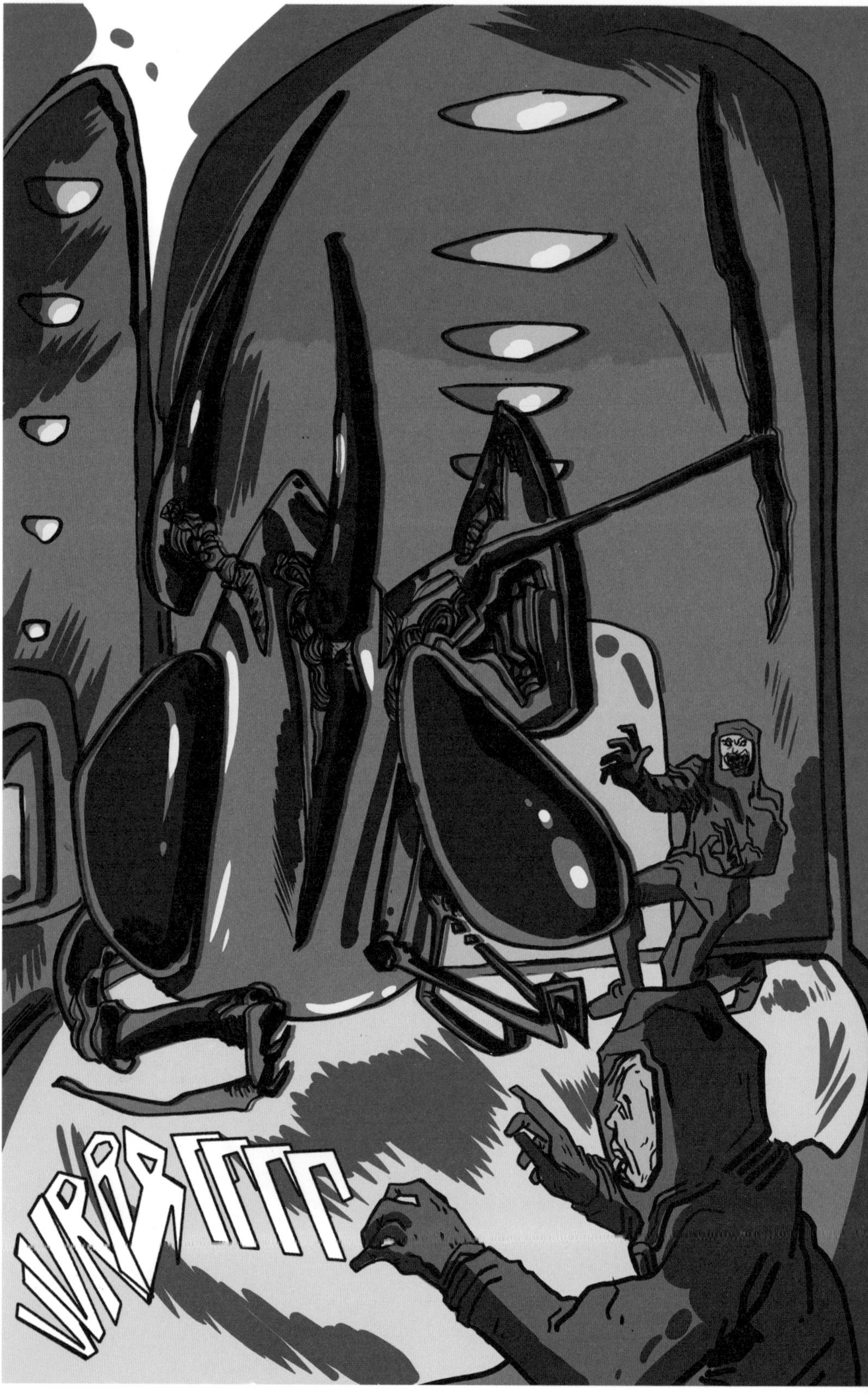

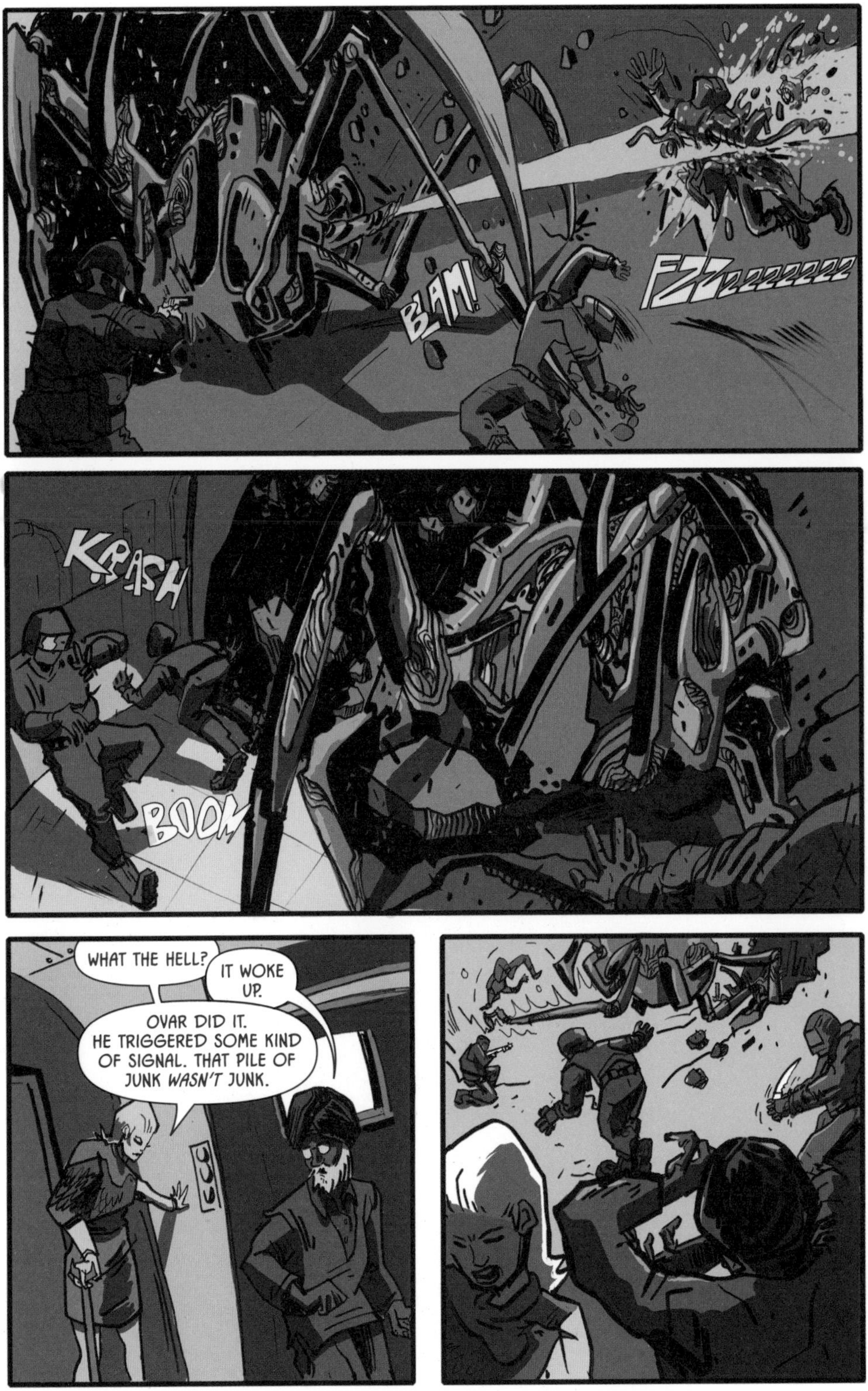
BLAM!
FZZzzzzzzzz
KRASH
BOOM
WHAT THE HELL?
IT WOKE UP.
OVAR DID IT. HE TRIGGERED SOME KIND OF SIGNAL. THAT PILE OF JUNK *WASN'T* JUNK.

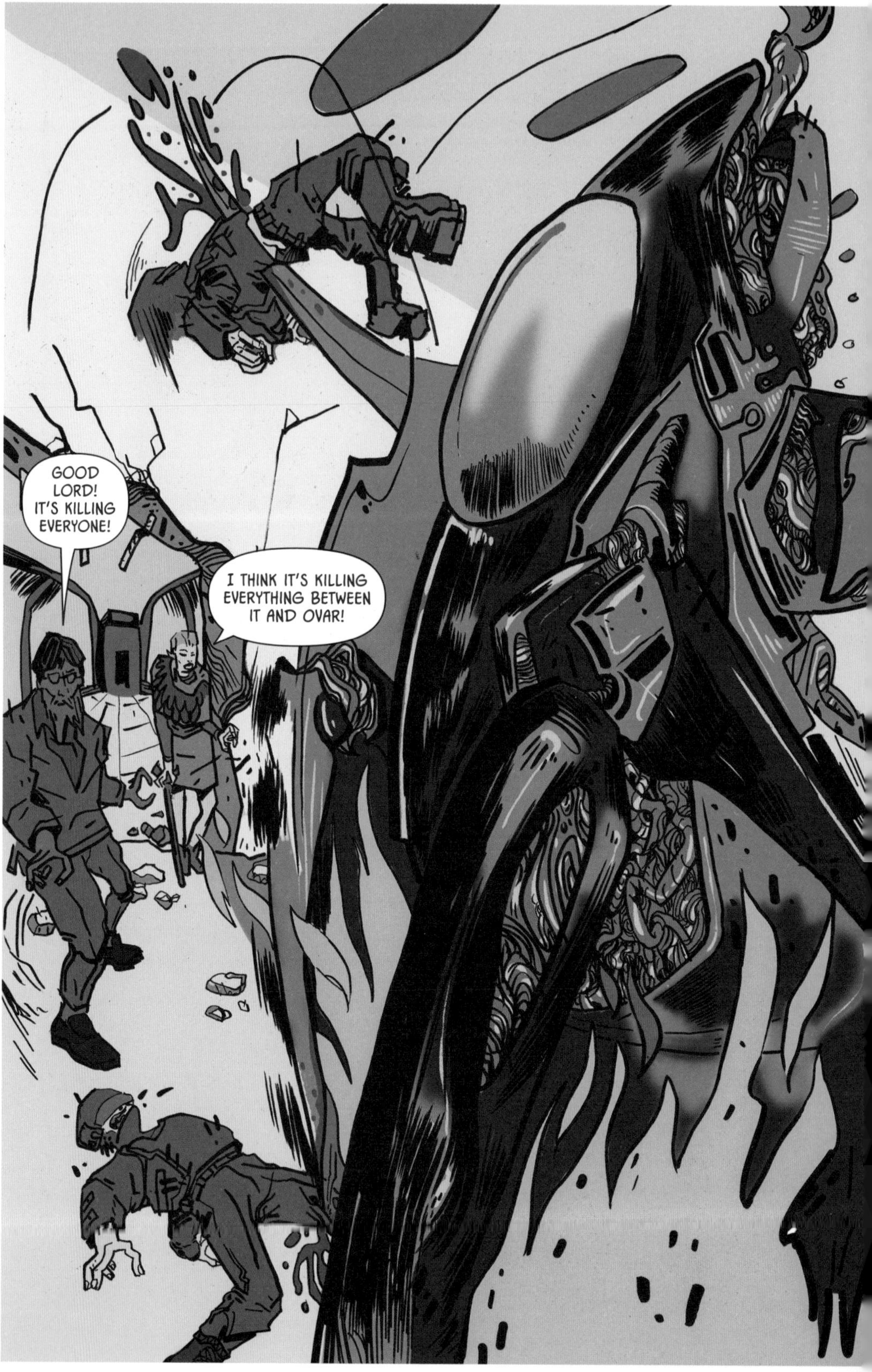
GOOD LORD! IT'S KILLING EVERYONE!
I THINK IT'S KILLING EVERYTHING BETWEEN IT AND OVAR!

HOW ARE WE GOING TO EXPLAIN THIS?

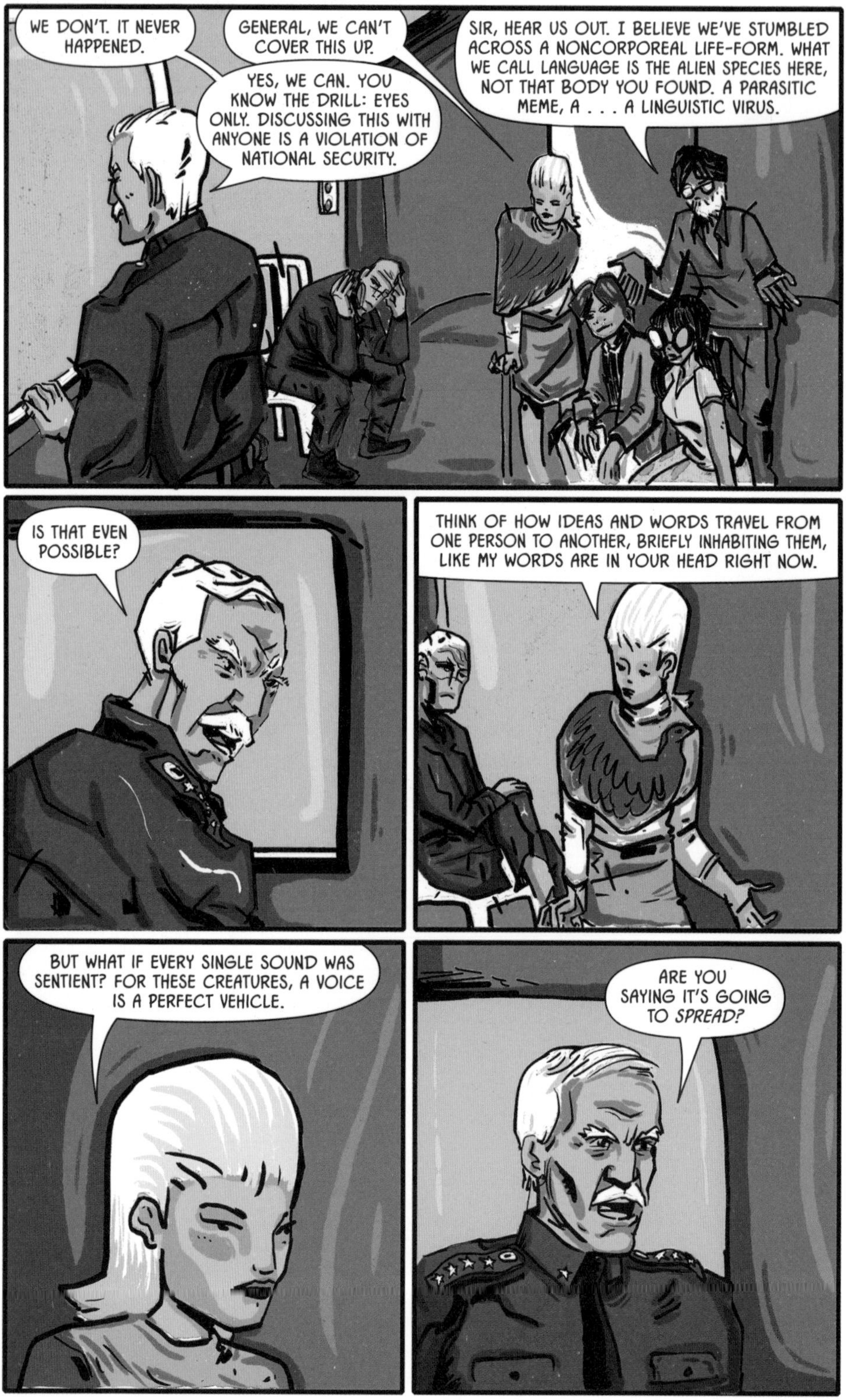
WE DON'T. IT NEVER HAPPENED.
GENERAL, WE CAN'T COVER THIS UP.
YES, WE CAN. YOU KNOW THE DRILL: EYES ONLY. DISCUSSING THIS WITH ANYONE IS A VIOLATION OF NATIONAL SECURITY.
SIR, HEAR US OUT. I BELIEVE WE'VE STUMBLED ACROSS A NONCORPOREAL LIFE-FORM. WHAT WE CALL LANGUAGE IS THE ALIEN SPECIES HERE, NOT THAT BODY YOU FOUND. A PARASITIC MEME, A . . . A LINGUISTIC VIRUS.
IS THAT EVEN POSSIBLE?
THINK OF HOW IDEAS AND WORDS TRAVEL FROM ONE PERSON TO ANOTHER, BRIEFLY INHABITING THEM, LIKE MY WORDS ARE IN YOUR HEAD RIGHT NOW.
BUT WHAT IF EVERY SINGLE SOUND WAS SENTIENT? FOR THESE CREATURES, A VOICE IS A PERFECT VEHICLE.
ARE YOU SAYING IT'S GOING TO *SPREAD?*

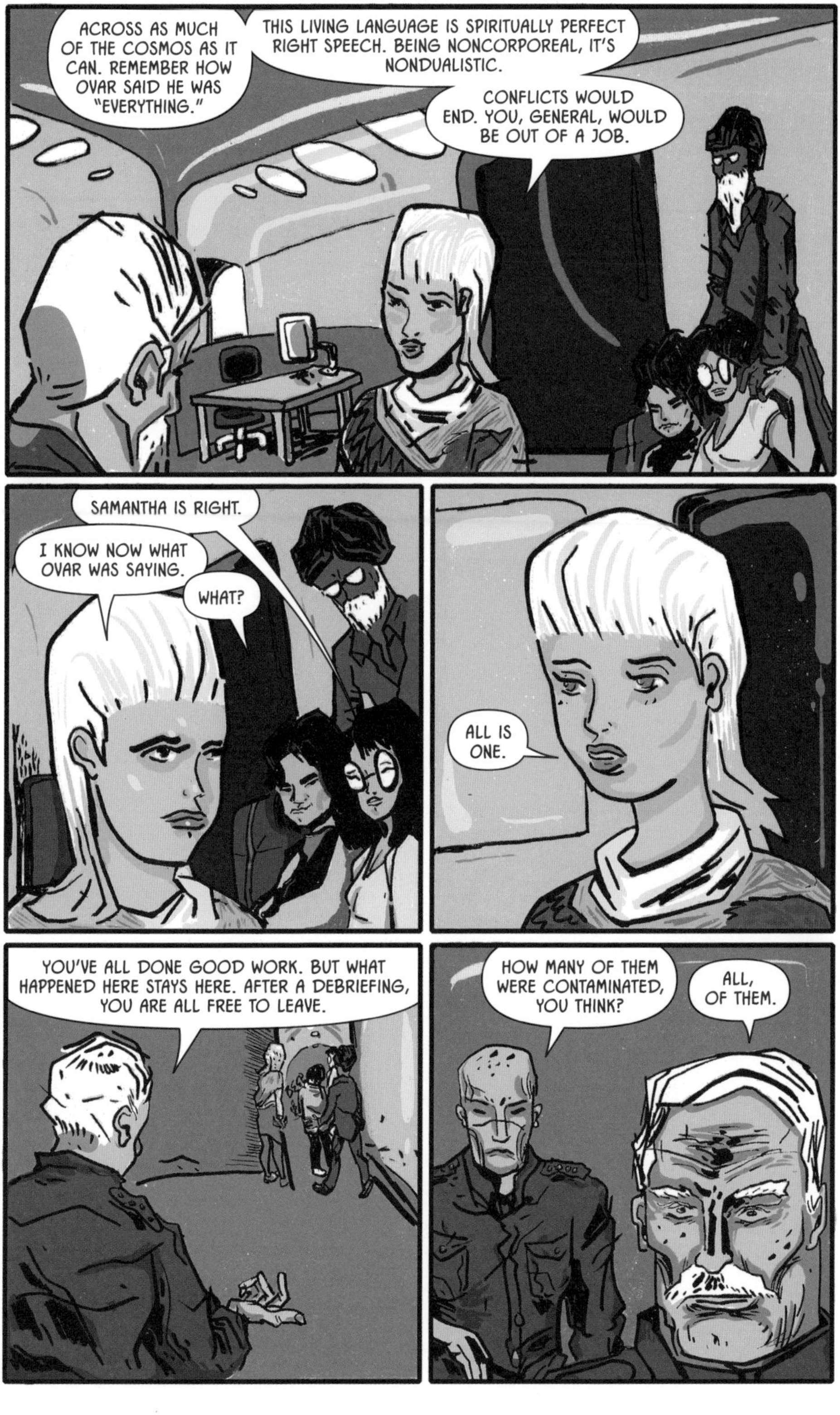
ACROSS AS MUCH OF THE COSMOS AS IT CAN. REMEMBER HOW OVAR SAID HE WAS "EVERYTHING."
THIS LIVING LANGUAGE IS SPIRITUALLY PERFECT RIGHT SPEECH. BEING NONCORPOREAL, IT'S NONDUALISTIC.
CONFLICTS WOULD END. YOU, GENERAL, WOULD BE OUT OF A JOB.
SAMANTHA IS RIGHT.
I KNOW NOW WHAT OVAR WAS SAYING.
WHAT?
ALL IS ONE.
YOU'VE ALL DONE GOOD WORK. BUT WHAT HAPPENED HERE STAYS HERE. AFTER A DEBRIEFING, YOU ARE ALL FREE TO LEAVE.
HOW MANY OF THEM WERE CONTAMINATED, YOU THINK?
ALL, OF THEM.

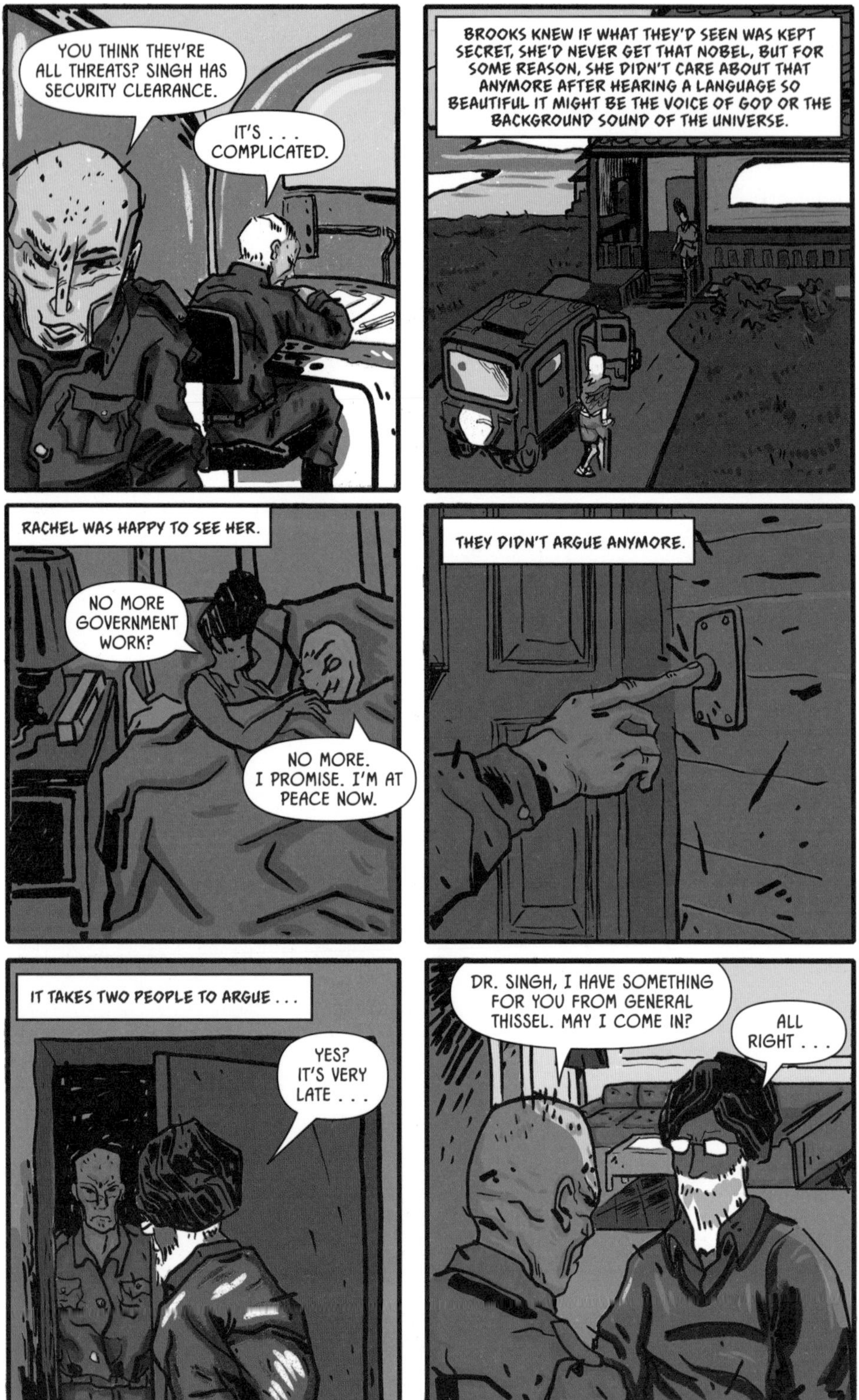
YOU THINK THEY'RE ALL THREATS? SINGH HAS SECURITY CLEARANCE.
IT'S . . . COMPLICATED.
BROOKS KNEW IF WHAT THEY'D SEEN WAS KEPT SECRET, SHE'D NEVER GET THAT NOBEL, BUT FOR SOME REASON, SHE DIDN'T CARE ABOUT THAT ANYMORE AFTER HEARING A LANGUAGE SO BEAUTIFUL IT MIGHT BE THE VOICE OF GOD OR THE BACKGROUND SOUND OF THE UNIVERSE.
RACHEL WAS HAPPY TO SEE HER.
NO MORE GOVERNMENT WORK?
NO MORE. I PROMISE. I'M AT PEACE NOW.
THEY DIDN'T ARGUE ANYMORE.
IT TAKES TWO PEOPLE TO ARGUE . . .
YES? IT'S VERY LATE . . .
DR. SINGH, I HAVE SOMETHING FOR YOU FROM GENERAL THISSEL. MAY I COME IN?
ALL RIGHT . . .

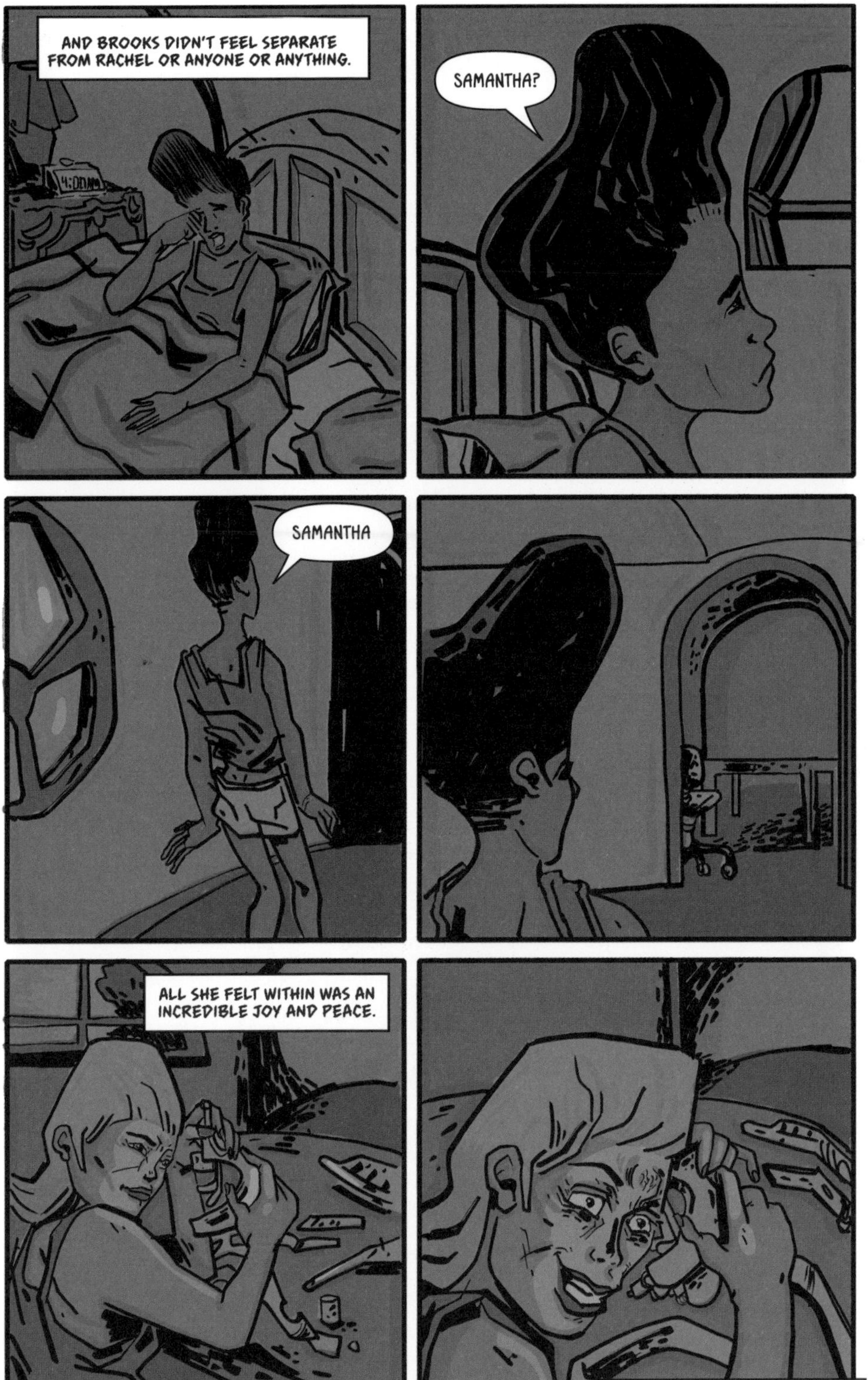
AND BROOKS DIDN'T FEEL SEPARATE FROM RACHEL OR ANYONE OR ANYTHING.
SAMANTHA?
SAMANTHA
ALL SHE FELT WITHIN WAS AN INCREDIBLE JOY AND PEACE.
AND THEN THE DOORBELL RANG.

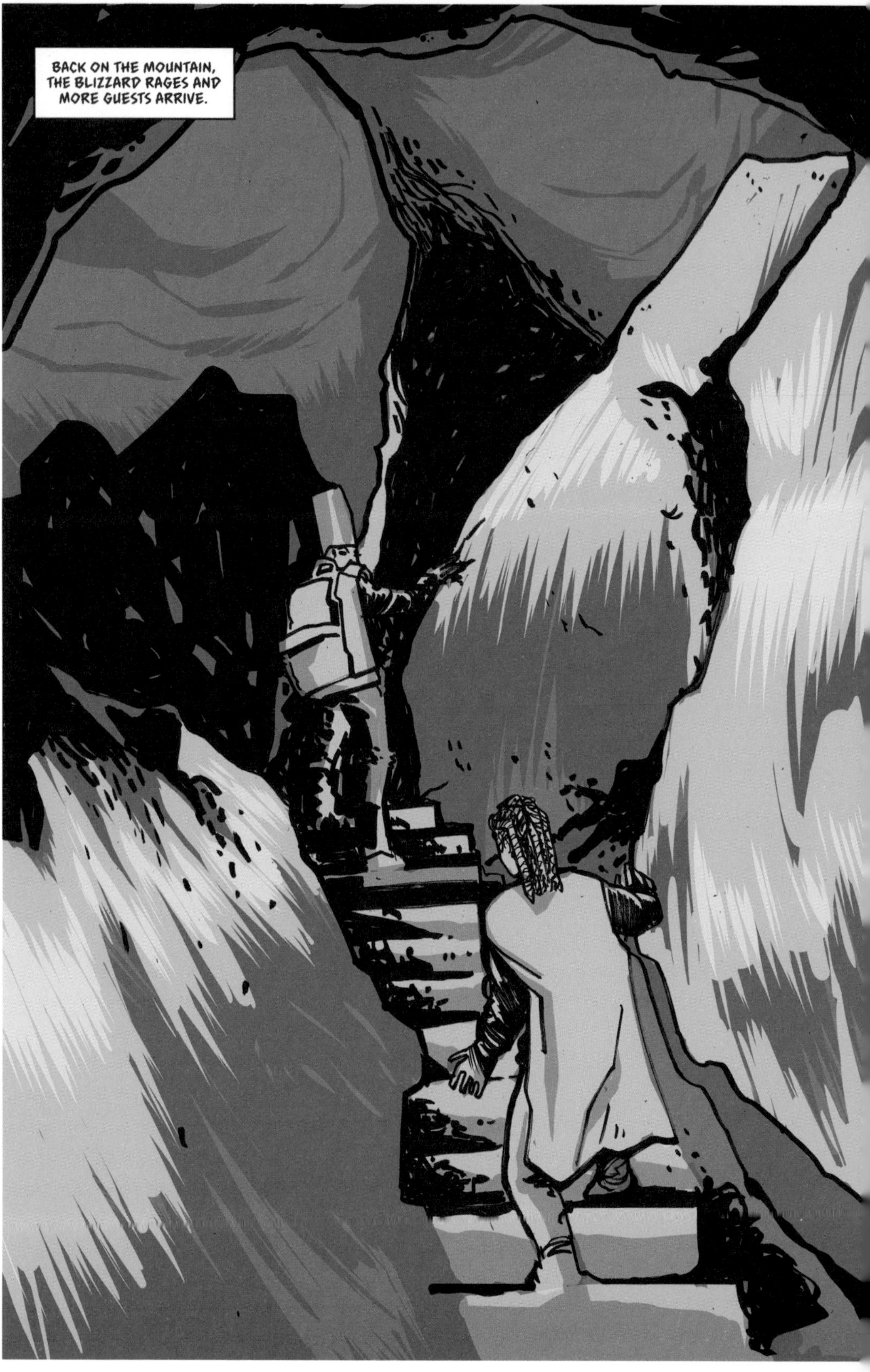
BACK ON THE MOUNTAIN, THE BLIZZARD RAGES AND MORE GUESTS ARRIVE.

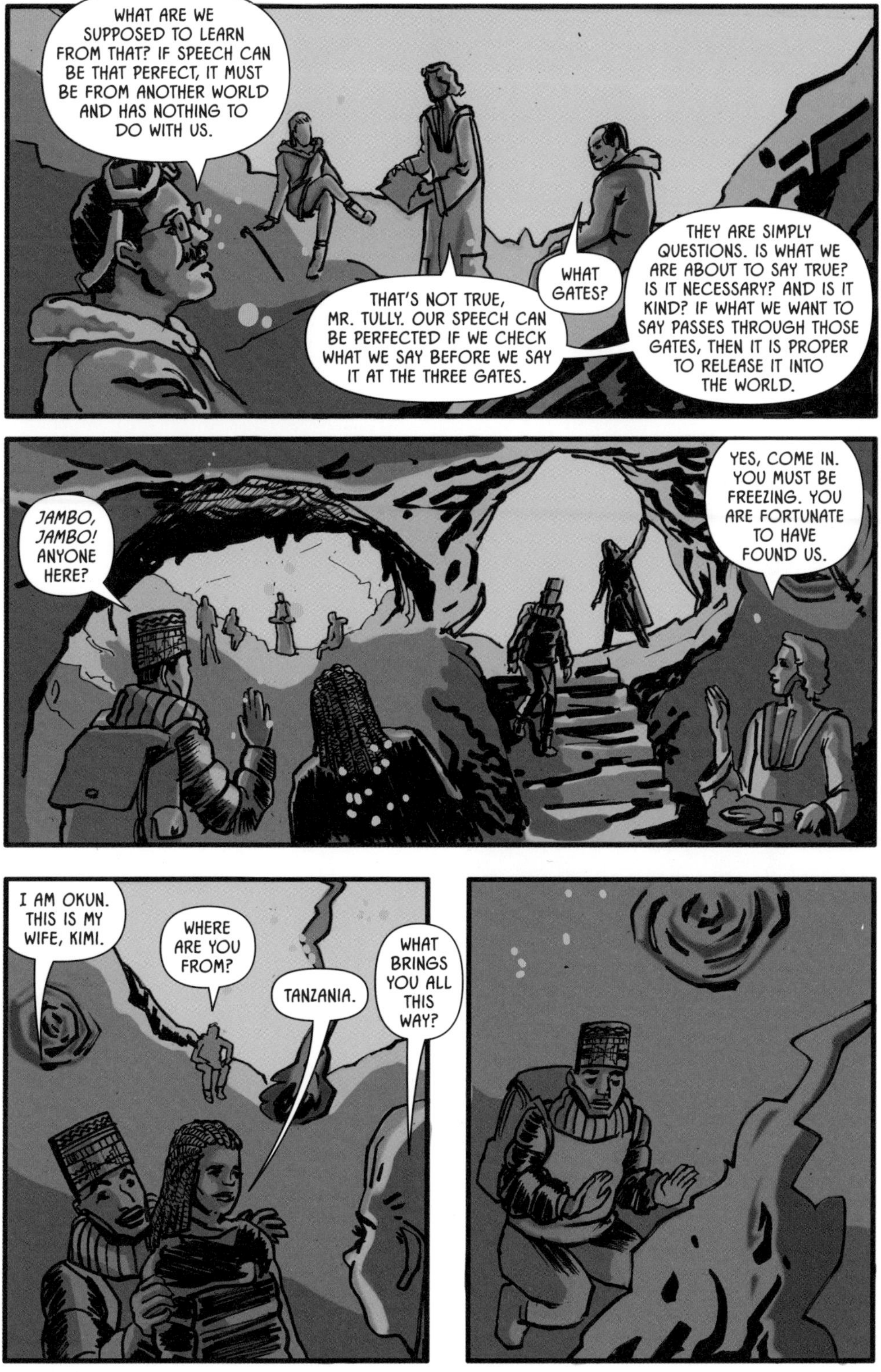
WHAT ARE WE SUPPOSED TO LEARN FROM THAT? IF SPEECH CAN BE THAT PERFECT, IT MUST BE FROM ANOTHER WORLD AND HAS NOTHING TO DO WITH US.
THAT'S NOT TRUE, MR. TULLY. OUR SPEECH CAN BE PERFECTED IF WE CHECK WHAT WE SAY BEFORE WE SAY IT AT THE THREE GATES.
WHAT GATES?
THEY ARE SIMPLY QUESTIONS. IS WHAT WE ARE ABOUT TO SAY TRUE? IS IT NECESSARY? AND IS IT KIND? IF WHAT WE WANT TO SAY PASSES THROUGH THOSE GATES, THEN IT IS PROPER TO RELEASE IT INTO THE WORLD.
JAMBO, JAMBO! ANYONE HERE?
YES, COME IN. YOU MUST BE FREEZING. YOU ARE FORTUNATE TO HAVE FOUND US.
I AM OKUN. THIS IS MY WIFE, KIMI.
WHERE ARE YOU FROM?
TANZANIA.
WHAT BRINGS YOU ALL THIS WAY?

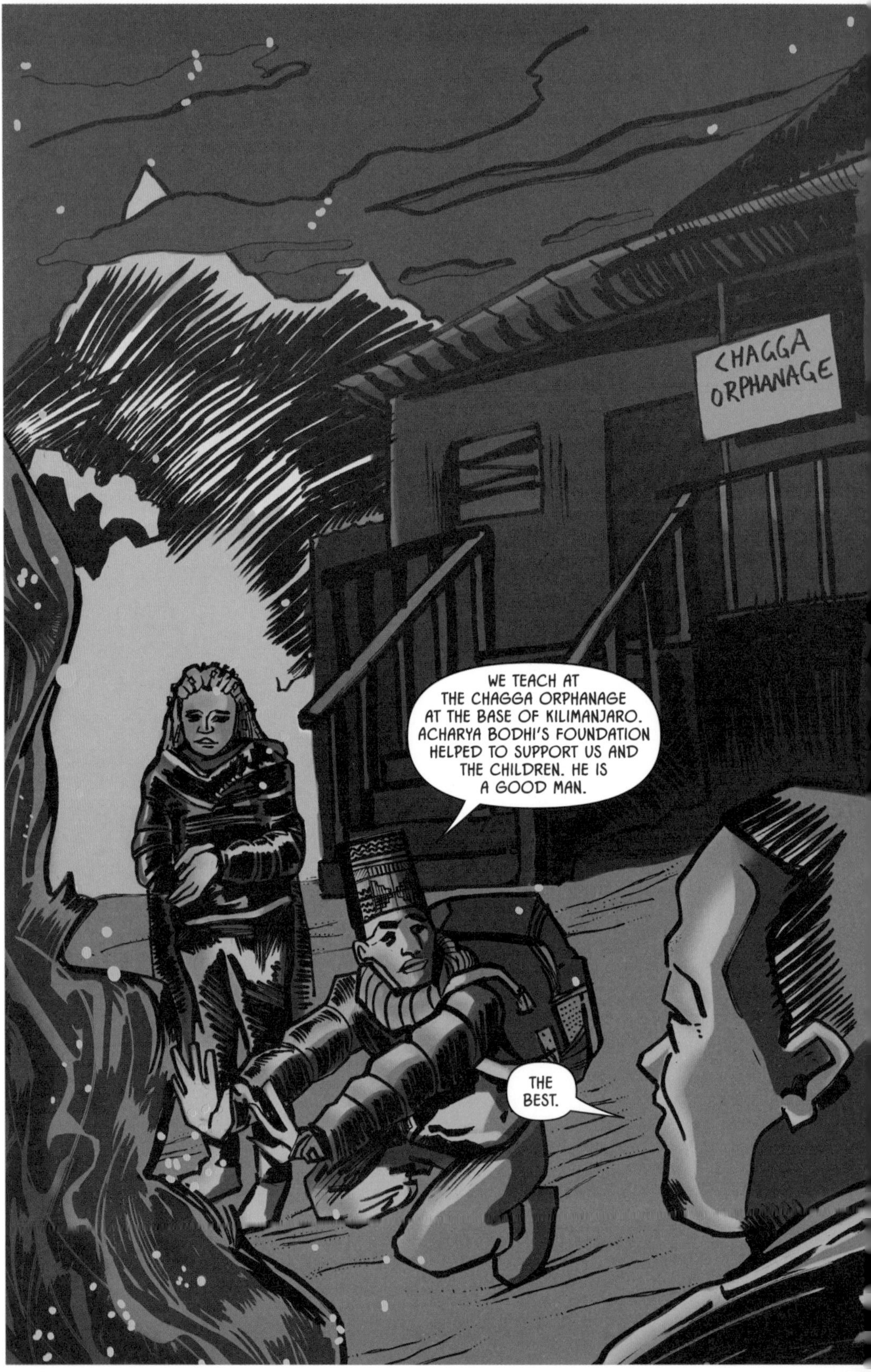
CHAGGA ORPHANAGE
WE TEACH AT THE CHAGGA ORPHANAGE AT THE BASE OF KILIMANJARO. ACHARYA BODHI'S FOUNDATION HELPED TO SUPPORT US AND THE CHILDREN. HE IS A GOOD MAN.
THE BEST.

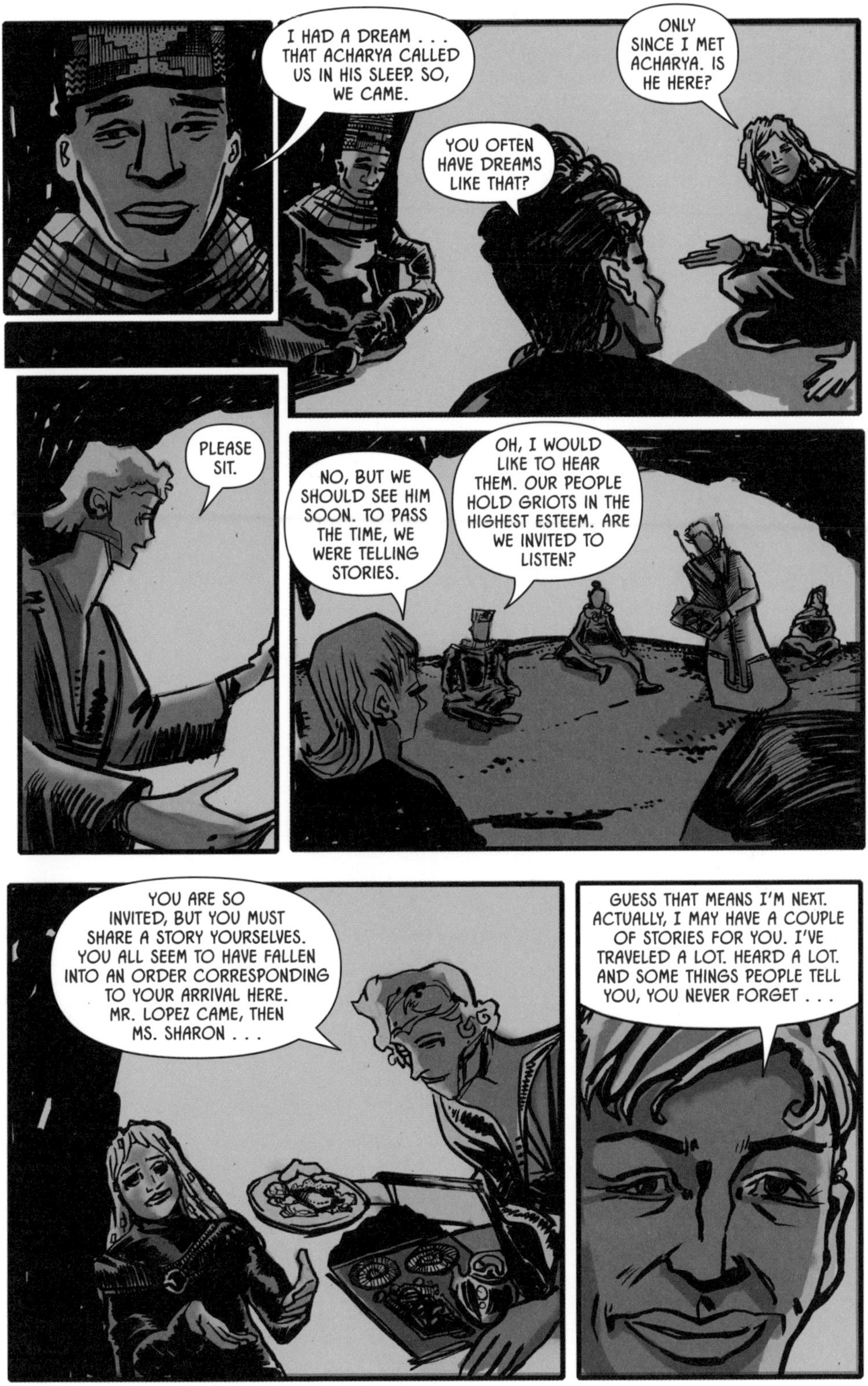
I HAD A DREAM . . . THAT ACHARYA CALLED US IN HIS SLEEP. SO, WE CAME.
YOU OFTEN HAVE DREAMS LIKE THAT?
ONLY SINCE I MET ACHARYA. IS HE HERE?
PLEASE SIT.
NO, BUT WE SHOULD SEE HIM SOON. TO PASS THE TIME, WE WERE TELLING STORIES.
OH, I WOULD LIKE TO HEAR THEM. OUR PEOPLE HOLD GRIOTS IN THE HIGHEST ESTEEM. ARE WE INVITED TO LISTEN?
YOU ARE SO INVITED, BUT YOU MUST SHARE A STORY YOURSELVES. YOU ALL SEEM TO HAVE FALLEN INTO AN ORDER CORRESPONDING TO YOUR ARRIVAL HERE. MR. LOPEZ CAME, THEN MS. SHARON . . .
GUESS THAT MEANS I'M NEXT. ACTUALLY, I MAY HAVE A COUPLE OF STORIES FOR YOU. I'VE TRAVELED A LOT. HEARD A LOT. AND SOME THINGS PEOPLE TELL YOU, YOU NEVER FORGET . . .

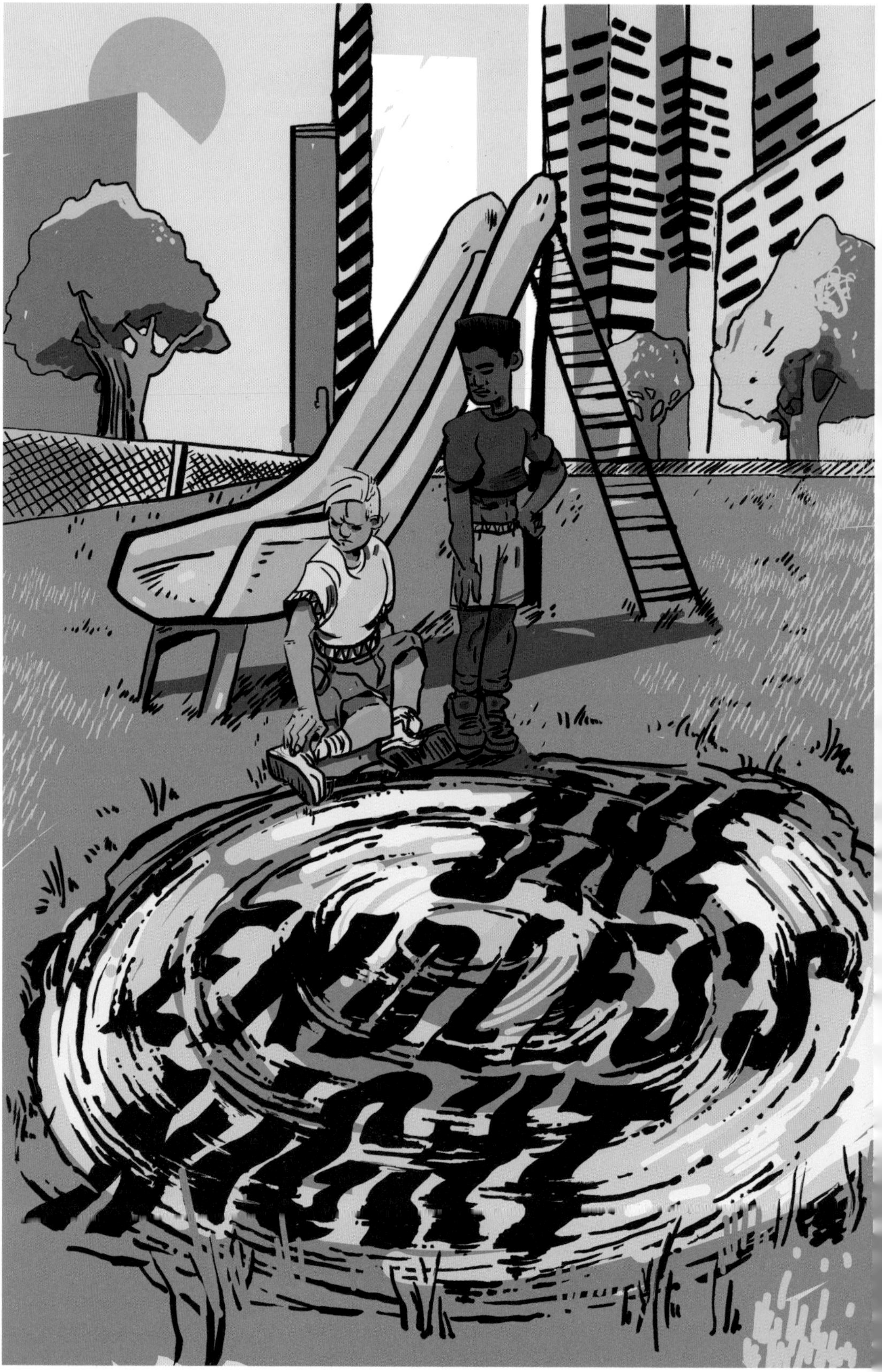

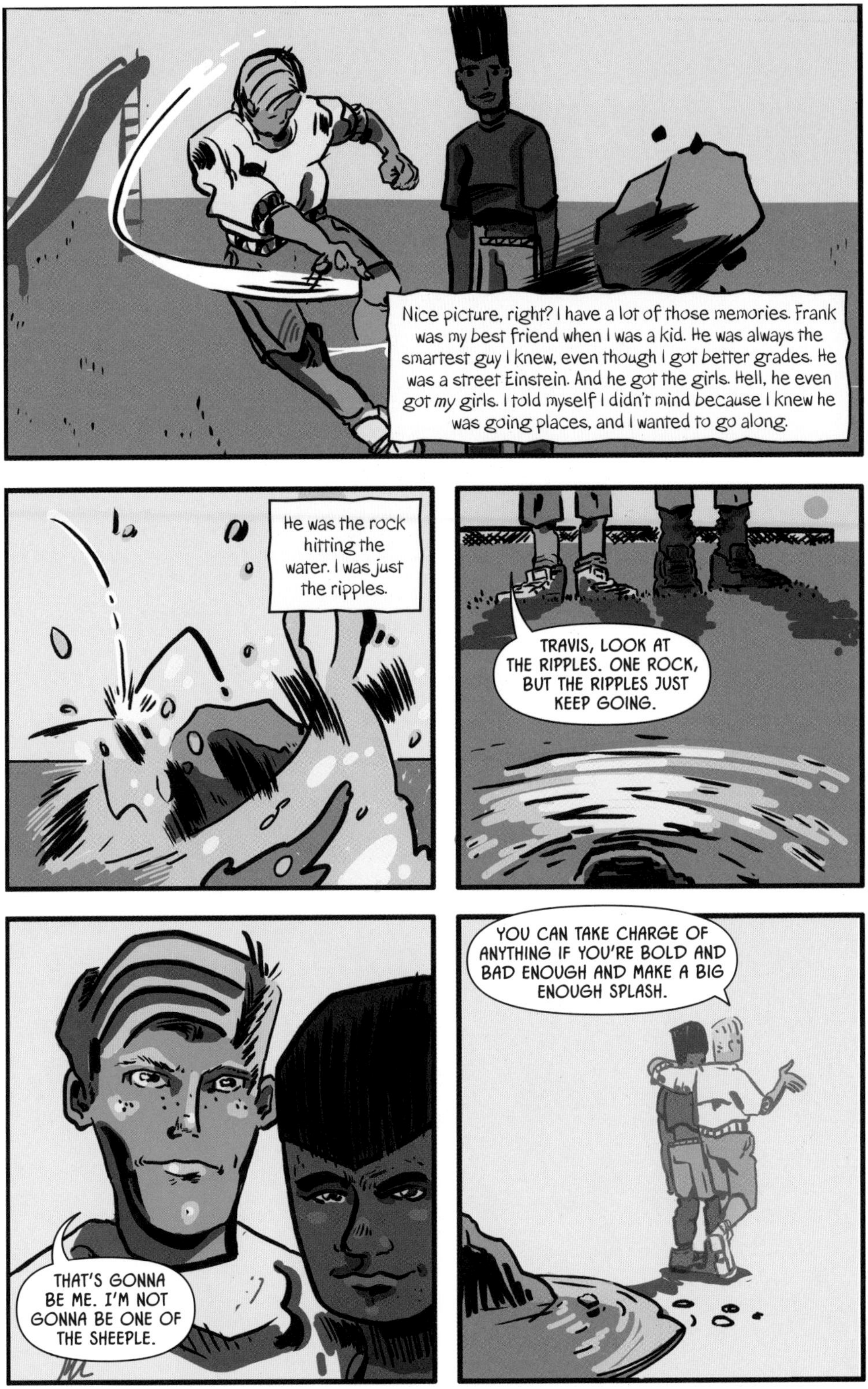
Nice picture, right? I have a lot of those memories. Frank was my best friend when I was a kid. He was always the smartest guy I knew, even though I got better grades. He was a street Einstein. And he got the girls. Hell, he even got *my* girls. I told myself I didn't mind because I knew he was going places, and I wanted to go along.
He was the rock hitting the water. I was just the ripples.
TRAVIS, LOOK AT THE RIPPLES. ONE ROCK, BUT THE RIPPLES JUST KEEP GOING.
THAT'S GONNA BE ME. I'M NOT GONNA BE ONE OF THE SHEEPLE.
YOU CAN TAKE CHARGE OF ANYTHING IF YOU'RE BOLD AND BAD ENOUGH AND MAKE A BIG ENOUGH SPLASH.

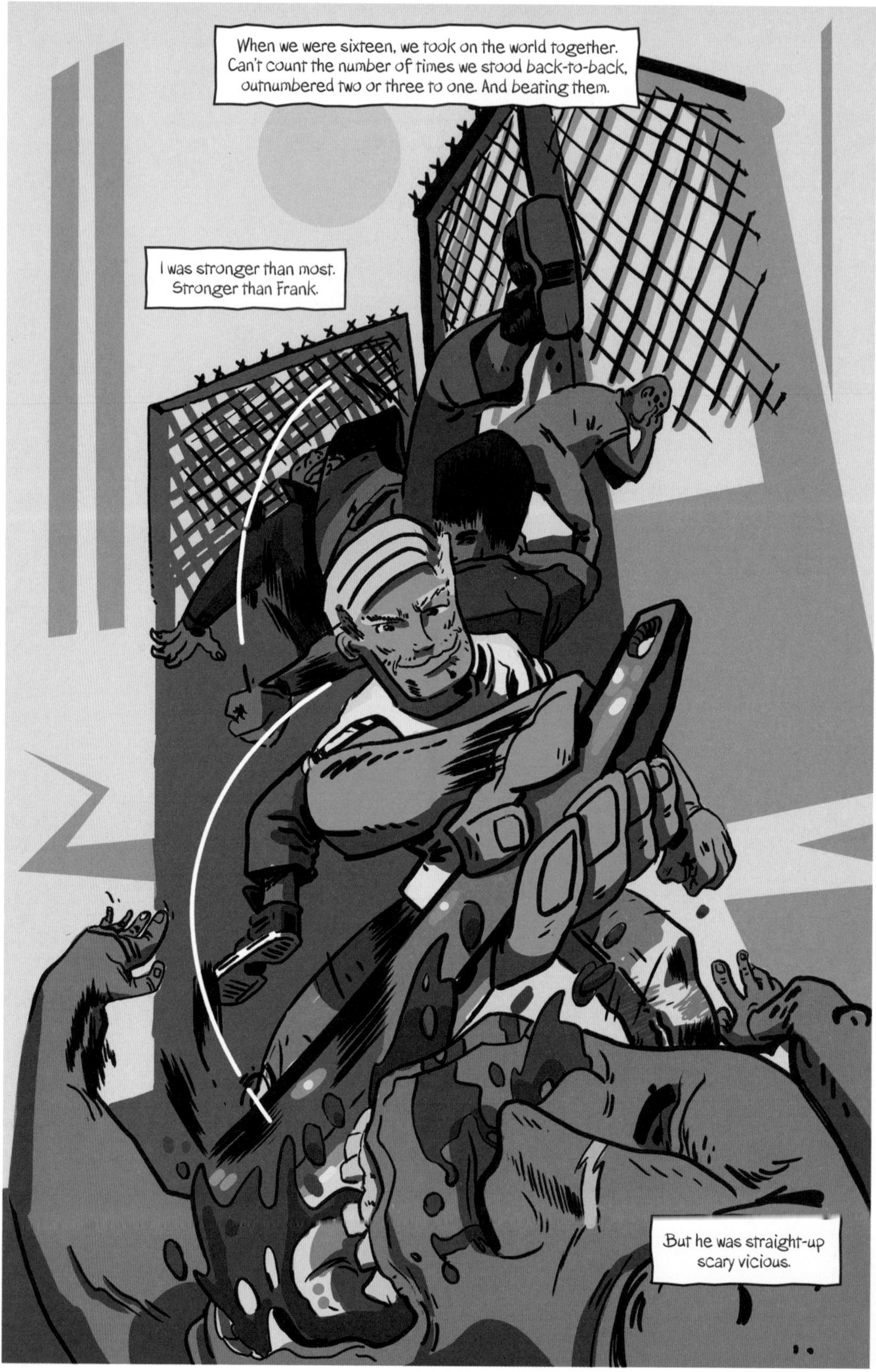
When we were sixteen, we took on the world together. Can't count the number of times we stood back-to-back, outnumbered two or three to one. And beating them.
I was stronger than most. Stronger than Frank.
But he was straight-up scary vicious.

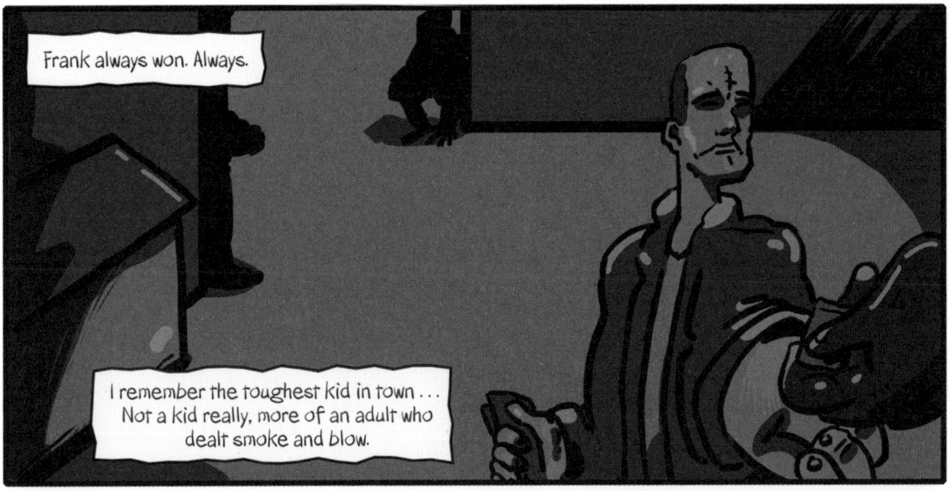
Frank always won. Always.
I remember the toughest kid in town . . . Not a kid really, more of an adult who dealt smoke and blow.

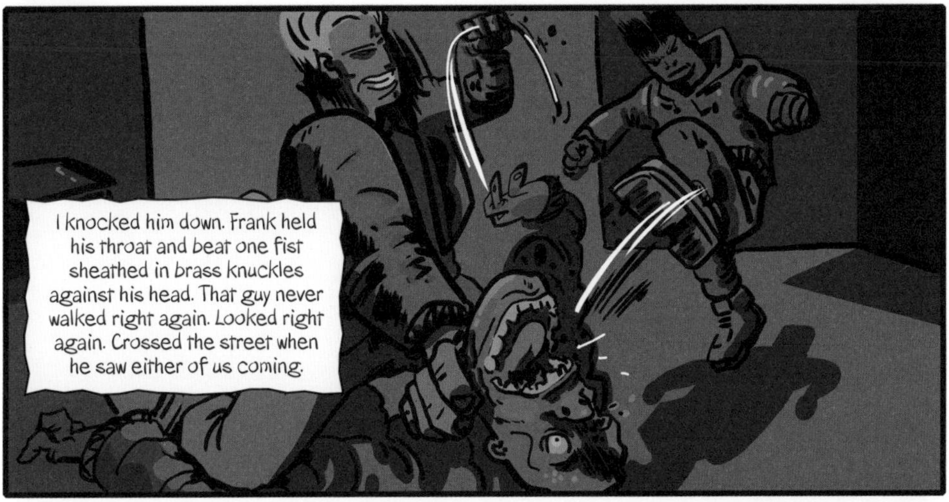
I knocked him down. Frank held his throat and beat one fist sheathed in brass knuckles against his head. That guy never walked right again. Looked right again. Crossed the street when he saw either of us coming.

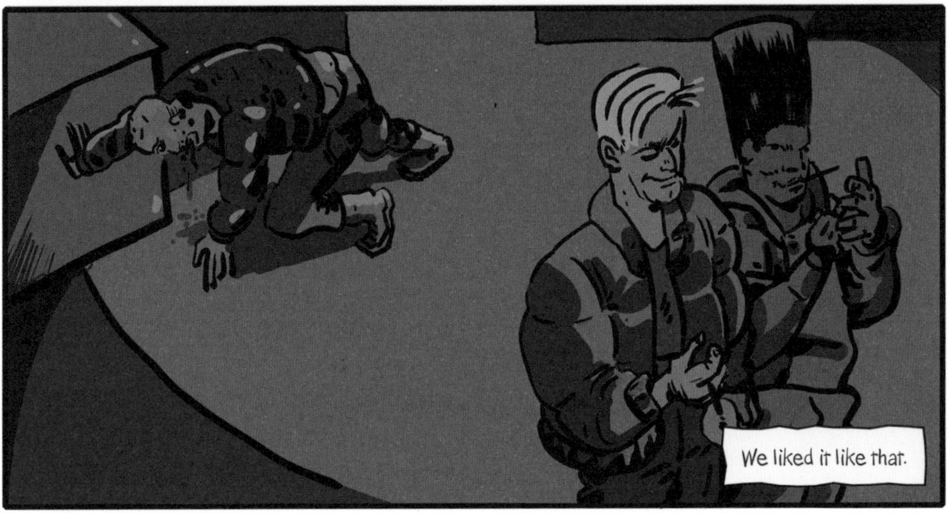
We liked it like that.

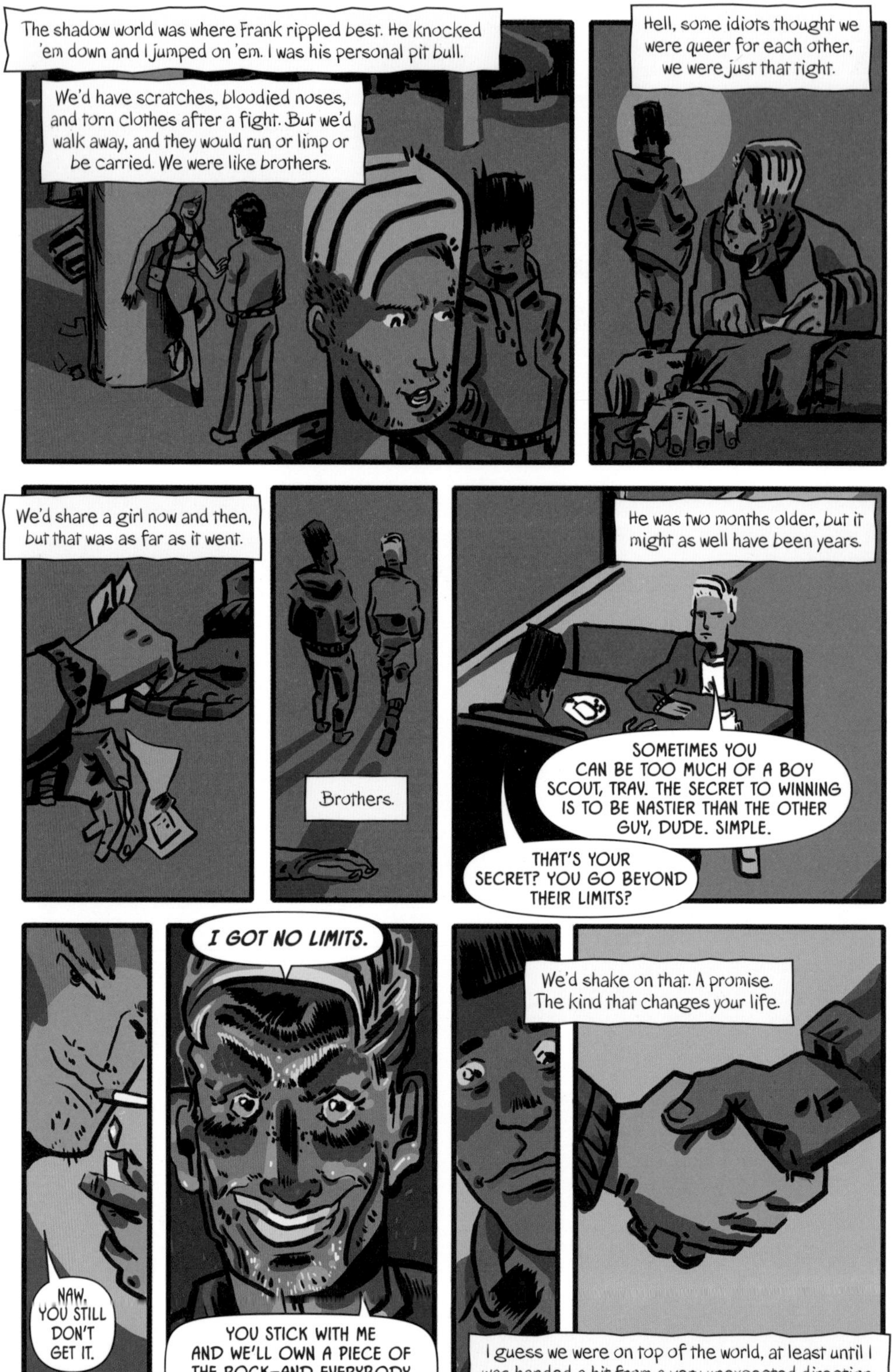

The shadow world was where Frank rippled best. He knocked 'em down and I jumped on 'em. I was his personal pit bull.
We'd have scratches, bloodied noses, and torn clothes after a fight. But we'd walk away, and they would run or limp or be carried. We were like brothers.
Hell, some idiots thought we were queer for each other, we were just that tight.
We'd share a girl now and then, but that was as far as it went.
Brothers.
He was two months older, but it might as well have been years.
SOMETIMES YOU CAN BE TOO MUCH OF A BOY SCOUT, TRAV. THE SECRET TO WINNING IS TO BE NASTIER THAN THE OTHER GUY, DUDE. SIMPLE.
THAT'S YOUR SECRET? YOU GO BEYOND THEIR LIMITS?
NAW, YOU STILL DON'T GET IT.
I GOT NO LIMITS.
YOU STICK WITH ME AND WE'LL OWN A PIECE OF THE ROCK—AND EVERYBODY ELSE'S CHUNK, TOO.
We'd shake on that. A promise. The kind that changes your life.
I guess we were on top of the world, at least until I was handed a hit from a very unexpected direction.

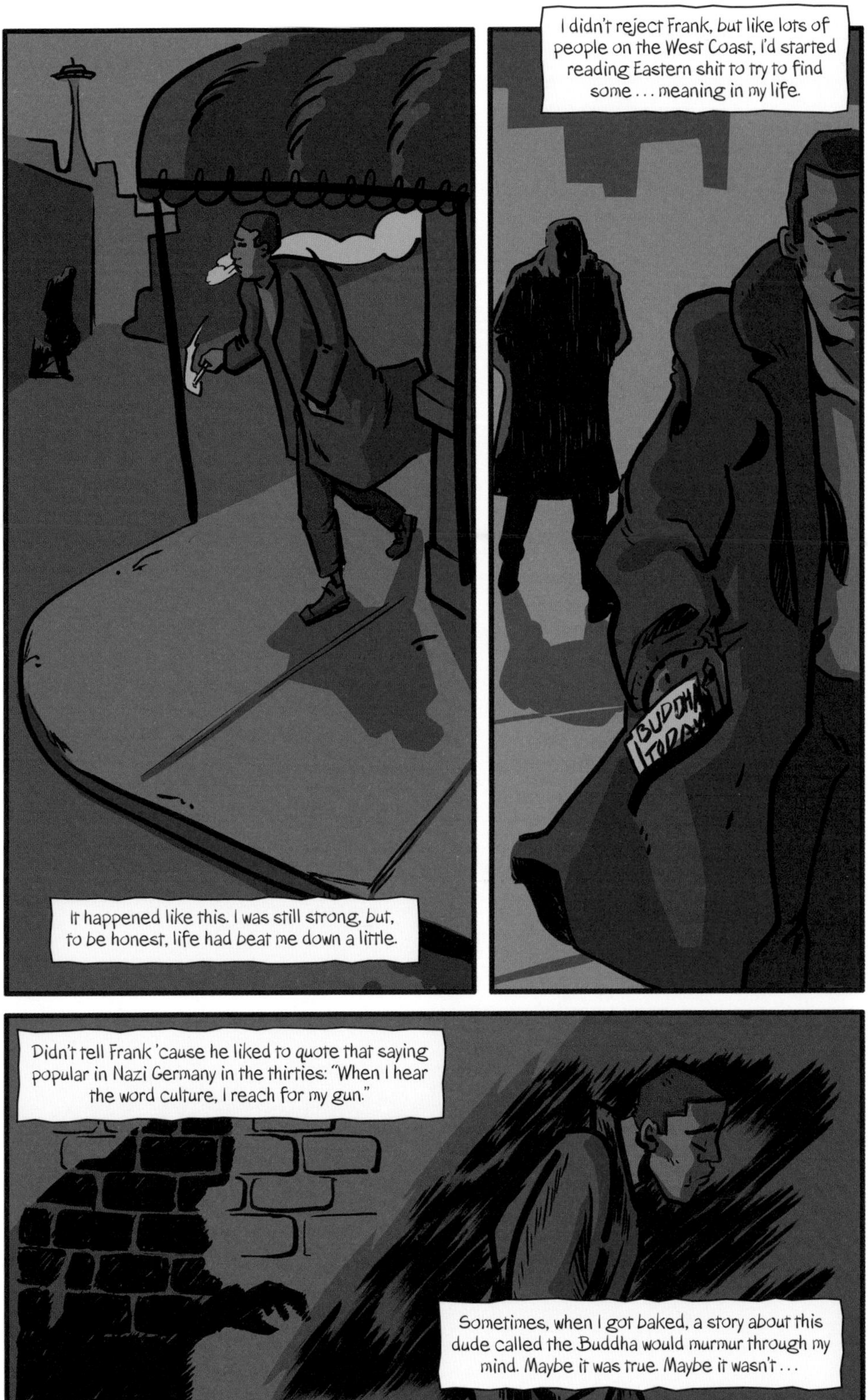
It happened like this. I was still strong, but, to be honest, life had beat me down a little.
I didn't reject Frank, but like lots of people on the West Coast, I'd started reading Eastern shit to try to find some . . . meaning in my life.
Didn't tell Frank 'cause he liked to quote that saying popular in Nazi Germany in the thirties: "When I hear the word culture, I reach for my gun."
Sometimes, when I got baked, a story about this dude called the Buddha would murmur through my mind. Maybe it was true. Maybe it wasn't . . .

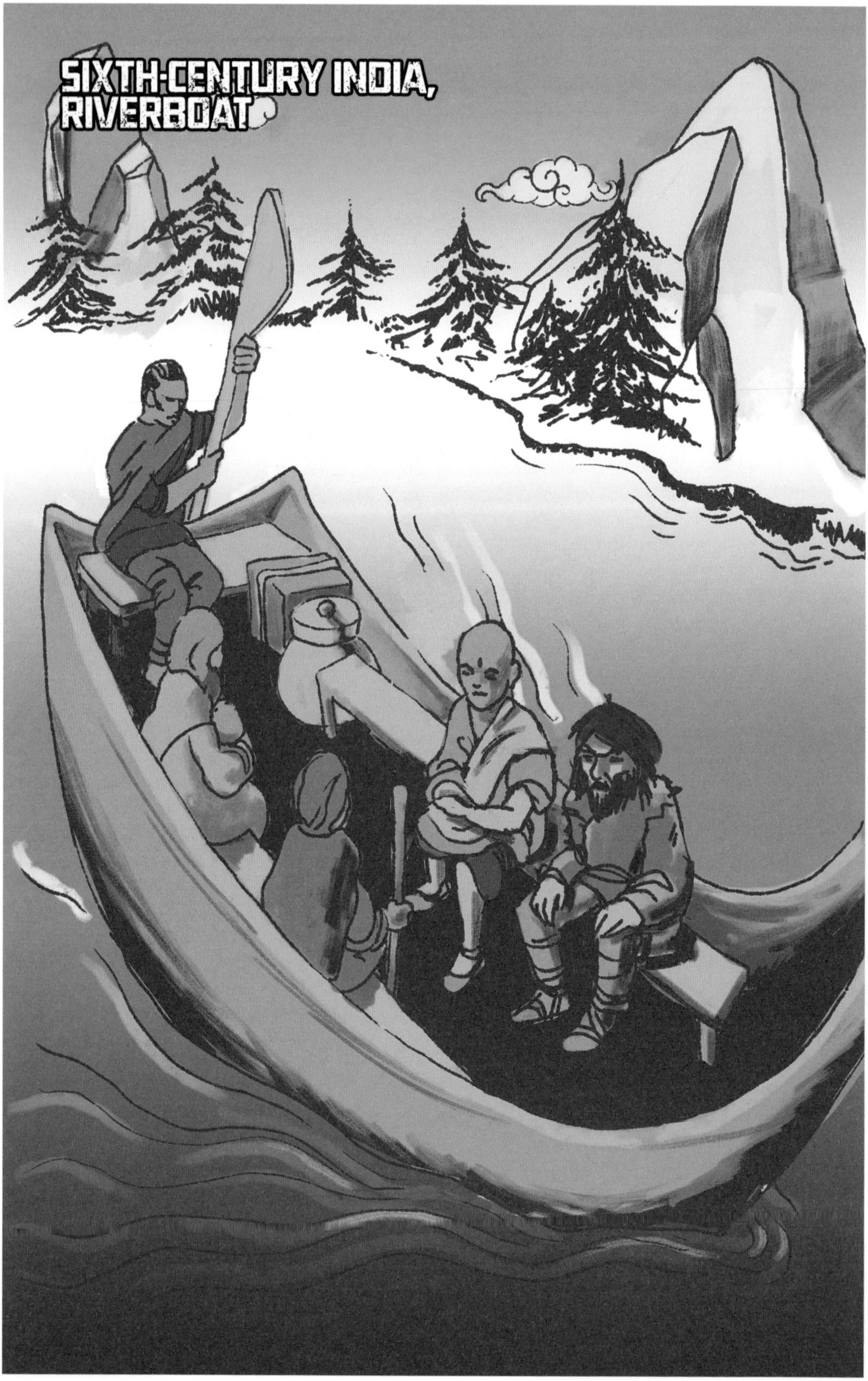
SIXTH-CENTURY INDIA,
RIVERBOAT

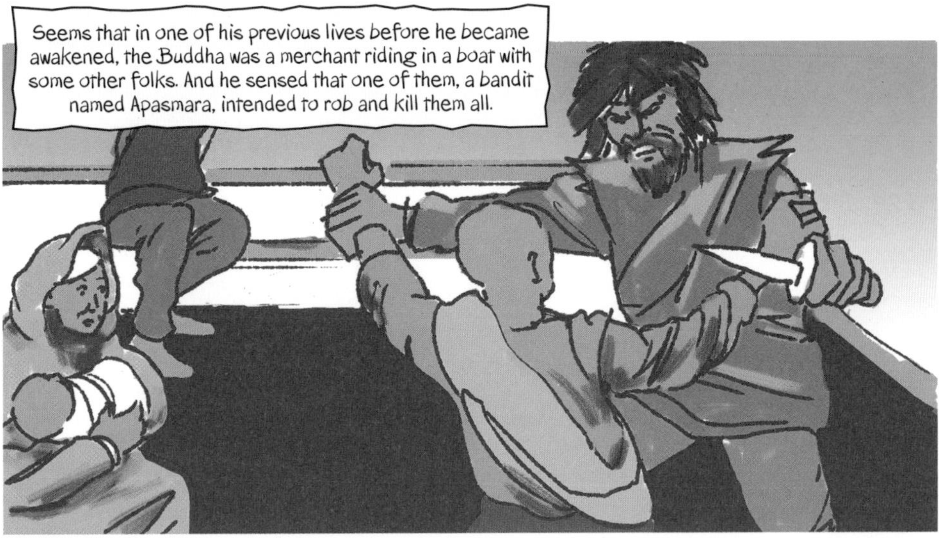
Seems that in one of his previous lives before he became awakened, the Buddha was a merchant riding in a boat with some other folks. And he sensed that one of them, a bandit named Apasmara, intended to rob and kill them all.

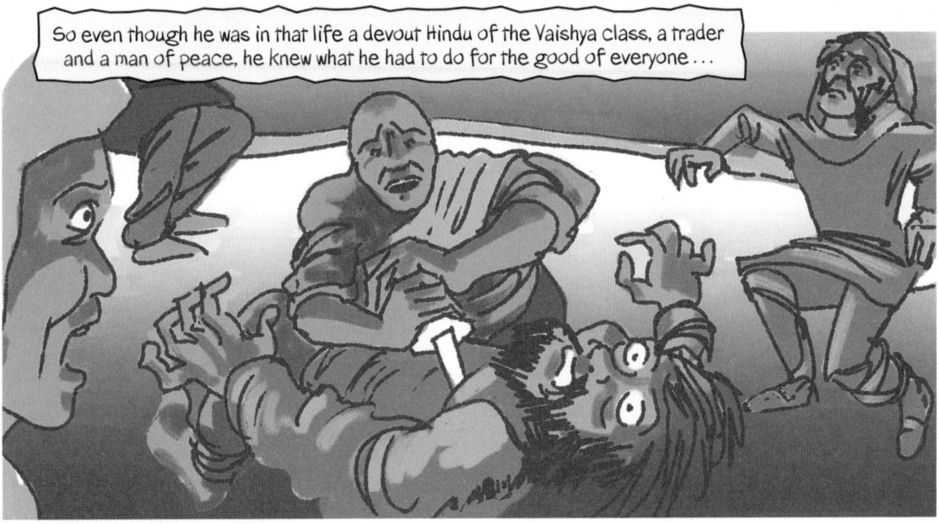
So even though he was in that life a devout Hindu of the Vaishya class, a trader and a man of peace, he knew what he had to do for the good of everyone . . .

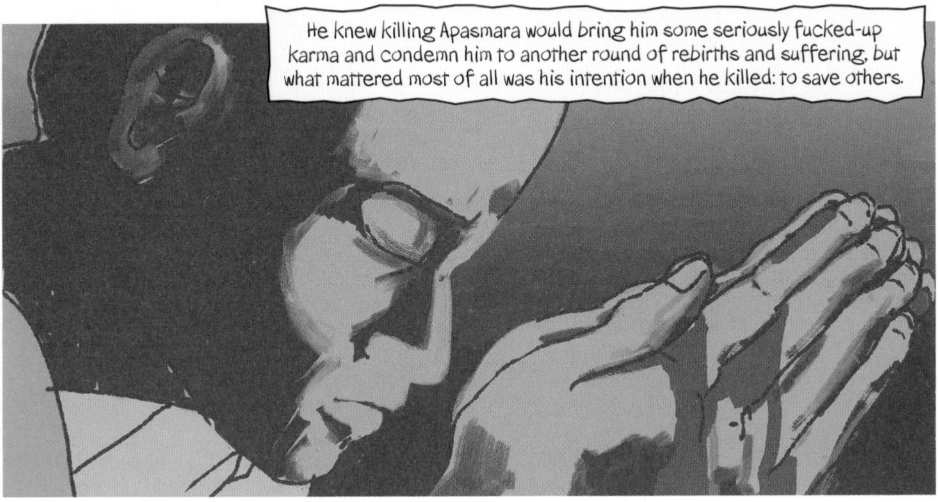
He knew killing Apasmara would bring him some seriously fucked-up karma and condemn him to another round of rebirths and suffering, but what mattered most of all was his intention when he killed: to save others.

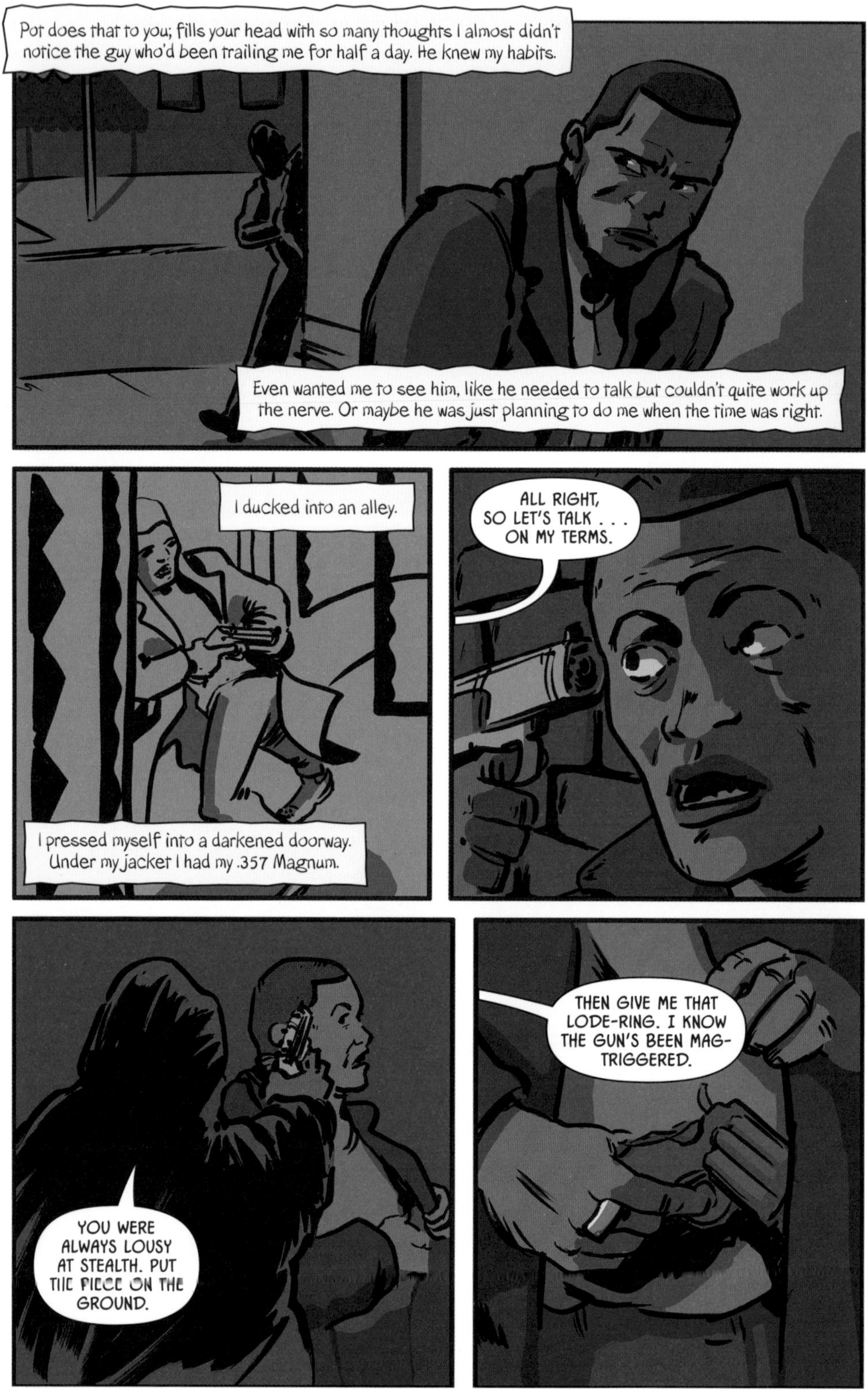
Pot does that to you; fills your head with so many thoughts I almost didn't notice the guy who'd been trailing me for half a day. He knew my habits.
Even wanted me to see him, like he needed to talk but couldn't quite work up the nerve. Or maybe he was just planning to do me when the time was right.
I ducked into an alley.
I pressed myself into a darkened doorway. Under my jacket I had my .357 Magnum.
ALL RIGHT, SO LET'S TALK . . . ON MY TERMS.
YOU WERE ALWAYS LOUSY AT STEALTH. PUT THE PIECE ON THE GROUND.
THEN GIVE ME THAT LODE-RING. I KNOW THE GUN'S BEEN MAG-TRIGGERED.

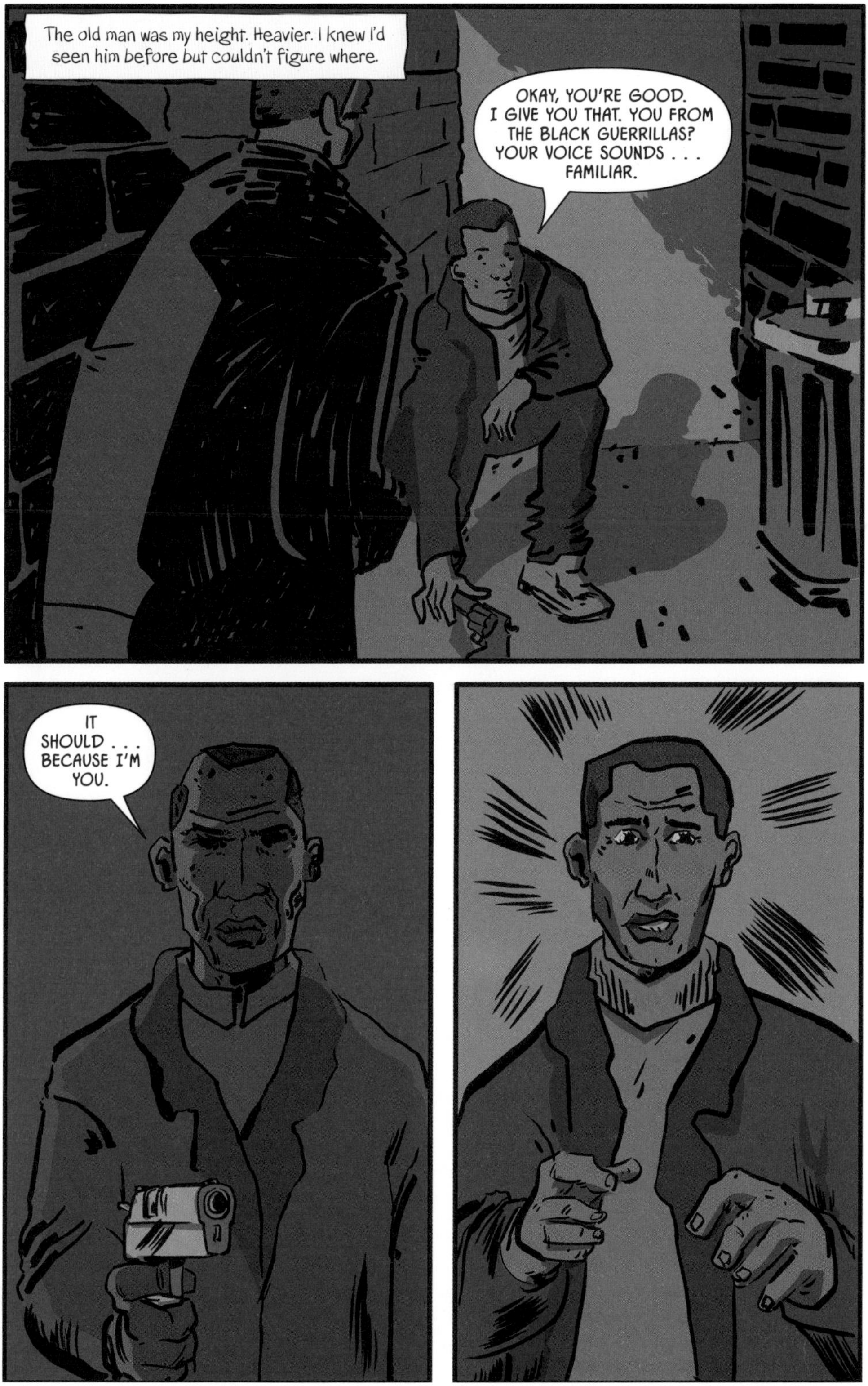
The old man was my height. Heavier. I knew I'd seen him before but couldn't figure where.
OKAY, YOU'RE GOOD. I GIVE YOU THAT. YOU FROM THE BLACK GUERRILLAS? YOUR VOICE SOUNDS . . . FAMILIAR.
IT SHOULD . . . BECAUSE I'M YOU.

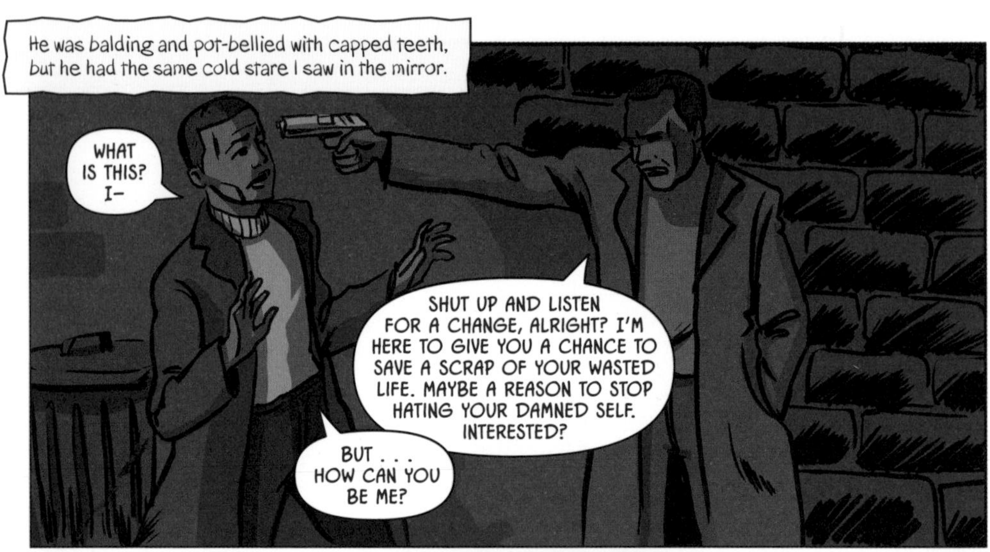
He was balding and pot-bellied with capped teeth, but he had the same cold stare I saw in the mirror.
WHAT IS THIS? I–
SHUT UP AND LISTEN FOR A CHANGE, ALRIGHT? I'M HERE TO GIVE YOU A CHANCE TO SAVE A SCRAP OF YOUR WASTED LIFE. MAYBE A REASON TO STOP HATING YOUR DAMNED SELF. INTERESTED?
BUT . . . HOW CAN YOU BE ME?

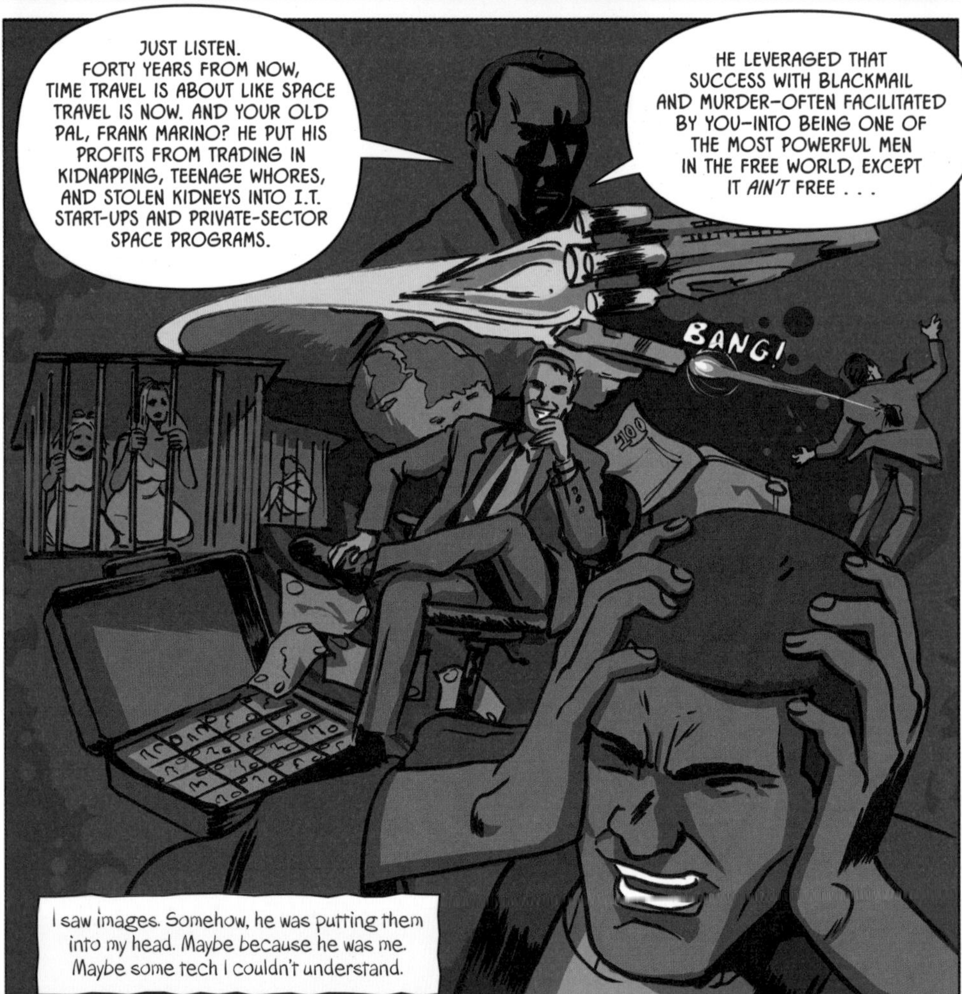
JUST LISTEN. FORTY YEARS FROM NOW, TIME TRAVEL IS ABOUT LIKE SPACE TRAVEL IS NOW. AND YOUR OLD PAL, FRANK MARINO? HE PUT HIS PROFITS FROM TRADING IN KIDNAPPING, TEENAGE WHORES, AND STOLEN KIDNEYS INTO I.T. START-UPS AND PRIVATE-SECTOR SPACE PROGRAMS.
HE LEVERAGED THAT SUCCESS WITH BLACKMAIL AND MURDER–OFTEN FACILITATED BY YOU–INTO BEING ONE OF THE MOST POWERFUL MEN IN THE FREE WORLD, EXCEPT IT *AIN'T* FREE . . .
BANG!
I saw images. Somehow, he was putting them into my head. Maybe because he was me. Maybe some tech I couldn't understand.

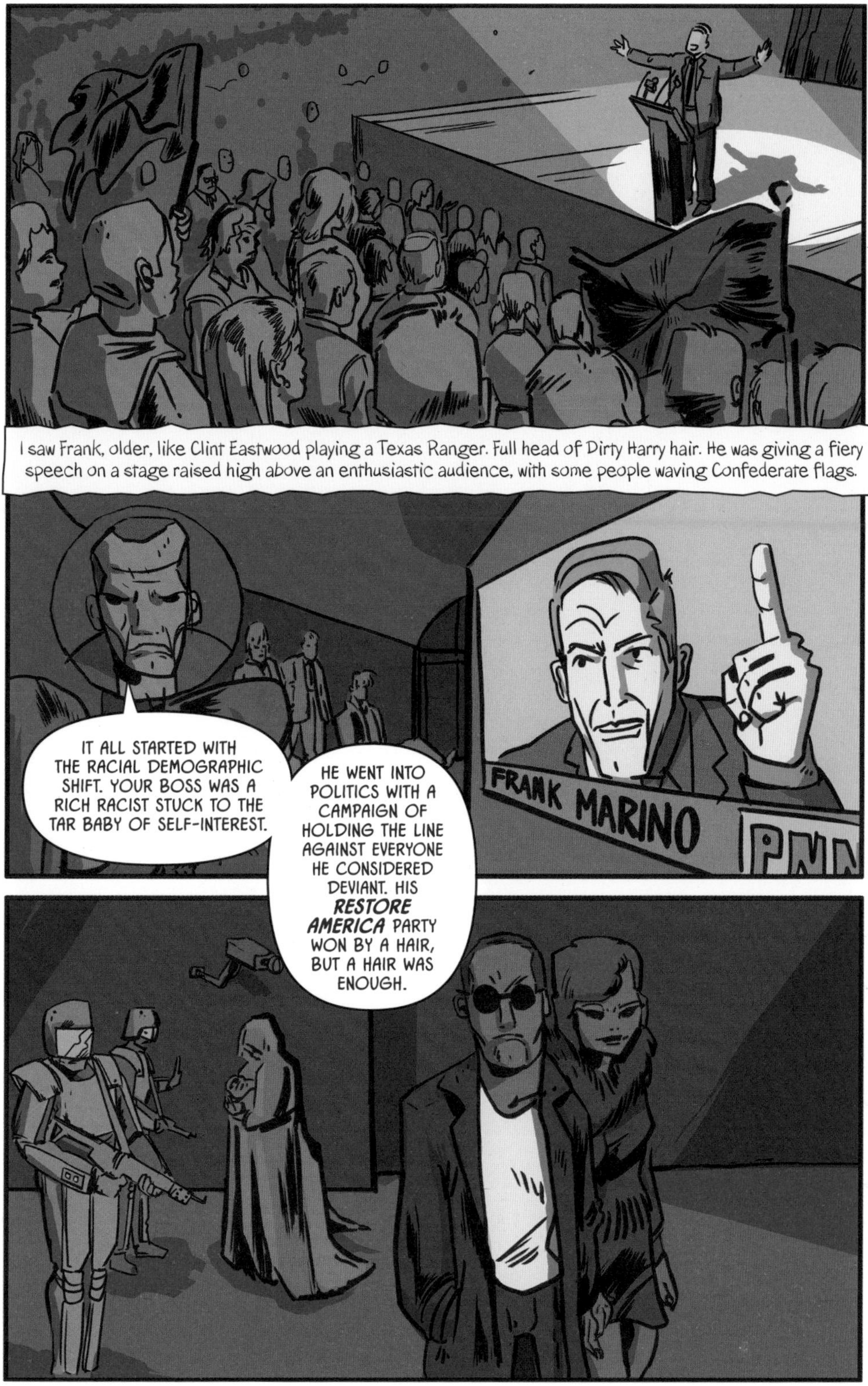
I saw Frank, older, like Clint Eastwood playing a Texas Ranger. Full head of Dirty Harry hair. He was giving a fiery speech on a stage raised high above an enthusiastic audience, with some people waving Confederate flags.
IT ALL STARTED WITH THE RACIAL DEMOGRAPHIC SHIFT. YOUR BOSS WAS A RICH RACIST STUCK TO THE TAR BABY OF SELF-INTEREST.
FRANK MARINO
HE WENT INTO POLITICS WITH A CAMPAIGN OF HOLDING THE LINE AGAINST EVERYONE HE CONSIDERED DEVIANT. HIS ***RESTORE AMERICA*** PARTY WON BY A HAIR, BUT A HAIR WAS ENOUGH.

"DURING HIS FIRST TERM, HE PLAYED HIS HAND CAREFULLY. HIS DEPARTMENT OF JUSTICE AND SUPREME COURT PICKS LET AFFIRMATIVE ACTION DIE AND SOCIETY SLOWLY RESEGREGATE ITSELF ALONG TRIBAL LINES."

"GRADUALLY, A NEW CASTE SYSTEM TOOK HOLD. THE WAR ON TERROR TURNED INWARD."

"THEN THE ETHNIC CLEANSING BEGAN."

MARINO ENGINEERED BOMBINGS OF FEDERAL BUILDINGS. THE GOVERNMENT INVOKED EMERGENCY POWERS TO DEAL WITH A MANUFACTURED CRISIS.

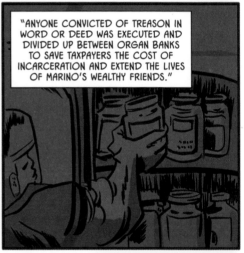

"ANYONE CONVICTED OF TREASON IN WORD OR DEED WAS EXECUTED AND DIVIDED UP BETWEEN ORGAN BANKS TO SAVE TAXPAYERS THE COST OF INCARCERATION AND EXTEND THE LIVES OF MARINO'S WEALTHY FRIENDS."

THE ONLY REASON I'M ALIVE IS BECAUSE PRESIDENT MARINO LIKES ME BECAUSE—YOU—CLEANED UP PROBLEMS FOR HIM BACK IN THE DAY WHEN HE WAS JUST ANOTHER THUG.

I GET IT NOW. THIS WEED MUST BE DUSTED. YOU'RE NOT REAL. SAY WHATEVER YOU WANT. THE FUTURE IS CRAP? SO, WHAT ELSE IS NEW? WHAT DO YOU WANT ME TO DO ABOUT IT?

KILL HIM.

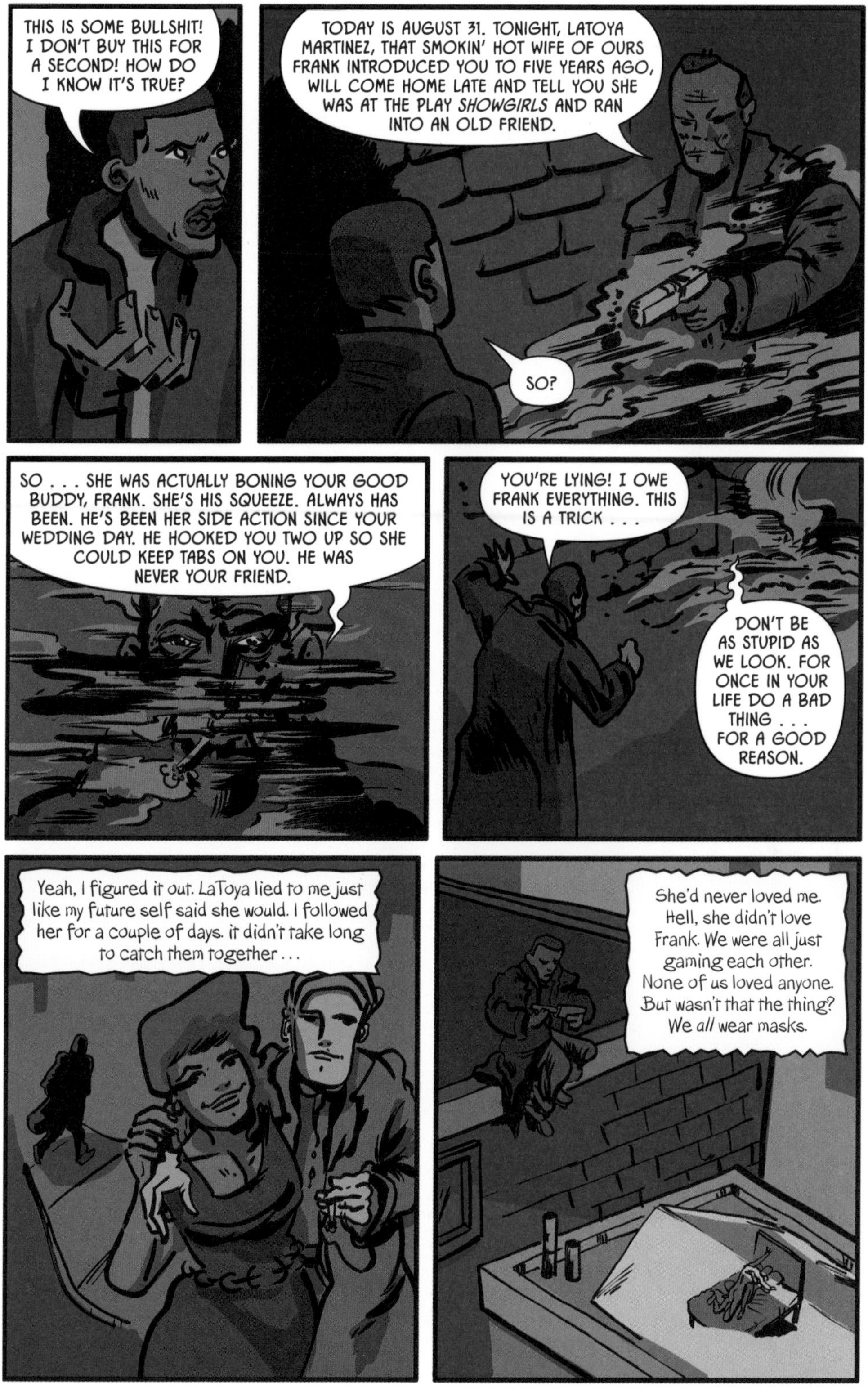
THIS IS SOME BULLSHIT! I DON'T BUY THIS FOR A SECOND! HOW DO I KNOW IT'S TRUE?
TODAY IS AUGUST 31. TONIGHT, LATOYA MARTINEZ, THAT SMOKIN' HOT WIFE OF OURS FRANK INTRODUCED YOU TO FIVE YEARS AGO, WILL COME HOME LATE AND TELL YOU SHE WAS AT THE PLAY *SHOWGIRLS* AND RAN INTO AN OLD FRIEND.
SO?
SO . . . SHE WAS ACTUALLY BONING YOUR GOOD BUDDY, FRANK. SHE'S HIS SQUEEZE. ALWAYS HAS BEEN. HE'S BEEN HER SIDE ACTION SINCE YOUR WEDDING DAY. HE HOOKED YOU TWO UP SO SHE COULD KEEP TABS ON YOU. HE WAS NEVER YOUR FRIEND.
YOU'RE LYING! I OWE FRANK EVERYTHING. THIS IS A TRICK . . .
DON'T BE AS STUPID AS WE LOOK. FOR ONCE IN YOUR LIFE DO A BAD THING . . . FOR A GOOD REASON.
Yeah, I figured it out. LaToya lied to me just like my future self said she would. I followed her for a couple of days. it didn't take long to catch them together . . .
She'd never loved me. Hell, she didn't love Frank. We were all just gaming each other. None of us loved anyone. But wasn't that the thing? We *all* wear masks.

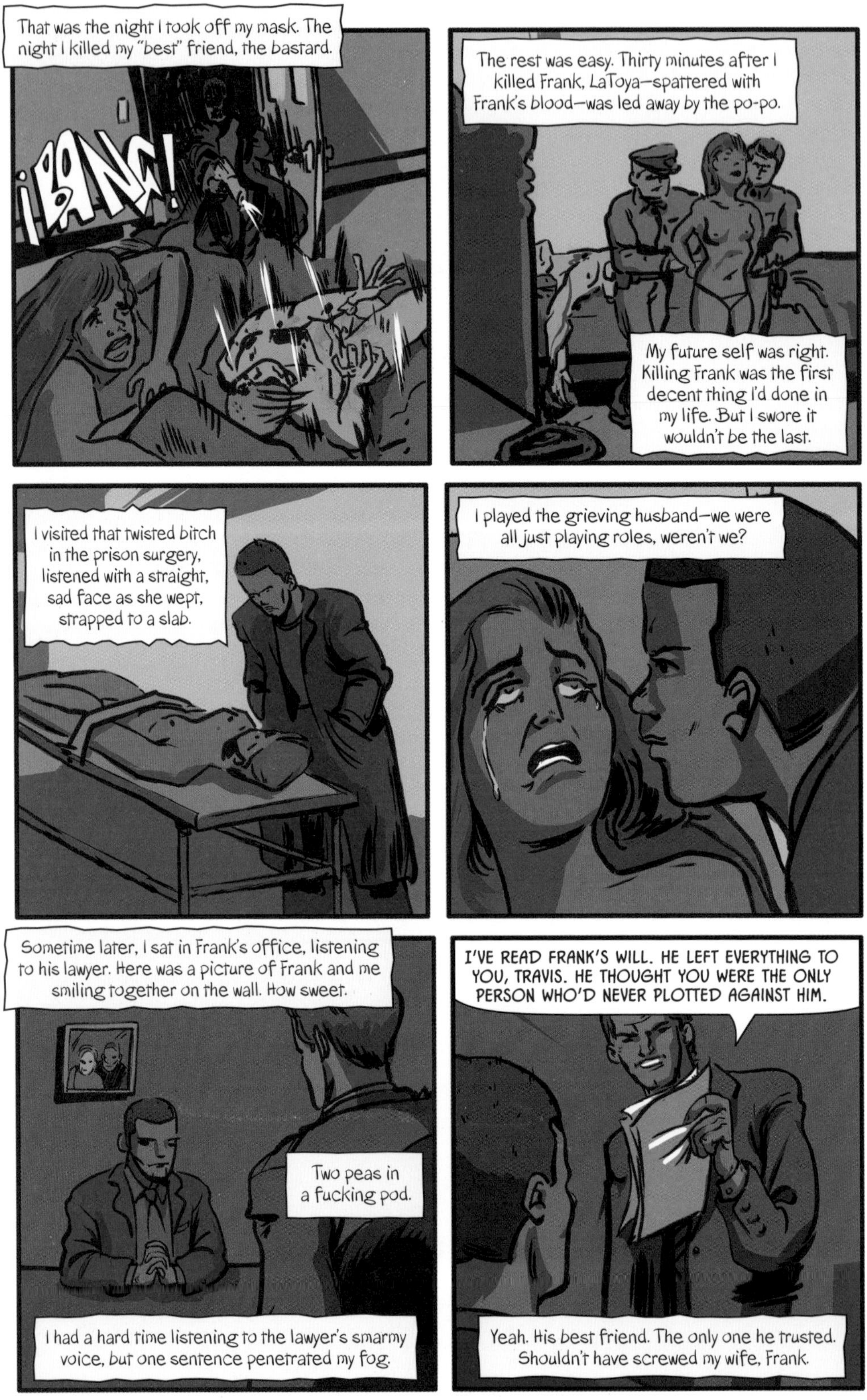
That was the night I took off my mask. The night I killed my "best" friend, the bastard.
¡BANG!
The rest was easy. Thirty minutes after I killed Frank, LaToya—spattered with Frank's blood—was led away by the po-po.
My future self was right. Killing Frank was the first decent thing I'd done in my life. But I swore it wouldn't be the last.
I visited that twisted bitch in the prison surgery, listened with a straight, sad face as she wept, strapped to a slab.
I played the grieving husband—we were all just playing roles, weren't we?
Sometime later, I sat in Frank's office, listening to his lawyer. Here was a picture of Frank and me smiling together on the wall. How sweet.
Two peas in a fucking pod.
I had a hard time listening to the lawyer's smarmy voice, but one sentence penetrated my fog.
I'VE READ FRANK'S WILL. HE LEFT EVERYTHING TO YOU, TRAVIS. HE THOUGHT YOU WERE THE ONLY PERSON WHO'D NEVER PLOTTED AGAINST HIM.
Yeah. His best friend. The only one he trusted. Shouldn't have screwed my wife, Frank.

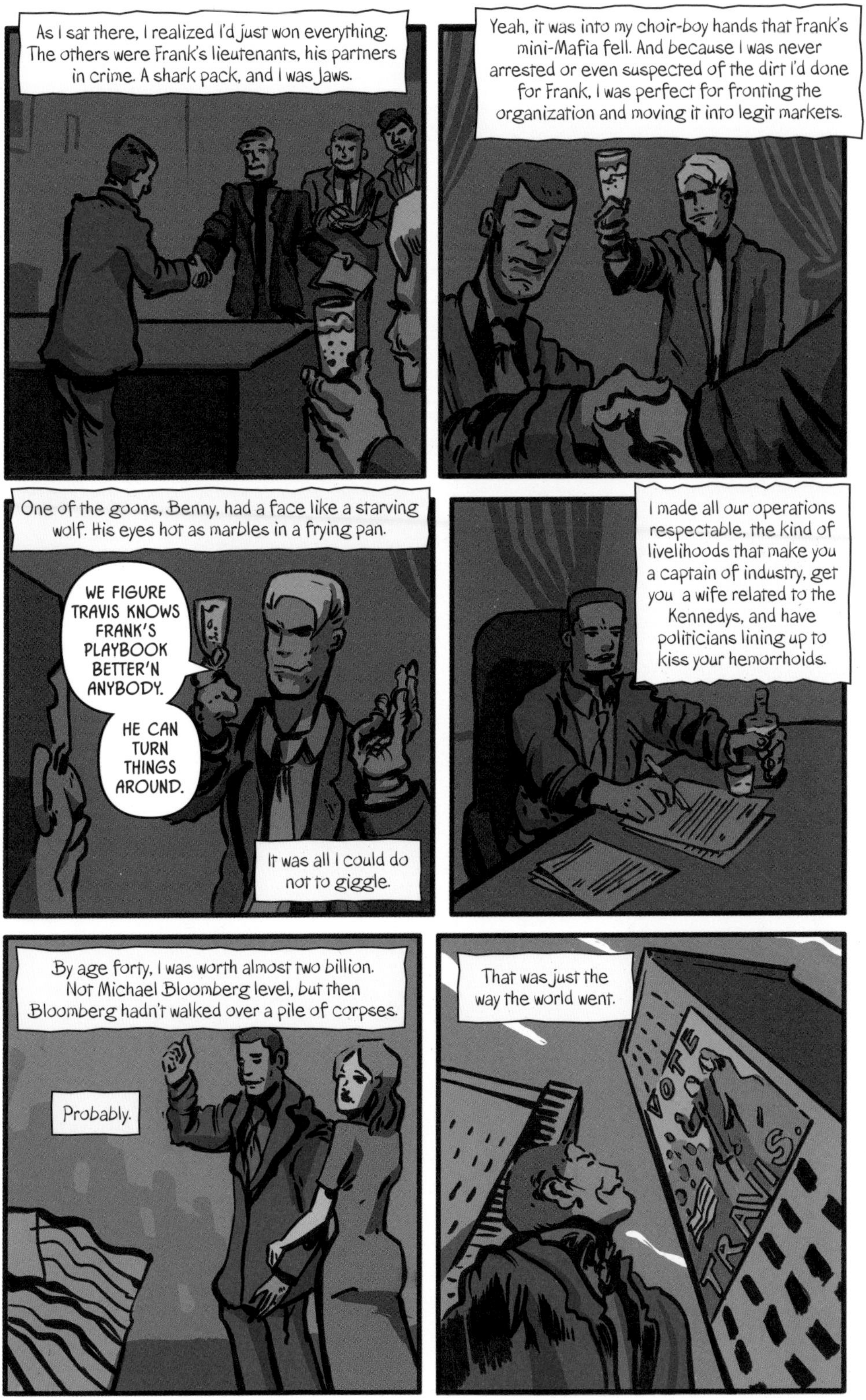
As I sat there, I realized I'd just won everything. The others were Frank's lieutenants, his partners in crime. A shark pack, and I was Jaws.
Yeah, it was into my choir-boy hands that Frank's mini-Mafia fell. And because I was never arrested or even suspected of the dirt I'd done for Frank, I was perfect for fronting the organization and moving it into legit markets.
One of the goons, Benny, had a face like a starving wolf. His eyes hot as marbles in a frying pan.
WE FIGURE TRAVIS KNOWS FRANK'S PLAYBOOK BETTER'N ANYBODY.
HE CAN TURN THINGS AROUND.
It was all I could do not to giggle.
I made all our operations respectable, the kind of livelihoods that make you a captain of industry, get you a wife related to the Kennedys, and have politicians lining up to kiss your hemorrhoids.
By age forty, I was worth almost two billion. Not Michael Bloomberg level, but then Bloomberg hadn't walked over a pile of corpses.
Probably.
That was just the way the world went.
VOTE
TRAVIS

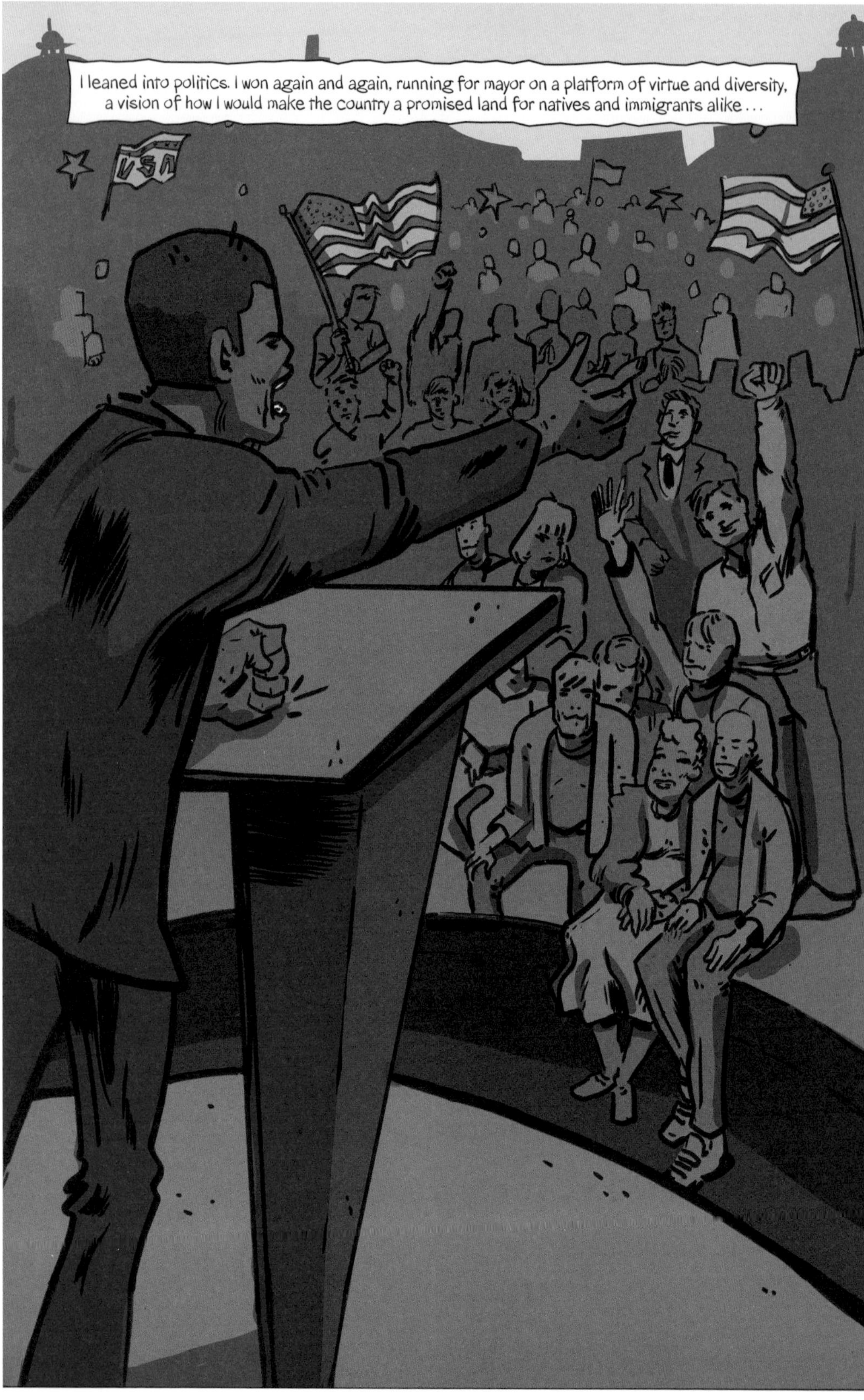
I leaned into politics. I won again and again, running for mayor on a platform of virtue and diversity, a vision of how I would make the country a promised land for natives and immigrants alike . . .
USA

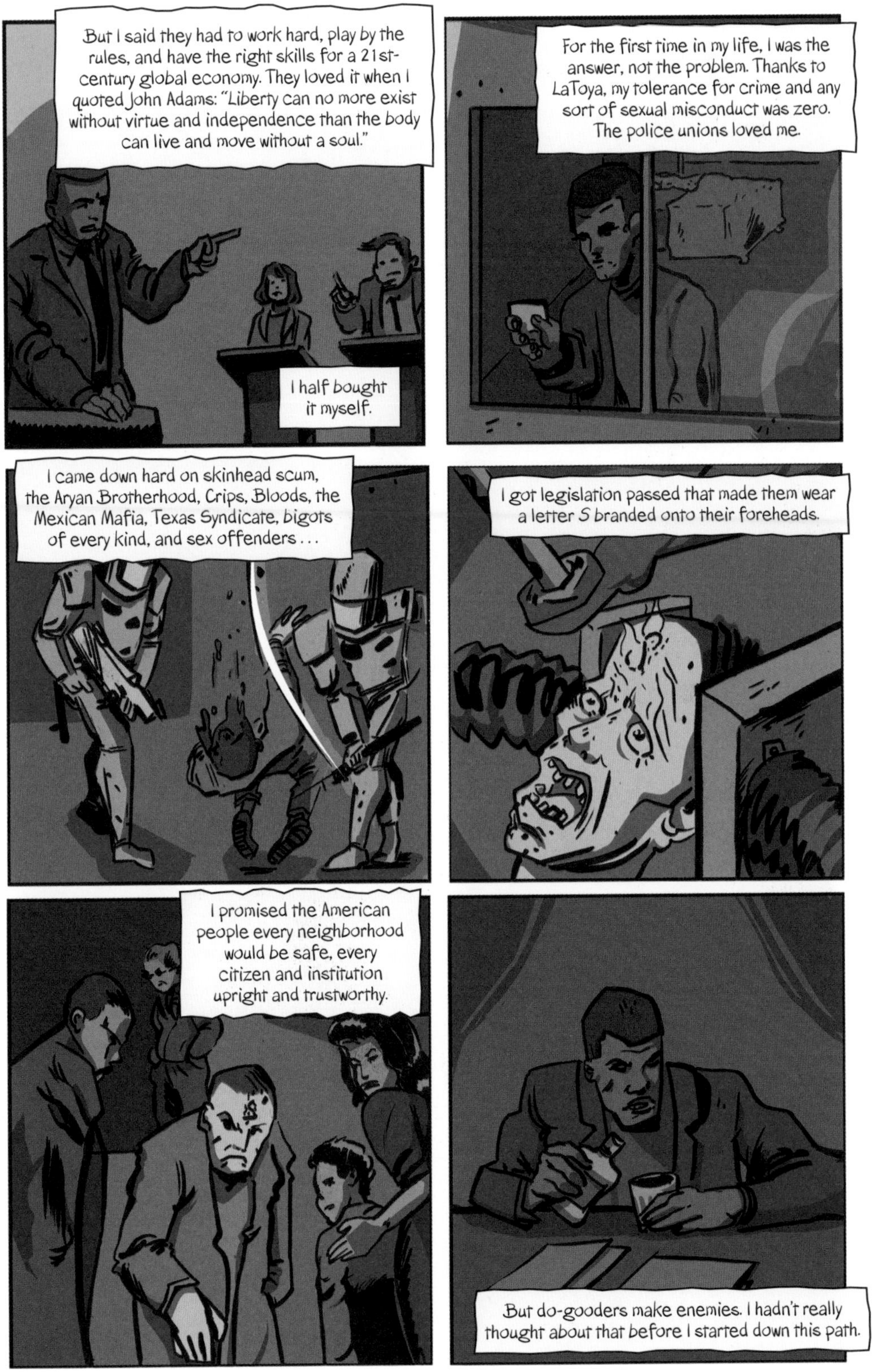
But I said they had to work hard, play by the rules, and have the right skills for a 21st-century global economy. They loved it when I quoted John Adams: "Liberty can no more exist without virtue and independence than the body can live and move without a soul."
I half bought it myself.
For the first time in my life, I was the answer, not the problem. Thanks to LaToya, my tolerance for crime and any sort of sexual misconduct was zero. The police unions loved me.
I came down hard on skinhead scum, the Aryan Brotherhood, Crips, Bloods, the Mexican Mafia, Texas Syndicate, bigots of every kind, and sex offenders . . .
I got legislation passed that made them wear a letter S branded onto their foreheads.
I promised the American people every neighborhood would be safe, every citizen and institution upright and trustworthy.
But do-gooders make enemies. I hadn't really thought about that before I started down this path.

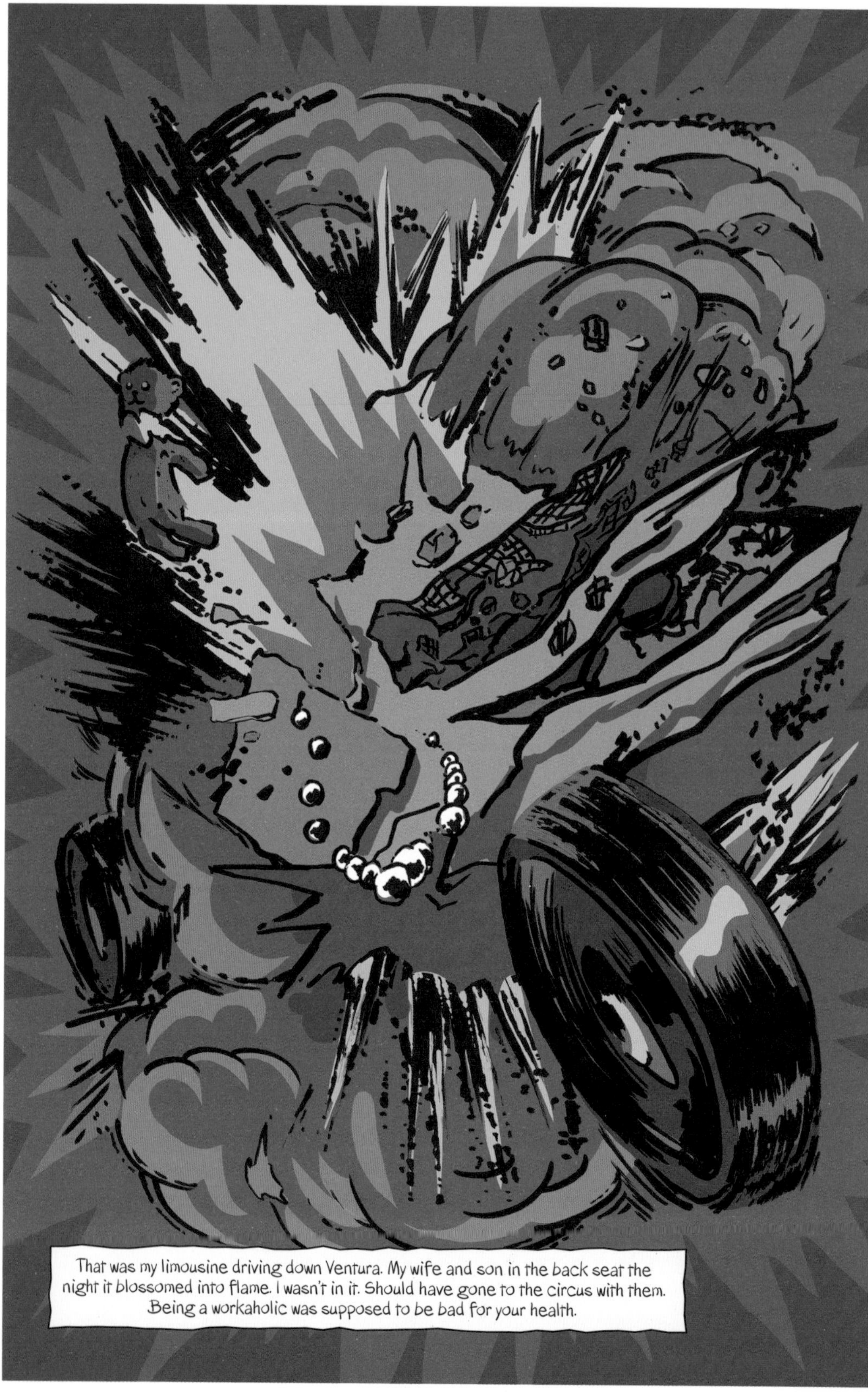
That was my limousine driving down Ventura. My wife and son in the back seat the night it blossomed into flame. I wasn't in it. Should have gone to the circus with them. Being a workaholic was supposed to be bad for your health.

The funeral was held in the rain. I liked that, because it was the first time in years I'd cried, and damned if I wanted to do that in public.

I'd tried to be an unselfish public servant. Voters knew that. After my beloved family was murdered, my path to the White House was clear.

And one of my first acts was to sign the National Emergencies Act.

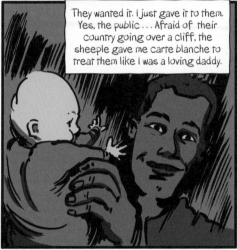

They wanted it. I just gave it to them. Yes, the public... Afraid of their country going over a cliff, the sheeple gave me carte blanche to treat them like I was a loving daddy.

I dropped Adams and switched to quoting Edmund Burke: "Society cannot exist unless a controlling power upon will and appetite be placed somewhere, and the less of it there is within, the more there is without." Corporate and Middle America, and the military, loved it.

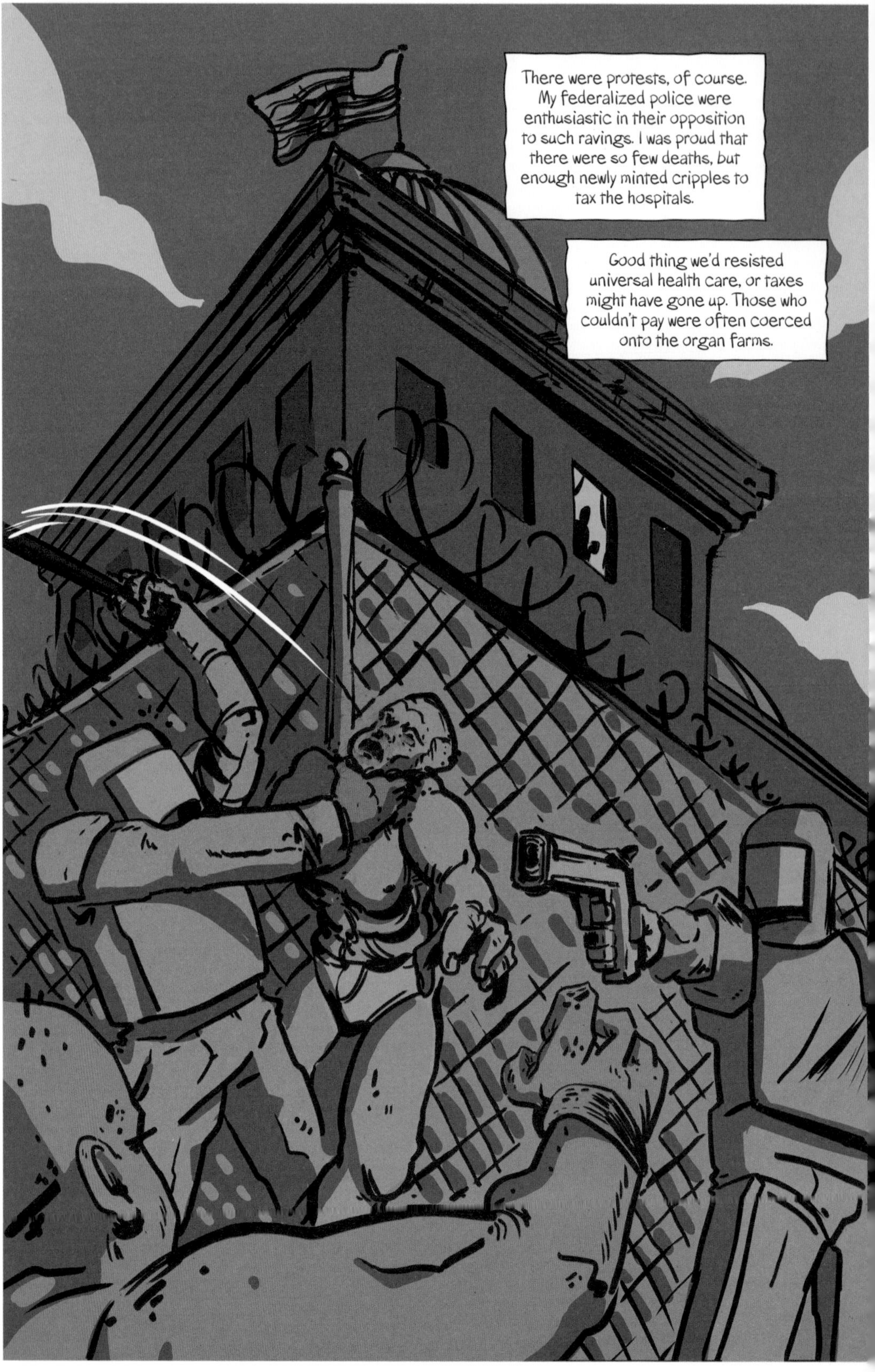
There were protests, of course. My federalized police were enthusiastic in their opposition to such ravings. I was proud that there were so few deaths, but enough newly minted cripples to tax the hospitals.
Good thing we'd resisted universal health care, or taxes might have gone up. Those who couldn't pay were often coerced onto the organ farms.

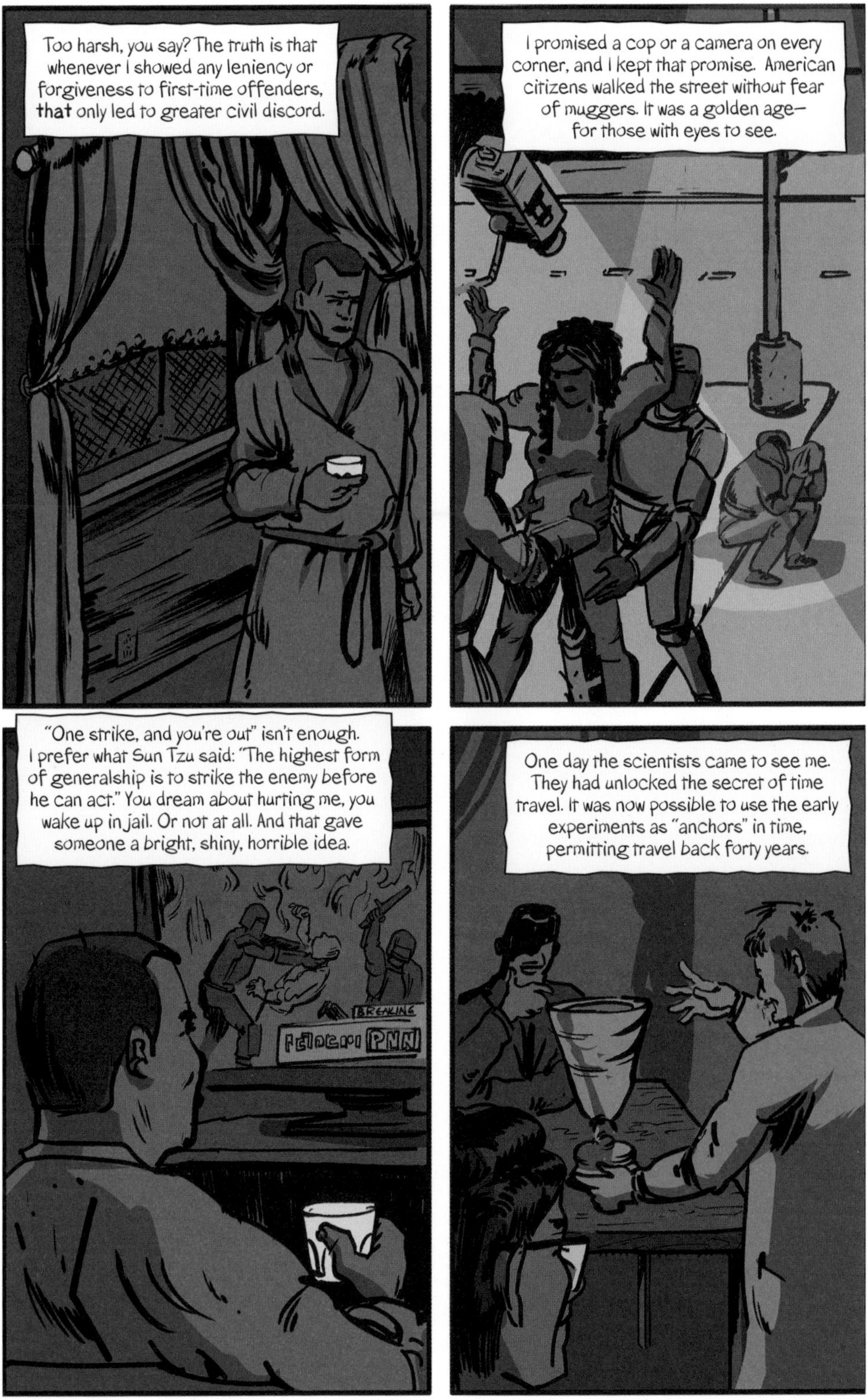
Too harsh, you say? The truth is that whenever I showed any leniency or forgiveness to first-time offenders, **that** only led to greater civil discord.
I promised a cop or a camera on every corner, and I kept that promise. American citizens walked the street without fear of muggers. It was a golden age—for those with eyes to see.
"One strike, and you're out" isn't enough. I prefer what Sun Tzu said: "The highest form of generalship is to strike the enemy before he can act." You dream about hurting me, you wake up in jail. Or not at all. And that gave someone a bright, shiny, horrible idea.
BREAKING
PNN
One day the scientists came to see me. They had unlocked the secret of time travel. It was now possible to use the early experiments as "anchors" in time, permitting travel back forty years.

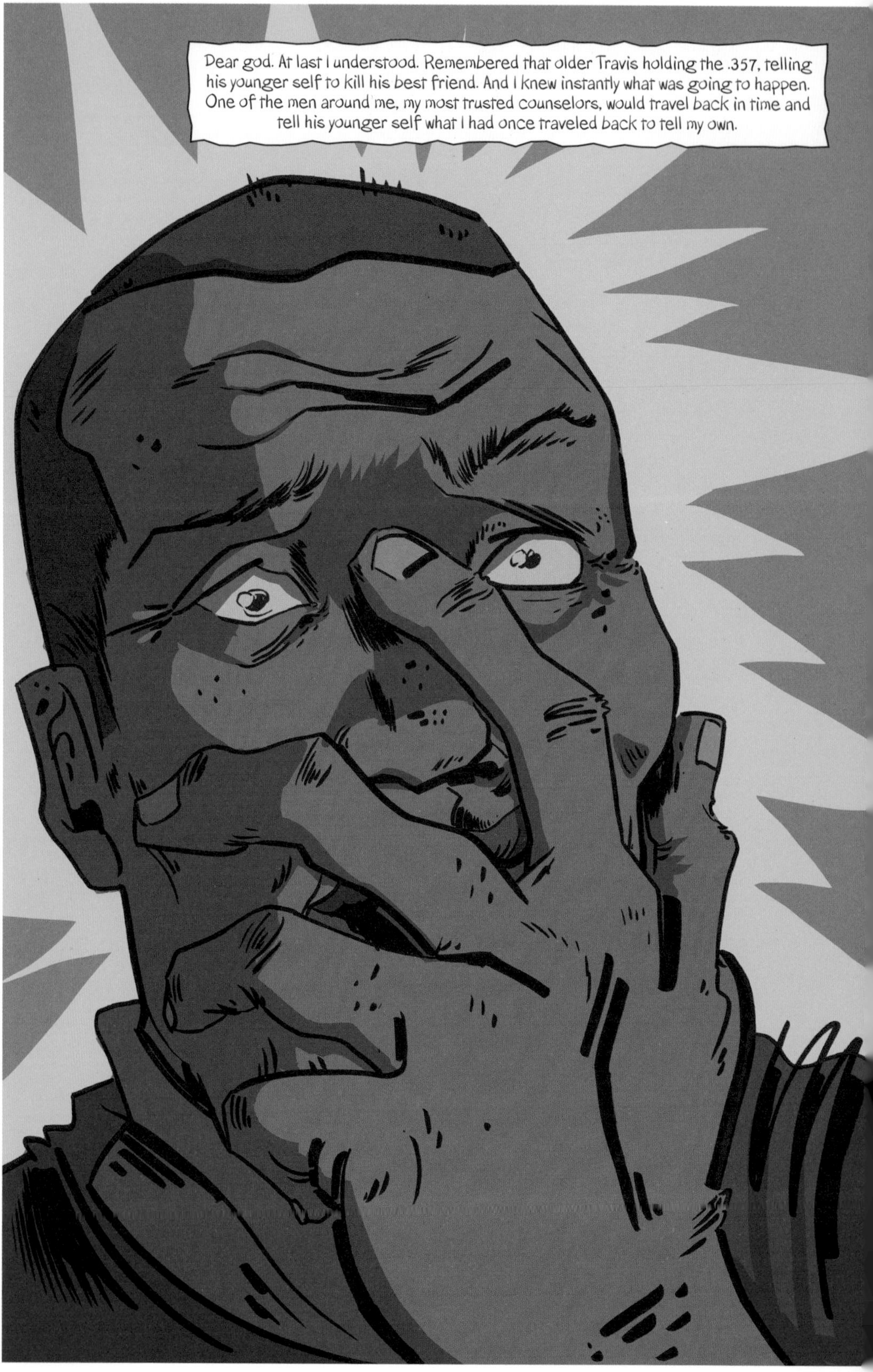
Dear god. At last I understood. Remembered that older Travis holding the .357, telling his younger self to kill his best friend. And I knew instantly what was going to happen. One of the men around me, my most trusted counselors, would travel back in time and tell his younger self what I had once traveled back to tell my own.

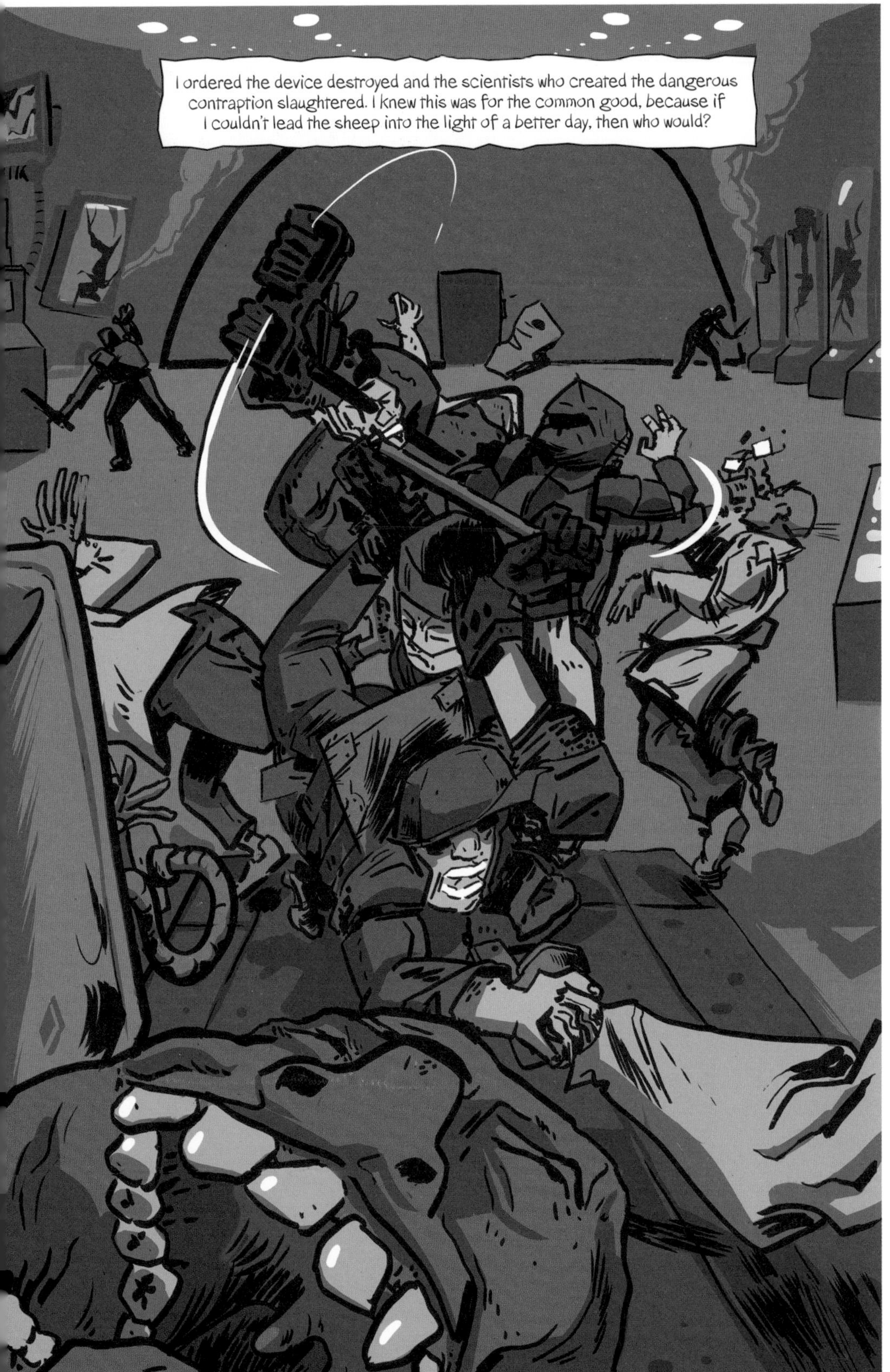
I ordered the device destroyed and the scientists who created the dangerous contraption slaughtered. I knew this was for the common good, because if I couldn't lead the sheep into the light of a better day, then who would?

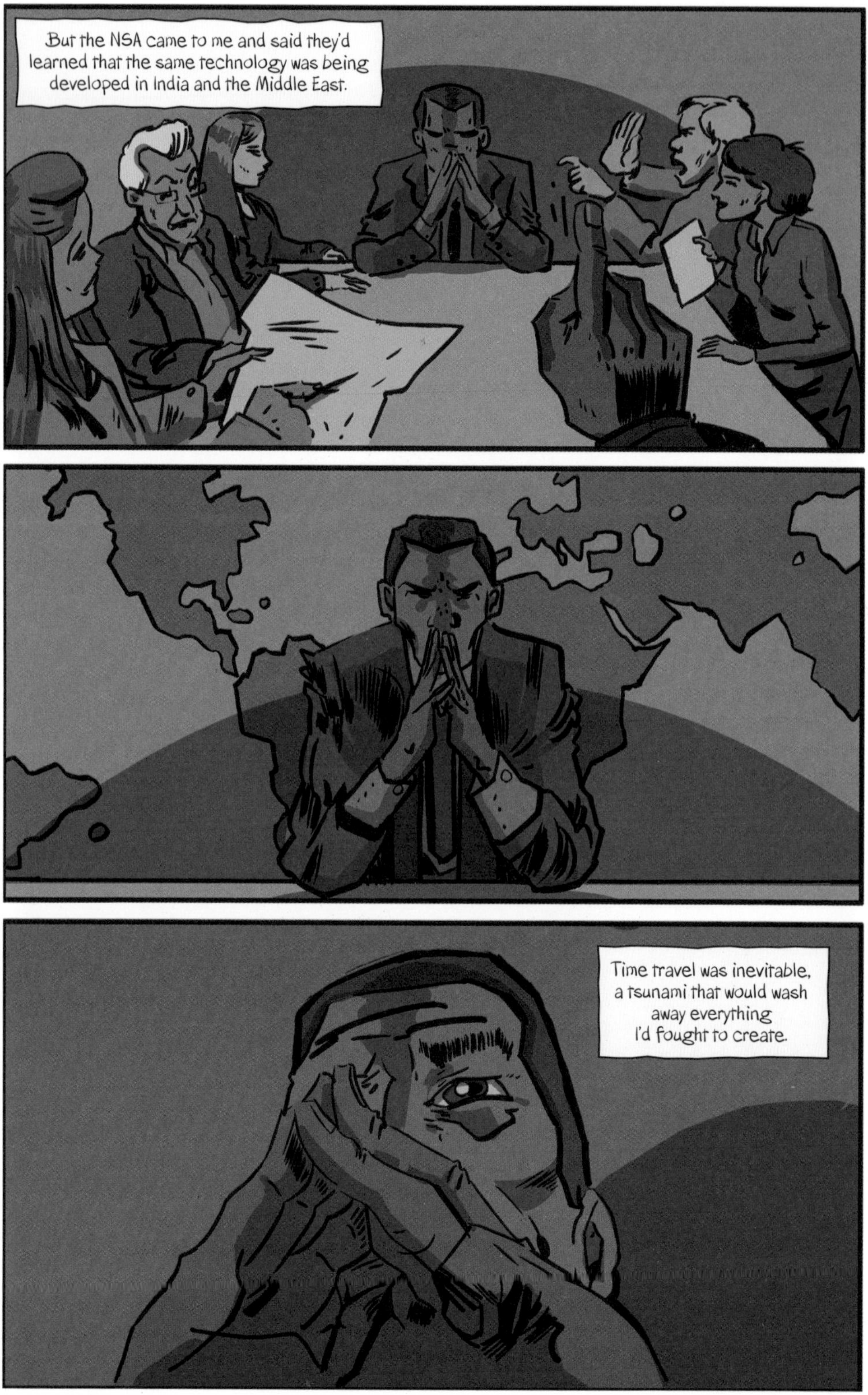
But the NSA came to me and said they'd learned that the same technology was being developed in India and the Middle East.
Time travel was inevitable, a tsunami that would wash away everything I'd fought to create.

I remember scanning the Situation Room. Ten men and women, all seemingly innocent, but gleaming deep in their eyes was a hunger for power.

I couldn't kill everyone plotting against me. And even if I did, their successors would eventually travel back in time and destroy me. It was then I realized how completely I'd become that which I truly despised.

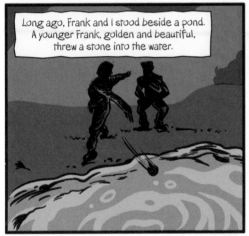

Long ago, Frank and I stood beside a pond. A younger Frank, golden and beautiful, threw a stone into the water.

I see it clearly now. Reality protected itself.

You could make ripples, but they vanished like a bubble in a stream or lightning flashing in a summer cloud.

But history was more like a mighty river flowing in one direction, its waves irreversible. Things changed. Nothing changed. World without end, amen.

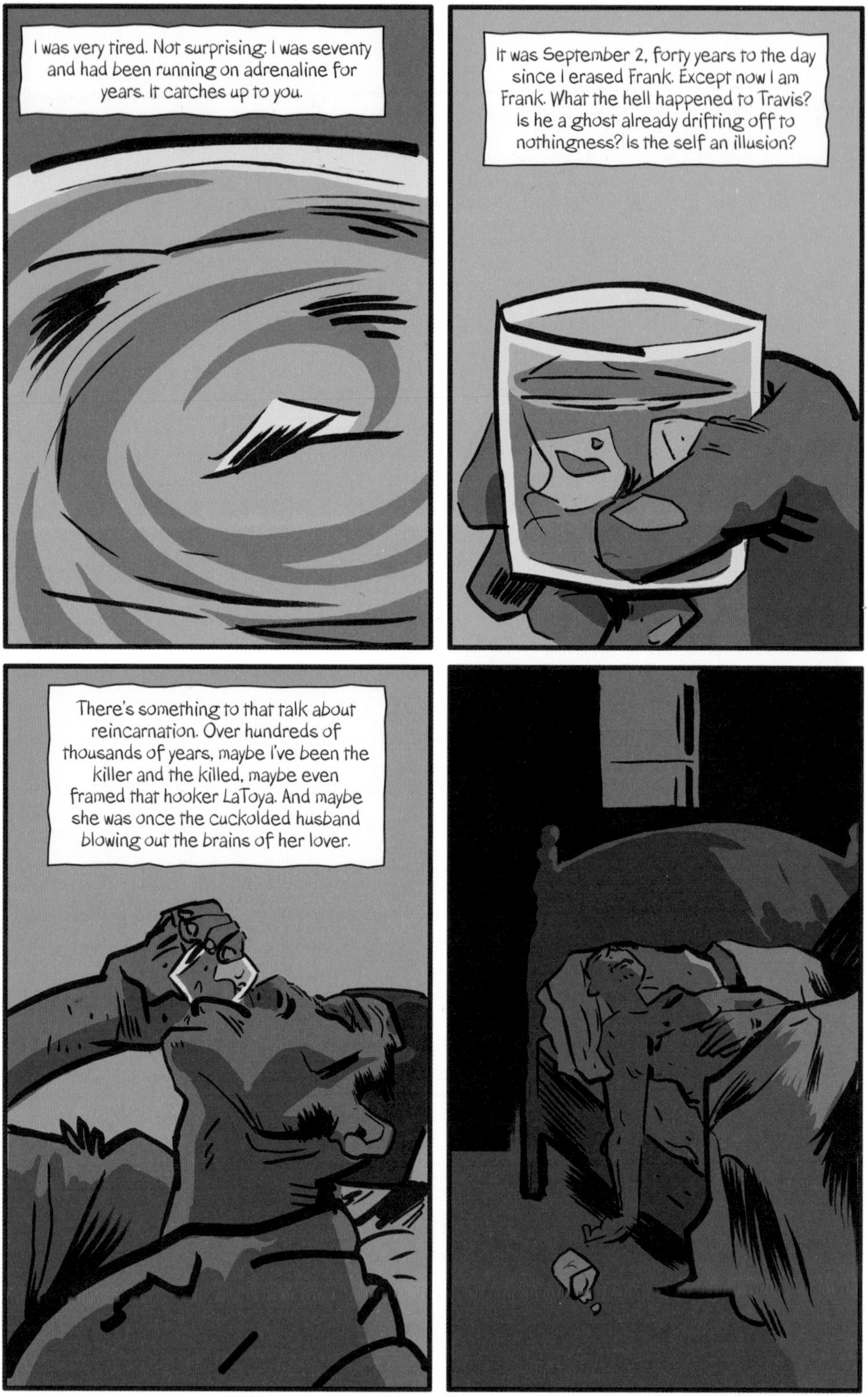
I was very tired. Not surprising: I was seventy and had been running on adrenaline for years. It catches up to you.
It was September 2, forty years to the day since I erased Frank. Except now I am Frank. What the hell happened to Travis? Is he a ghost already drifting off to nothingness? Is the self an illusion?
There's something to that talk about reincarnation. Over hundreds of thousands of years, maybe I've been the killer and the killed, maybe even framed that hooker LaToya. And maybe she was once the cuckolded husband blowing out the brains of her lover.

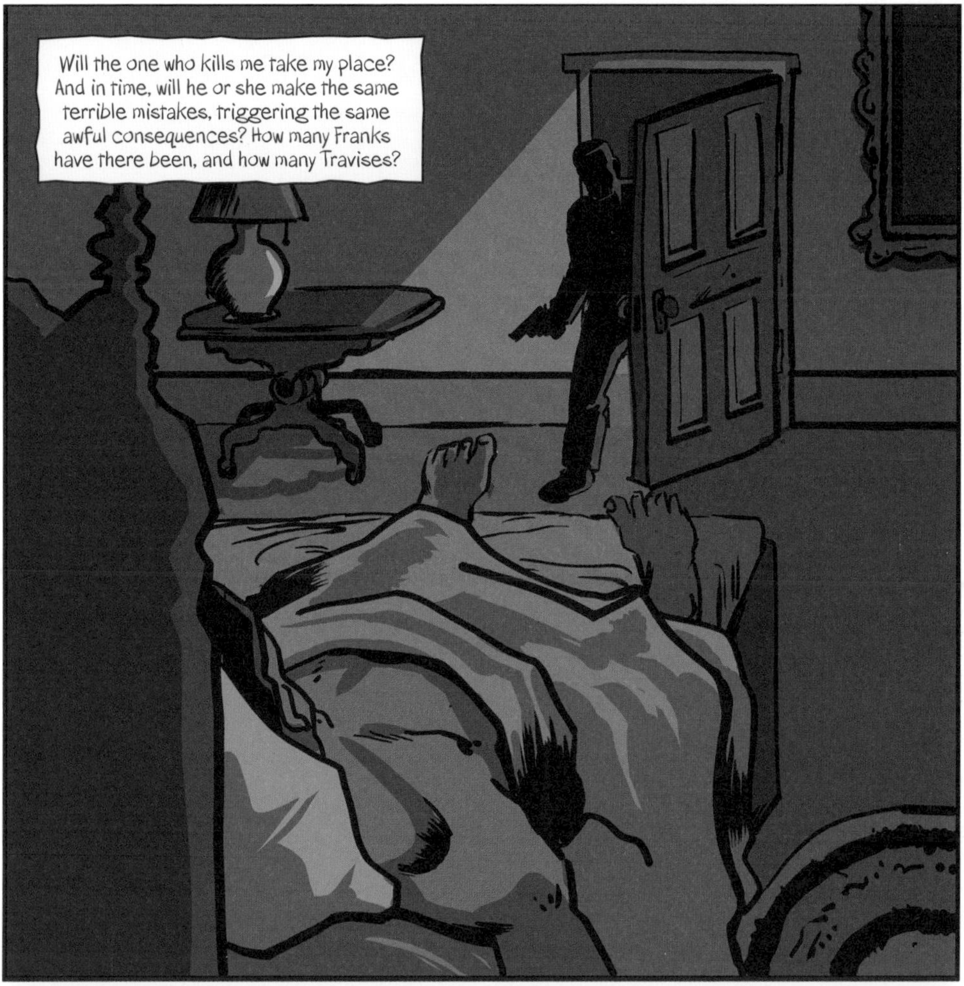
Will the one who kills me take my place? And in time, will he or she make the same terrible mistakes, triggering the same awful consequences? How many Franks have there been, and how many Travises?

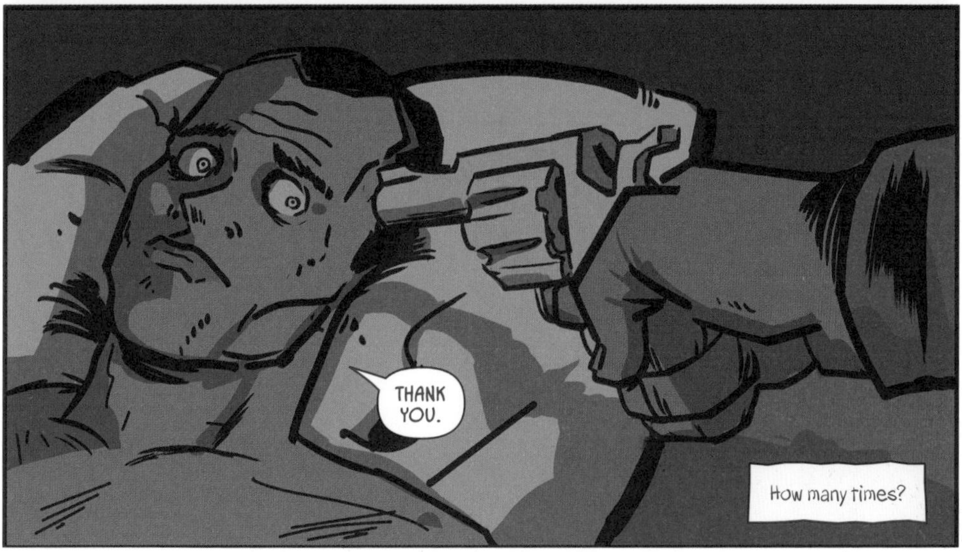
THANK YOU.
How many times?

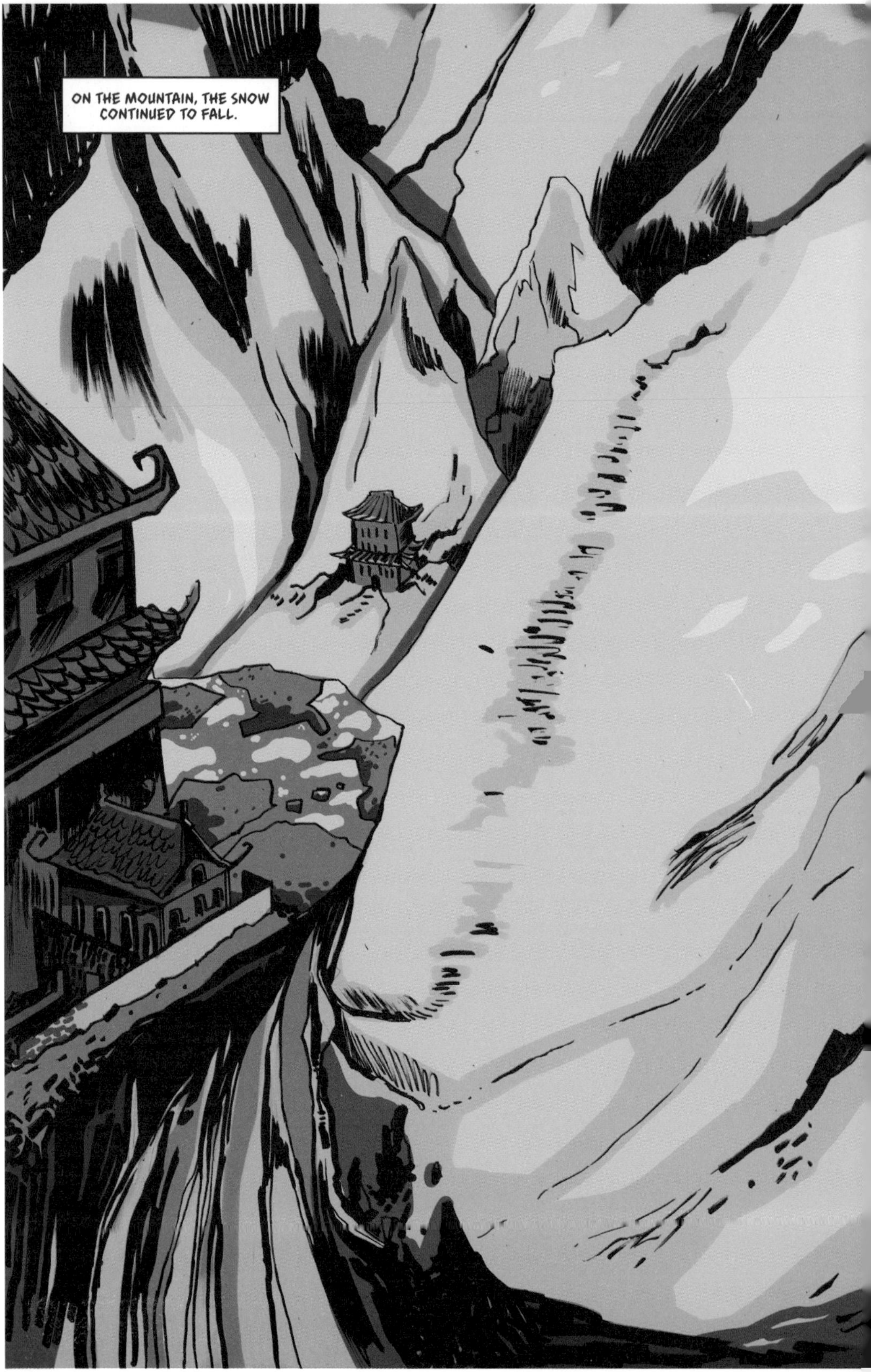
ON THE MOUNTAIN, THE SNOW CONTINUED TO FALL.

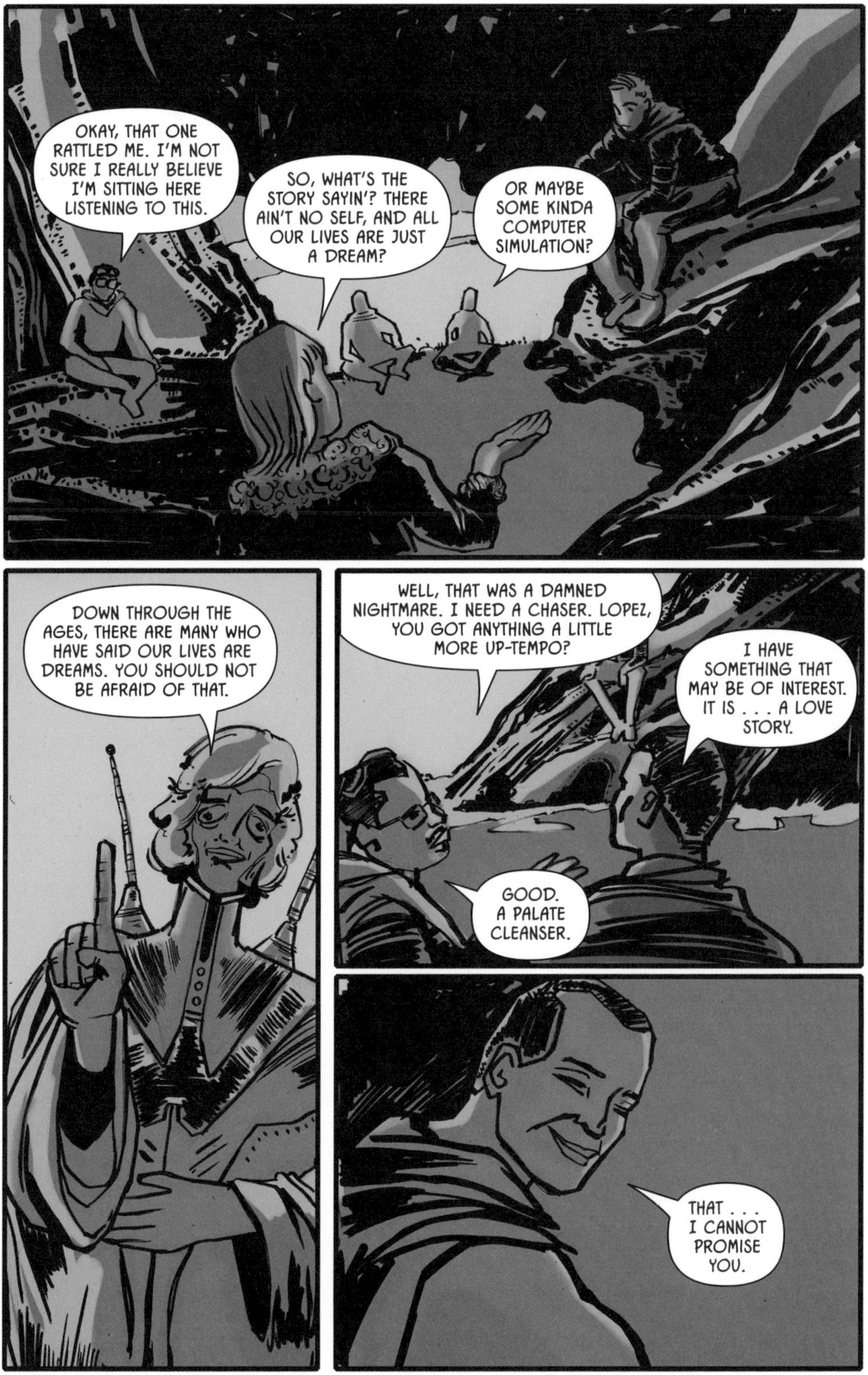
OKAY, THAT ONE RATTLED ME. I'M NOT SURE I REALLY BELIEVE I'M SITTING HERE LISTENING TO THIS.
SO, WHAT'S THE STORY SAYIN'? THERE AIN'T NO SELF, AND ALL OUR LIVES ARE JUST A DREAM?
OR MAYBE SOME KINDA COMPUTER SIMULATION?
DOWN THROUGH THE AGES, THERE ARE MANY WHO HAVE SAID OUR LIVES ARE DREAMS. YOU SHOULD NOT BE AFRAID OF THAT.
WELL, THAT WAS A DAMNED NIGHTMARE. I NEED A CHASER. LOPEZ, YOU GOT ANYTHING A LITTLE MORE UP-TEMPO?
I HAVE SOMETHING THAT MAY BE OF INTEREST. IT IS . . . A LOVE STORY.
GOOD. A PALATE CLEANSER.
THAT . . . I CANNOT PROMISE YOU.

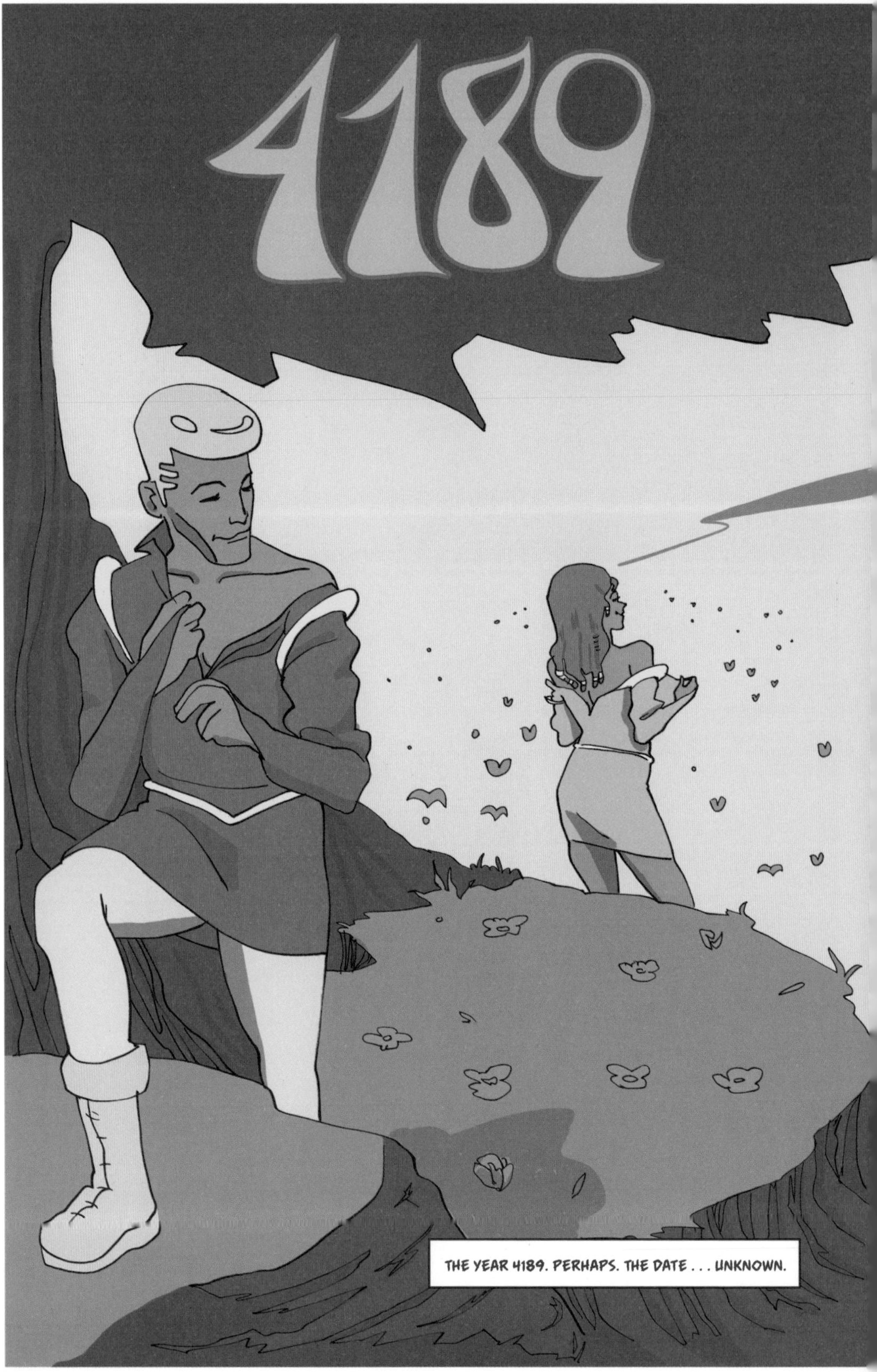
4189
THE YEAR 4189. PERHAPS. THE DATE . . . UNKNOWN.

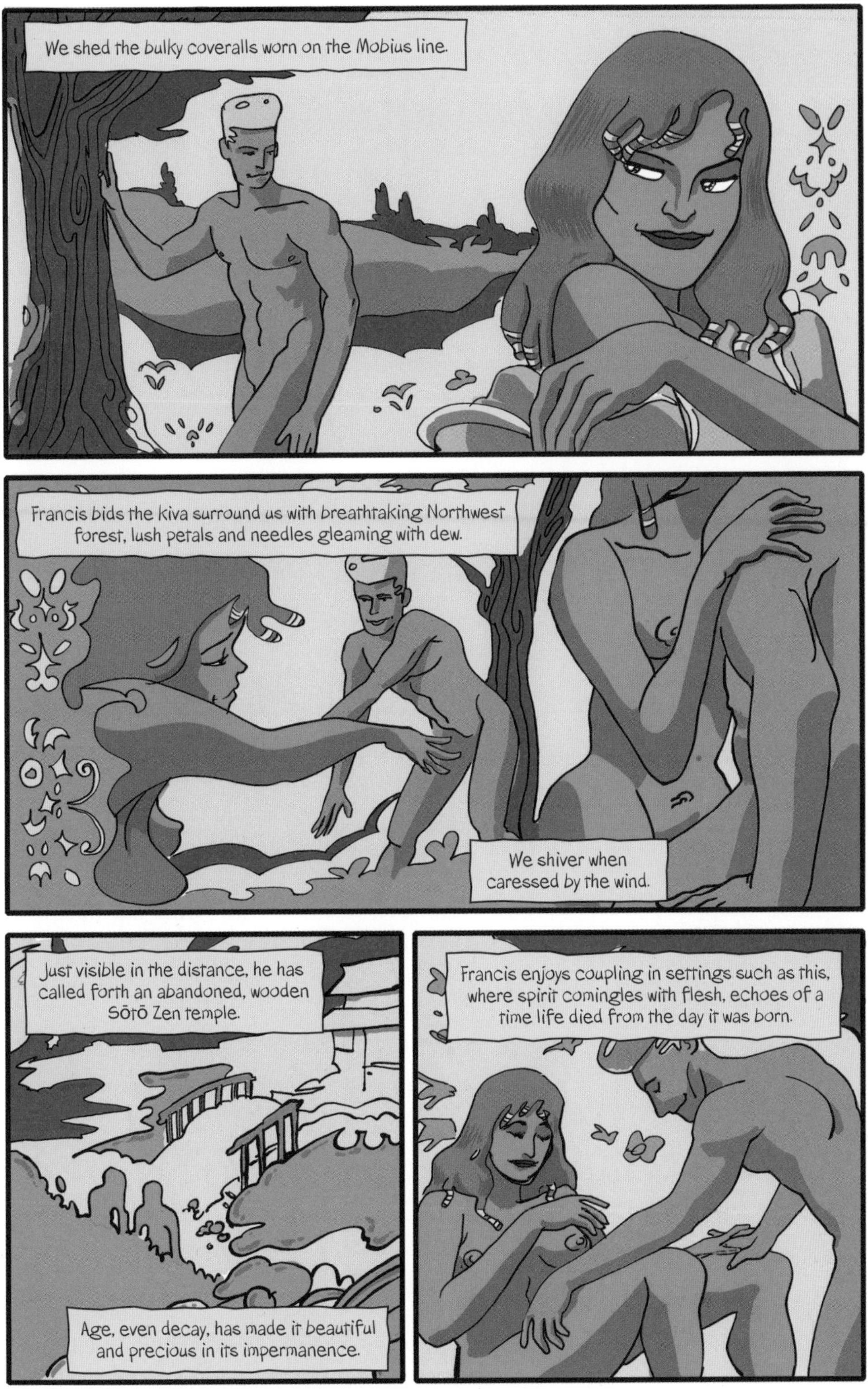
We shed the bulky coveralls worn on the Mobius line.
Francis bids the kiva surround us with breathtaking Northwest forest, lush petals and needles gleaming with dew.
We shiver when caressed by the wind.
Just visible in the distance, he has called forth an abandoned, wooden Sōtō Zen temple.
Age, even decay, has made it beautiful and precious in its impermanence.
Francis enjoys coupling in settings such as this, where spirit comingles with flesh, echoes of a time life died from the day it was born.

I open the thumb-sized vial of Thanadose.

Illegal as self-murder, and worth every erg.

For a time, the microsynthes crawling through our veins stop whispering eternity and we can glimpse an ending, as once our ancestors did.

After a year of trysts, we know each other's heats and tastes and textures.

He is so beautiful, as perfect as a pleasure doll.

He could have anyone. A mere fluke of luck that he wants me.

We melt into one another . . .

. . . and finally lie in each other's arms, sipping one another's breaths.

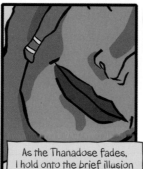

As the Thanadose fades, I hold onto the brief illusion that I will die. But that is a lie.

We will have endless tomorrows. Without change. Without suffering. Without growth.

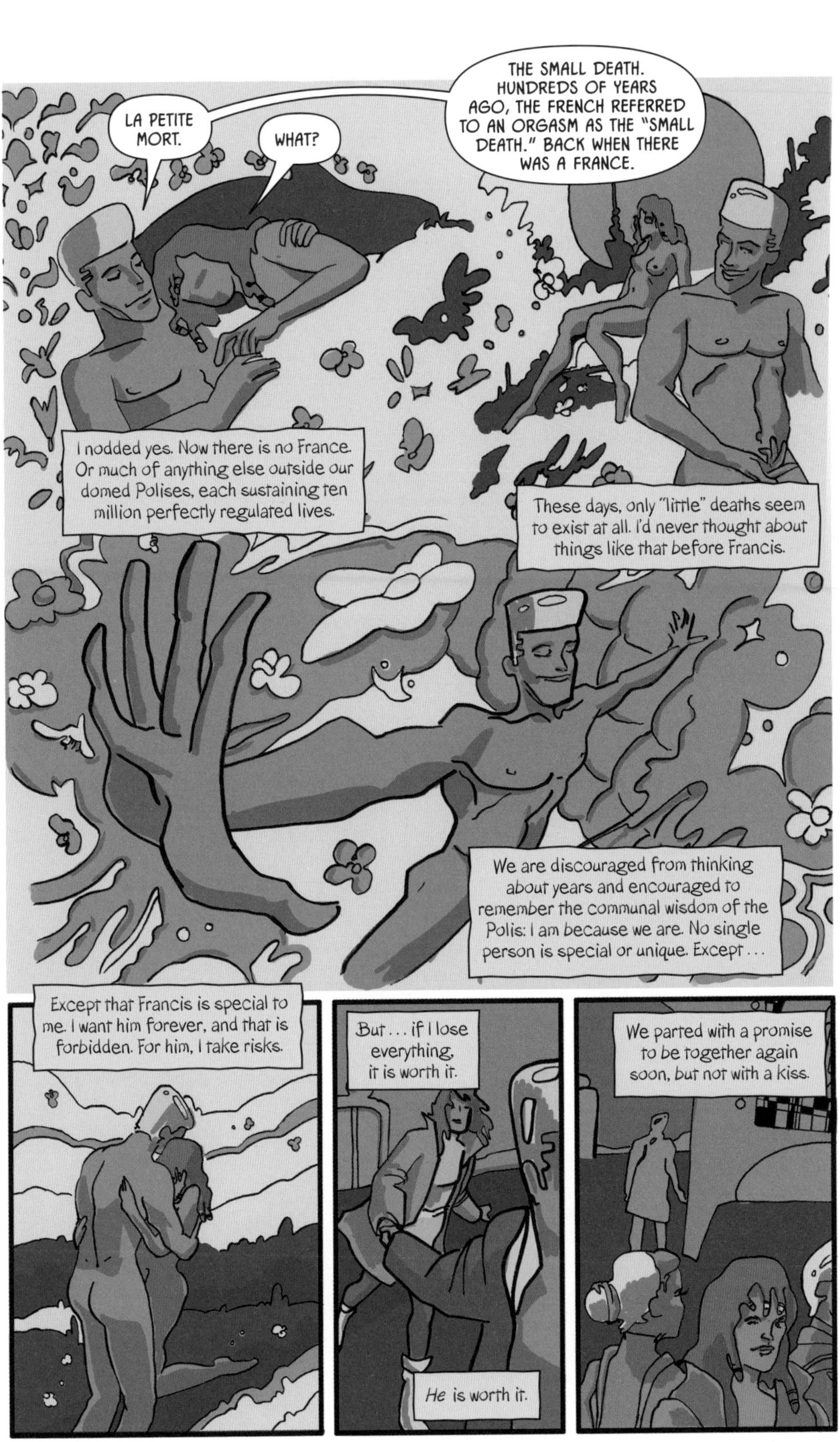
LA PETITE MORT.
WHAT?
THE SMALL DEATH. HUNDREDS OF YEARS AGO, THE FRENCH REFERRED TO AN ORGASM AS THE "SMALL DEATH." BACK WHEN THERE WAS A FRANCE.
I nodded yes. Now there is no France. Or much of anything else outside our domed Polises, each sustaining ten million perfectly regulated lives.
These days, only "little" deaths seem to exist at all. I'd never thought about things like that before Francis.
We are discouraged from thinking about years and encouraged to remember the communal wisdom of the Polis: I am because we are. No single person is special or unique. Except . . .
Except that Francis is special to me. I want him forever, and that is forbidden. For him, I take risks.
But . . . if I lose everything, it is worth it.
He is worth it.
We parted with a promise to be together again soon, but not with a kiss.

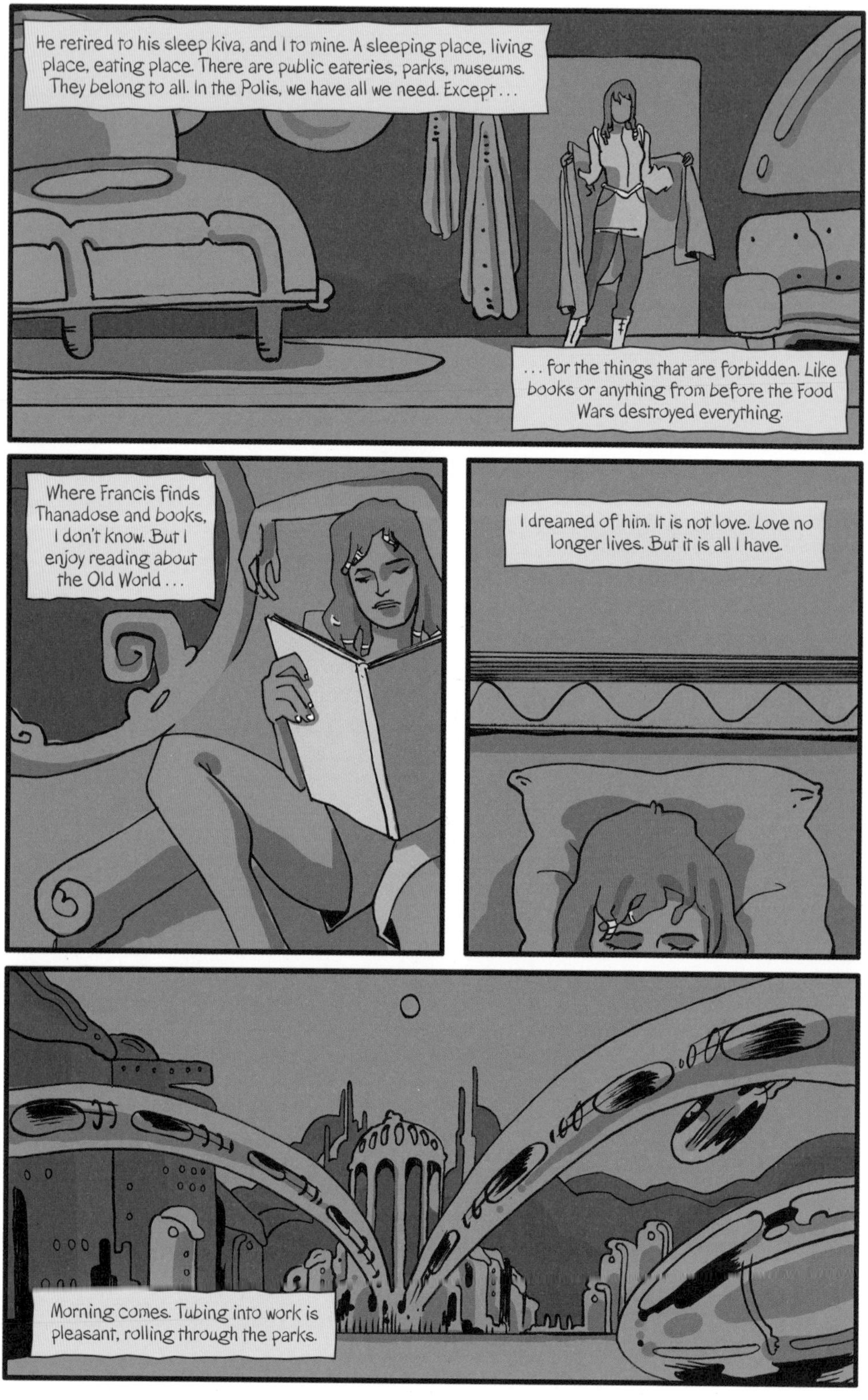
He retired to his sleep kiva, and I to mine. A sleeping place, living place, eating place. There are public eateries, parks, museums. They belong to all. In the Polis, we have all we need. Except . . .
. . . for the things that are forbidden. Like books or anything from before the Food Wars destroyed everything.
Where Francis finds Thanadose and books, I don't know. But I enjoy reading about the Old World . . .
I dreamed of him. It is not love. Love no longer lives. But it is all I have.
Morning comes. Tubing into work is pleasant, rolling through the parks.

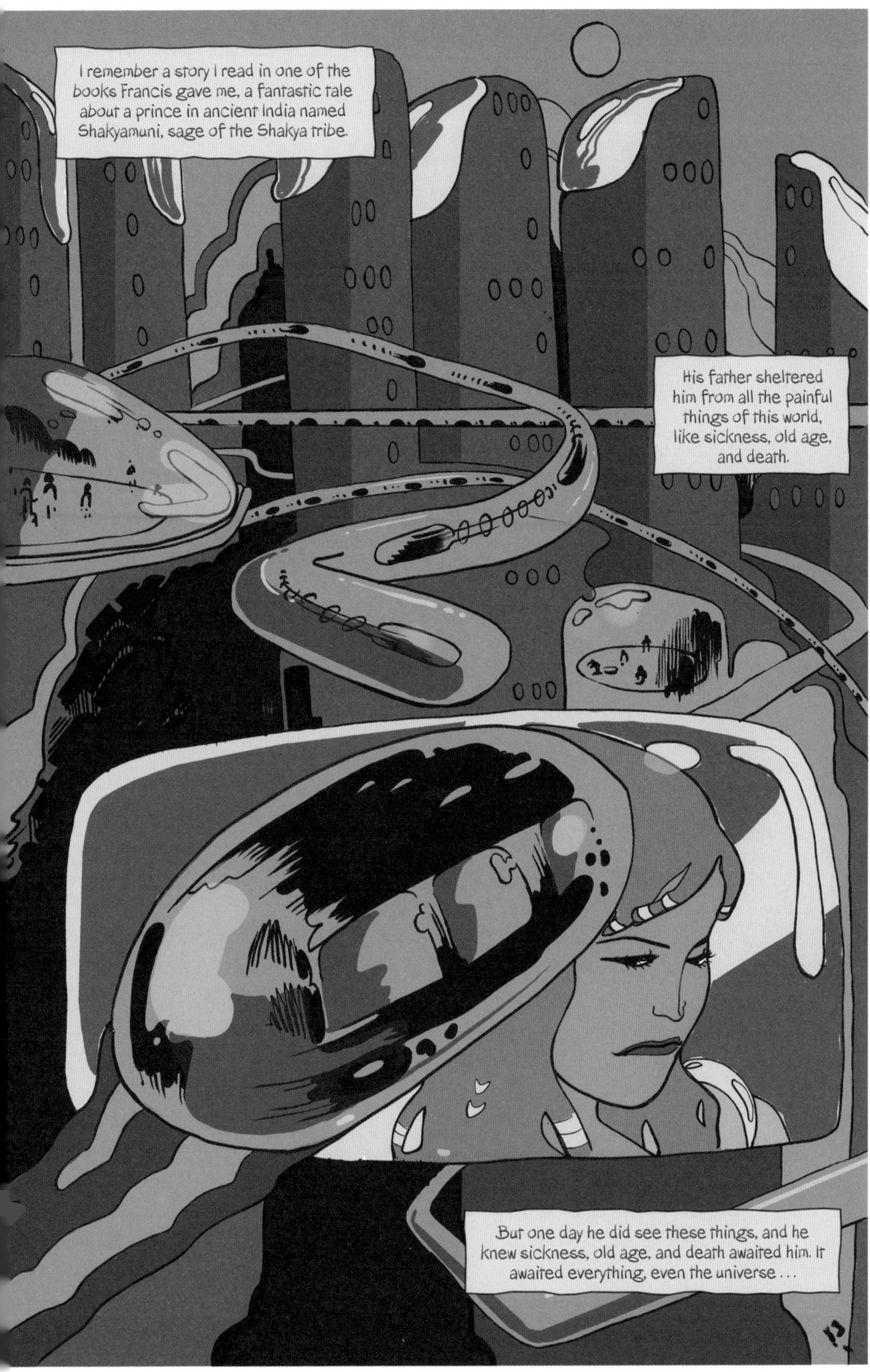
I remember a story I read in one of the books Francis gave me, a fantastic tale about a prince in ancient India named Shakyamuni, sage of the Shakya tribe.
His father sheltered him from all the painful things of this world, like sickness, old age, and death.
But one day he did see these things, and he knew sickness, old age, and death awaited him. It awaited everything, even the universe . . .

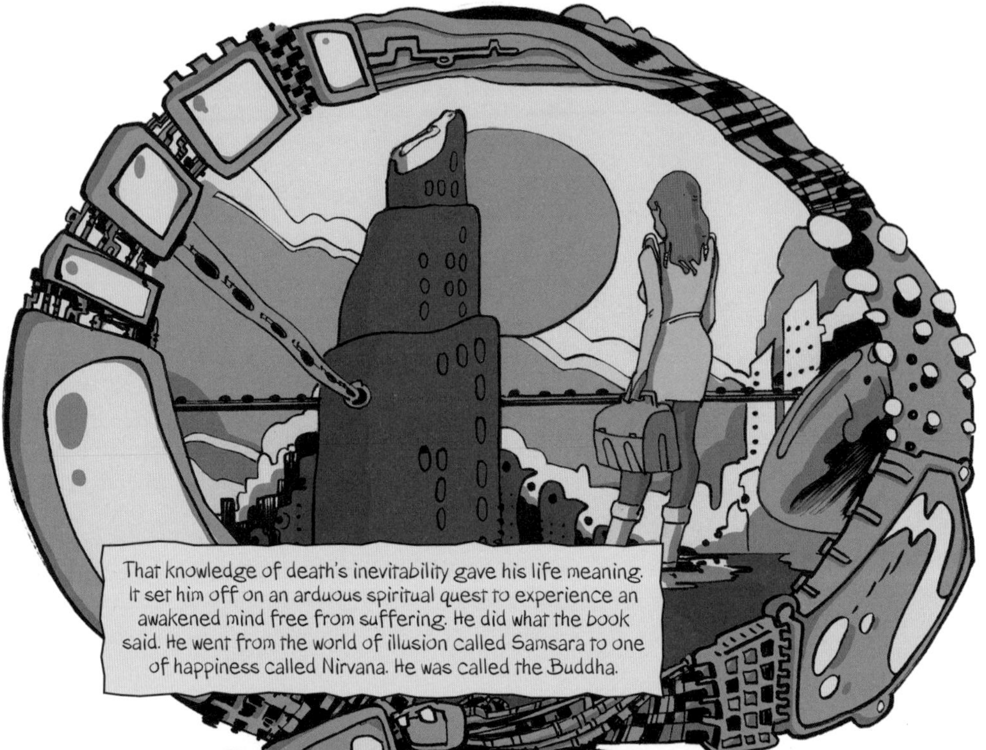
That knowledge of death's inevitability gave his life meaning. It set him off on an arduous spiritual quest to experience an awakened mind free from suffering. He did what the book said. He went from the world of illusion called Samsara to one of happiness called Nirvana. He was called the Buddha.

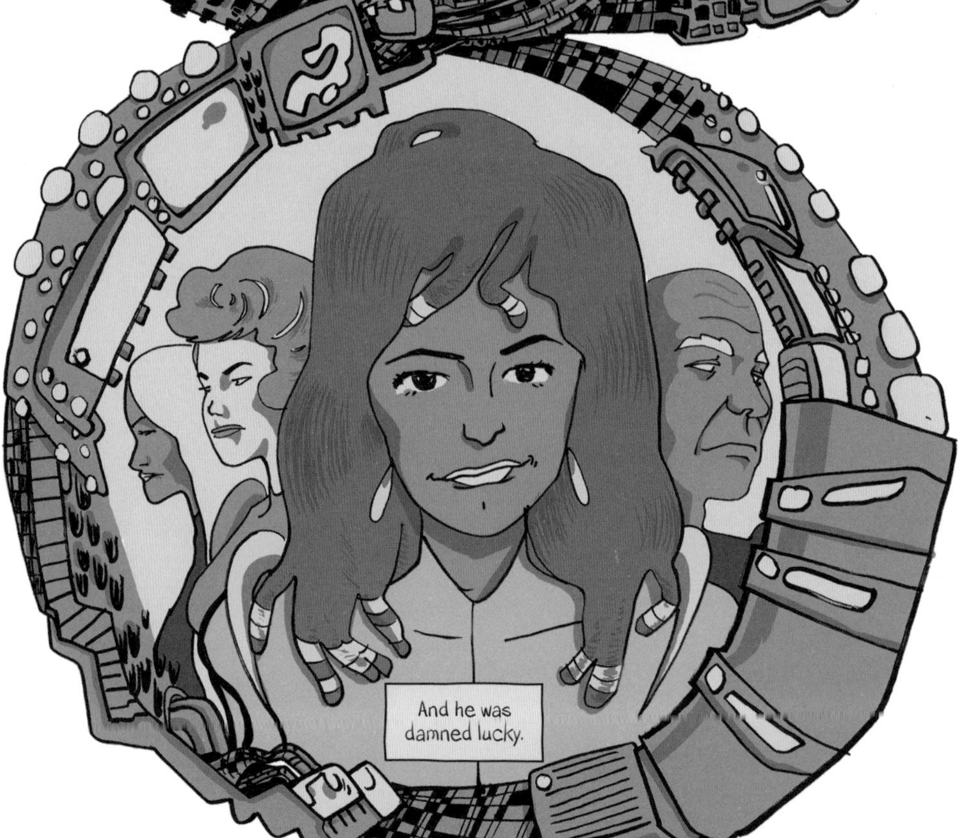
And he was damned lucky.

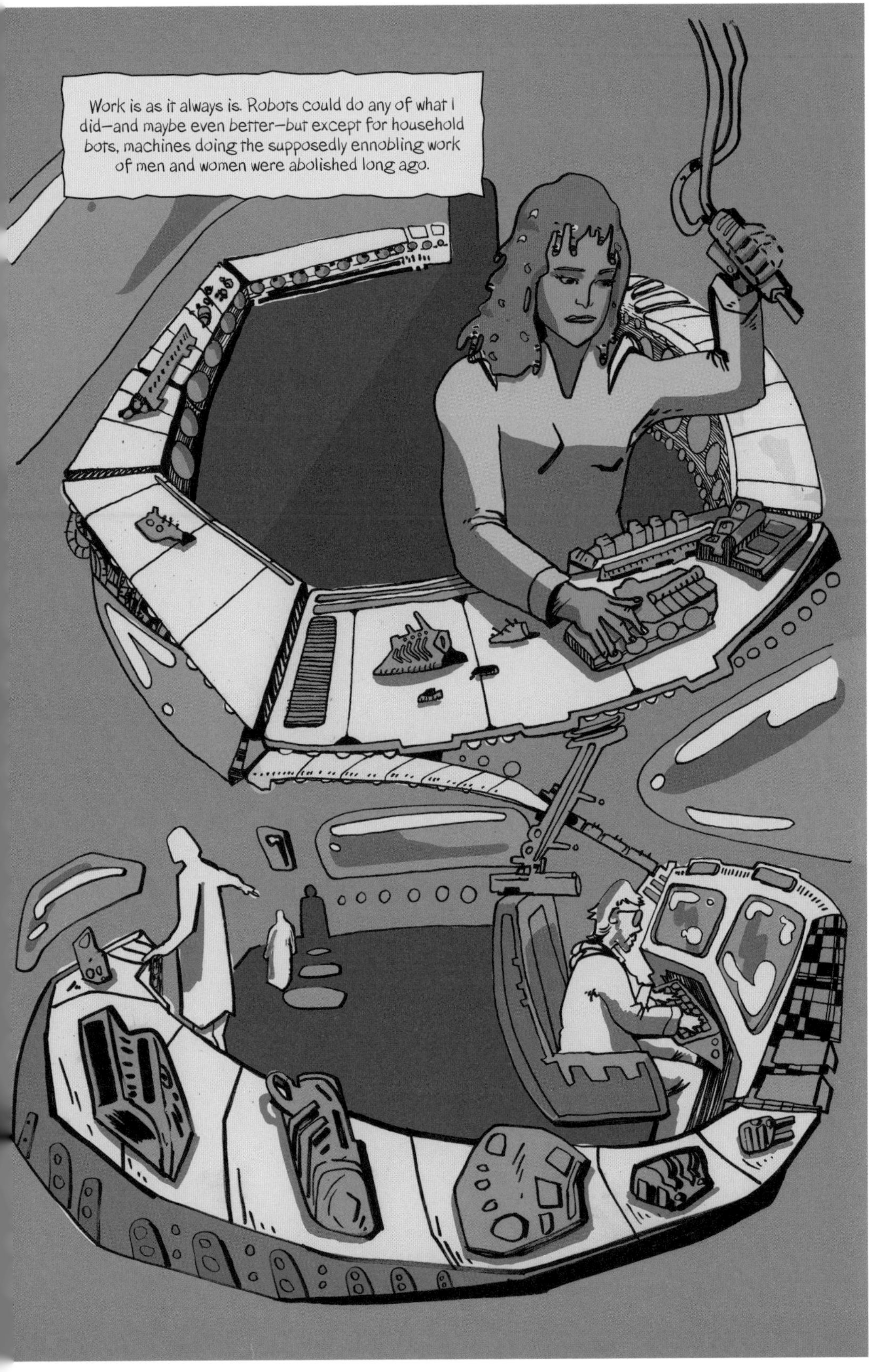
Work is as it always is. Robots could do any of what I did—and maybe even better—but except for household bots, machines doing the supposedly ennobling work of men and women were abolished long ago.

A machine I had not seen before came down the line. I pulled it off, researched it, and spent half the day exploring and renewing the thing.

I put it back on the line, where it mysteriously trundled on to whatever ultimate destiny fate had decreed. Where did it go?

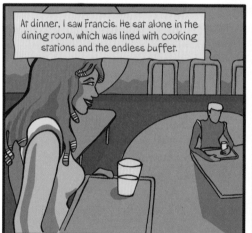

At dinner, I saw Francis. He sat alone in the dining room, which was lined with cooking stations and the endless buffet.

I sat with him, and he acknowledged me with a nod. He seemed withdrawn.

CAN I SEE YOU TONIGHT?

I DON'T THINK THAT'S A GOOD IDEA.

WHY?

I WANT MORE. WE WERE CLOSE. SO CLOSE.

YES, WE WERE.

IT WAS LIKE STEPPING RIGHT TO THE EDGE OF A CLIFF, THEN AT THE LAST MOMENT . . . WE BACKED AWAY.

I just stared at him, afraid to speak.

WE HAVE TO DO THIS. WE HAVE TO DIE.

TOGETHER.

Hours later, back in my sleep kiva, I could still feel the thrill that flooded me when Francis had the courage to give voice to thoughts I dared not fully formulate.

We had to die. It was that simple. Together, at the height of our passion, we would face eternity together.

Death. Forbidden fruit. I wondered what it would feel like to nibble at that illicit flesh. To be . . .

Free.

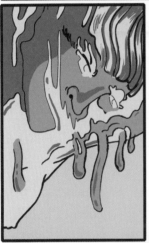

Free.

Fucking microsynthes. We had to die.

But in order to do that, I had to find the Death Dealers.

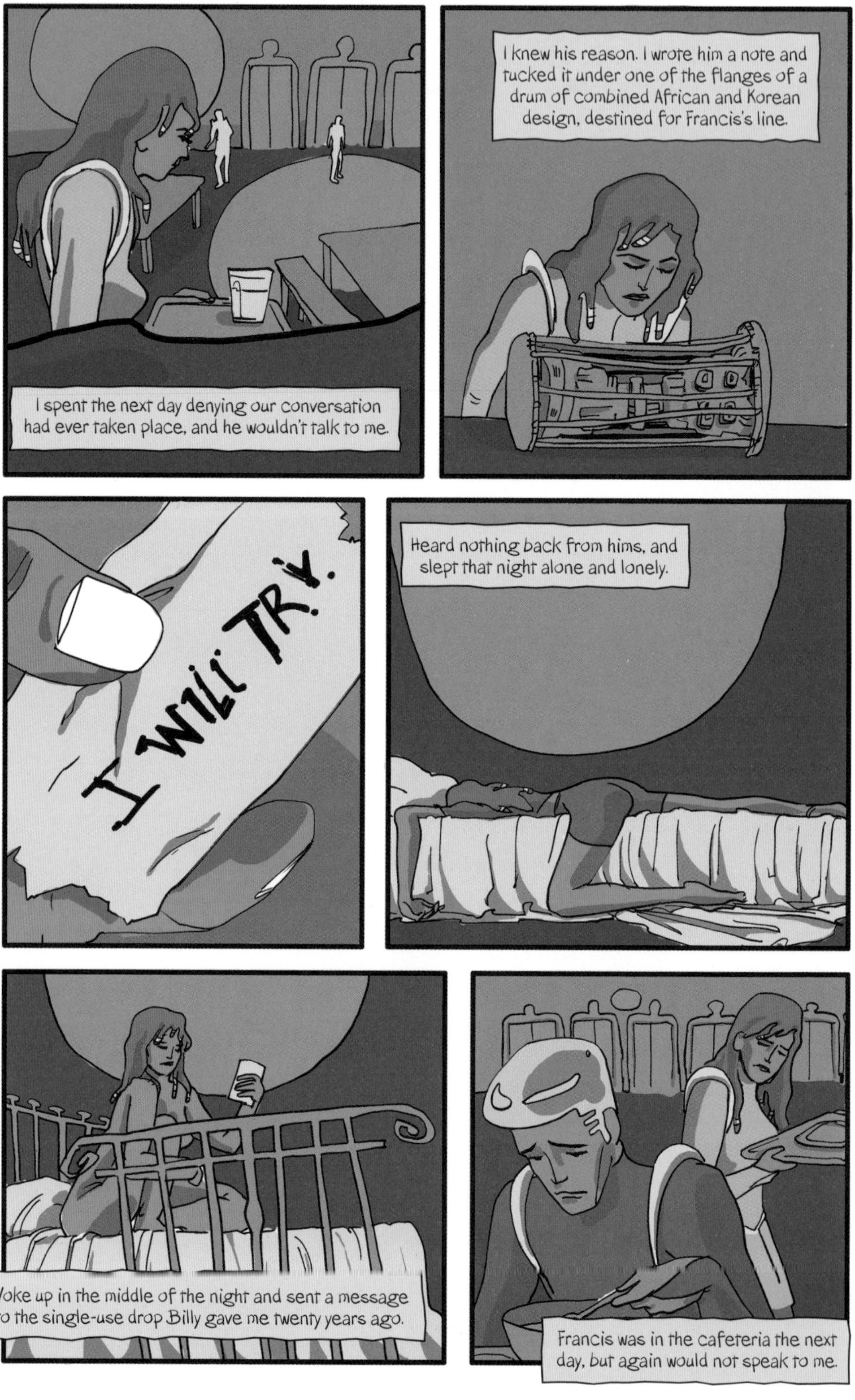
I spent the next day denying our conversation had ever taken place, and he wouldn't talk to me.
I knew his reason. I wrote him a note and tucked it under one of the flanges of a drum of combined African and Korean design, destined for Francis's line.
I WILL TRY.
Heard nothing back from hims, and slept that night alone and lonely.
Woke up in the middle of the night and sent a message to the single-use drop Billy gave me twenty years ago.
Francis was in the cafeteria the next day, but again would not speak to me.

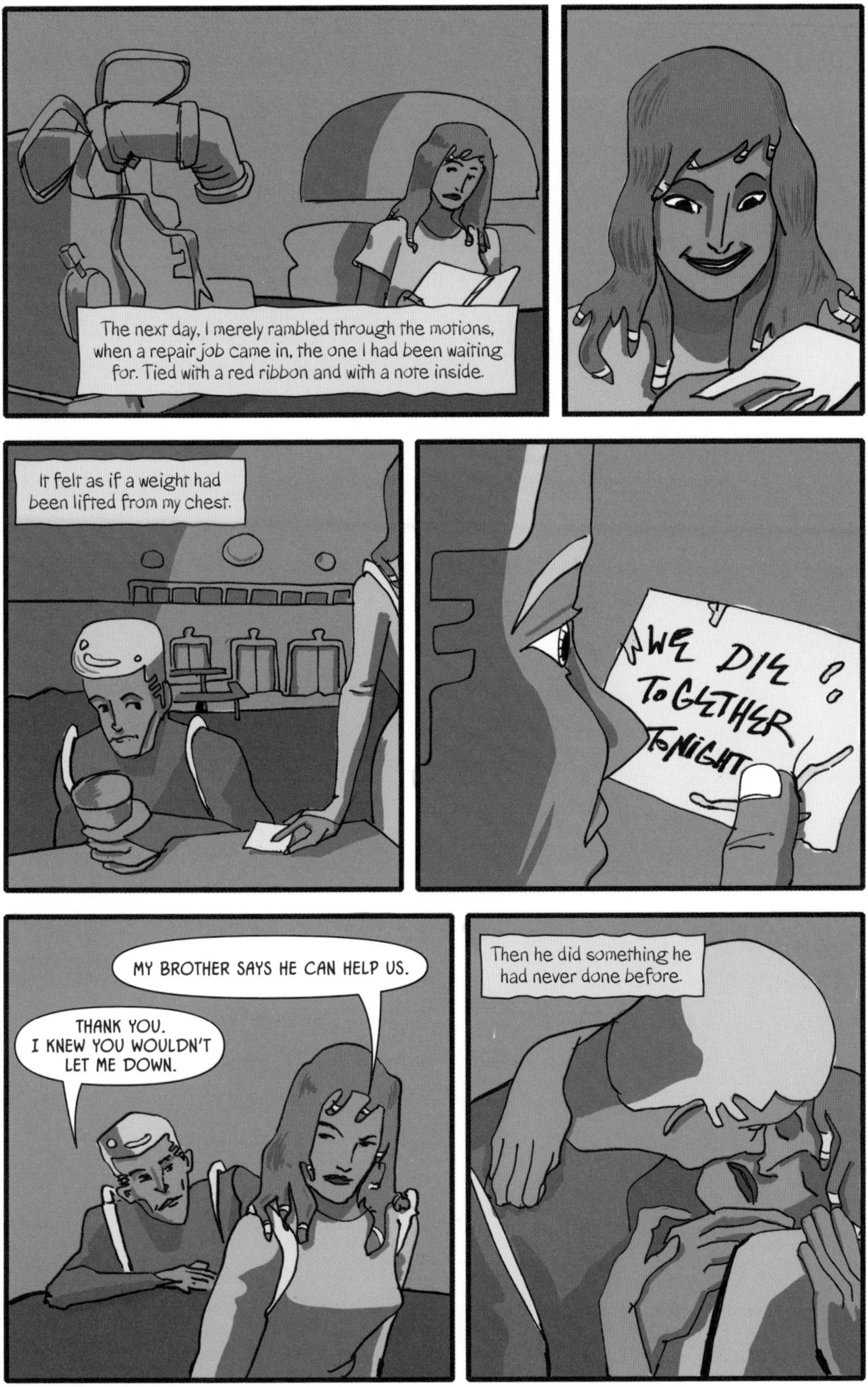

The next day, I merely rambled through the motions, when a repair job came in, the one I had been waiting for. Tied with a red ribbon and with a note inside.
It felt as if a weight had been lifted from my chest.
WE DIE TOGETHER TONIGHT
MY BROTHER SAYS HE CAN HELP US.
THANK YOU. I KNEW YOU WOULDN'T LET ME DOWN.
Then he did something he had never done before.

IT'S GOING TO BE SO GOOD.

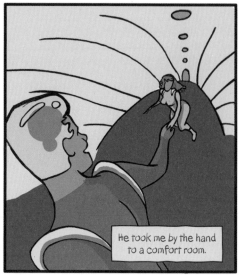

He took me by the hand to a comfort room.

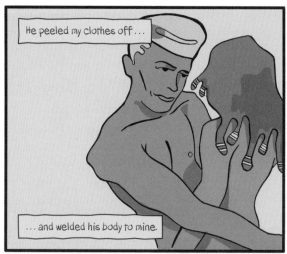

He peeled my clothes off...

... and welded his body to mine.

He was like a furnace.

It had never been like that before.

And would never be again.

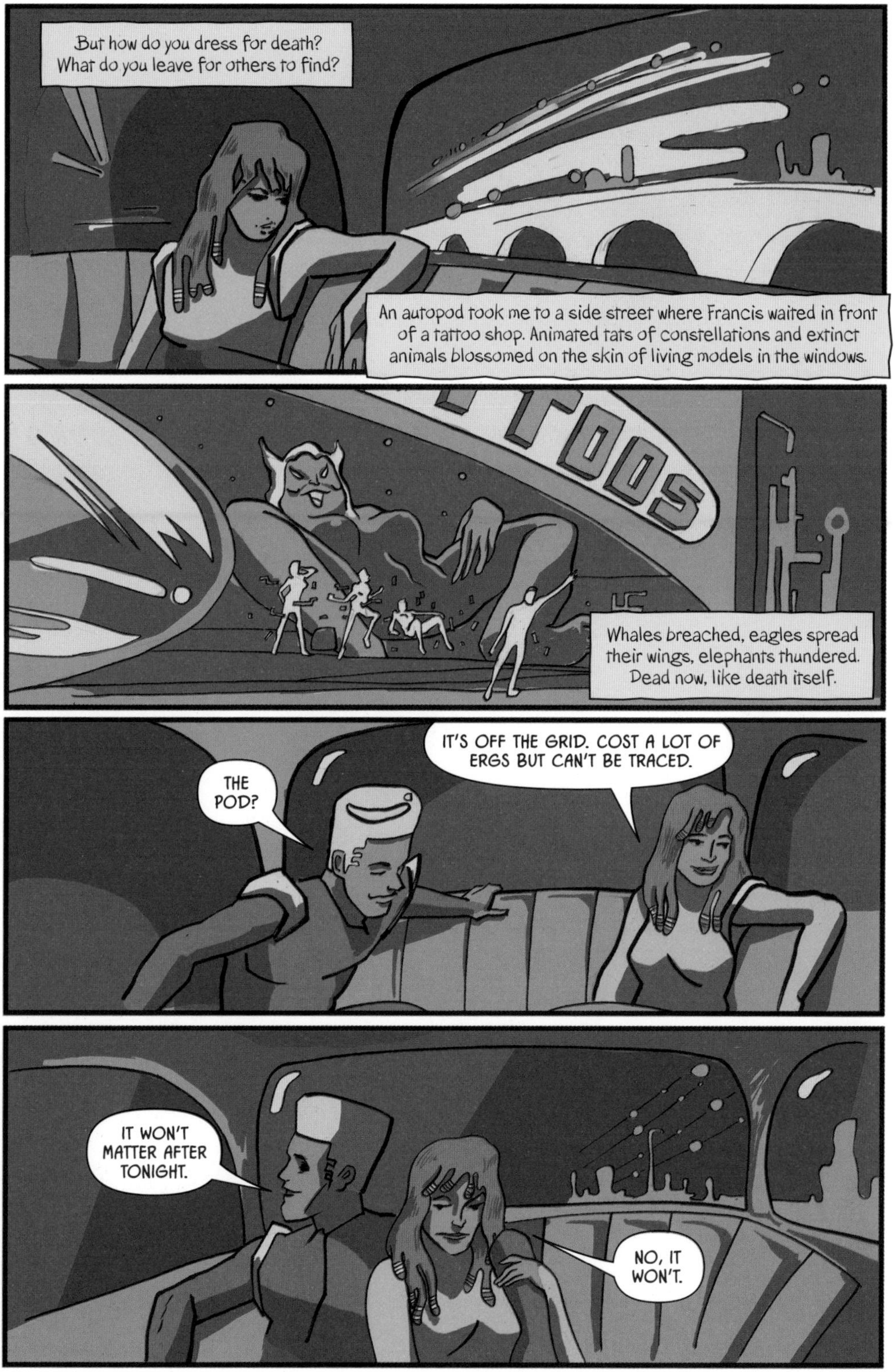
But how do you dress for death? What do you leave for others to find?
An autopod took me to a side street where Francis waited in front of a tattoo shop. Animated tats of constellations and extinct animals blossomed on the skin of living models in the windows.
TOOS
Whales breached, eagles spread their wings, elephants thundered. Dead now, like death itself.
THE POD?
IT'S OFF THE GRID. COST A LOT OF ERGS BUT CAN'T BE TRACED.
IT WON'T MATTER AFTER TONIGHT.
NO, IT WON'T.

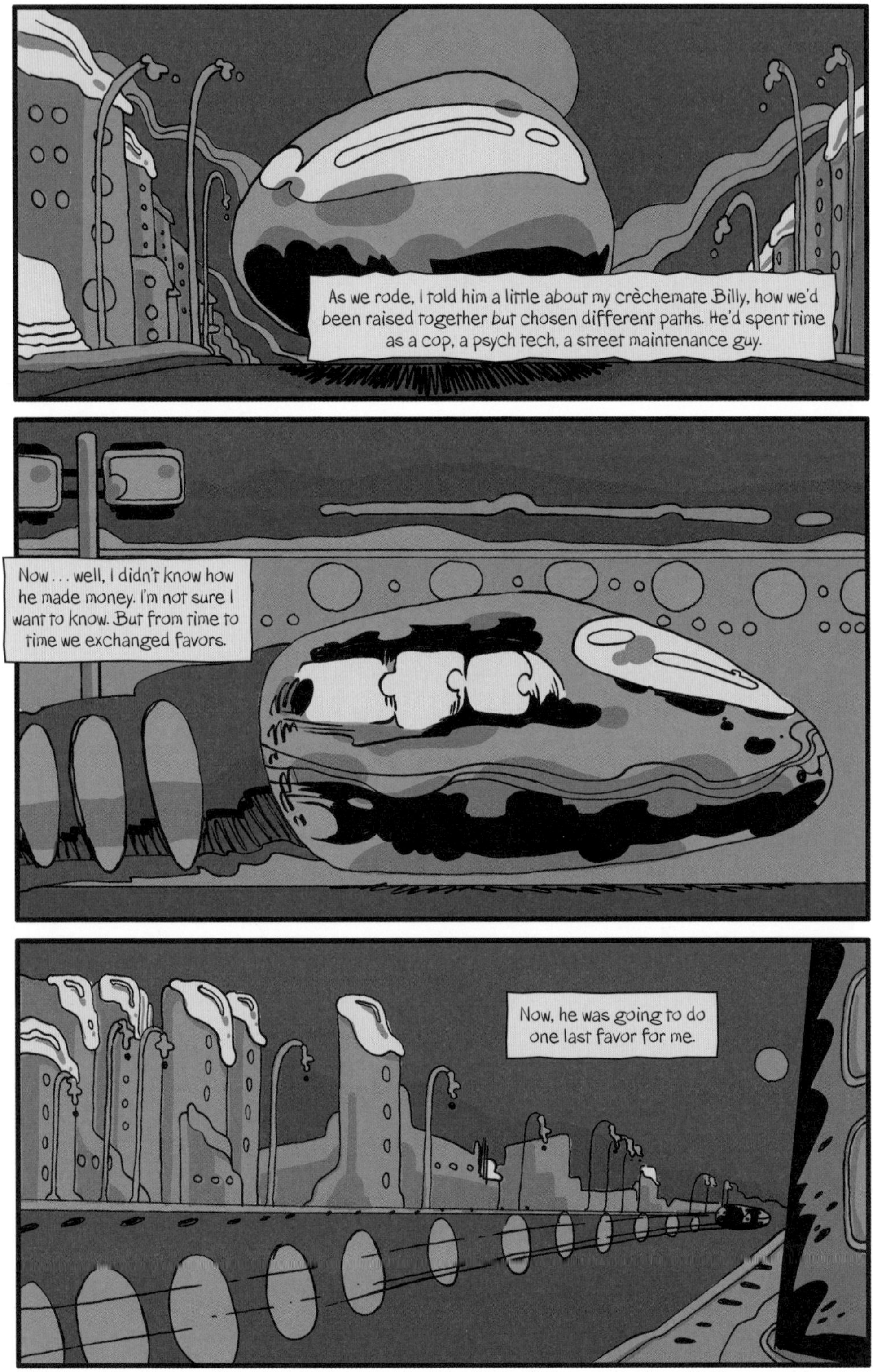
As we rode, I told him a little about my crèchemate Billy, how we'd been raised together but chosen different paths. He'd spent time as a cop, a psych tech, a street maintenance guy.
Now . . . well, I didn't know how he made money. I'm not sure I want to know. But from time to time we exchanged favors.
Now, he was going to do one last favor for me.

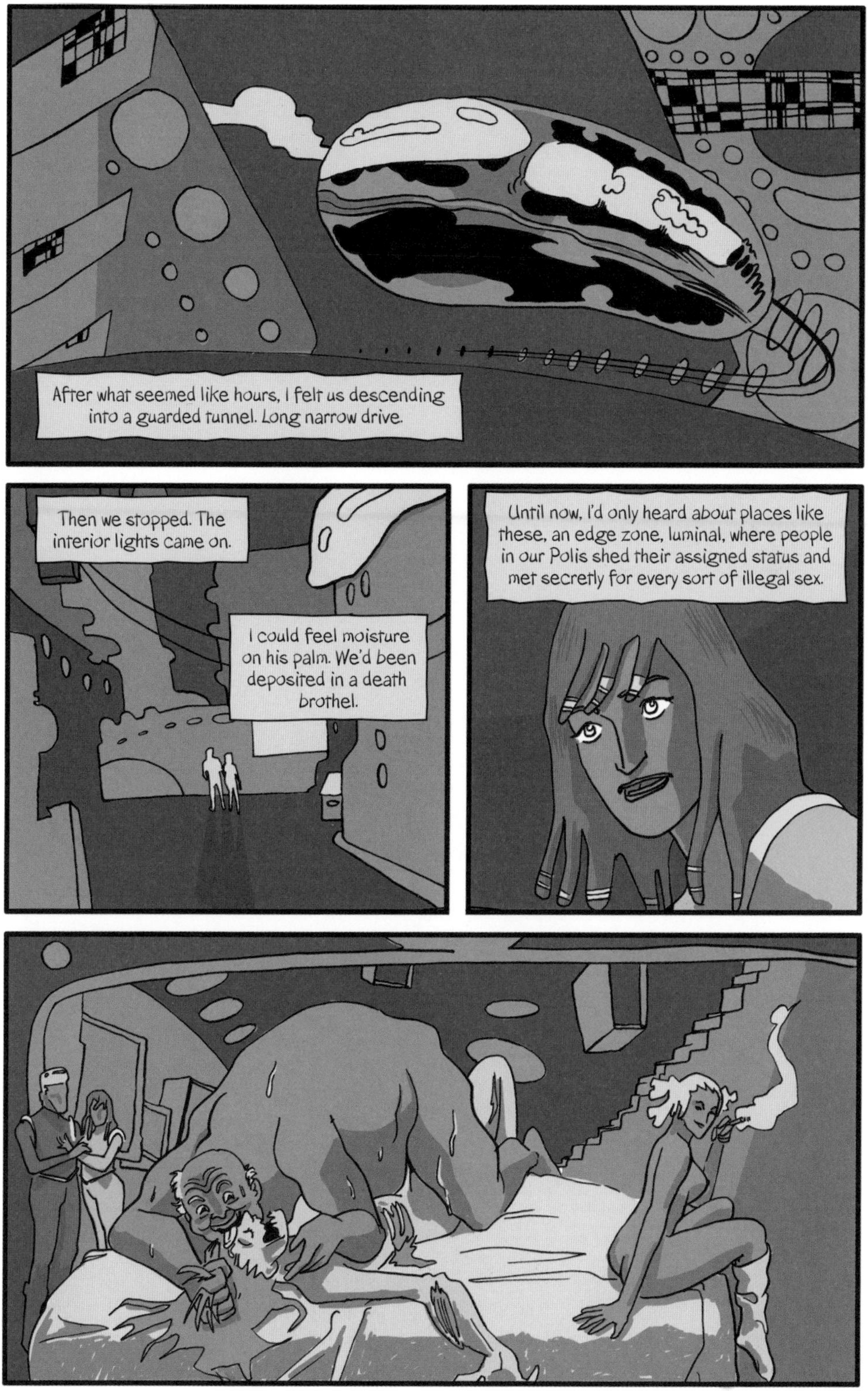
After what seemed like hours, I felt us descending into a guarded tunnel. Long narrow drive.
Then we stopped. The interior lights came on.
I could feel moisture on his palm. We'd been deposited in a death brothel.
Until now, I'd only heard about places like these, an edge zone, luminal, where people in our Polis shed their assigned status and met secretly for every sort of illegal sex.

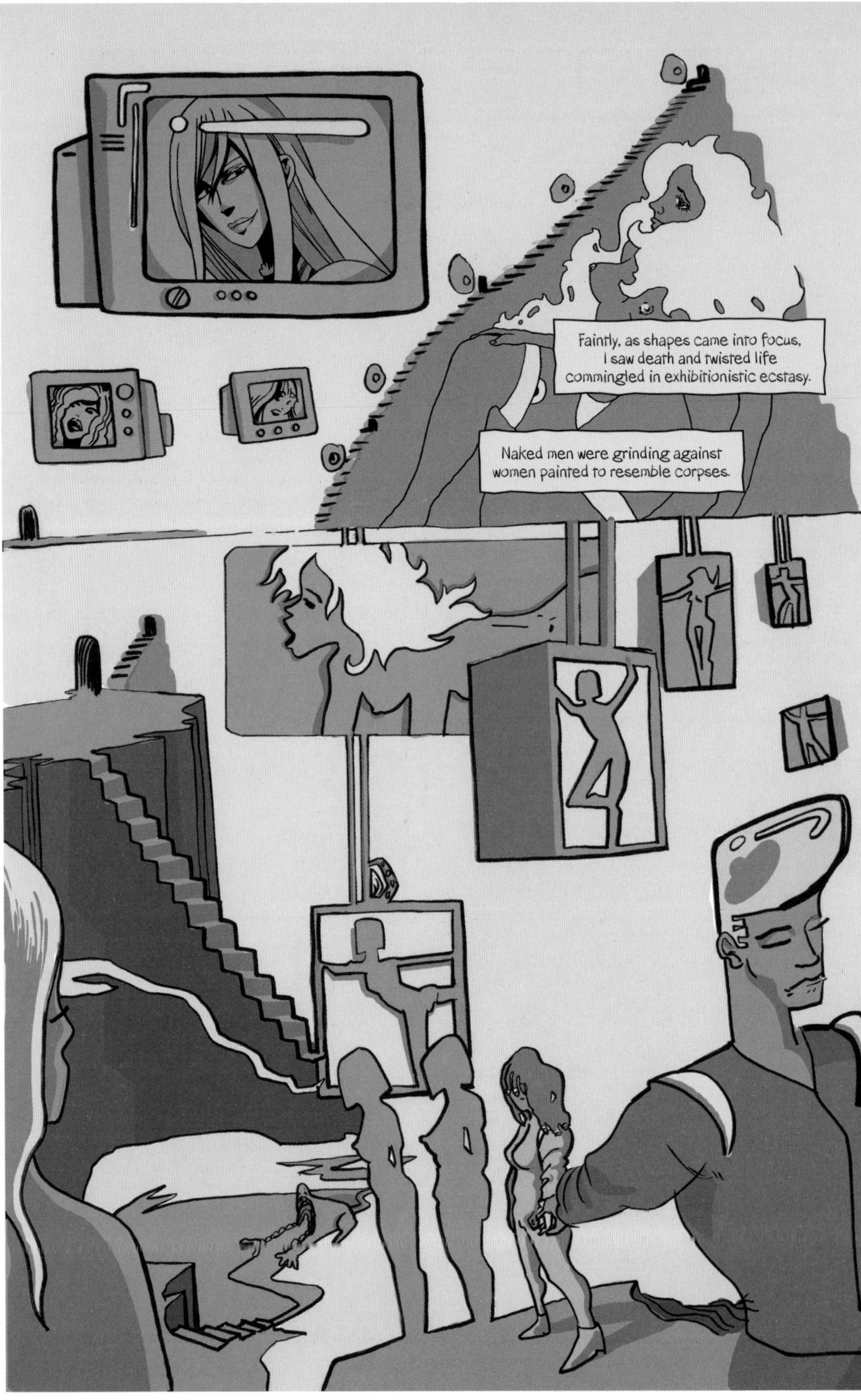
Faintly, as shapes came into focus, I saw death and twisted life commingled in exhibitionistic ecstasy.
Naked men were grinding against women painted to resemble corpses.

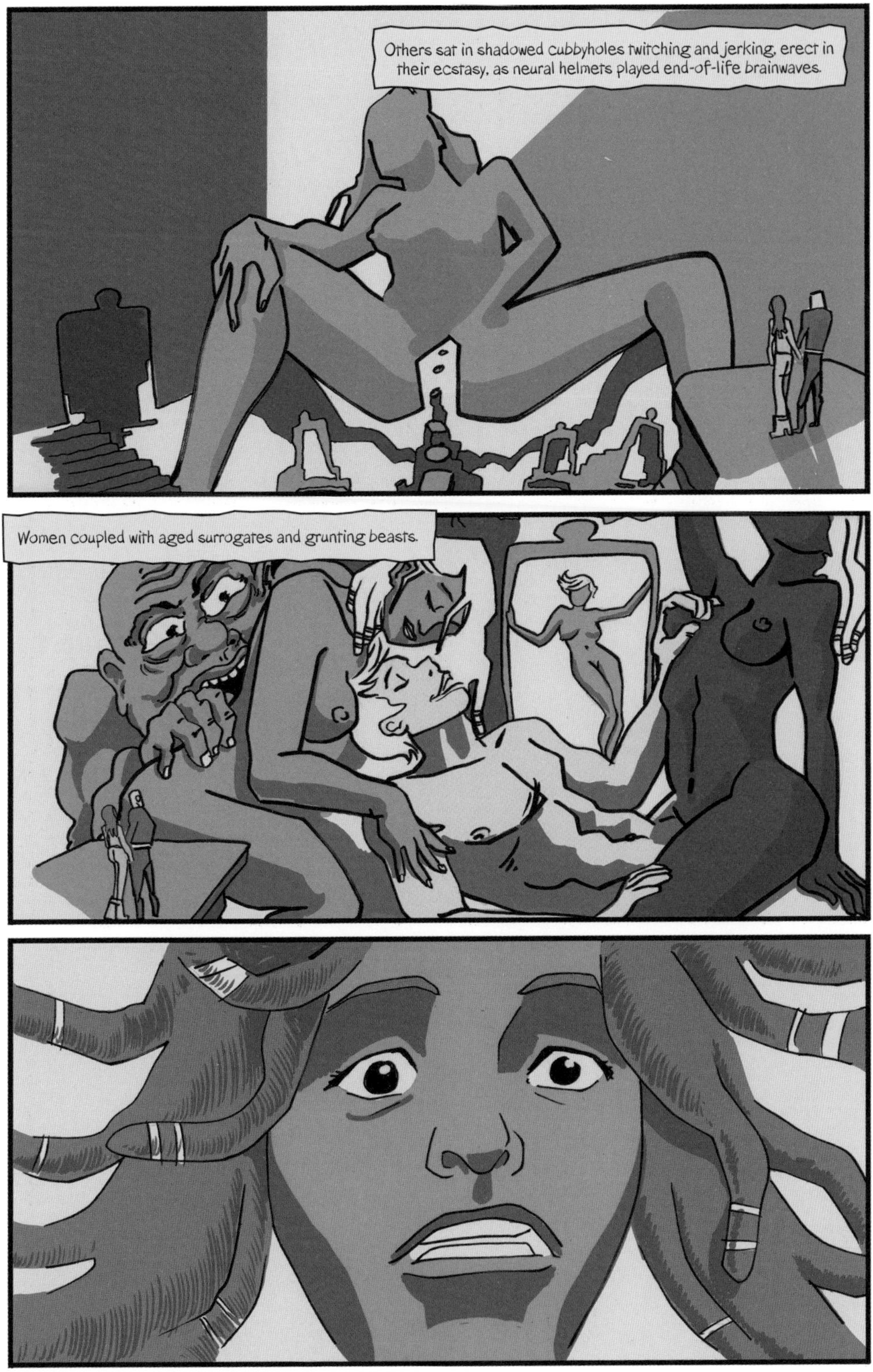
Others sat in shadowed cubbyholes twitching and jerking, erect in their ecstasy, as neural helmets played end-of-life brainwaves.
Women coupled with aged surrogates and grunting beasts.

My mind reeled from the scent of sex mingled with the stench of decomposition.

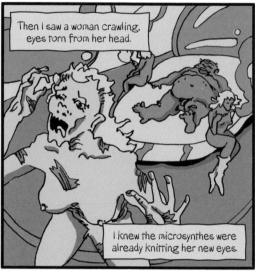

Then I saw a woman crawling, eyes torn from her head.

I knew the microsynthes were already knitting her new eyes.

I SAW IT . . .

I SAW IT . . . CAN'T YOU SEE IT?

And then, suddenly and without a sound, Billy materialized at my side

NEVER FIGURED TO SEE YOU IN A PLACE LIKE THIS, SISTER.

YOU ALWAYS WERE JUMPY, CHANDRA. MORE NERVOUS THAN ANYONE ELSE IN OUR LITTER.

HE THE ONE?

YEAH . . .

96

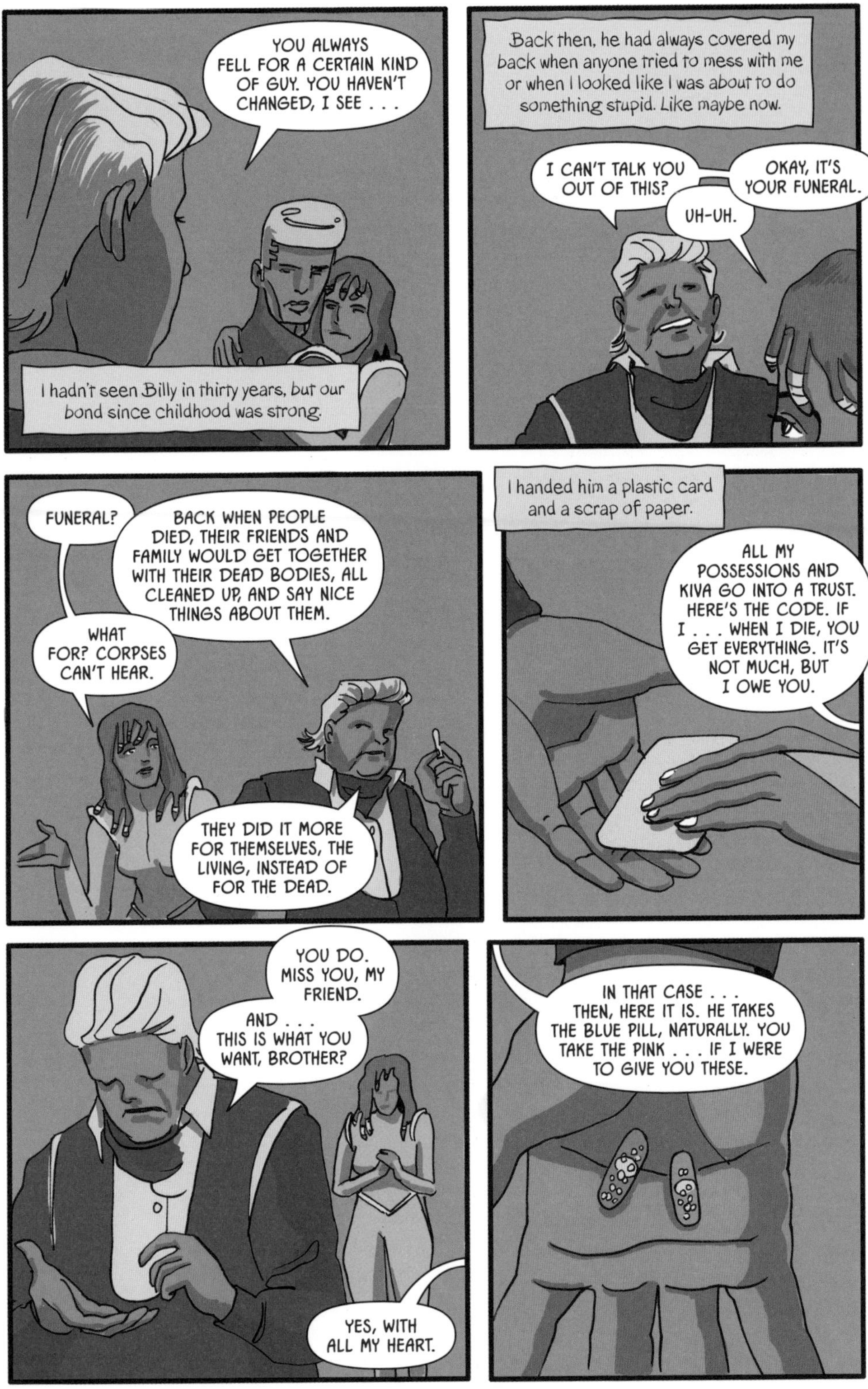
YOU ALWAYS FELL FOR A CERTAIN KIND OF GUY. YOU HAVEN'T CHANGED, I SEE . . .
I hadn't seen Billy in thirty years, but our bond since childhood was strong.
Back then, he had always covered my back when anyone tried to mess with me or when I looked like I was about to do something stupid. Like maybe now.
I CAN'T TALK YOU OUT OF THIS?
UH-UH.
OKAY, IT'S YOUR FUNERAL.
FUNERAL?
BACK WHEN PEOPLE DIED, THEIR FRIENDS AND FAMILY WOULD GET TOGETHER WITH THEIR DEAD BODIES, ALL CLEANED UP, AND SAY NICE THINGS ABOUT THEM.
WHAT FOR? CORPSES CAN'T HEAR.
THEY DID IT MORE FOR THEMSELVES, THE LIVING, INSTEAD OF FOR THE DEAD.
I handed him a plastic card and a scrap of paper.
ALL MY POSSESSIONS AND KIVA GO INTO A TRUST. HERE'S THE CODE. IF I . . . WHEN I DIE, YOU GET EVERYTHING. IT'S NOT MUCH, BUT I OWE YOU.
YOU DO. MISS YOU, MY FRIEND.
AND . . . THIS IS WHAT YOU WANT, BROTHER?
YES, WITH ALL MY HEART.
IN THAT CASE . . . THEN, HERE IT IS. HE TAKES THE BLUE PILL, NATURALLY. YOU TAKE THE PINK . . . IF I WERE TO GIVE YOU THESE.

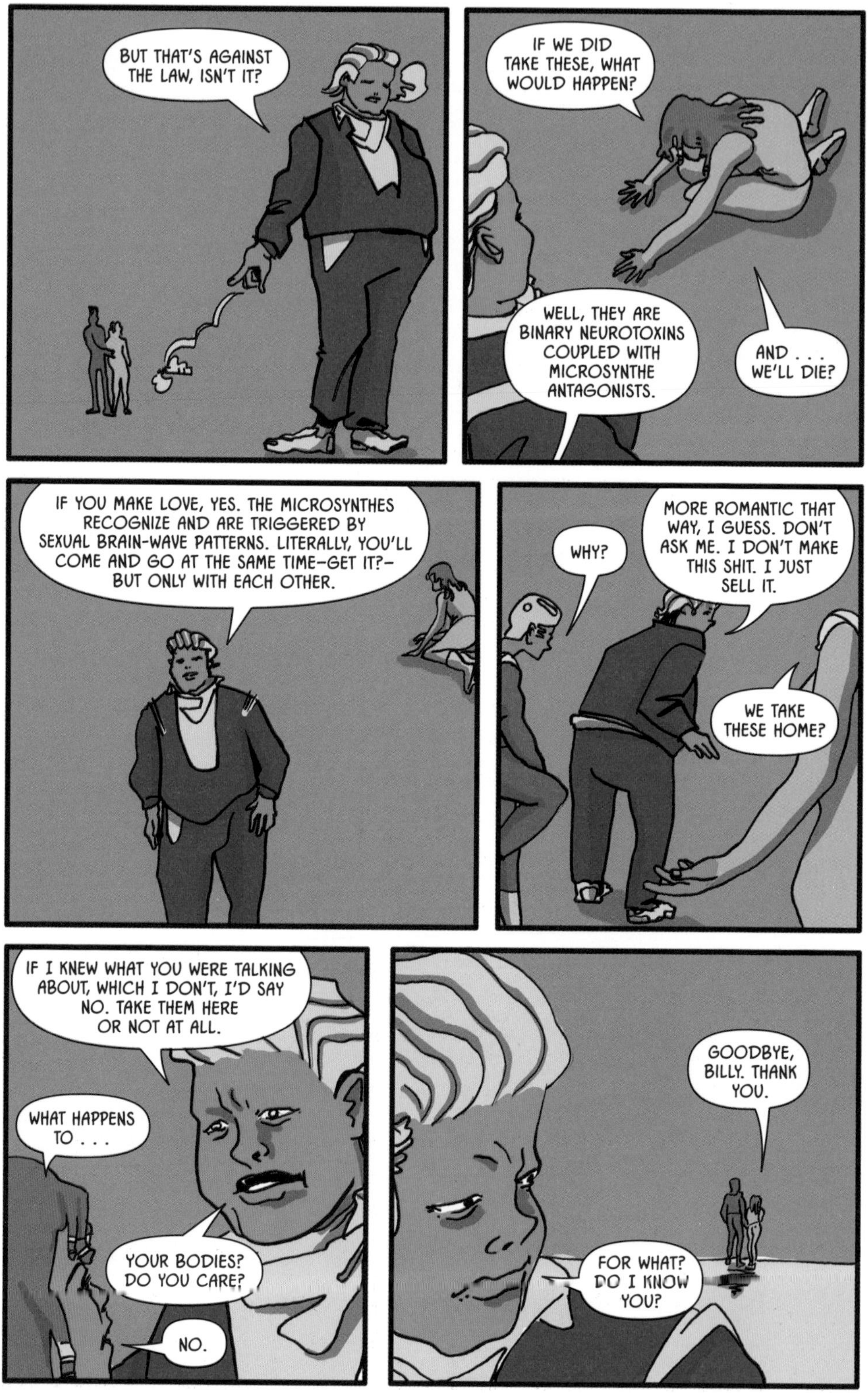
BUT THAT'S AGAINST THE LAW, ISN'T IT?
IF WE DID TAKE THESE, WHAT WOULD HAPPEN?
WELL, THEY ARE BINARY NEUROTOXINS COUPLED WITH MICROSYNTHE ANTAGONISTS.
AND . . . WE'LL DIE?
IF YOU MAKE LOVE, YES. THE MICROSYNTHES RECOGNIZE AND ARE TRIGGERED BY SEXUAL BRAIN-WAVE PATTERNS. LITERALLY, YOU'LL COME AND GO AT THE SAME TIME—GET IT?— BUT ONLY WITH EACH OTHER.
WHY?
MORE ROMANTIC THAT WAY, I GUESS. DON'T ASK ME. I DON'T MAKE THIS SHIT. I JUST SELL IT.
WE TAKE THESE HOME?
IF I KNEW WHAT YOU WERE TALKING ABOUT, WHICH I DON'T, I'D SAY NO. TAKE THEM HERE OR NOT AT ALL.
WHAT HAPPENS TO . . .
YOUR BODIES? DO YOU CARE?
NO.
GOODBYE, BILLY. THANK YOU.
FOR WHAT? DO I KNOW YOU?

The masked man beckoned to us. He opened the door, grinning, and we entered a little cubical with a bed. It was better than we had expected.

SO . . . THIS IS IT.

I ALWAYS WONDERED WHAT MY LAST SIGHT WOULD BE.

COULD IT BE ME?

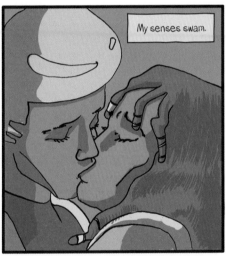

My senses swam.

YOU'VE NEVER KISSED ME LIKE THAT BEFORE.

I DON'T THINK I'VE EVER KISSED ANYONE LIKE THAT.

WHY? WHY HERE? WHY NOW?

THERE'S A LAST TIME FOR EVERYTHING. ARE YOU READY?

YES.

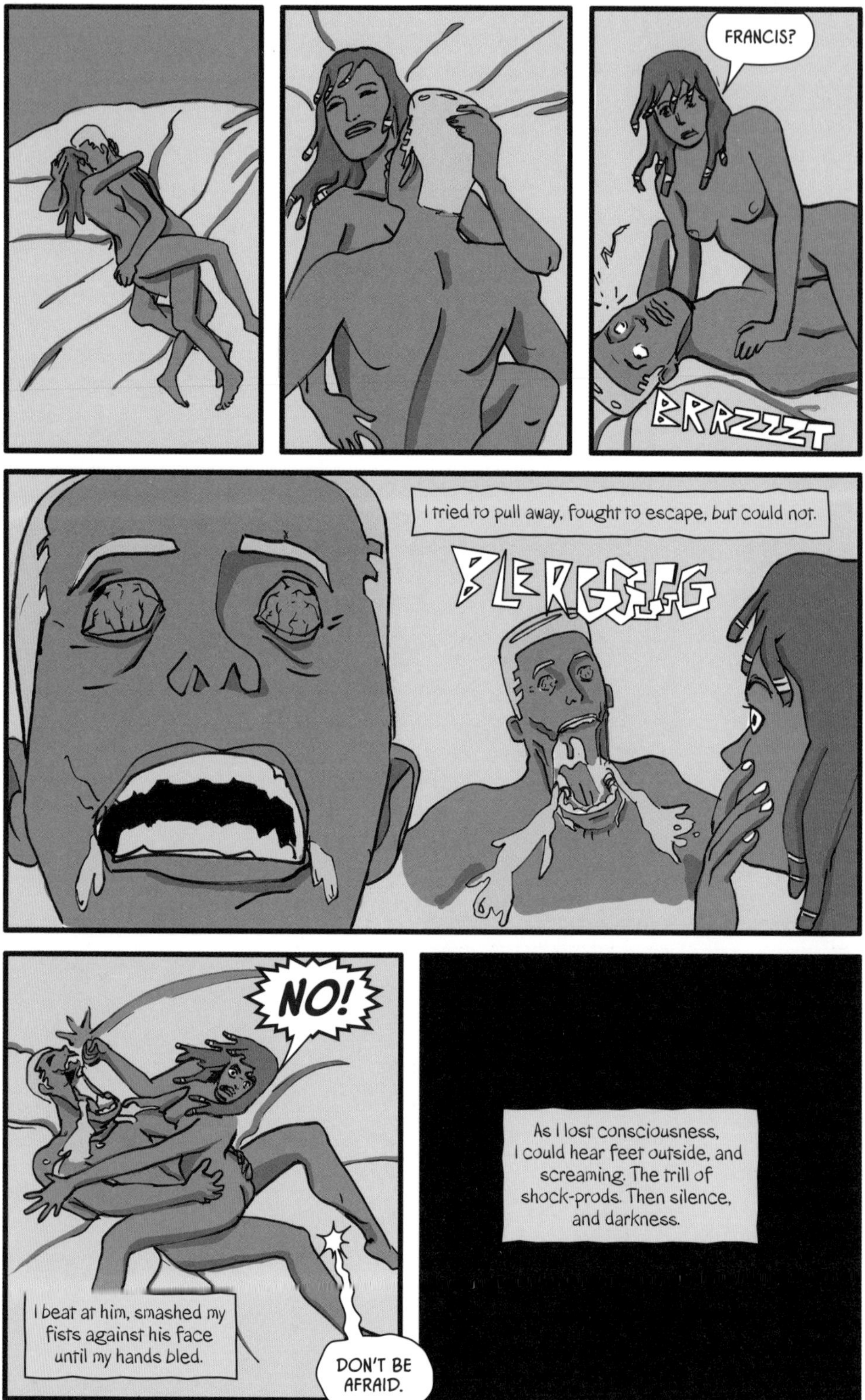
FRANCIS?
BRRZZZT
I tried to pull away, fought to escape, but could not.
BLERGGGG
NO!
I beat at him, smashed my fists against his face until my hands bled.
DON'T BE AFRAID.
As I lost consciousness, I could hear feet outside, and screaming. The trill of shock-prods. Then silence, and darkness.

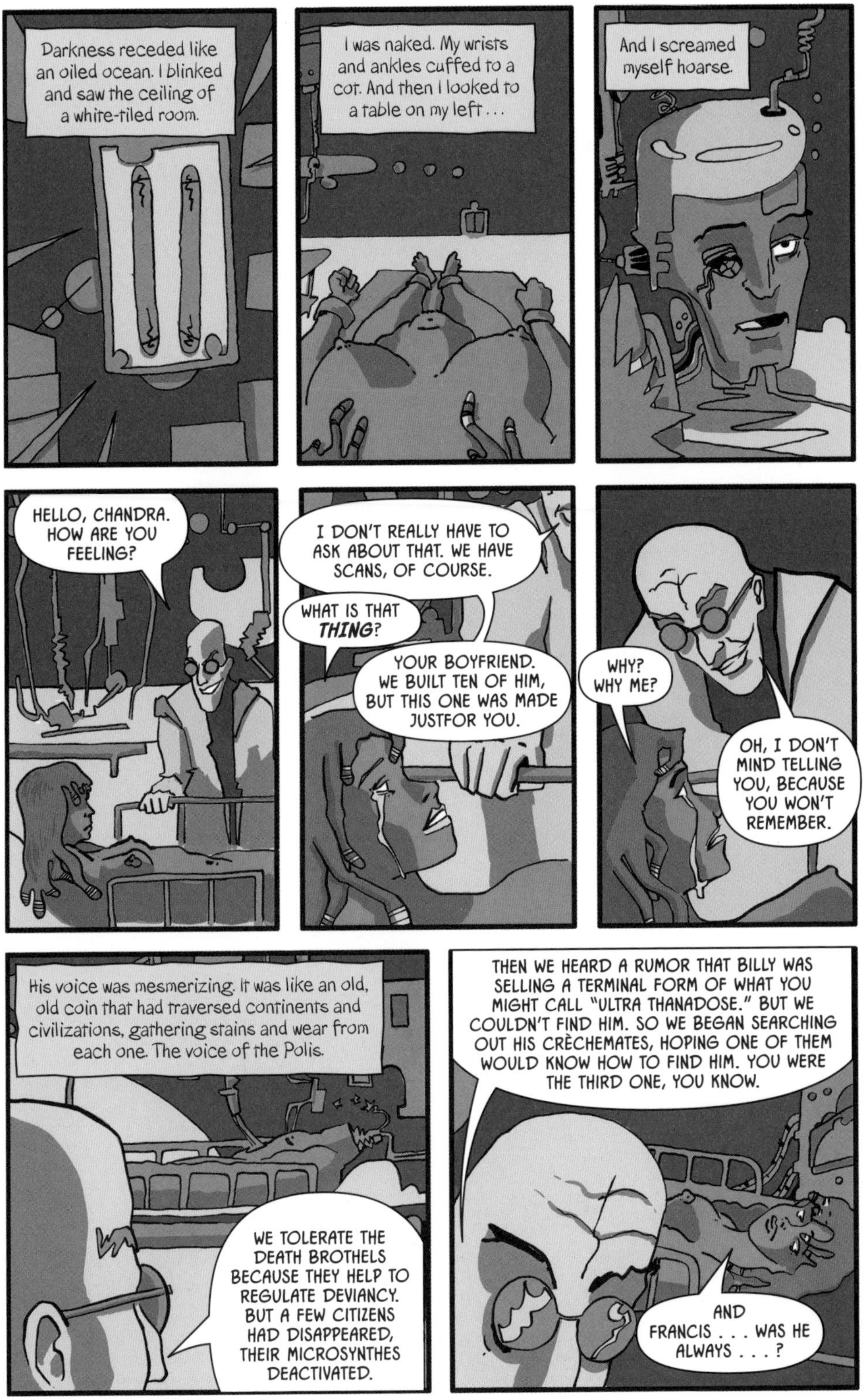
Darkness receded like an oiled ocean. I blinked and saw the ceiling of a white-tiled room.
I was naked. My wrists and ankles cuffed to a cot. And then I looked to a table on my left . . .
And I screamed myself hoarse.
HELLO, CHANDRA. HOW ARE YOU FEELING?
I DON'T REALLY HAVE TO ASK ABOUT THAT. WE HAVE SCANS, OF COURSE.
WHAT IS THAT *THING*?
YOUR BOYFRIEND. WE BUILT TEN OF HIM, BUT THIS ONE WAS MADE JUSTFOR YOU.
WHY? WHY ME?
OH, I DON'T MIND TELLING YOU, BECAUSE YOU WON'T REMEMBER.
His voice was mesmerizing. It was like an old, old coin that had traversed continents and civilizations, gathering stains and wear from each one. The voice of the Polis.
WE TOLERATE THE DEATH BROTHELS BECAUSE THEY HELP TO REGULATE DEVIANCY. BUT A FEW CITIZENS HAD DISAPPEARED, THEIR MICROSYNTHES DEACTIVATED.
THEN WE HEARD A RUMOR THAT BILLY WAS SELLING A TERMINAL FORM OF WHAT YOU MIGHT CALL "ULTRA THANADOSE." BUT WE COULDN'T FIND HIM. SO WE BEGAN SEARCHING OUT HIS CRÈCHEMATES, HOPING ONE OF THEM WOULD KNOW HOW TO FIND HIM. YOU WERE THE THIRD ONE, YOU KNOW.
AND FRANCIS . . . WAS HE ALWAYS . . . ?

YES. A SEX DOLL RECONFIGURED FOR ANALYSIS, CAPABLE OF BREAKING DOWN THE COMPOUNDS TO BE CERTAIN WE HAD THE REAL SAMPLE. WE RAIDED. NOW WE CAN RECONFIGURE THE MICROSYNTHES TO COMPENSATE.

IS BILLY . . .

DEAD? OH, HEAVENS NO! WE WASTE NOTHING. LIKE YOU, HE BELONGS TO ALL OF US. AND WE CARE ABOUT EVERYONE. WE ALWAYS HAVE EVERYONE'S BEST INTERESTS IN MIND.

I SUSPECT THAT'S SOMETHING YOU FORGOT.

There was a sound, and I finally recognized it. No way out. No way out . . . It was my own voice.

COME NOW, YOU'VE BEEN GIVEN A GIFT FOR WHICH KINGS AND PHARAOHS WOULD HAVE GLADLY EXCHANGED THEIR CROWNS.

I DON'T WANT IT.

WHAT YOU—OR ANY OF US—WANT ISN'T IMPORTANT. WE'RE ALL AN ESSENTIAL PART OF THE POLIS. THE CLAN. THE FAMILY. BECAUSE THERE IS A PLACE FOR EVERYTHING, AND EVERYTHING SHOULD BE IN ITS PLACE.

IT IS SELFISH TO SEE ONESELF AS SEPARATE OR SPECIAL WITHIN THE COLLECTIVE.

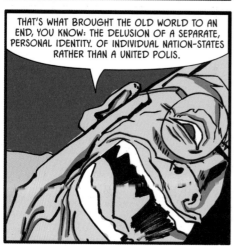

THAT'S WHAT BROUGHT THE OLD WORLD TO AN END, YOU KNOW: THE DELUSION OF A SEPARATE, PERSONAL IDENTITY. OF INDIVIDUAL NATION-STATES RATHER THAN A UNITED POLIS.

BUT I'M NOT HAPPY.

I KNOW. OCCASIONALLY SOCIETY PRODUCES MALCONTENTS WHO SEE THEMSELVES AS THE HEROES IN THEIR OWN SEPARATE STORIES.

WELL, I CAN FIX THOSE ANTISOCIAL IMAGININGS.

That was the moment real panic hit me.

NO! NO . . . THEY'RE ALL I HAVE. THEY'RE ALL OF ME THAT'S LEFT. ALL THAT'S MINE.

THERE IS NO YOU OR ME. NO MINE OR YOURS. ONLY WE.

Slowly, the edges of my visual field began to burn away.

Chandra awakened at home, although it took her a little time to determine where she was.

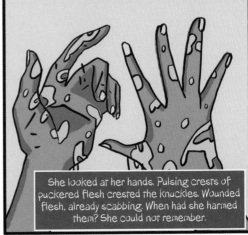

She looked at her hands. Pulsing crests of puckered flesh crested the knuckles. Wounded flesh, already scabbing. When had she harmed them? She could not remember.

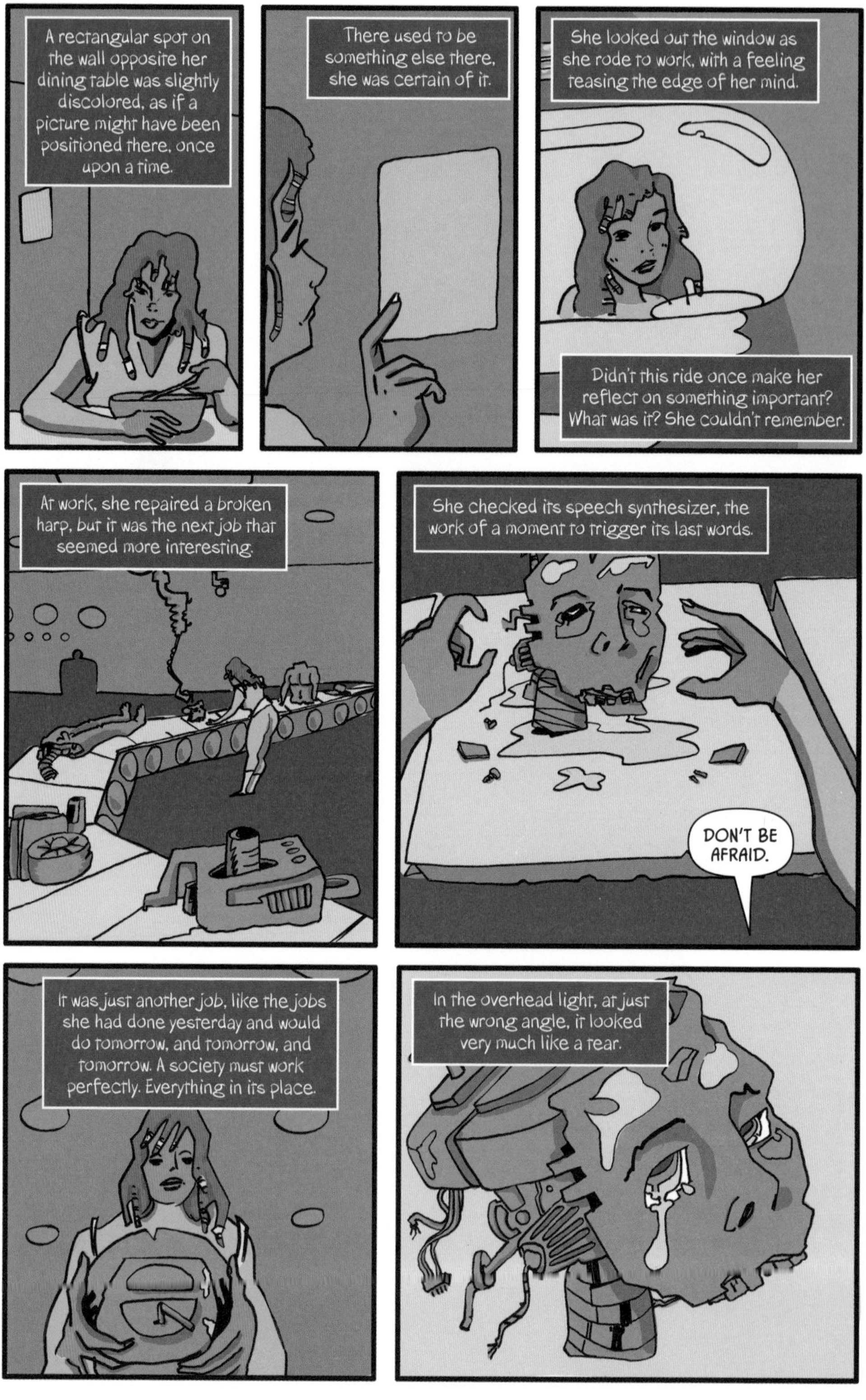
A rectangular spot on the wall opposite her dining table was slightly discolored, as if a picture might have been positioned there, once upon a time.
There used to be something else there, she was certain of it.
She looked out the window as she rode to work, with a feeling teasing the edge of her mind.
Didn't this ride once make her reflect on something important? What was it? She couldn't remember.
At work, she repaired a broken harp, but it was the next job that seemed more interesting.
She checked its speech synthesizer, the work of a moment to trigger its last words.
DON'T BE AFRAID.
It was just another job, like the jobs she had done yesterday and would do tomorrow, and tomorrow, and tomorrow. A society must work perfectly. Everything in its place.
In the overhead light, at just the wrong angle, it looked very much like a tear.

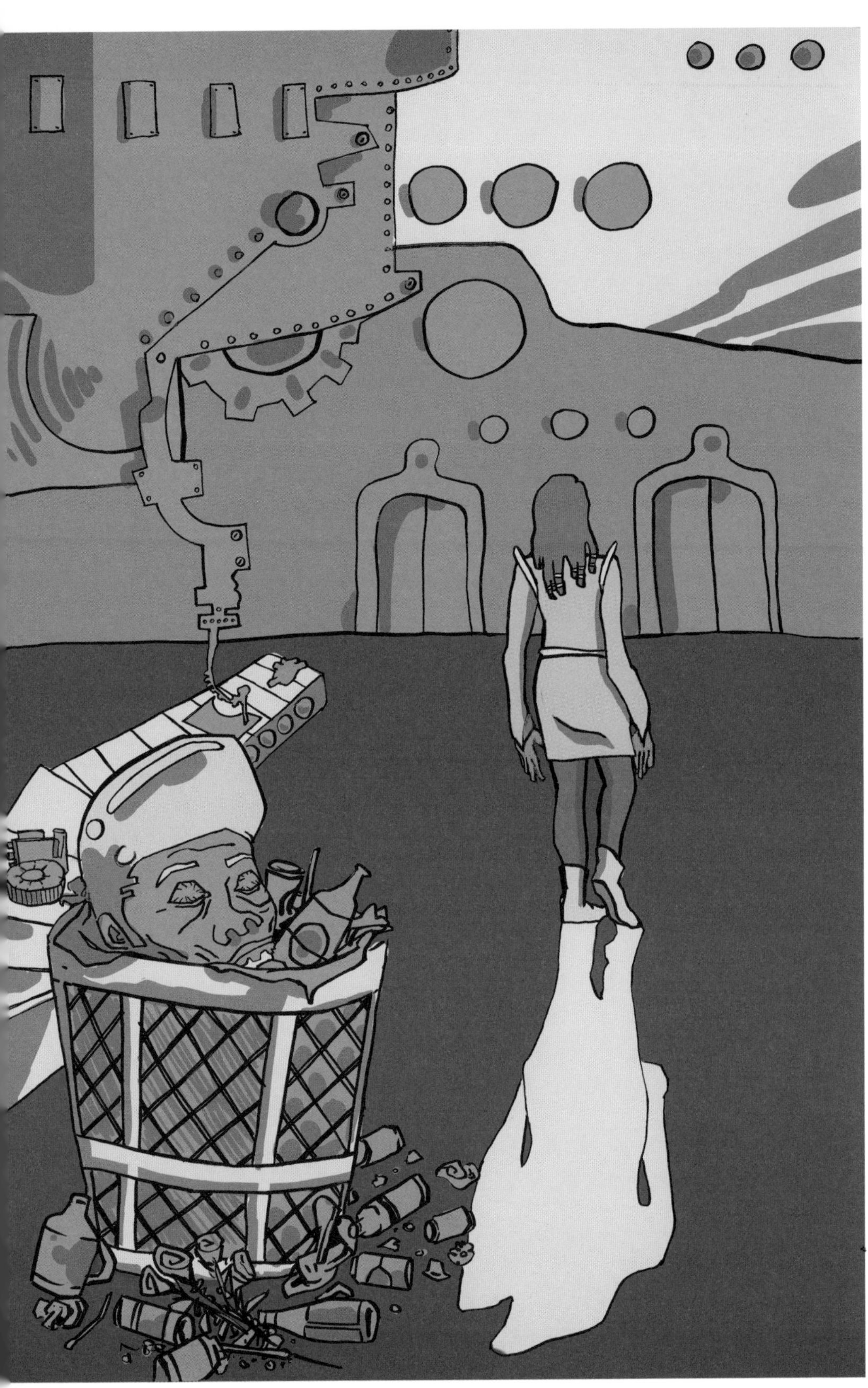

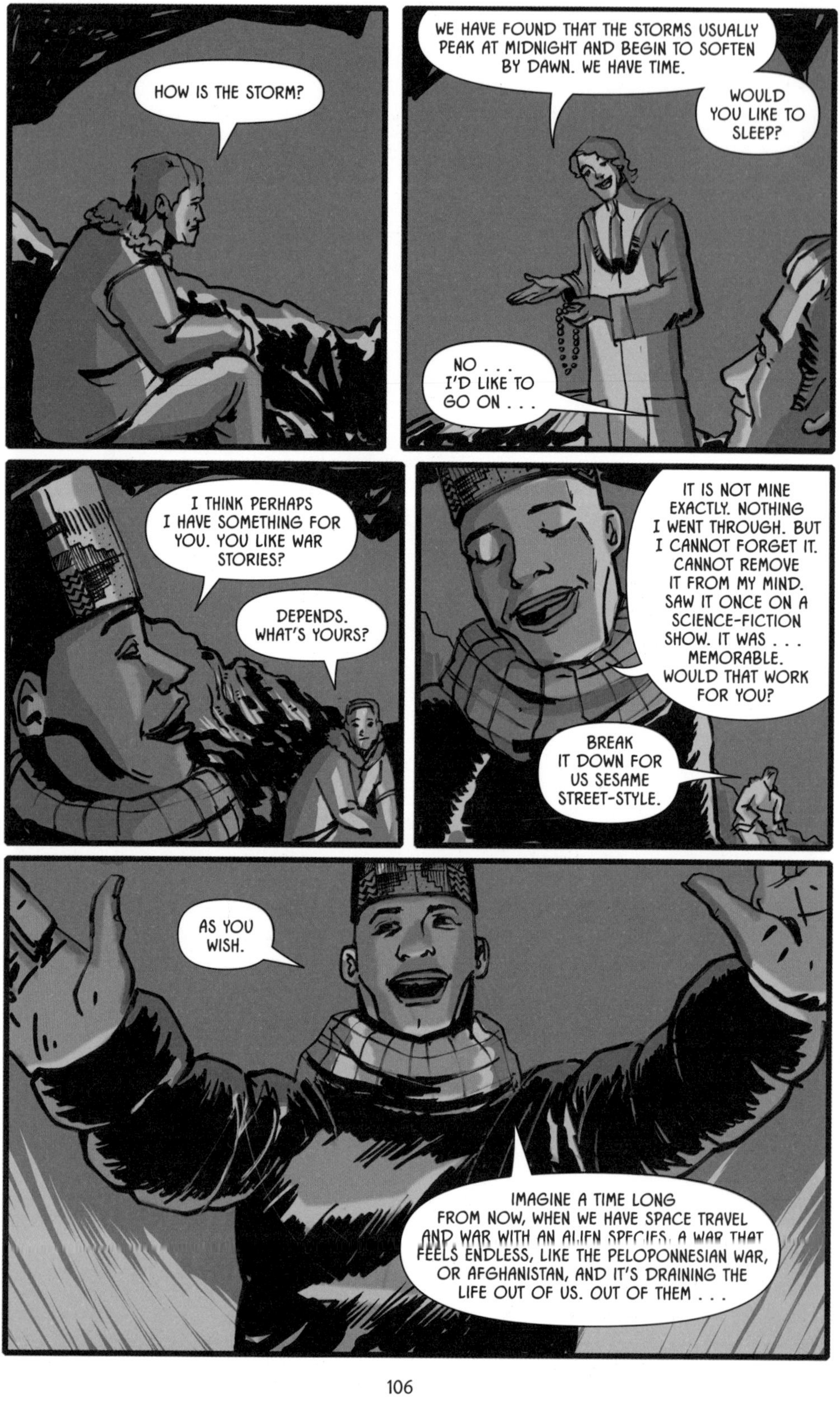
HOW IS THE STORM?
WE HAVE FOUND THAT THE STORMS USUALLY PEAK AT MIDNIGHT AND BEGIN TO SOFTEN BY DAWN. WE HAVE TIME.
WOULD YOU LIKE TO SLEEP?
NO . . . I'D LIKE TO GO ON . . .
I THINK PERHAPS I HAVE SOMETHING FOR YOU. YOU LIKE WAR STORIES?
DEPENDS. WHAT'S YOURS?
IT IS NOT MINE EXACTLY. NOTHING I WENT THROUGH. BUT I CANNOT FORGET IT. CANNOT REMOVE IT FROM MY MIND. SAW IT ONCE ON A SCIENCE-FICTION SHOW. IT WAS . . . MEMORABLE. WOULD THAT WORK FOR YOU?
BREAK IT DOWN FOR US SESAME STREET-STYLE.
AS YOU WISH.
IMAGINE A TIME LONG FROM NOW, WHEN WE HAVE SPACE TRAVEL AND WAR WITH AN ALIEN SPECIES, A WAR THAT FEELS ENDLESS, LIKE THE PELOPONNESIAN WAR, OR AFGHANISTAN, AND IT'S DRAINING THE LIFE OUT OF US. OUT OF THEM . . .

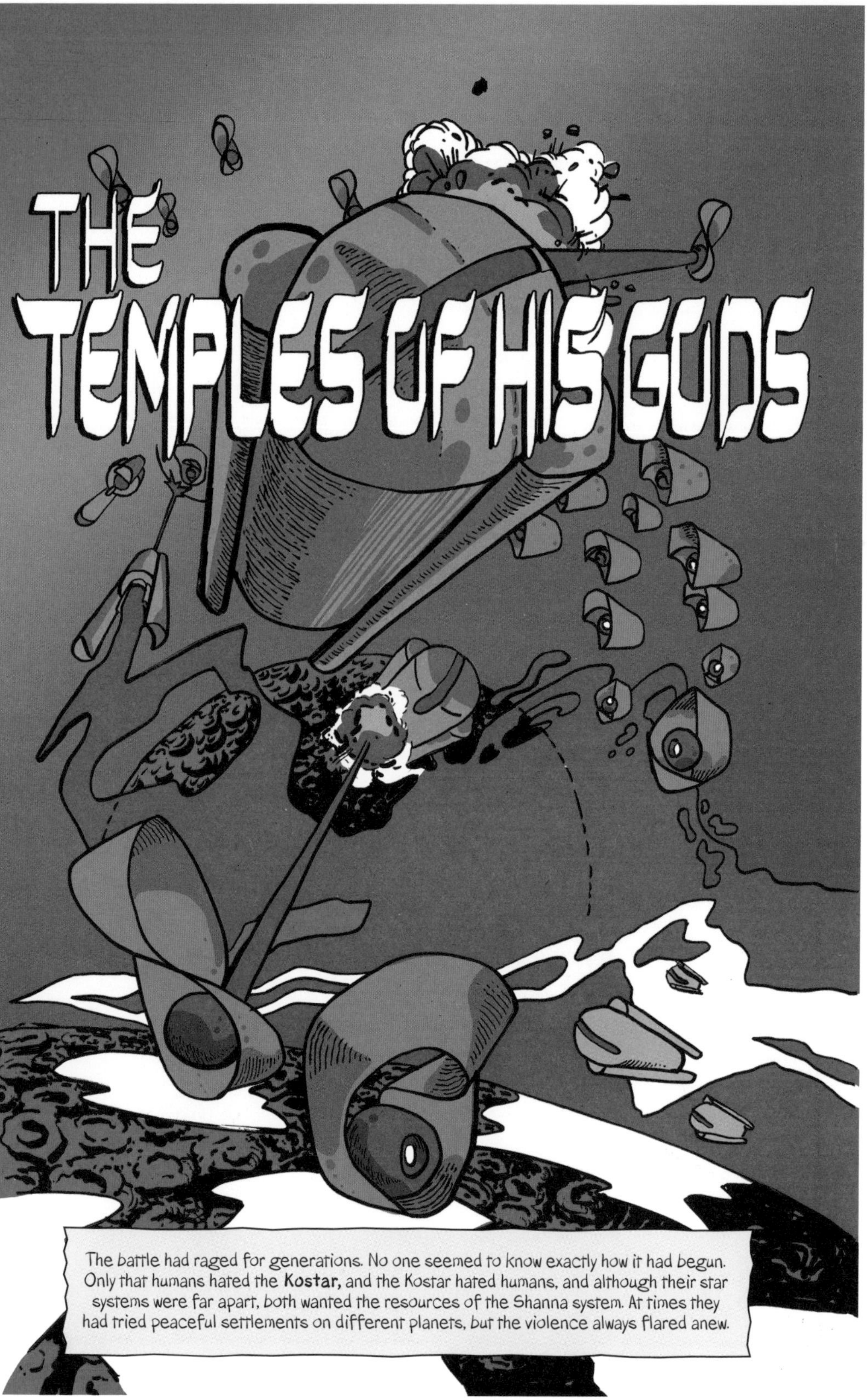
THE TEMPLES OF HIS GODS
The battle had raged for generations. No one seemed to know exactly how it had begun. Only that humans hated the **Kostar,** and the Kostar hated humans, and although their star systems were far apart, both wanted the resources of the Shanna system. At times they had tried peaceful settlements on different planets, but the violence always flared anew.

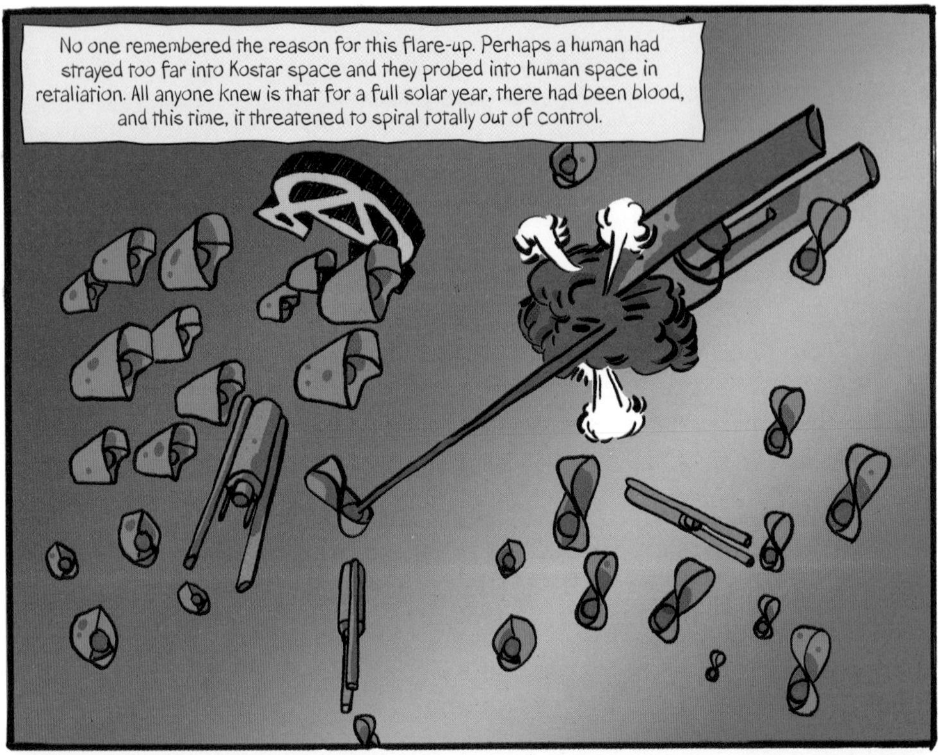
No one remembered the reason for this flare-up. Perhaps a human had strayed too far into Kostar space and they probed into human space in retaliation. All anyone knew is that for a full solar year, there had been blood, and this time, it threatened to spiral totally out of control.

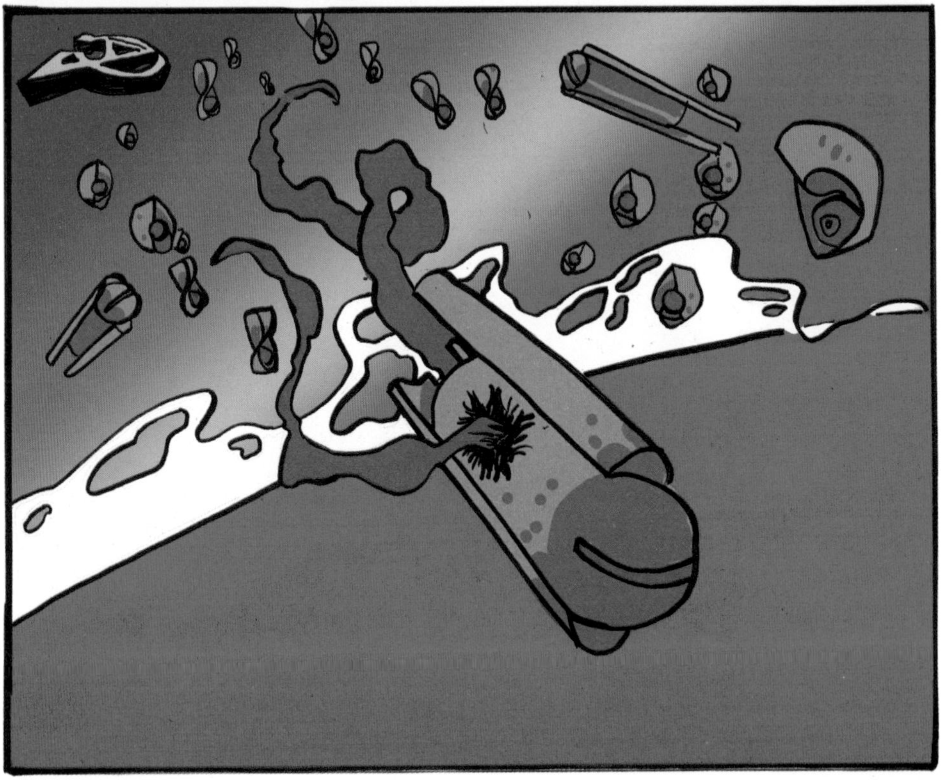

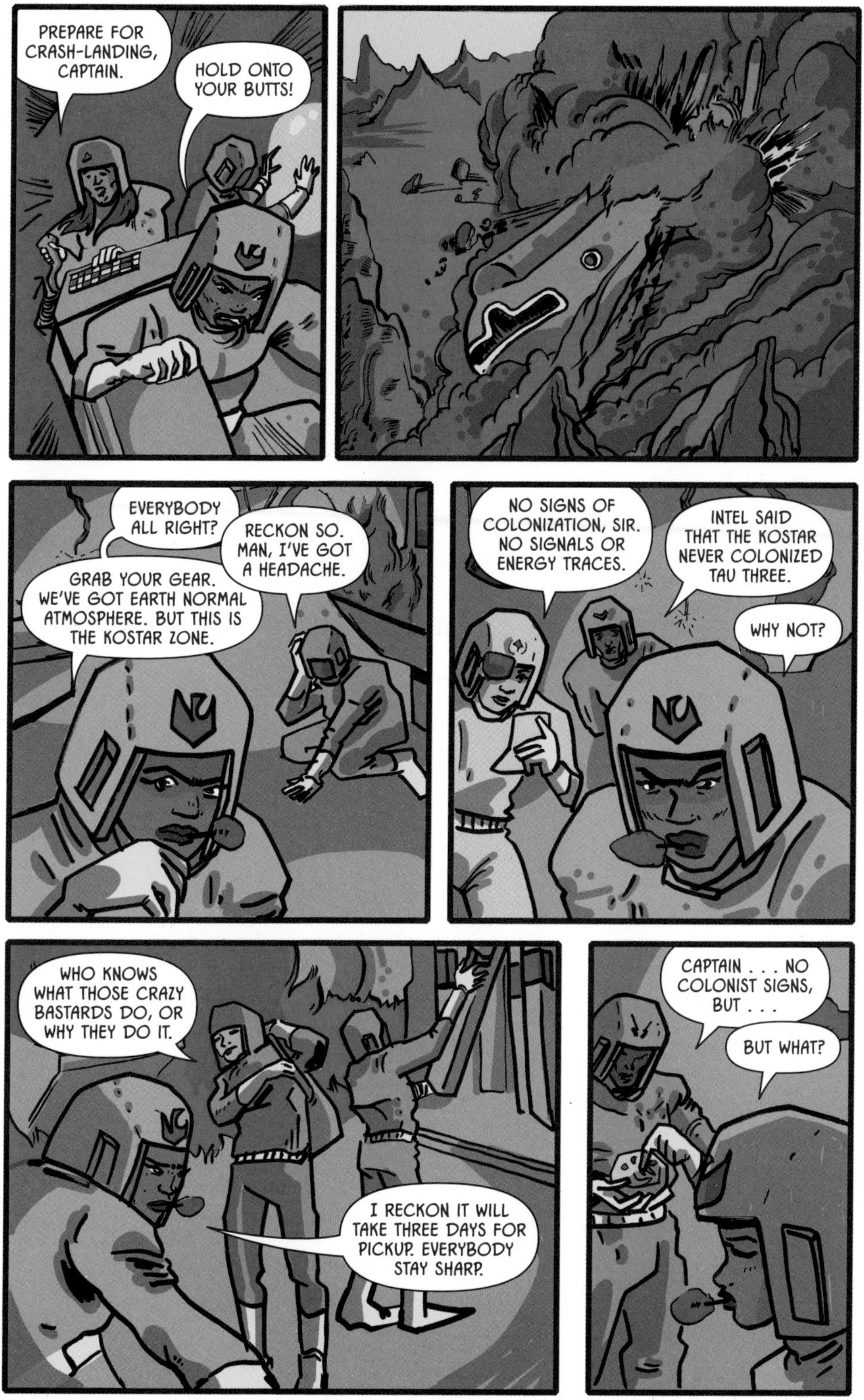
PREPARE FOR CRASH-LANDING, CAPTAIN.
HOLD ONTO YOUR BUTTS!
EVERYBODY ALL RIGHT?
RECKON SO. MAN, I'VE GOT A HEADACHE.
GRAB YOUR GEAR. WE'VE GOT EARTH NORMAL ATMOSPHERE. BUT THIS IS THE KOSTAR ZONE.
NO SIGNS OF COLONIZATION, SIR. NO SIGNALS OR ENERGY TRACES.
INTEL SAID THAT THE KOSTAR NEVER COLONIZED TAU THREE.
WHY NOT?
WHO KNOWS WHAT THOSE CRAZY BASTARDS DO, OR WHY THEY DO IT.
I RECKON IT WILL TAKE THREE DAYS FOR PICKUP. EVERYBODY STAY SHARP.
CAPTAIN . . . NO COLONIST SIGNS, BUT . . .
BUT WHAT?

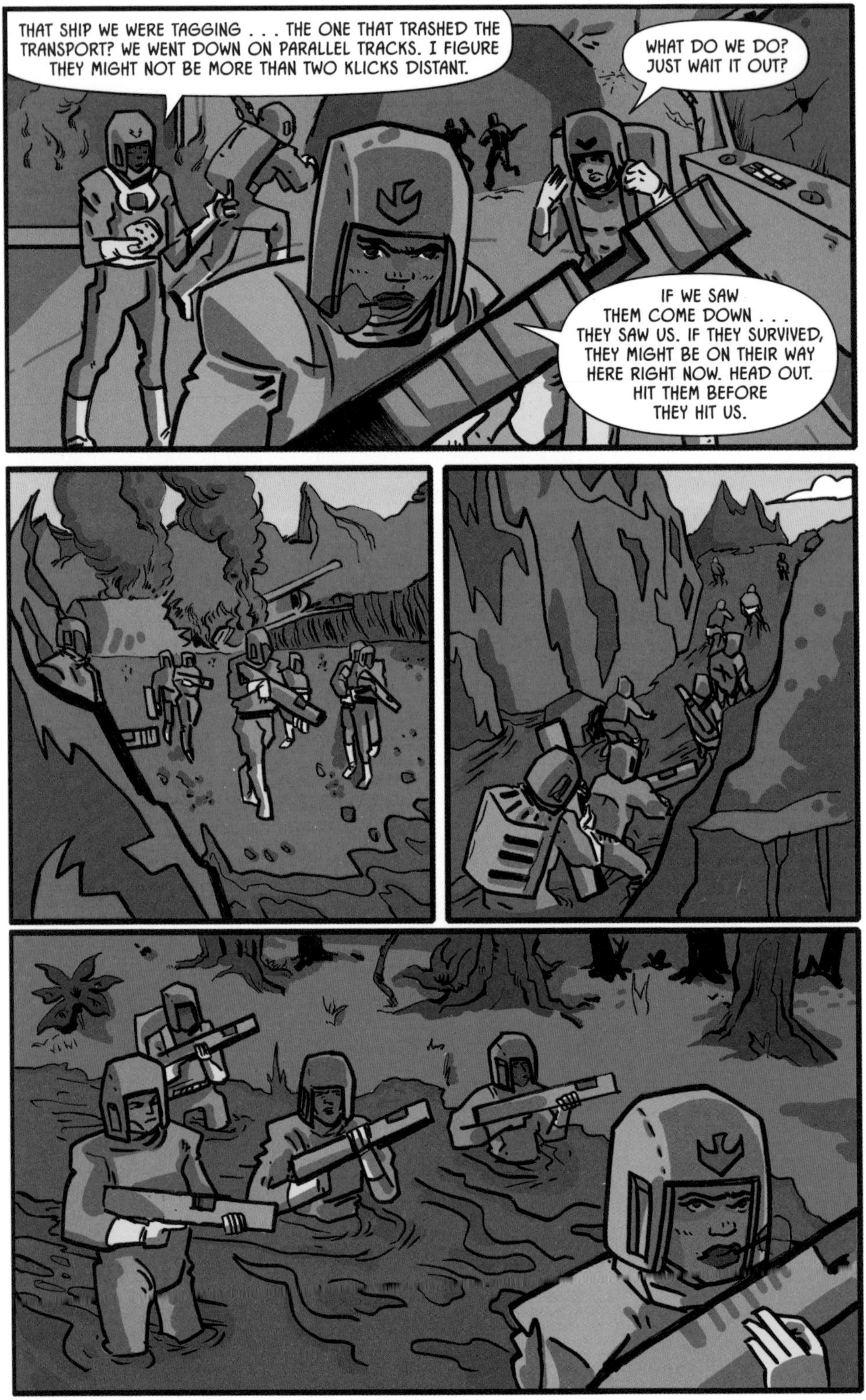
THAT SHIP WE WERE TAGGING . . . THE ONE THAT TRASHED THE TRANSPORT? WE WENT DOWN ON PARALLEL TRACKS. I FIGURE THEY MIGHT NOT BE MORE THAN TWO KLICKS DISTANT.
WHAT DO WE DO? JUST WAIT IT OUT?
IF WE SAW THEM COME DOWN . . . THEY SAW US. IF THEY SURVIVED, THEY MIGHT BE ON THEIR WAY HERE RIGHT NOW. HEAD OUT. HIT THEM BEFORE THEY HIT US.

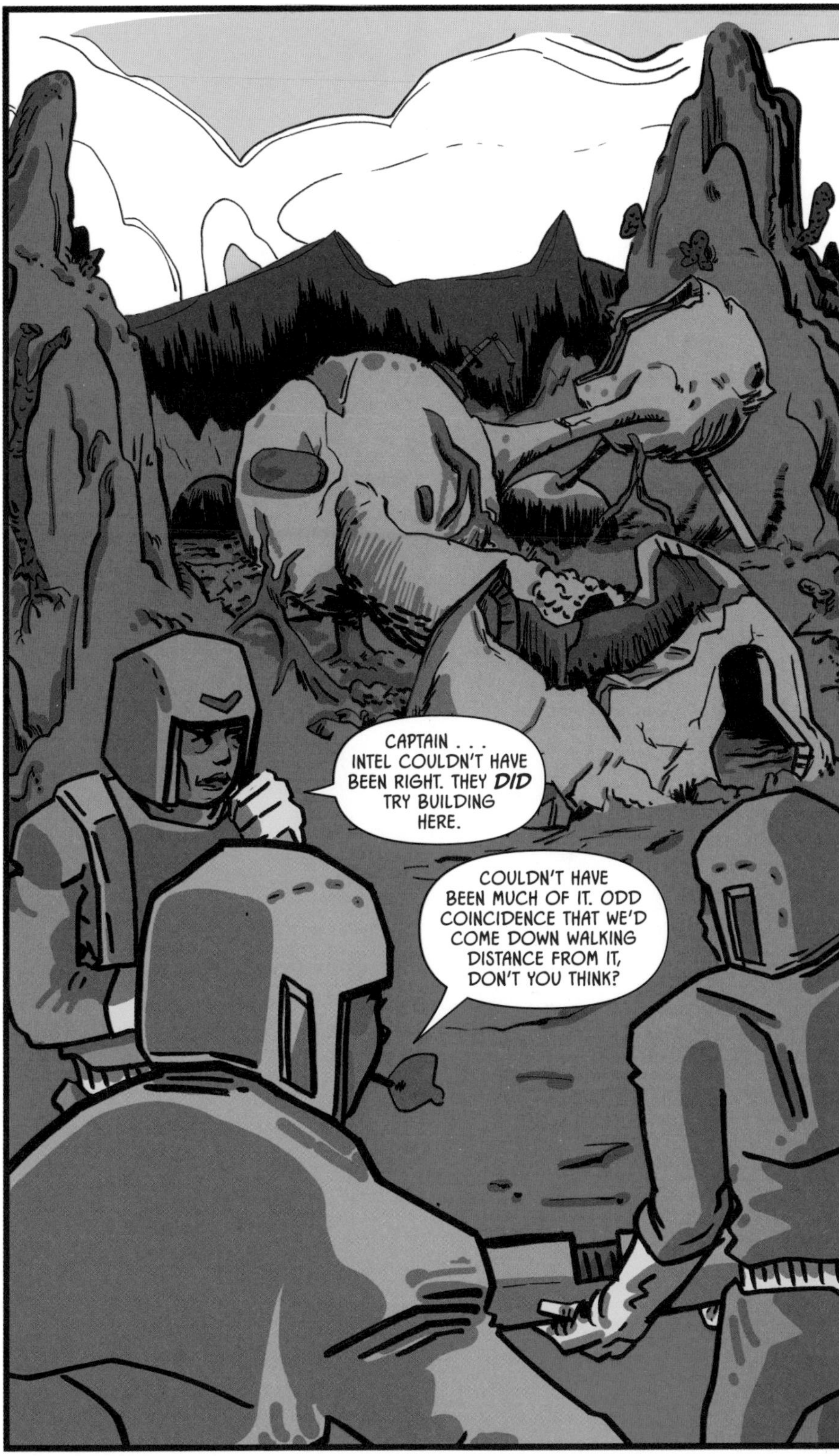
CAPTAIN . . . INTEL COULDN'T HAVE BEEN RIGHT. THEY *DID* TRY BUILDING HERE.
COULDN'T HAVE BEEN MUCH OF IT. ODD COINCIDENCE THAT WE'D COME DOWN WALKING DISTANCE FROM IT, DON'T YOU THINK?

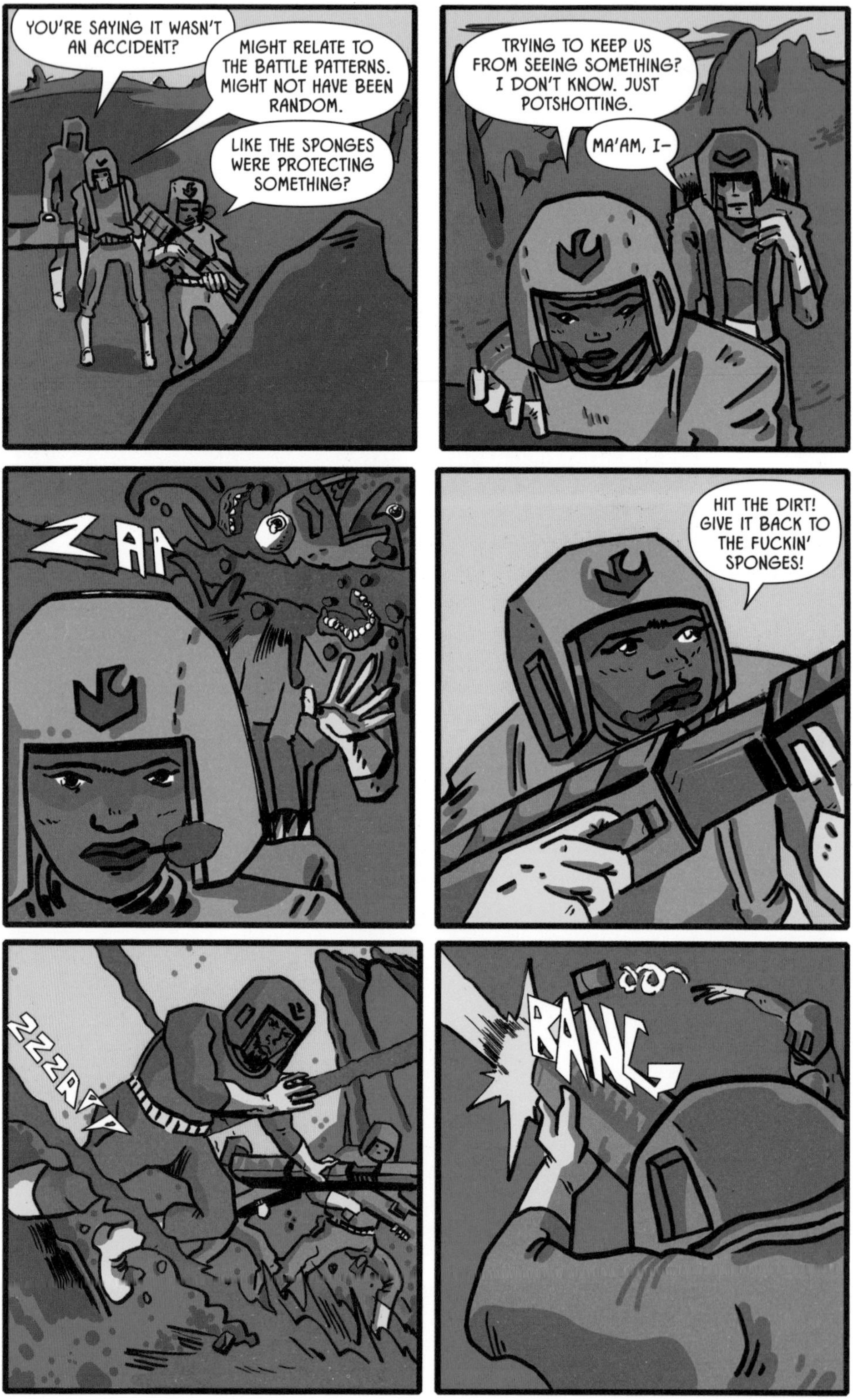

YOU'RE SAYING IT WASN'T AN ACCIDENT?
MIGHT RELATE TO THE BATTLE PATTERNS. MIGHT NOT HAVE BEEN RANDOM.
LIKE THE SPONGES WERE PROTECTING SOMETHING?
TRYING TO KEEP US FROM SEEING SOMETHING? I DON'T KNOW. JUST POTSHOTTING.
MA'AM, I–
ZAP
HIT THE DIRT! GIVE IT BACK TO THE FUCKIN' SPONGES!
ZZZAPP
BANG

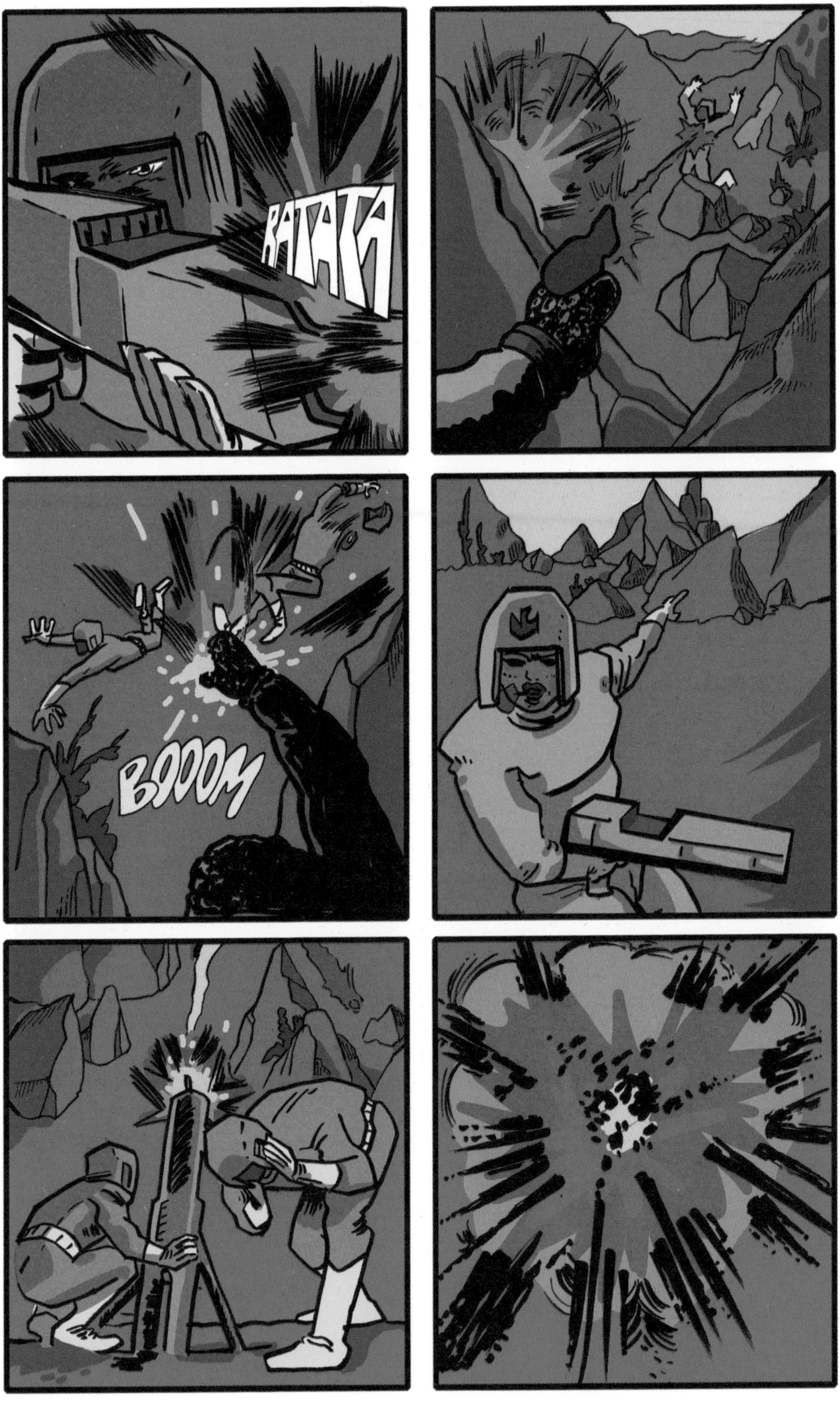
RATATA
BOOOM

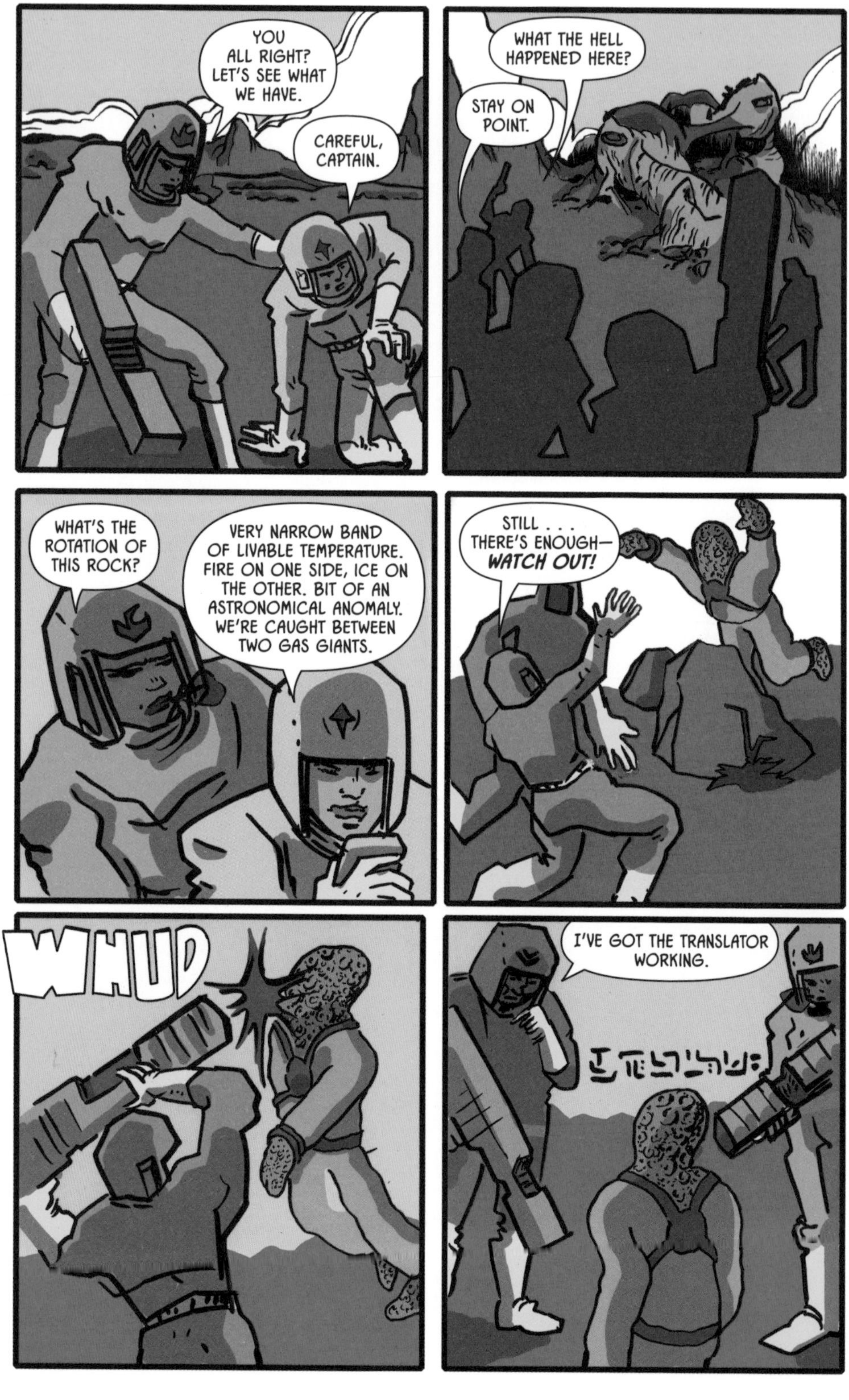
YOU ALL RIGHT? LET'S SEE WHAT WE HAVE.
CAREFUL, CAPTAIN.
WHAT THE HELL HAPPENED HERE?
STAY ON POINT.
WHAT'S THE ROTATION OF THIS ROCK?
VERY NARROW BAND OF LIVABLE TEMPERATURE. FIRE ON ONE SIDE, ICE ON THE OTHER. BIT OF AN ASTRONOMICAL ANOMALY. WE'RE CAUGHT BETWEEN TWO GAS GIANTS.
STILL . . . THERE'S ENOUGH— ***WATCH OUT!***
WHUD
I'VE GOT THE TRANSLATOR WORKING.

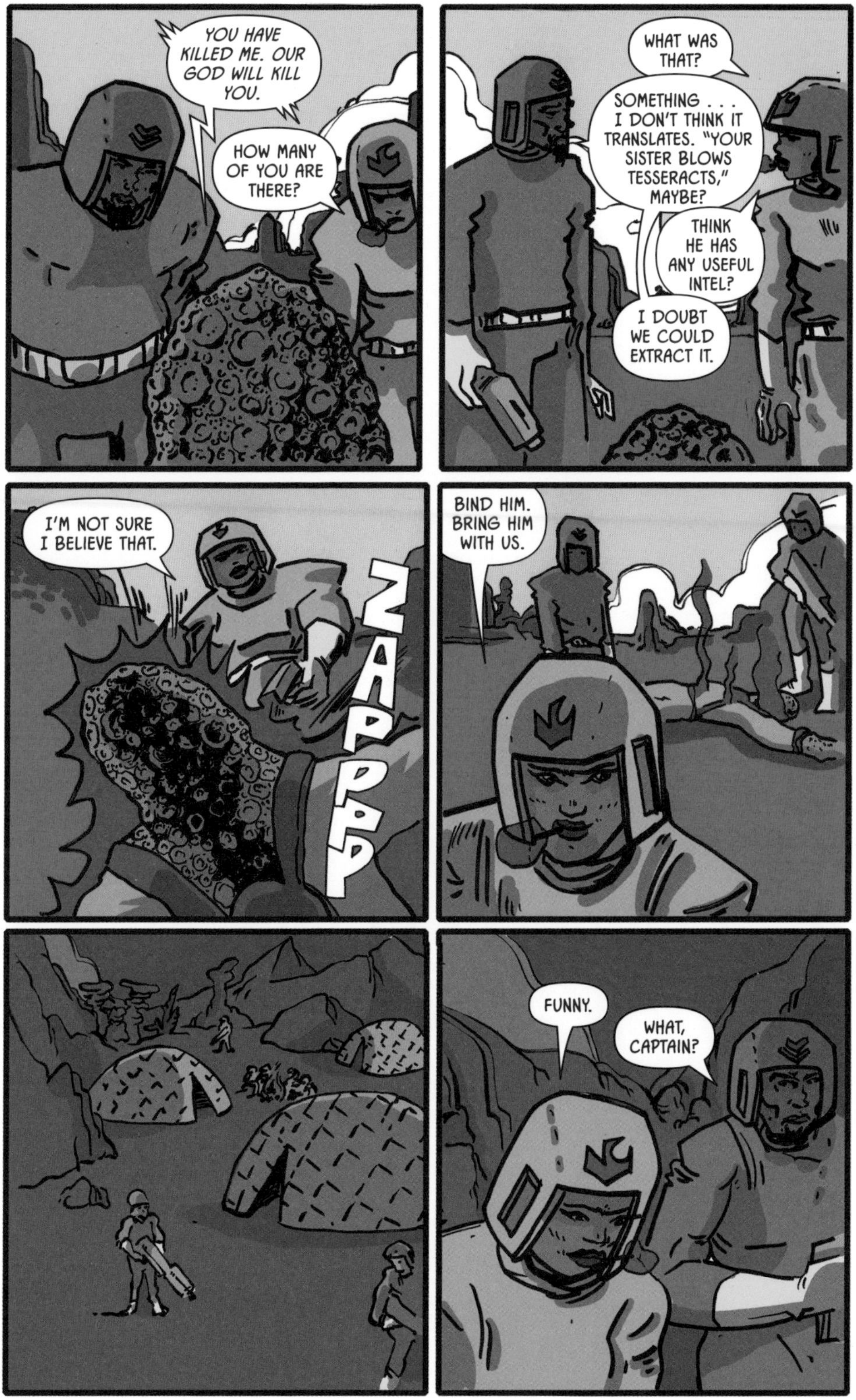
YOU HAVE KILLED ME. OUR GOD WILL KILL YOU.
HOW MANY OF YOU ARE THERE?
WHAT WAS THAT?
SOMETHING . . . I DON'T THINK IT TRANSLATES. "YOUR SISTER BLOWS TESSERACTS," MAYBE?
THINK HE HAS ANY USEFUL INTEL?
I DOUBT WE COULD EXTRACT IT.
I'M NOT SURE I BELIEVE THAT.
ZAPPP
BIND HIM. BRING HIM WITH US.
FUNNY.
WHAT, CAPTAIN?

EVERYONE THINKS THEIR GOD IS GOING TO BRING THEM JUSTICE. REVENGE. WHATEVER. WAY IT WAS ON EARTH, LEAST THAT'S WHAT THE HISTORY BOOKS SAY. SAME OUT HERE.

MAYBE. HAND ME THE RATIONS, WOULD YOU? SMELLS GOOD.

CAN DO. CAPTAIN?

I STUDIED XENOLINGUISTICS. CAN I LOOK AT THE TRANSLATOR? I NOTICED SOME-THING ODD.

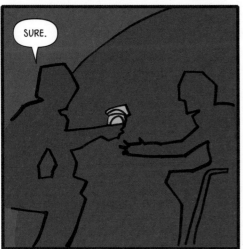

SURE.

OKAY. WE'VE ANALYZED THE SPONGES, AND THEY HAVE DIFFERENT TENSES FOR IMAGINARY AND PRACTICAL THINGS. I TRANSLATED A POEM OF THEIRS ONCE.

A SPONGE POEM?

YES. AND IT REFERRED TO A MYTHIC ANCESTOR WHO FOUGHT THE GODS. AND THE THING ABOUT IT WAS THAT WE WERE TOLD THE POEM NO LONGER MADE SENSE. IT WAS WRITTEN IN WHAT WE WOULD CALL THEIR BRONZE OR IRON AGE, LIKE WHEN OUR ANCESTORS WROTE THE OLD TESTAMENT.

YEAH?

WHAT WE WERE TOLD IS THAT DURING THAT PERIOD, THE GODS WERE CONSIDERED REAL. BUT AS THE SPONGES BECAME POST-TECHNOLOGICAL, THE GODS WERE CONSIDERED, WELL . . . MYTHIC. METAPHORICAL. AND SO, THE WORDS CHANGED TO REFLECT THAT, AND DESTROYED THE POETRY. AN ENTIRE POETIC FORM JUST . . . DIED.

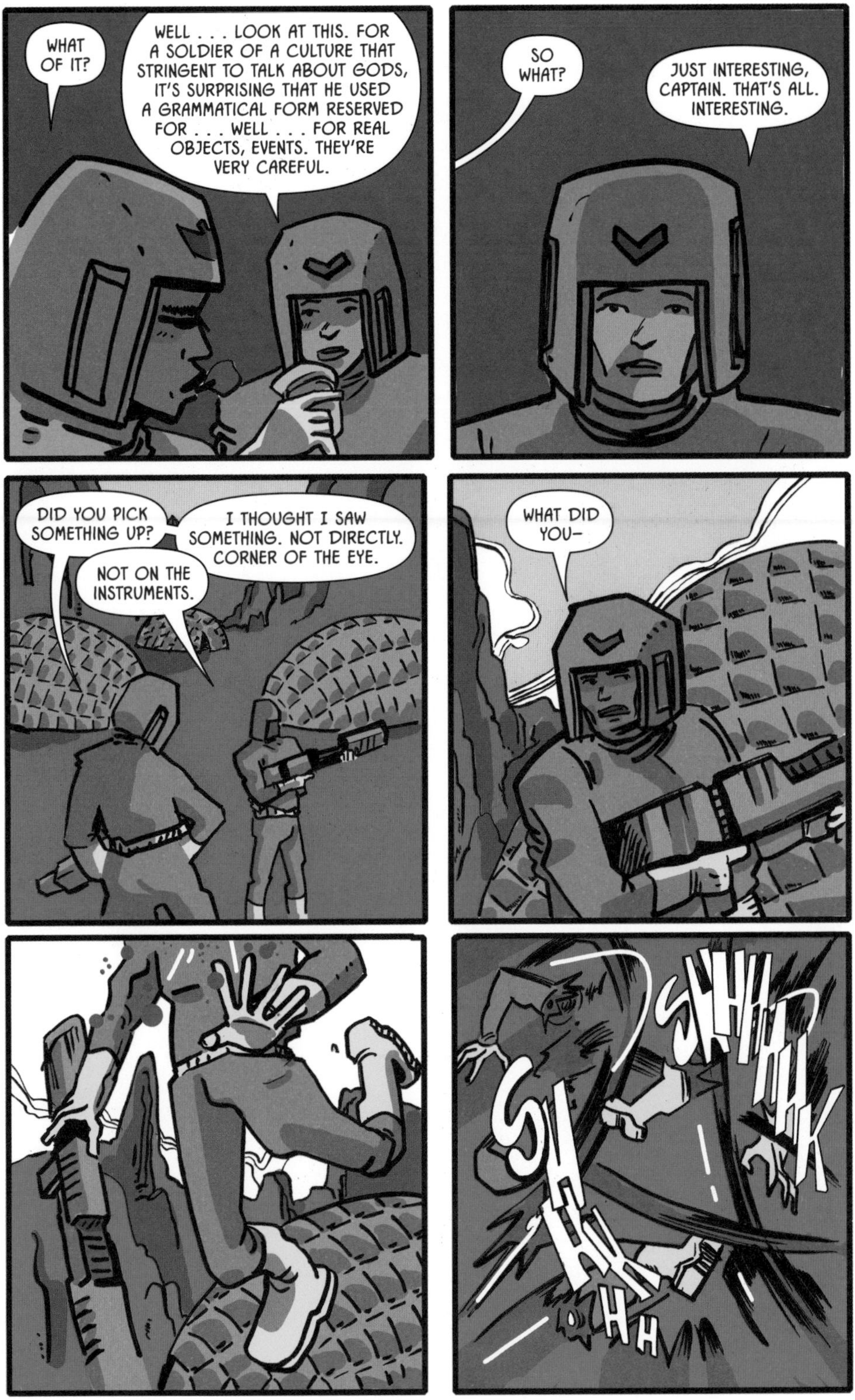
WHAT OF IT?
WELL . . . LOOK AT THIS. FOR A SOLDIER OF A CULTURE THAT STRINGENT TO TALK ABOUT GODS, IT'S SURPRISING THAT HE USED A GRAMMATICAL FORM RESERVED FOR . . . WELL . . . FOR REAL OBJECTS, EVENTS. THEY'RE VERY CAREFUL.
SO WHAT?
JUST INTERESTING, CAPTAIN. THAT'S ALL. INTERESTING.
DID YOU PICK SOMETHING UP?
I THOUGHT I SAW SOMETHING. NOT DIRECTLY. CORNER OF THE EYE.
NOT ON THE INSTRUMENTS.
WHAT DID YOU–
SHHHHHHHK
SHHHHHH

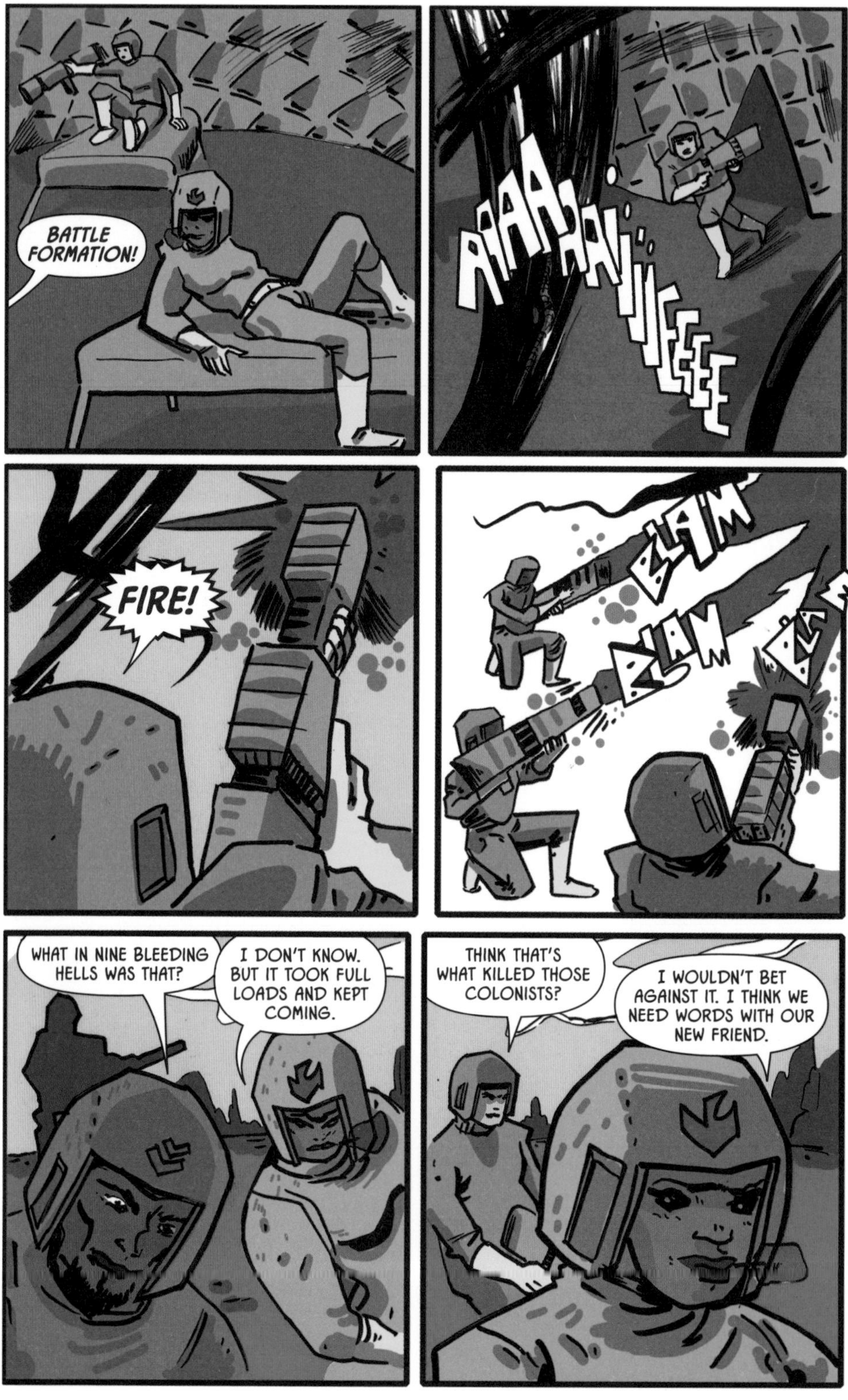

BATTLE FORMATION!
FIRE!
BLAM
BLAM
BLAM
WHAT IN NINE BLEEDING HELLS WAS THAT?
I DON'T KNOW. BUT IT TOOK FULL LOADS AND KEPT COMING.
THINK THAT'S WHAT KILLED THOSE COLONISTS?
I WOULDN'T BET AGAINST IT. I THINK WE NEED WORDS WITH OUR NEW FRIEND.

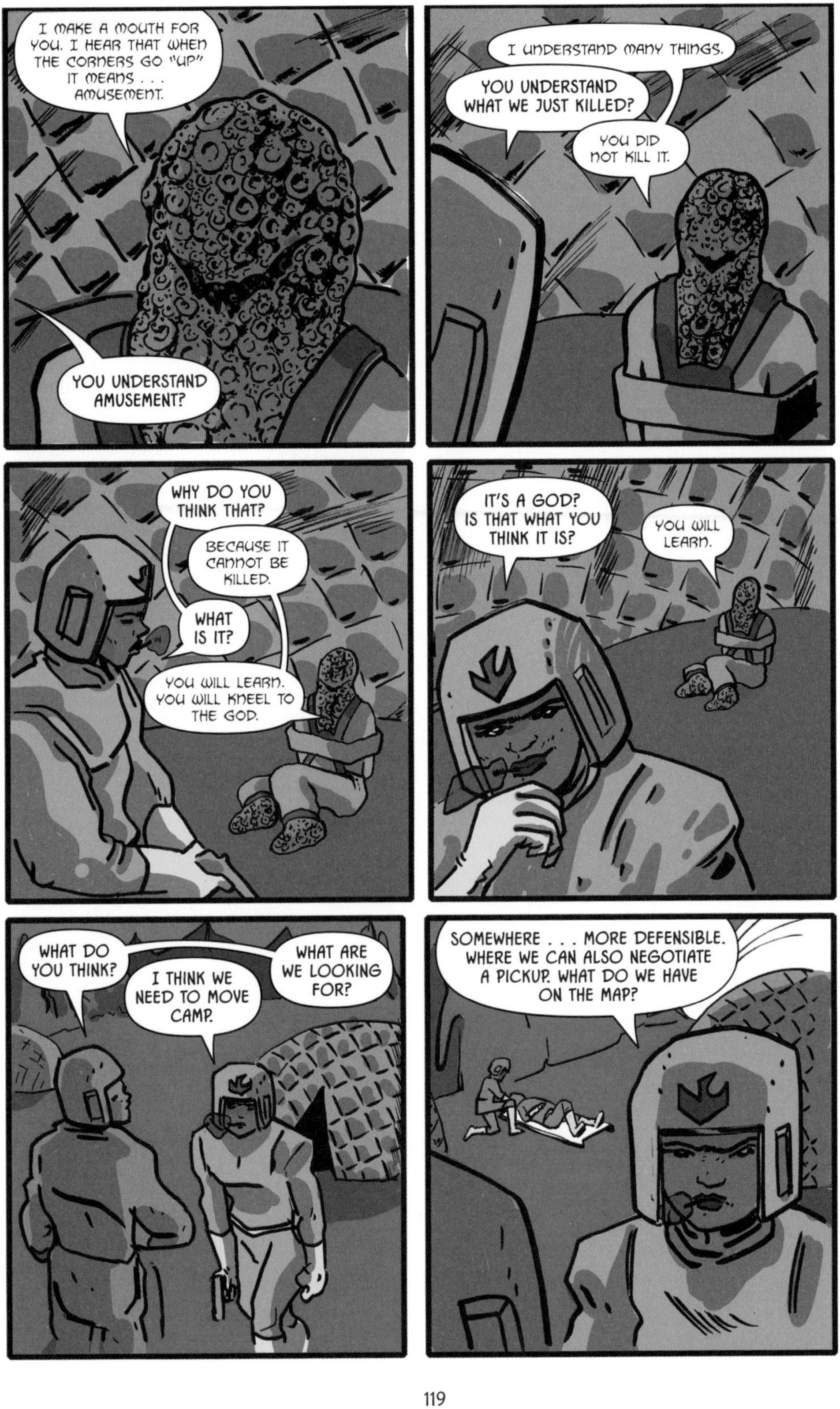
I MAKE A MOUTH FOR YOU. I HEAR THAT WHEN THE CORNERS GO "UP" IT MEANS . . . AMUSEMENT.
YOU UNDERSTAND AMUSEMENT?
I UNDERSTAND MANY THINGS.
YOU UNDERSTAND WHAT WE JUST KILLED?
YOU DID NOT KILL IT.
WHY DO YOU THINK THAT?
BECAUSE IT CANNOT BE KILLED.
WHAT IS IT?
YOU WILL LEARN. YOU WILL KNEEL TO THE GOD.
IT'S A GOD? IS THAT WHAT YOU THINK IT IS?
YOU WILL LEARN.
WHAT DO YOU THINK?
I THINK WE NEED TO MOVE CAMP.
WHAT ARE WE LOOKING FOR?
SOMEWHERE . . . MORE DEFENSIBLE. WHERE WE CAN ALSO NEGOTIATE A PICKUP. WHAT DO WE HAVE ON THE MAP?

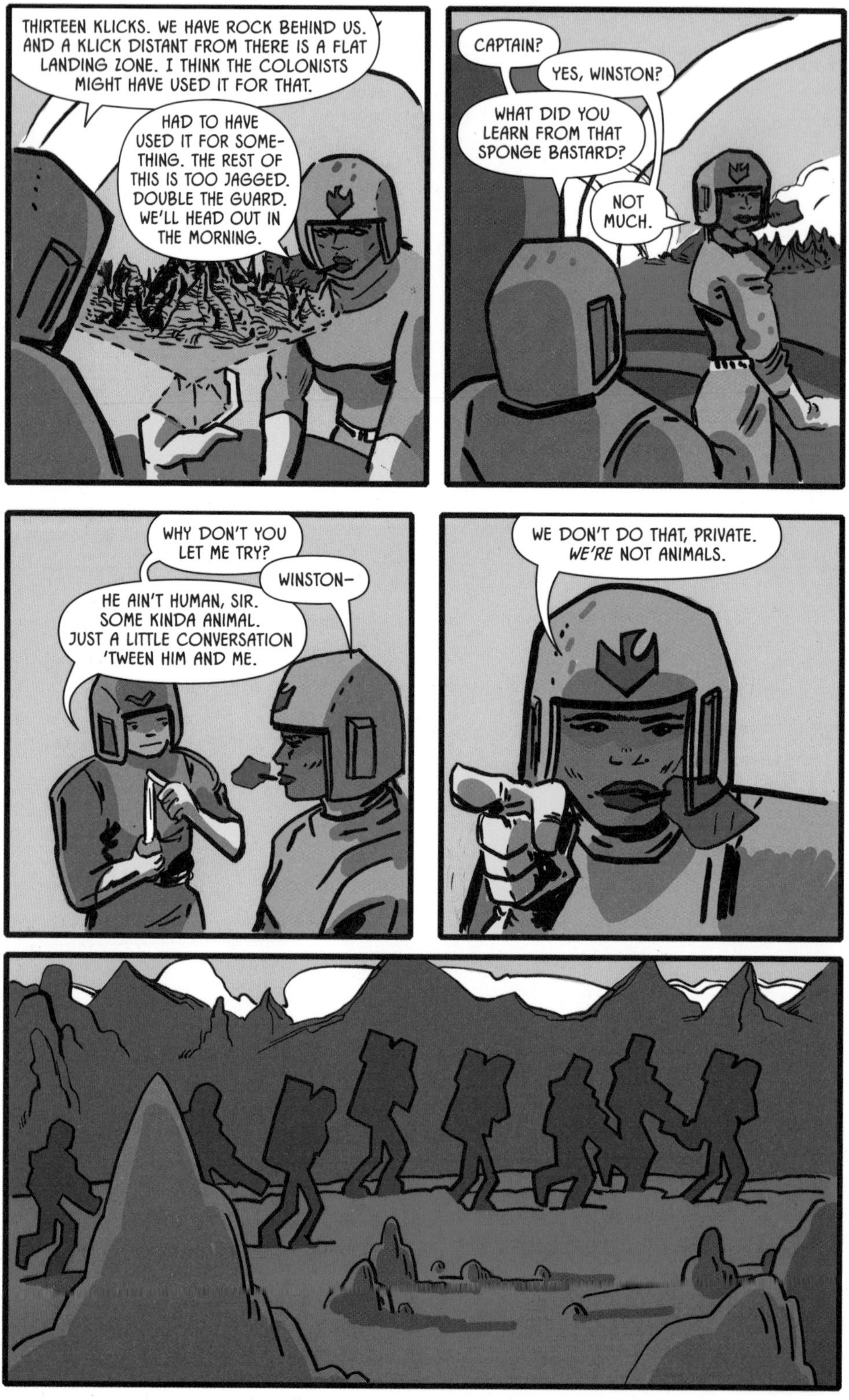
THIRTEEN KLICKS. WE HAVE ROCK BEHIND US. AND A KLICK DISTANT FROM THERE IS A FLAT LANDING ZONE. I THINK THE COLONISTS MIGHT HAVE USED IT FOR THAT.
HAD TO HAVE USED IT FOR SOMETHING. THE REST OF THIS IS TOO JAGGED. DOUBLE THE GUARD. WE'LL HEAD OUT IN THE MORNING.
CAPTAIN?
YES, WINSTON?
WHAT DID YOU LEARN FROM THAT SPONGE BASTARD?
NOT MUCH.
WHY DON'T YOU LET ME TRY?
WINSTON—
HE AIN'T HUMAN, SIR. SOME KINDA ANIMAL. JUST A LITTLE CONVERSATION 'TWEEN HIM AND ME.
WE DON'T DO THAT, PRIVATE. *WE'RE* NOT ANIMALS.

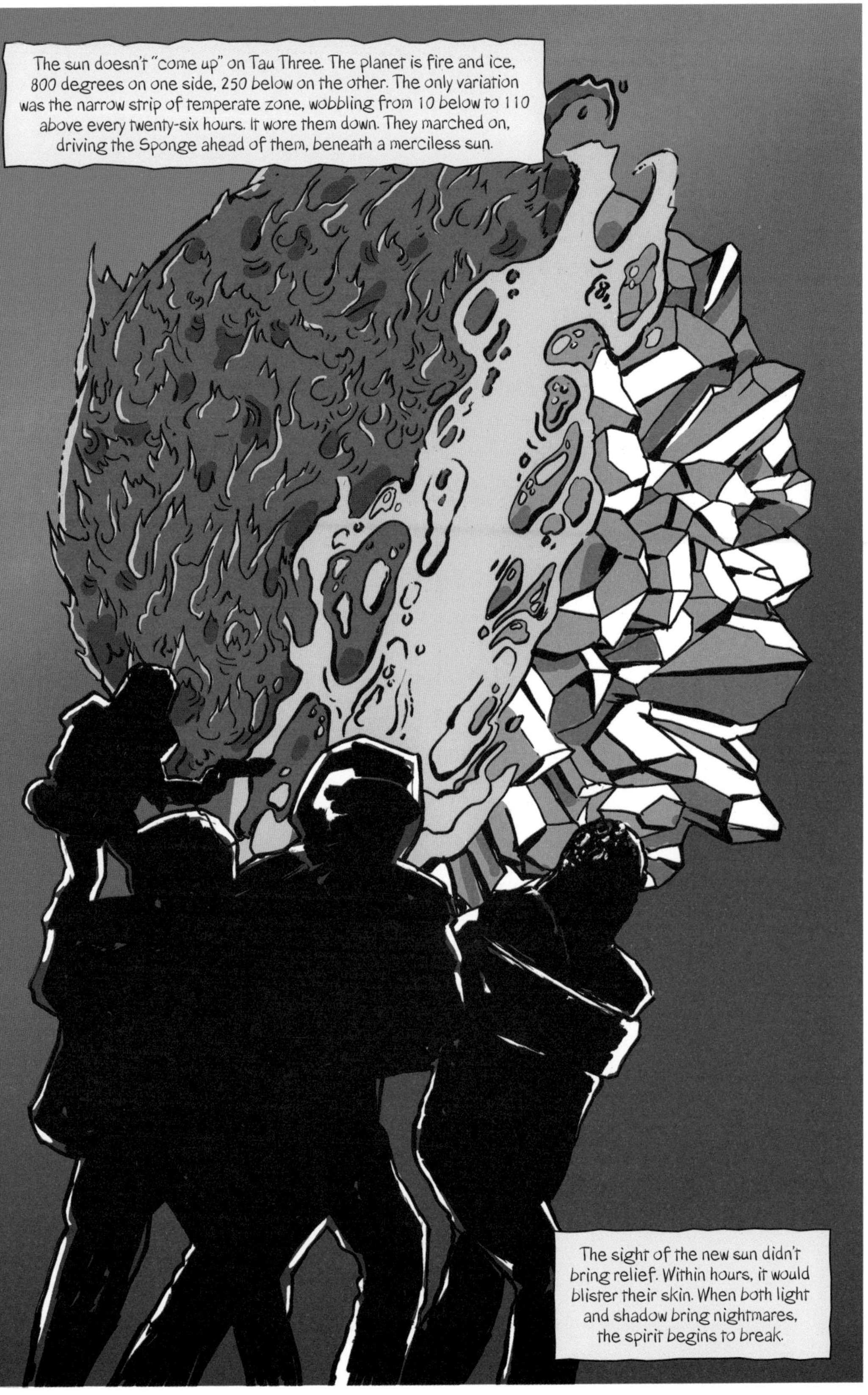
The sun doesn't "come up" on Tau Three. The planet is fire and ice, 800 degrees on one side, 250 below on the other. The only variation was the narrow strip of temperate zone, wobbling from 10 below to 110 above every twenty-six hours. It wore them down. They marched on, driving the Sponge ahead of them, beneath a merciless sun.
The sight of the new sun didn't bring relief. Within hours, it would blister their skin. When both light and shadow bring nightmares, the spirit begins to break.

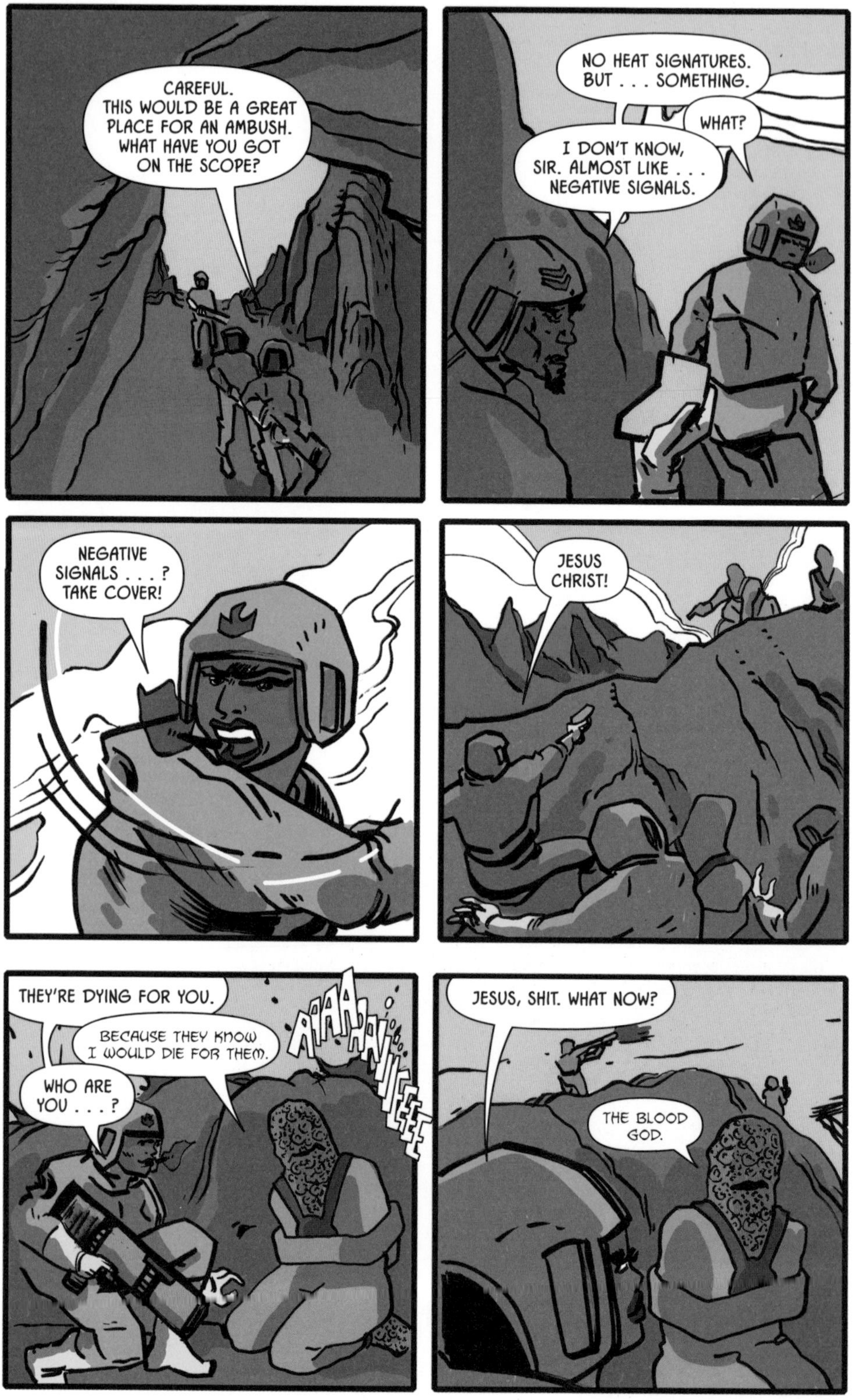
CAREFUL. THIS WOULD BE A GREAT PLACE FOR AN AMBUSH. WHAT HAVE YOU GOT ON THE SCOPE?
NO HEAT SIGNATURES. BUT . . . SOMETHING.
WHAT?
I DON'T KNOW, SIR. ALMOST LIKE . . . NEGATIVE SIGNALS.
NEGATIVE SIGNALS . . . ? TAKE COVER!
JESUS CHRIST!
THEY'RE DYING FOR YOU.
WHO ARE YOU . . . ?
BECAUSE THEY KNOW I WOULD DIE FOR THEM.
AAAAAIIEEEE
JESUS, SHIT. WHAT NOW?
THE BLOOD GOD.

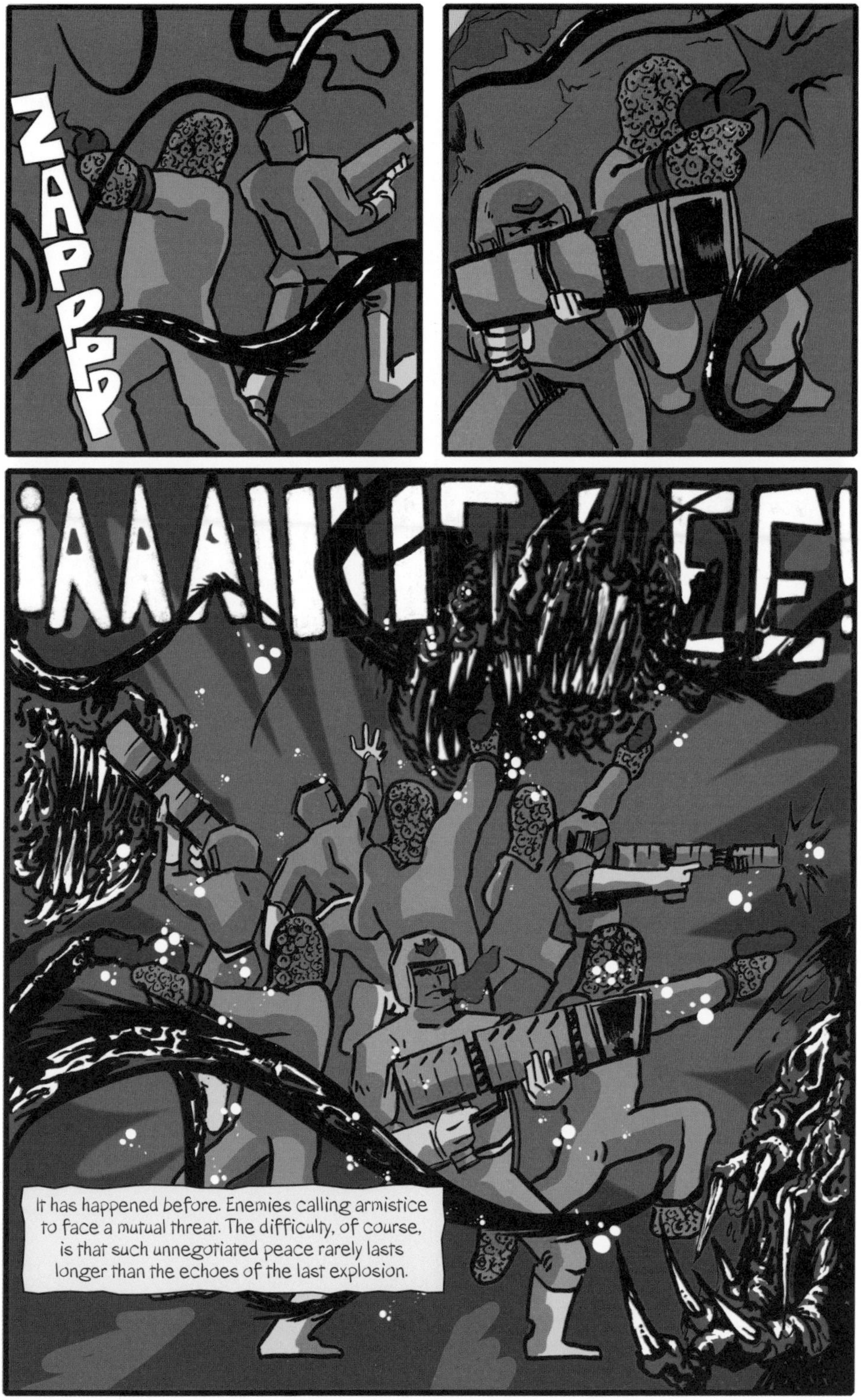
ZAPPPP
It has happened before. Enemies calling armistice to face a mutual threat. The difficulty, of course, is that such unnegotiated peace rarely lasts longer than the echoes of the last explosion.

ZAP

BANG

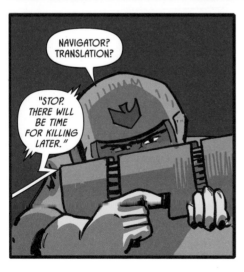

NAVIGATOR? TRANSLATION?

"STOP. THERE WILL BE TIME FOR KILLING LATER."

STAND DOWN!

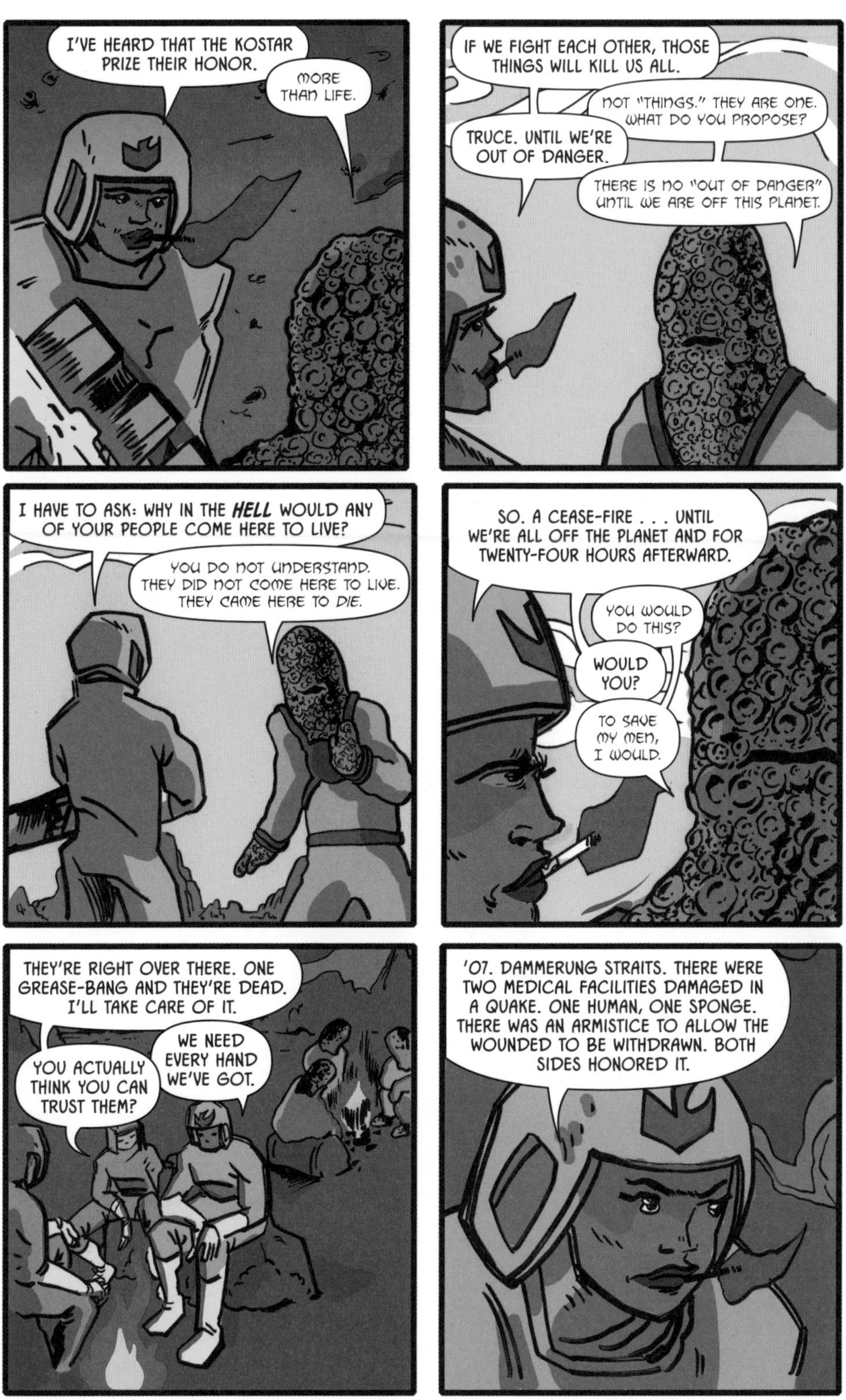

I'VE HEARD THAT THE KOSTAR PRIZE THEIR HONOR.
MORE THAN LIFE.
IF WE FIGHT EACH OTHER, THOSE THINGS WILL KILL US ALL.
NOT "THINGS." THEY ARE ONE. WHAT DO YOU PROPOSE?
TRUCE. UNTIL WE'RE OUT OF DANGER.
THERE IS NO "OUT OF DANGER" UNTIL WE ARE OFF THIS PLANET.
I HAVE TO ASK: WHY IN THE *HELL* WOULD ANY OF YOUR PEOPLE COME HERE TO LIVE?
YOU DO NOT UNDERSTAND. THEY DID NOT COME HERE TO LIVE. THEY CAME HERE TO *DIE*.
SO. A CEASE-FIRE . . . UNTIL WE'RE ALL OFF THE PLANET AND FOR TWENTY-FOUR HOURS AFTERWARD.
YOU WOULD DO THIS?
WOULD YOU?
TO SAVE MY MEN, I WOULD.
THEY'RE RIGHT OVER THERE. ONE GREASE-BANG AND THEY'RE DEAD. I'LL TAKE CARE OF IT.
YOU ACTUALLY THINK YOU CAN TRUST THEM?
WE NEED EVERY HAND WE'VE GOT.
'07. DAMMERUNG STRAITS. THERE WERE TWO MEDICAL FACILITIES DAMAGED IN A QUAKE. ONE HUMAN, ONE SPONGE. THERE WAS AN ARMISTICE TO ALLOW THE WOUNDED TO BE WITHDRAWN. BOTH SIDES HONORED IT.

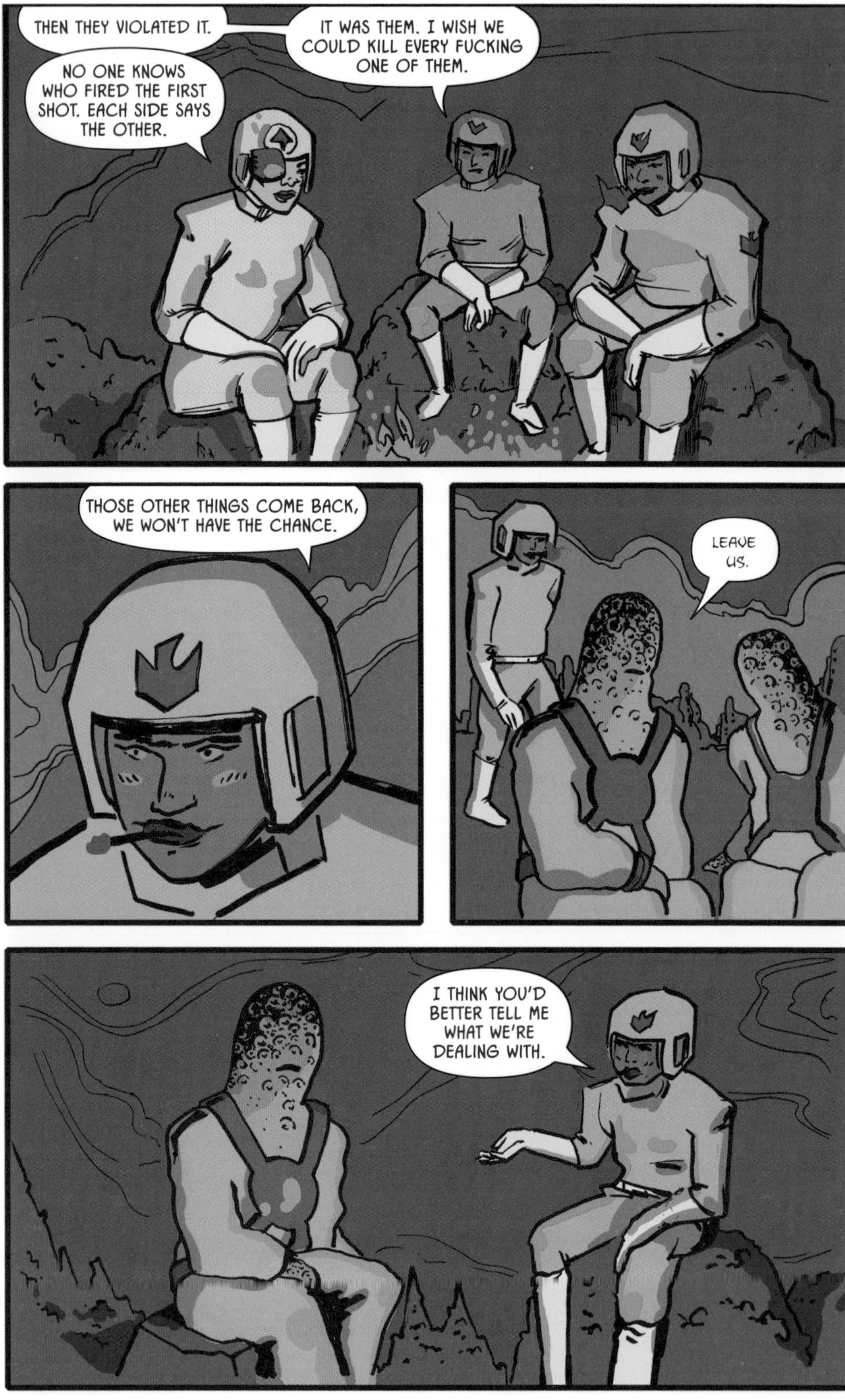
THEN THEY VIOLATED IT.
IT WAS THEM. I WISH WE COULD KILL EVERY FUCKING ONE OF THEM.
NO ONE KNOWS WHO FIRED THE FIRST SHOT. EACH SIDE SAYS THE OTHER.
THOSE OTHER THINGS COME BACK, WE WON'T HAVE THE CHANCE.
LEAVE US.
I THINK YOU'D BETTER TELL ME WHAT WE'RE DEALING WITH.

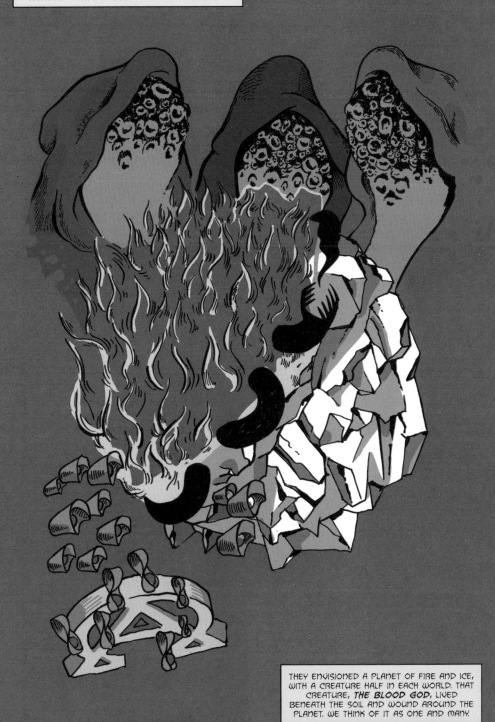

ONLY THREE HUNDRED YEARS AGO, WE FOUND THIS PLANET. AND WE FOUND IT BECAUSE WE SOUGHT IT. OUR HOLY FOLK HAD SEEN IT IN THEIR VISIONS . . .

THEY ENVISIONED A PLANET OF FIRE AND ICE, WITH A CREATURE HALF IN EACH WORLD. THAT CREATURE, *THE BLOOD GOD*, LIVED BENEATH THE SOIL AND WOUND AROUND THE PLANET. WE THINK OF IT AS ONE AND MANY.

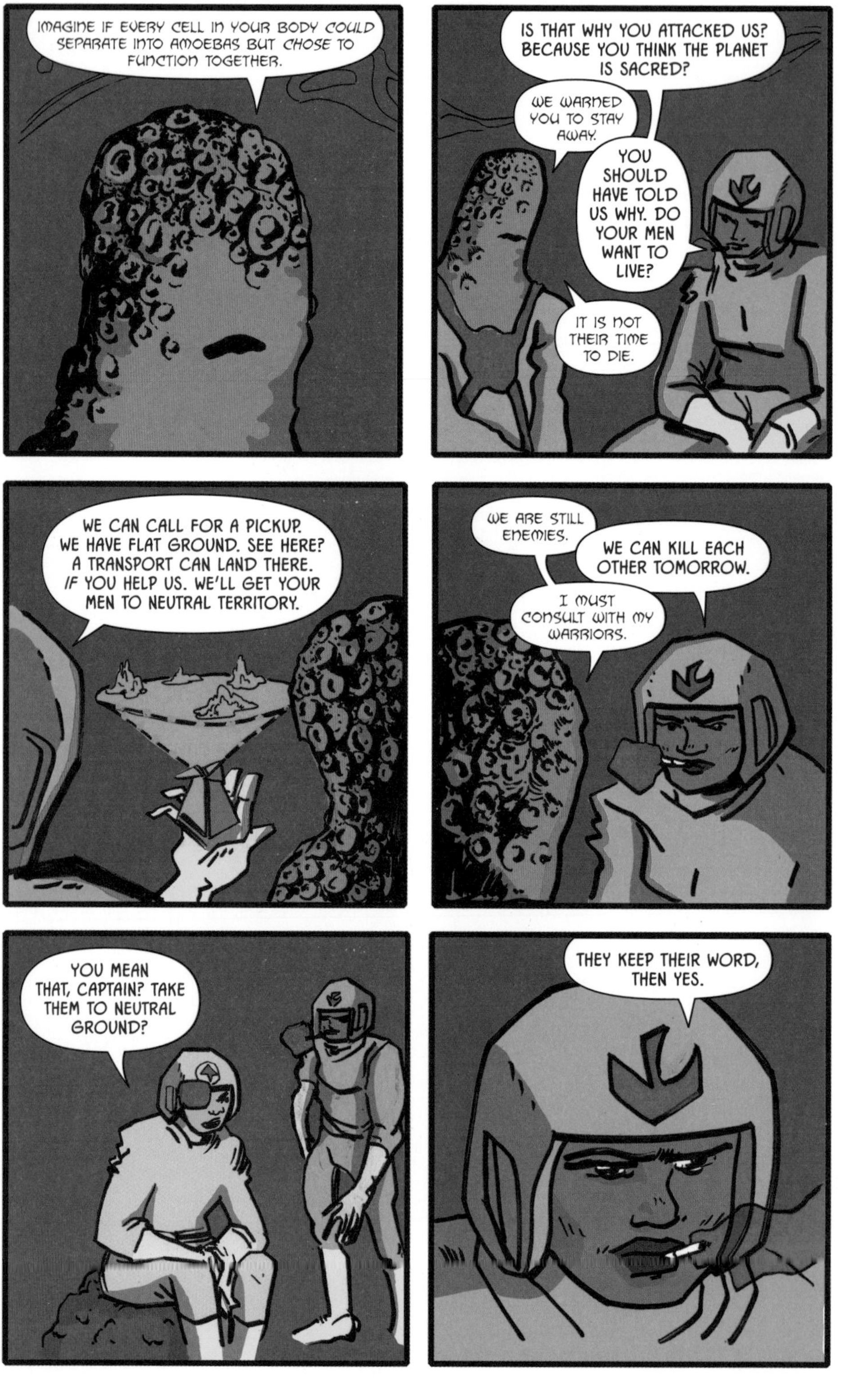
IMAGINE IF EVERY CELL IN YOUR BODY COULD SEPARATE INTO AMOEBAS BUT CHOSE TO FUNCTION TOGETHER.
IS THAT WHY YOU ATTACKED US? BECAUSE YOU THINK THE PLANET IS SACRED?
WE WARNED YOU TO STAY AWAY.
YOU SHOULD HAVE TOLD US WHY. DO YOUR MEN WANT TO LIVE?
IT IS NOT THEIR TIME TO DIE.
WE CAN CALL FOR A PICKUP. WE HAVE FLAT GROUND. SEE HERE? A TRANSPORT CAN LAND THERE. IF YOU HELP US. WE'LL GET YOUR MEN TO NEUTRAL TERRITORY.
WE ARE STILL ENEMIES.
WE CAN KILL EACH OTHER TOMORROW.
I MUST CONSULT WITH MY WARRIORS.
YOU MEAN THAT, CAPTAIN? TAKE THEM TO NEUTRAL GROUND?
THEY KEEP THEIR WORD, THEN YES.

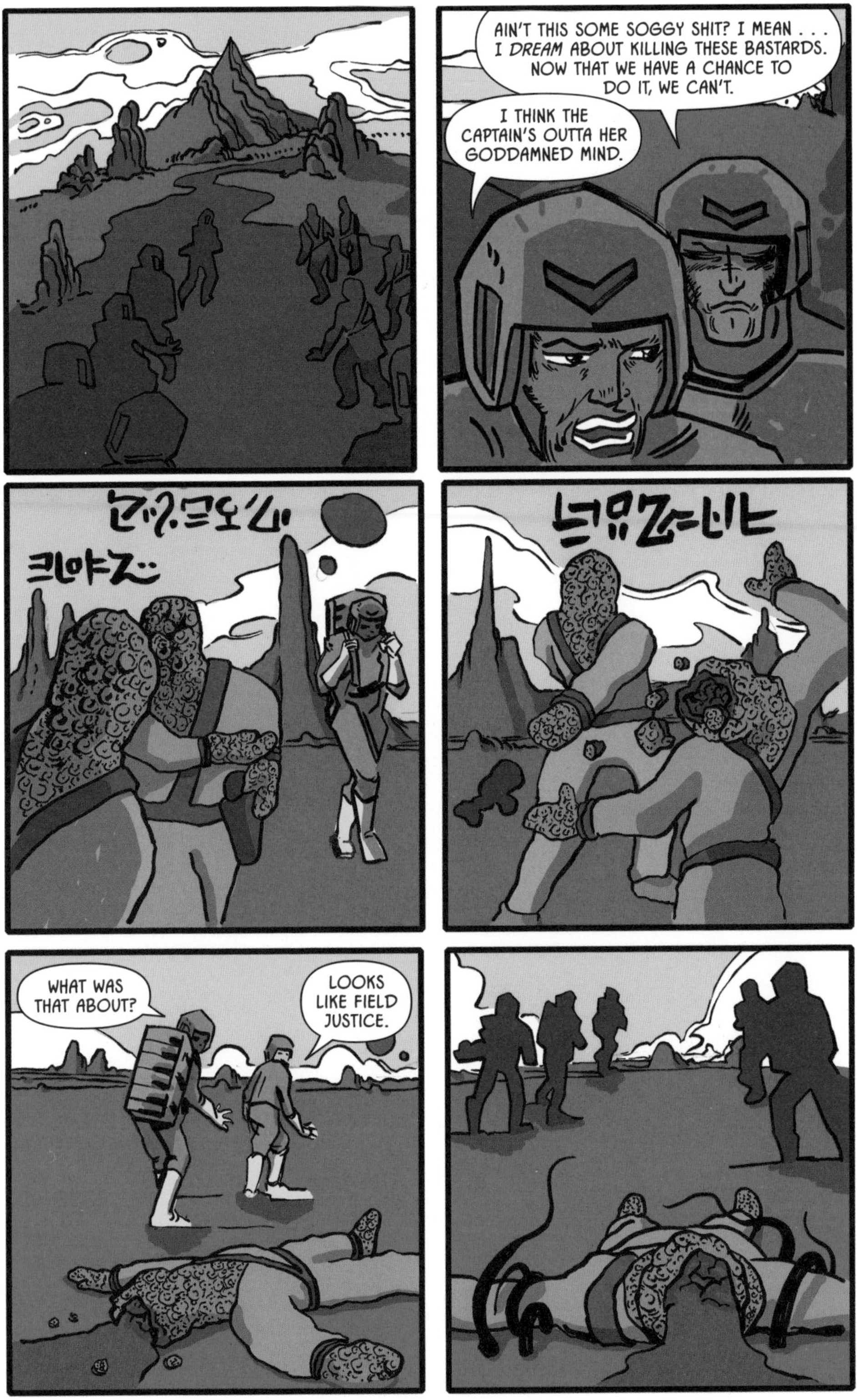
AIN'T THIS SOME SOGGY SHIT? I MEAN . . . I *DREAM* ABOUT KILLING THESE BASTARDS. NOW THAT WE HAVE A CHANCE TO DO IT, WE CAN'T.
I THINK THE CAPTAIN'S OUTTA HER GODDAMNED MIND.
WHAT WAS THAT ABOUT?
LOOKS LIKE FIELD JUSTICE.

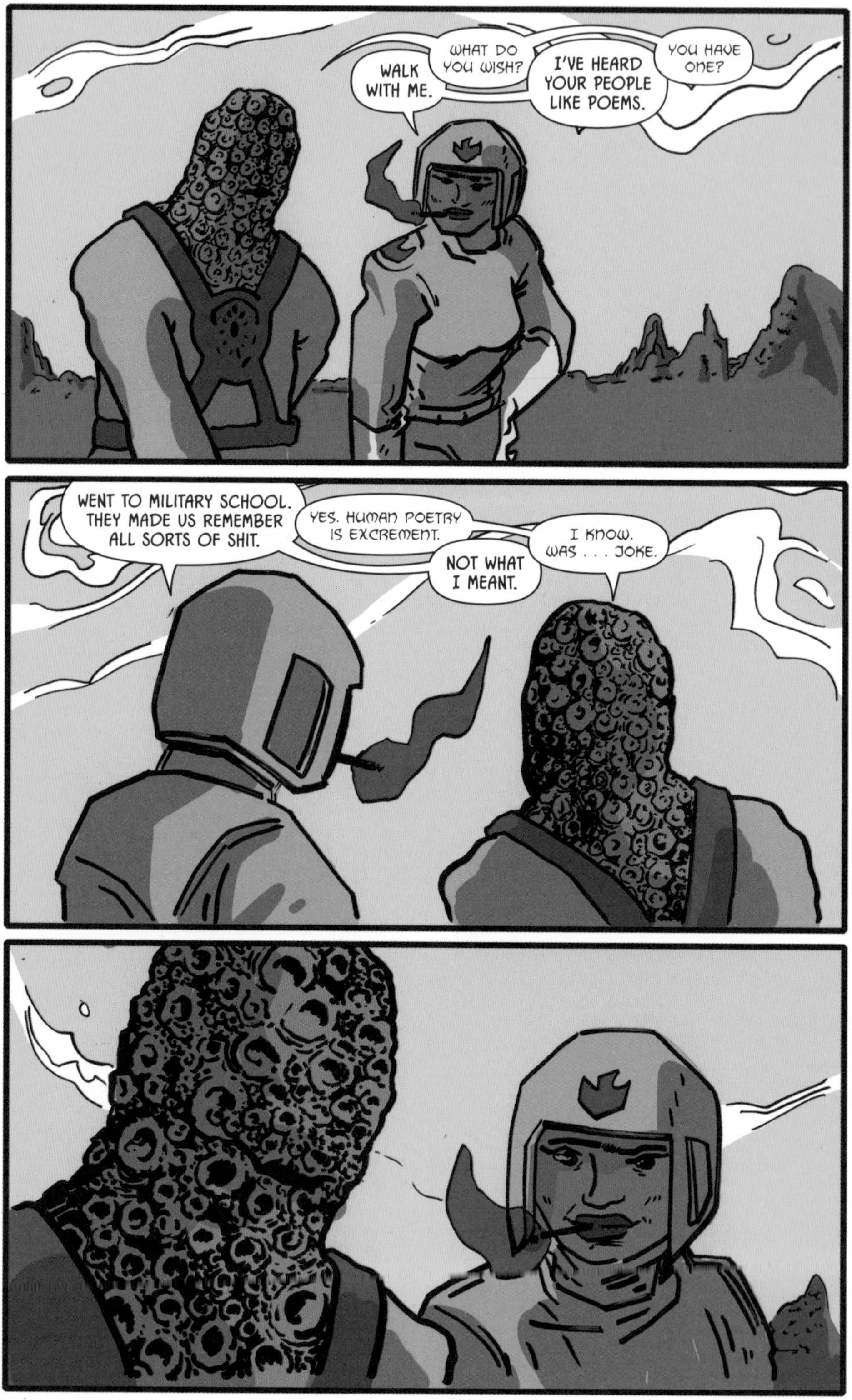
WALK WITH ME.
WHAT DO YOU WISH?
I'VE HEARD YOUR PEOPLE LIKE POEMS.
YOU HAVE ONE?
WENT TO MILITARY SCHOOL. THEY MADE US REMEMBER ALL SORTS OF SHIT.
YES. HUMAN POETRY IS EXCREMENT.
NOT WHAT I MEANT.
I KNOW. WAS . . . JOKE.

YOU HAVE THEM, TOO? POLITICIANS? THOSE WHO STAND IN THE WAY. HOW DO YOU KILL THEM?

WITH INSUFFICIENT FREQUENCY. ANYWAY . . . THE CITY FATHERS ASKED FOR VOLUNTEERS. MEN WILLING TO GUARD THE SINGLE BRIDGE INTO THE CITY FOR LONG ENOUGH FOR THE CITIZENS TO ESCAPE. IT WAS A SUICIDE JOB.

I LIKE THIS STORY. BUT I DIDN'T THINK SACRIFICE WAS THE HUMAN WAY.

"MOST OF THE HUMANS DID SAY HELL NO. BUT ONE DID NOT."

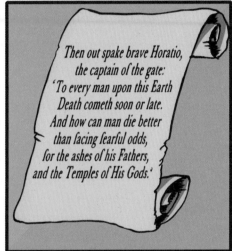

Then out spake brave Horatio, the captain of the gate: 'To every man upon this Earth Death cometh soon or late. And how can man die better than facing fearful odds, for the ashes of his Fathers, and the Temples of His Gods.'

IT IS A GOOD POEM.

CAPTAIN!

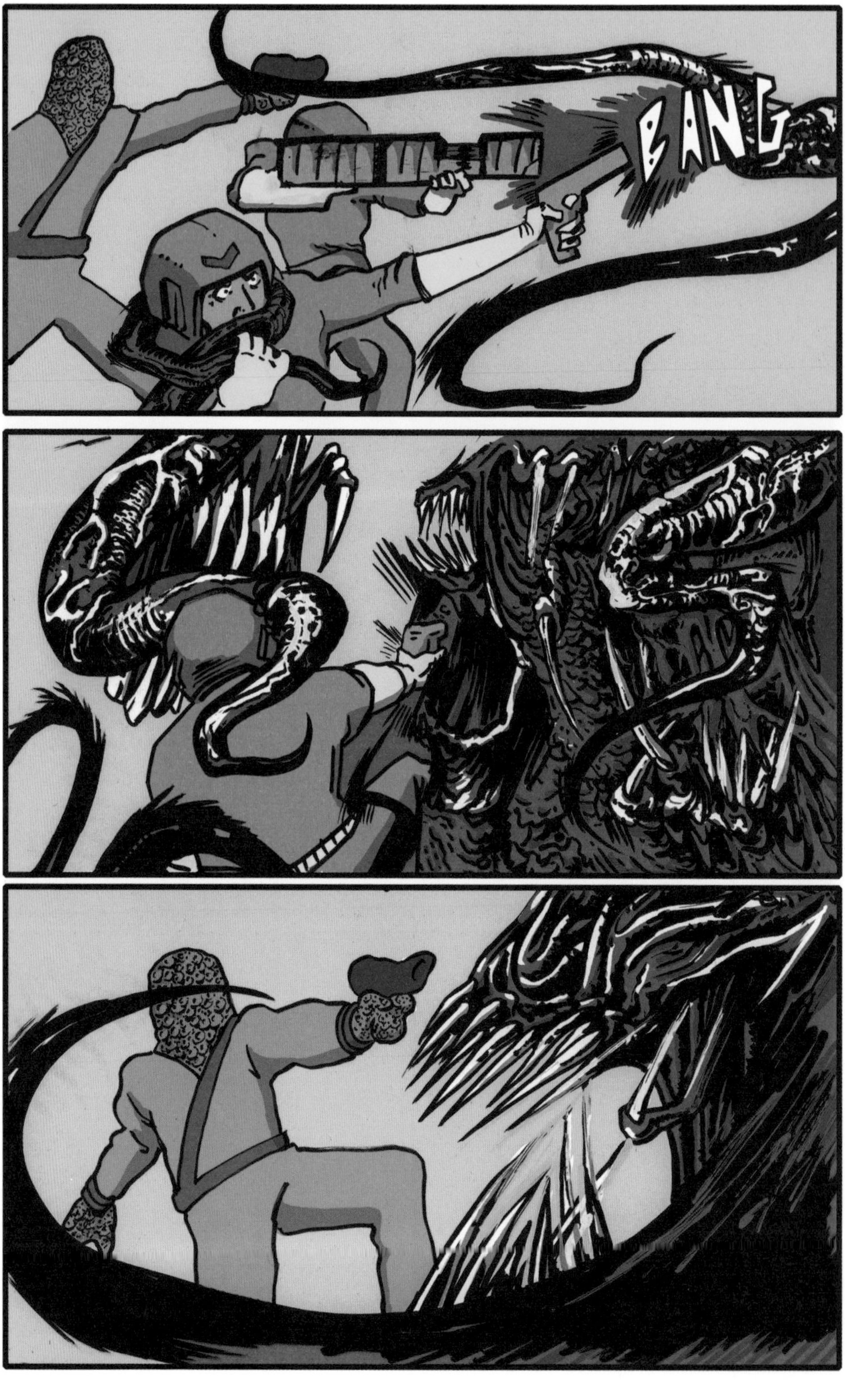
BANG

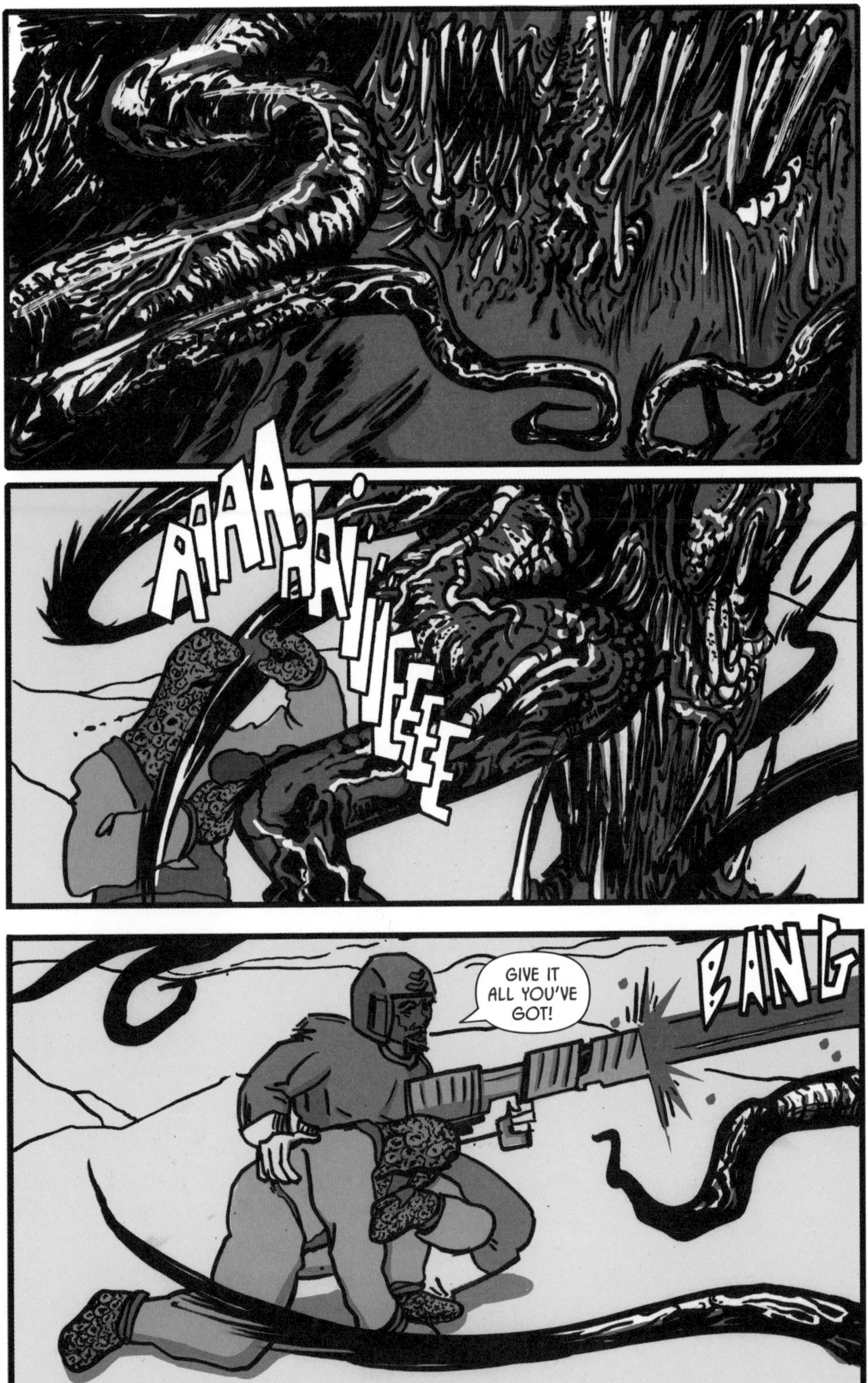
AAAAAAIIIEEEE
GIVE IT ALL YOU'VE GOT!
BANG

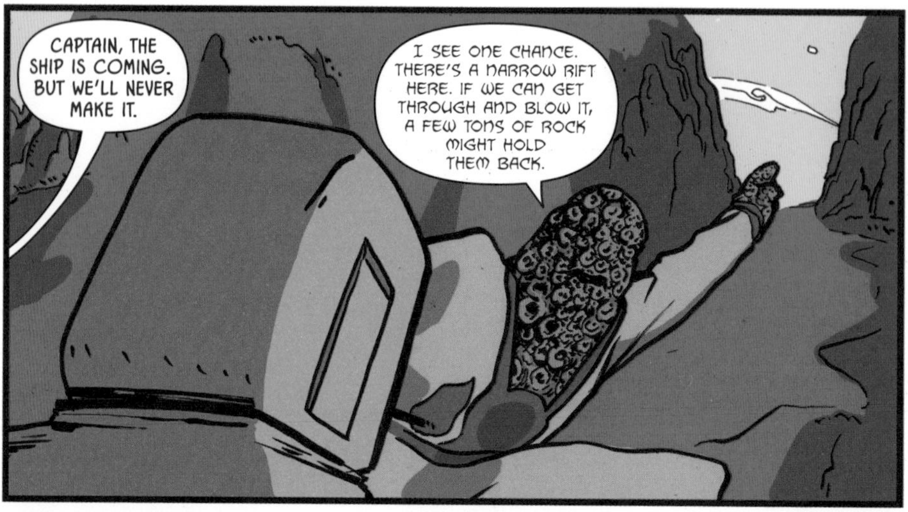
CAPTAIN, THE SHIP IS COMING. BUT WE'LL NEVER MAKE IT.
I SEE ONE CHANCE. THERE'S A NARROW RIFT HERE. IF WE CAN GET THROUGH AND BLOW IT, A FEW TONS OF ROCK MIGHT HOLD THEM BACK.

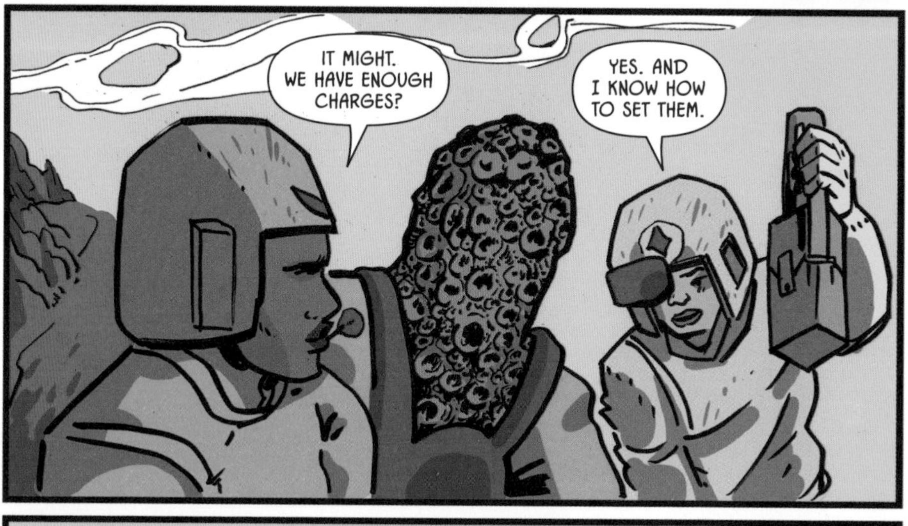
IT MIGHT. WE HAVE ENOUGH CHARGES?
YES. AND I KNOW HOW TO SET THEM.

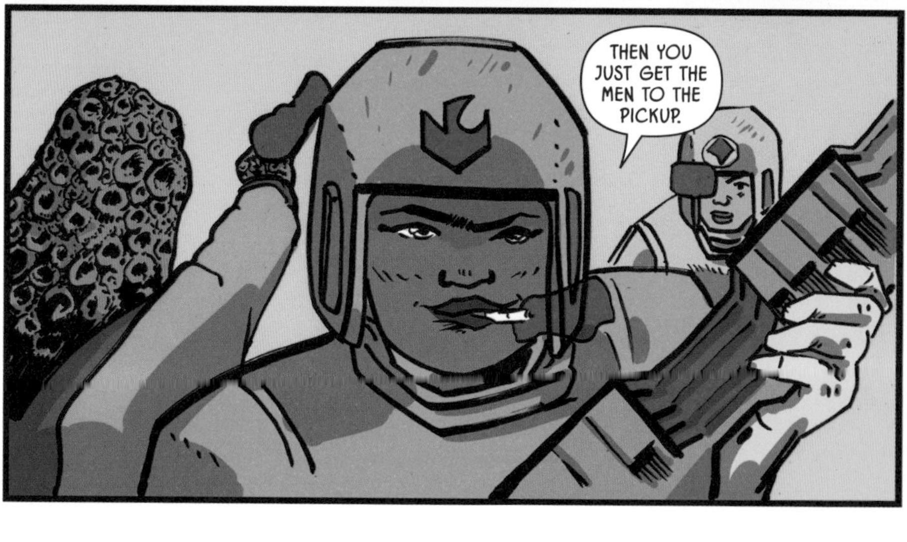
THEN YOU JUST GET THE MEN TO THE PICKUP.

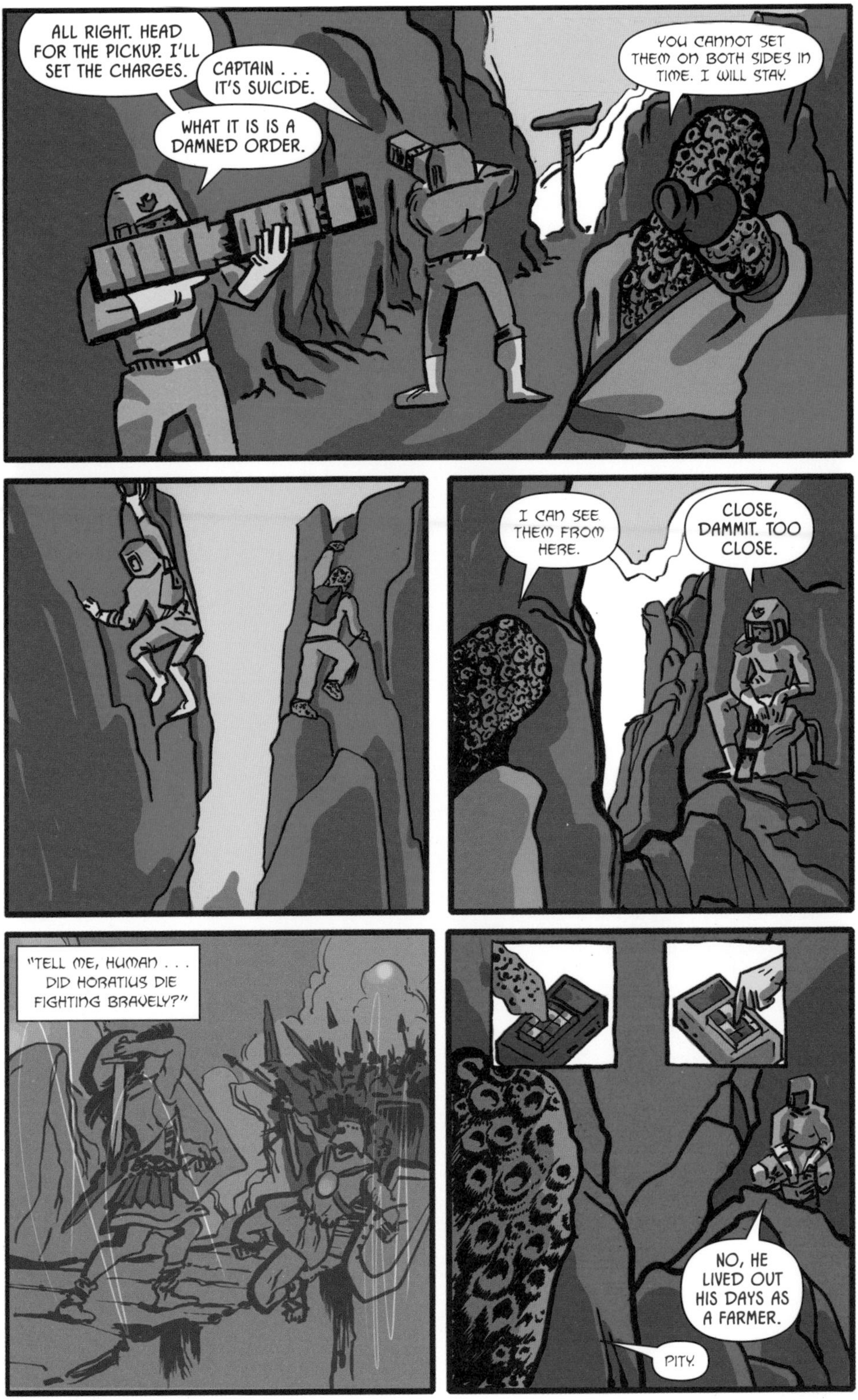
ALL RIGHT. HEAD FOR THE PICKUP. I'LL SET THE CHARGES.
CAPTAIN . . . IT'S SUICIDE.
WHAT IT IS IS A DAMNED ORDER.
YOU CANNOT SET THEM ON BOTH SIDES IN TIME. I WILL STAY.
I CAN SEE THEM FROM HERE.
CLOSE, DAMMIT. TOO CLOSE.
"TELL ME, HUMAN . . . DID HORATIUS DIE FIGHTING BRAVELY?"
NO, HE LIVED OUT HIS DAYS AS A FARMER.
PITY.

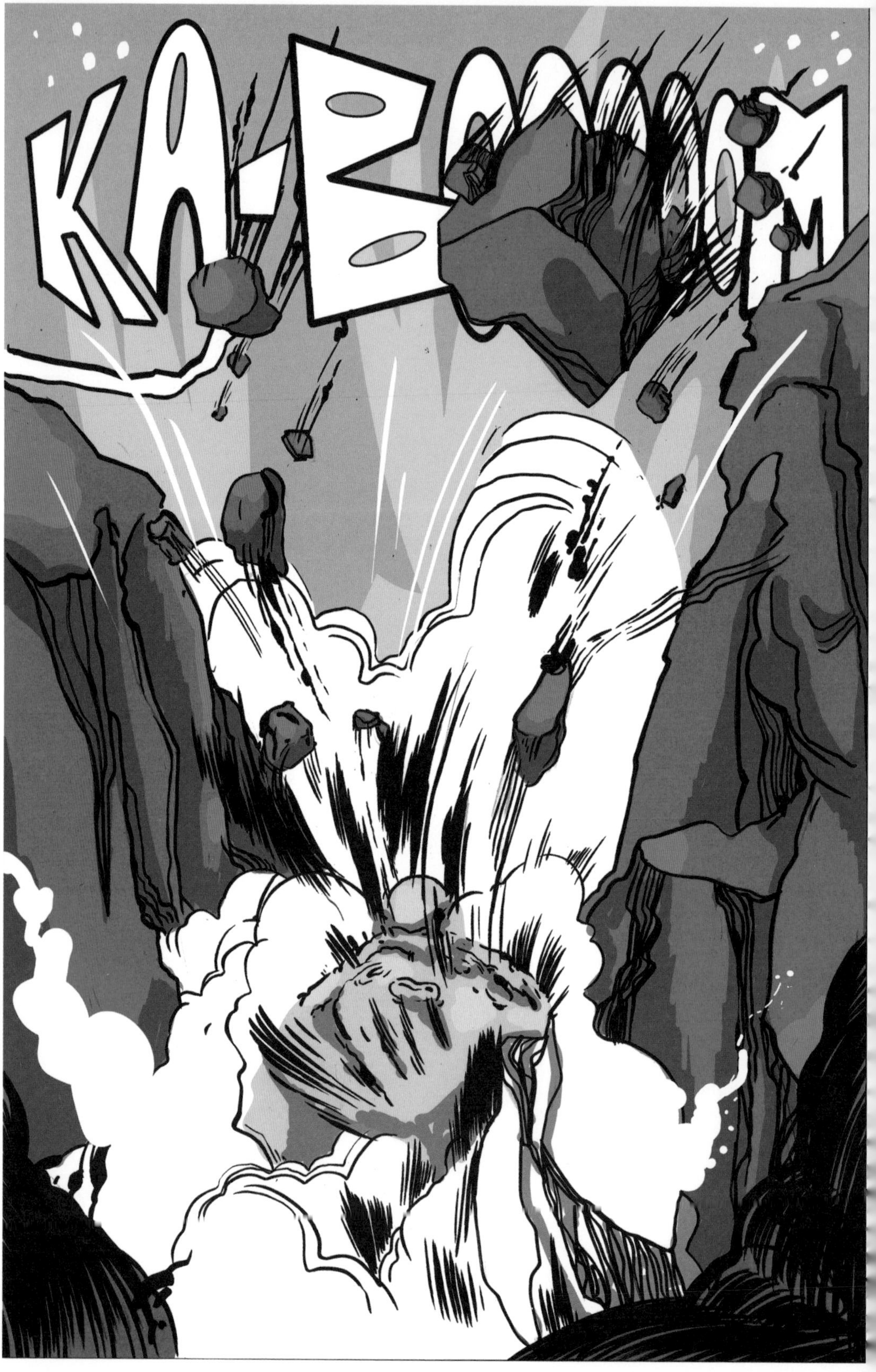
KA-BOOOOOM

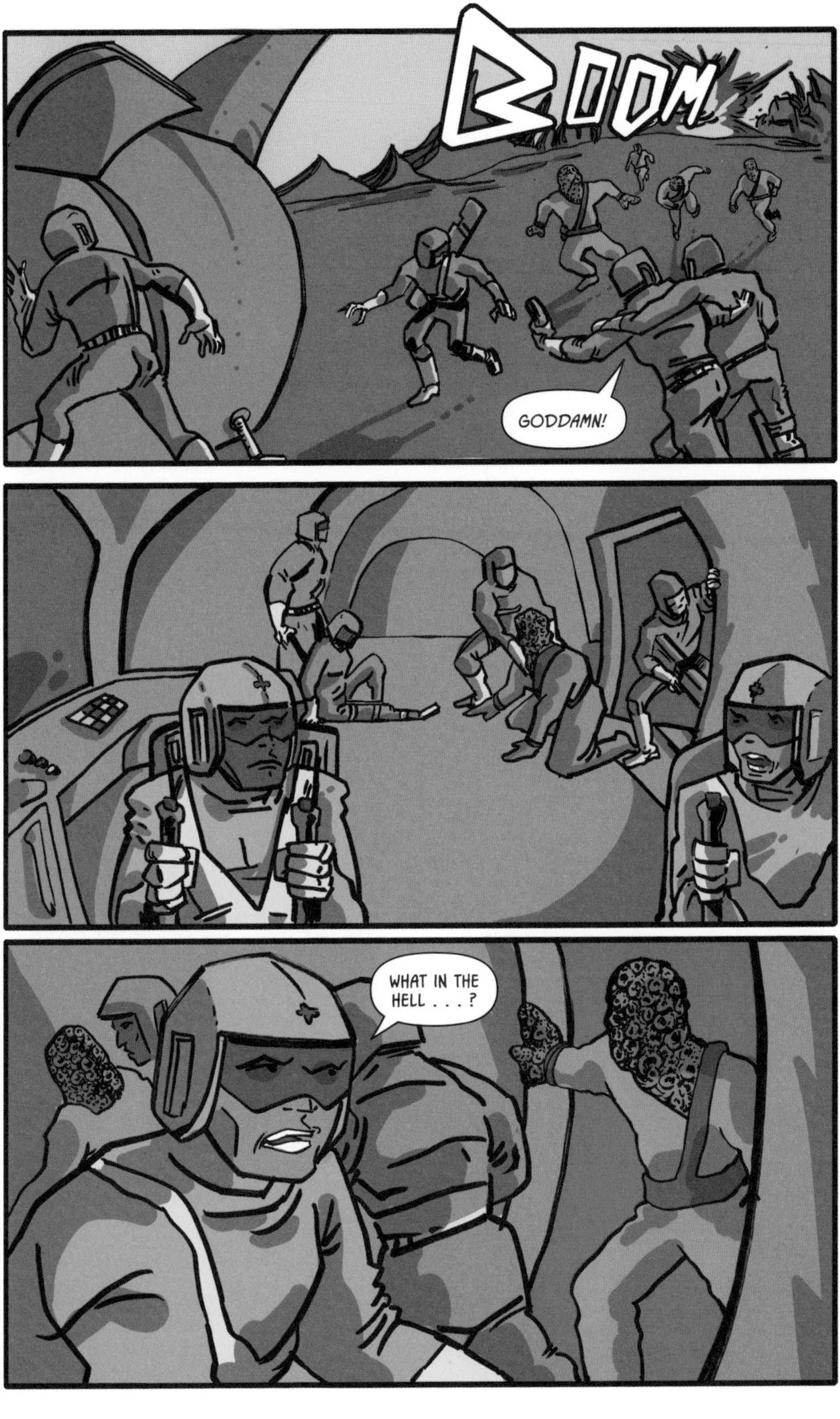
BOOM
GODDAMN!
WHAT IN THE HELL . . . ?

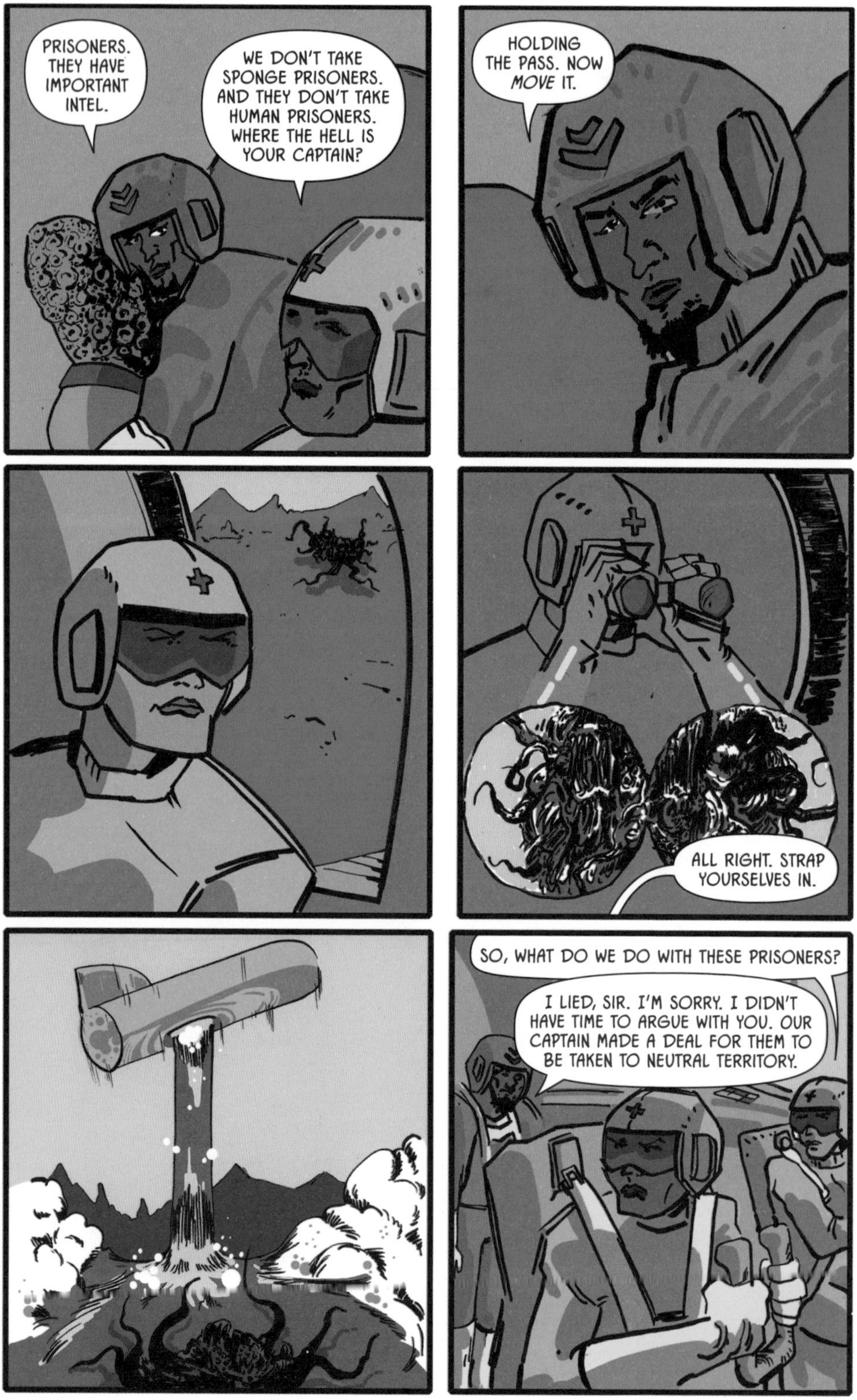
PRISONERS. THEY HAVE IMPORTANT INTEL.
WE DON'T TAKE SPONGE PRISONERS. AND THEY DON'T TAKE HUMAN PRISONERS. WHERE THE HELL IS YOUR CAPTAIN?
HOLDING THE PASS. NOW *MOVE* IT.
ALL RIGHT. STRAP YOURSELVES IN.
SO, WHAT DO WE DO WITH THESE PRISONERS?
I LIED, SIR. I'M SORRY. I DIDN'T HAVE TIME TO ARGUE WITH YOU. OUR CAPTAIN MADE A DEAL FOR THEM TO BE TAKEN TO NEUTRAL TERRITORY.

THIS IS BULLSHIT! MY KID SISTER DIED WITH THE 205TH ON OMEGA. I SAY WE SPACE 'EM.
THAT'S NOT GOING TO HAPPEN. MY CAPTAIN DIED TO SAVE US. THAT WAS THE DEAL SHE MADE. AND YOU WILL GODDAMNED WELL HONOR IT.
THIS IS MUTINY.
THIS IS KEEPING MY WORD.
ALL RIGHT. BUT YOU WILL BE PLACED UNDER ARREST.
I GAVE MY WORD.
CAPTAIN BLUE! TRACTOR BEAM. SPONGES! WE'RE FUCKED.
ALL INSTRUMENTATION DEAD. BEFORE IT DIED . . . THERE WAS A SIGNAL.
WHAT SORT OF SIGNAL?
FROM INSIDE ***OUR*** SHIP.

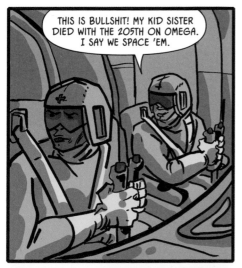

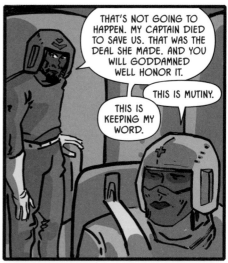

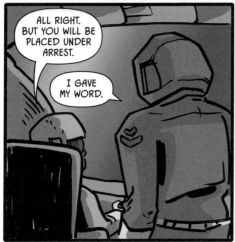

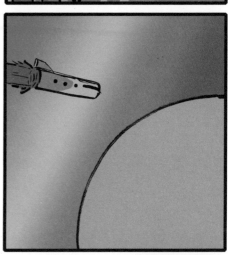

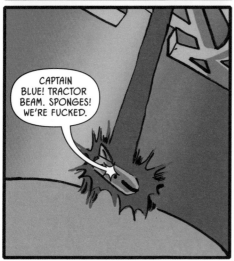

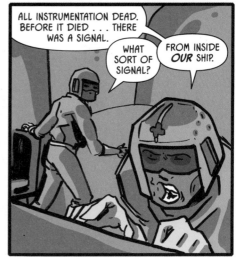

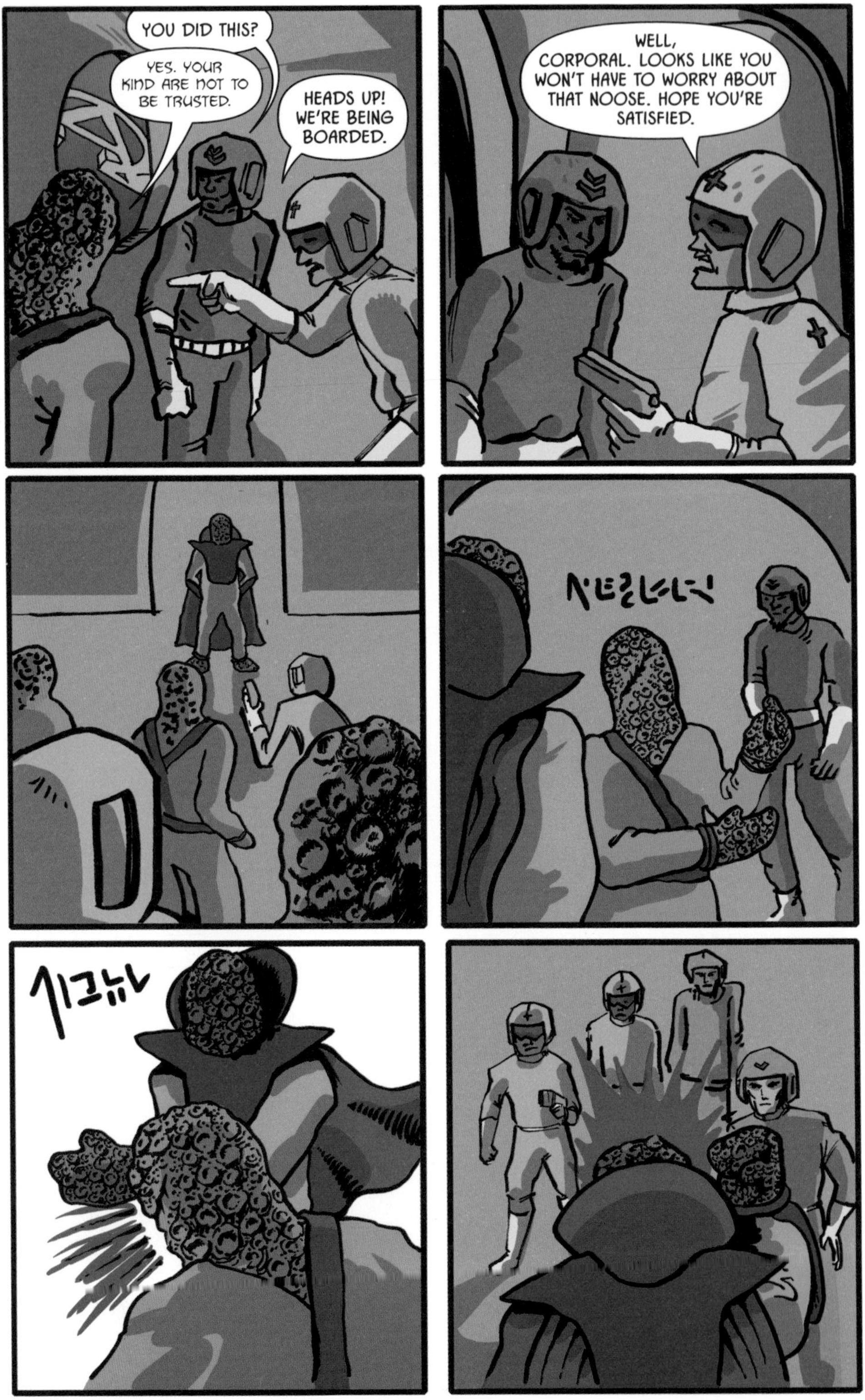
YOU DID THIS?
YES. YOUR KIND ARE NOT TO BE TRUSTED.
HEADS UP! WE'RE BEING BOARDED.
WELL, CORPORAL. LOOKS LIKE YOU WON'T HAVE TO WORRY ABOUT THAT NOOSE. HOPE YOU'RE SATISFIED.

WHAT DID HE SAY?

WAIT A MINUTE. GOT IT!

"THIS FOOL OF AN OFFICER MADE A COMMITMENT, SWEARING ON BLOODGOD. YOU SHOULD LEAVE. NOW. BEFORE I CHANGE MY MIND."

DON'T HAVE TO TELL ME TWICE.

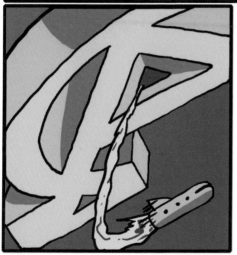

One year later...

It was said that within months, high-level, backdoor communications had opened between Sponges and human. And that when, a year later, a summit—the very first—was held on the neutral planet of D'Gere, the human corporal was called to testify on what had occurred on Tau Delta's third moon, known as Tau Three.

He testified to a joint body of humans and Sponges. But after his testimony, he was asked to step into a waiting area.

141

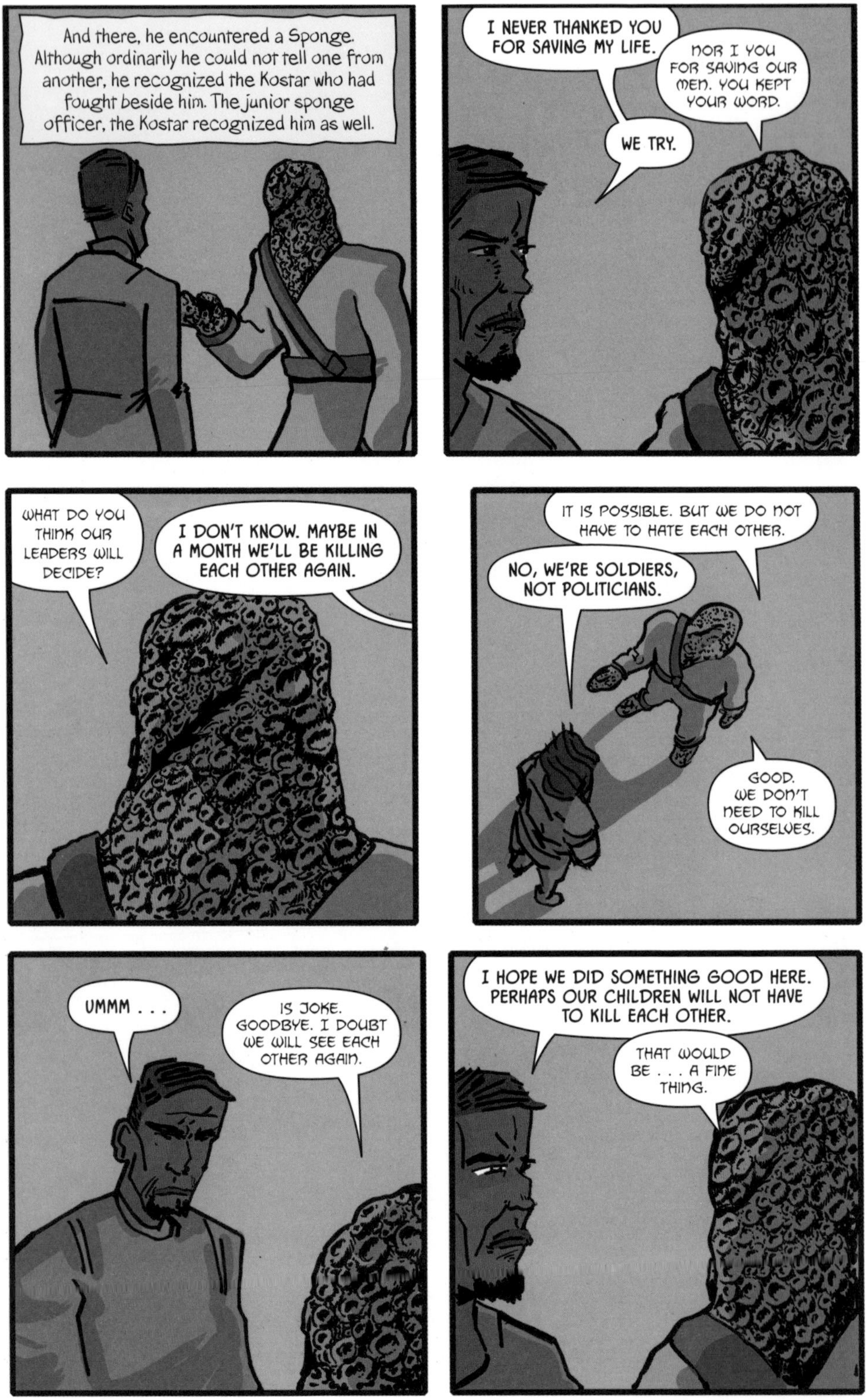
And there, he encountered a Sponge. Although ordinarily he could not tell one from another, he recognized the Kostar who had fought beside him. The junior sponge officer, the Kostar recognized him as well.
I NEVER THANKED YOU FOR SAVING MY LIFE.
WE TRY.
NOR I YOU FOR SAVING OUR MEN. YOU KEPT YOUR WORD.
WHAT DO YOU THINK OUR LEADERS WILL DECIDE?
I DON'T KNOW. MAYBE IN A MONTH WE'LL BE KILLING EACH OTHER AGAIN.
IT IS POSSIBLE. BUT WE DO NOT HAVE TO HATE EACH OTHER.
NO, WE'RE SOLDIERS, NOT POLITICIANS.
GOOD. WE DON'T NEED TO KILL OURSELVES.
UMMM . . .
IS JOKE. GOODBYE. I DOUBT WE WILL SEE EACH OTHER AGAIN.
I HOPE WE DID SOMETHING GOOD HERE. PERHAPS OUR CHILDREN WILL NOT HAVE TO KILL EACH OTHER.
THAT WOULD BE . . . A FINE THING.

Just as there will always be war, there will always be warriors to fight them. But if even brave Horatius could beat his sword into a plowshare . . . perhaps there is more cause for hope than fear.

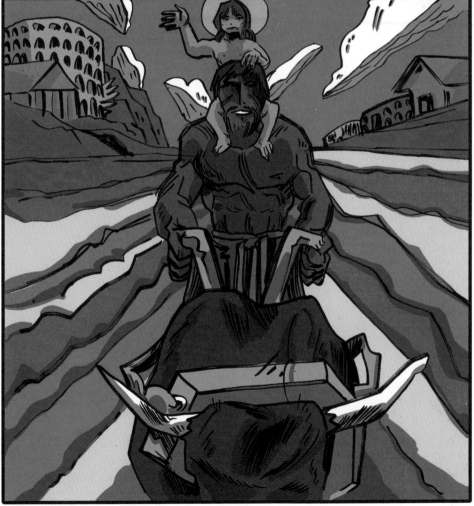

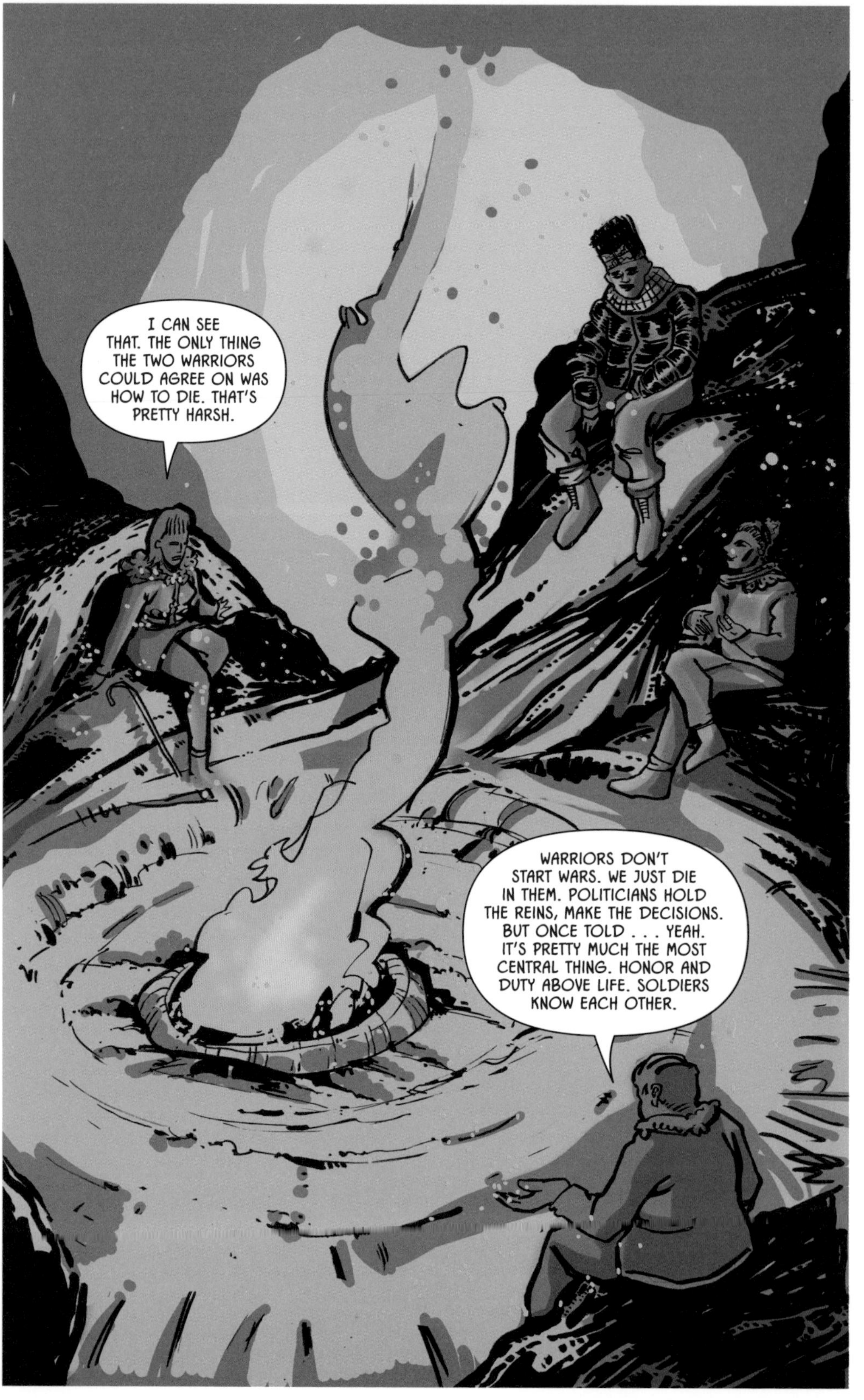
I CAN SEE THAT. THE ONLY THING THE TWO WARRIORS COULD AGREE ON WAS HOW TO DIE. THAT'S PRETTY HARSH.
WARRIORS DON'T START WARS. WE JUST DIE IN THEM. POLITICIANS HOLD THE REINS, MAKE THE DECISIONS. BUT ONCE TOLD . . . YEAH. IT'S PRETTY MUCH THE MOST CENTRAL THING. HONOR AND DUTY ABOVE LIFE. SOLDIERS KNOW EACH OTHER.

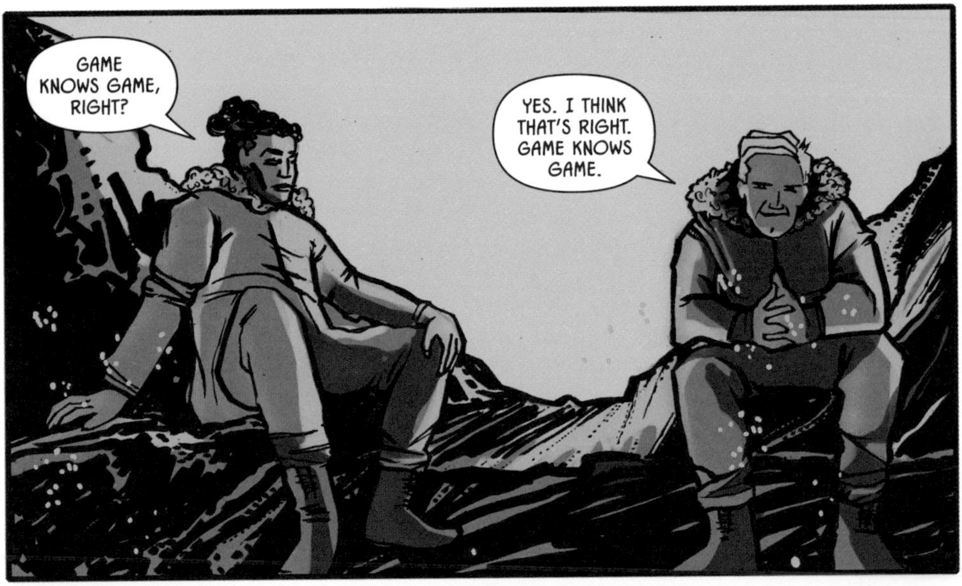
GAME KNOWS GAME, RIGHT?
YES. I THINK THAT'S RIGHT. GAME KNOWS GAME.

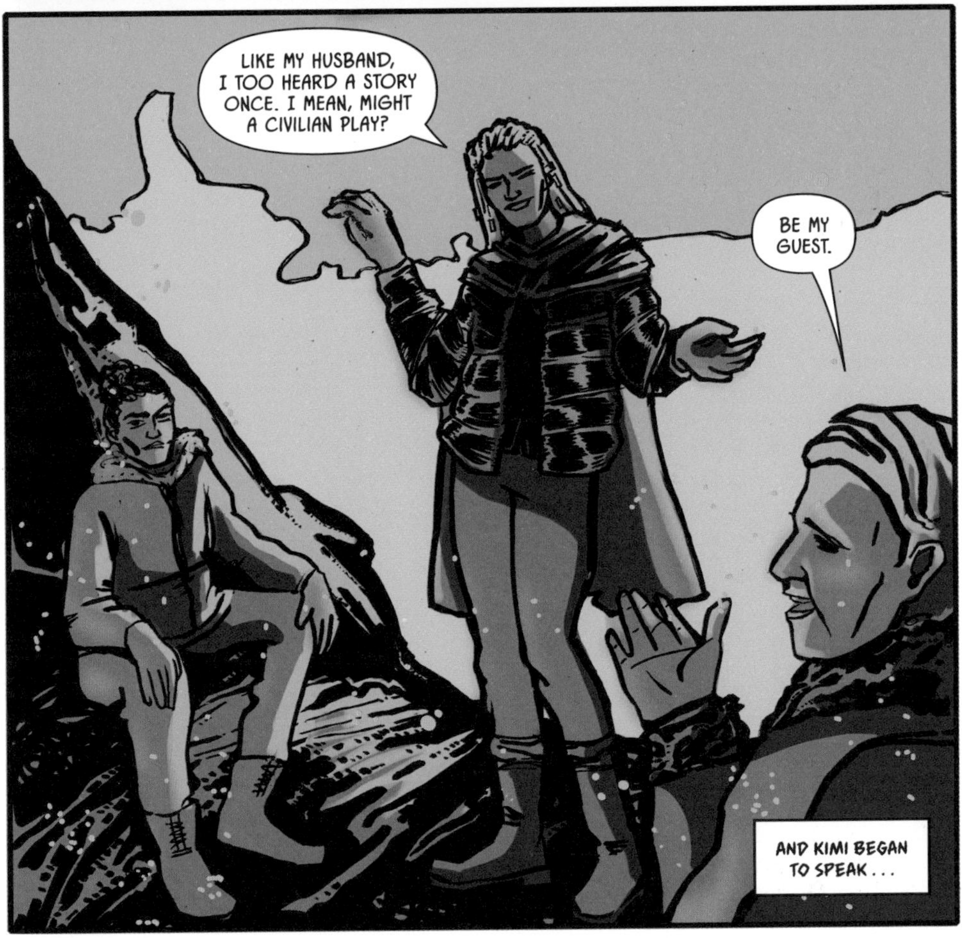
LIKE MY HUSBAND, I TOO HEARD A STORY ONCE. I MEAN, MIGHT A CIVILIAN PLAY?
BE MY GUEST.
AND KIMI BEGAN TO SPEAK . . .

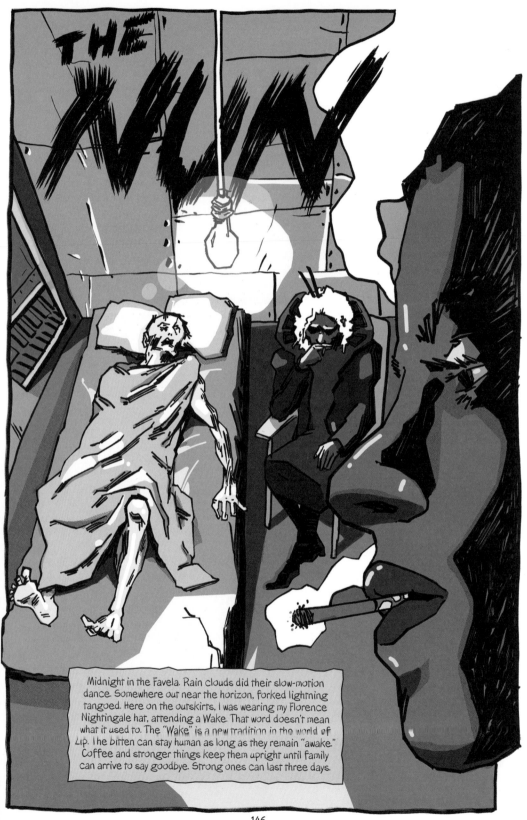

Midnight in the Favela. Rain clouds did their slow-motion dance. Somewhere out near the horizon, forked lightning tangoed. Here on the outskirts, I was wearing my Florence Nightingale hat, attending a Wake. That word doesn't mean what it used to. The "Wake" is a new tradition in the world of Zip. The bitten can stay human as long as they remain "awake." Coffee and stronger things keep them upright until family can arrive to say goodbye. Strong ones can last three days.

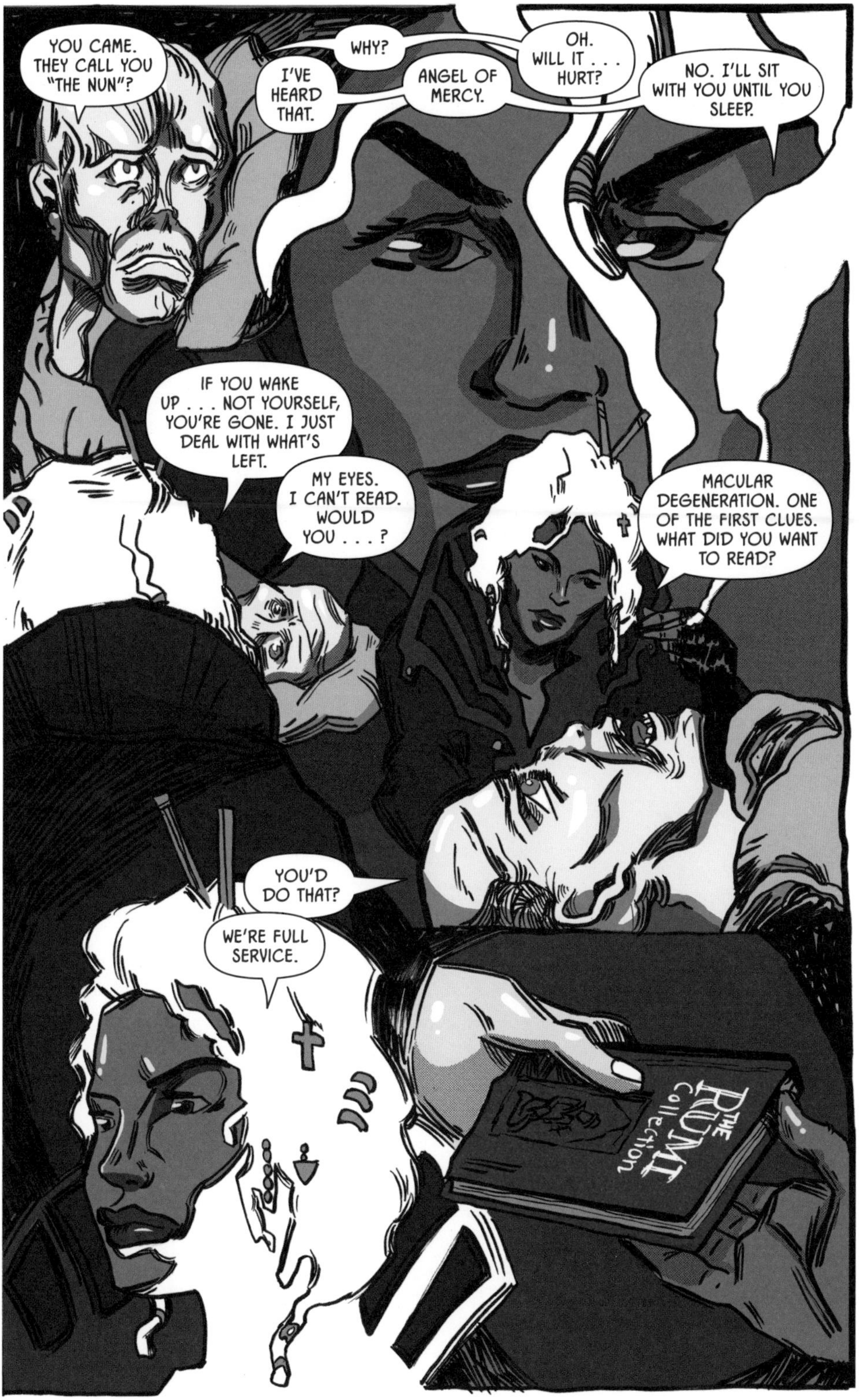
YOU CAME. THEY CALL YOU "THE NUN"?
I'VE HEARD THAT.
WHY?
ANGEL OF MERCY.
OH. WILL IT . . . HURT?
NO. I'LL SIT WITH YOU UNTIL YOU SLEEP.
IF YOU WAKE UP . . . NOT YOURSELF, YOU'RE GONE. I JUST DEAL WITH WHAT'S LEFT.
MY EYES. I CAN'T READ. WOULD YOU . . . ?
MACULAR DEGENERATION. ONE OF THE FIRST CLUES. WHAT DID YOU WANT TO READ?
YOU'D DO THAT?
WE'RE FULL SERVICE.
THE RUMI Collection

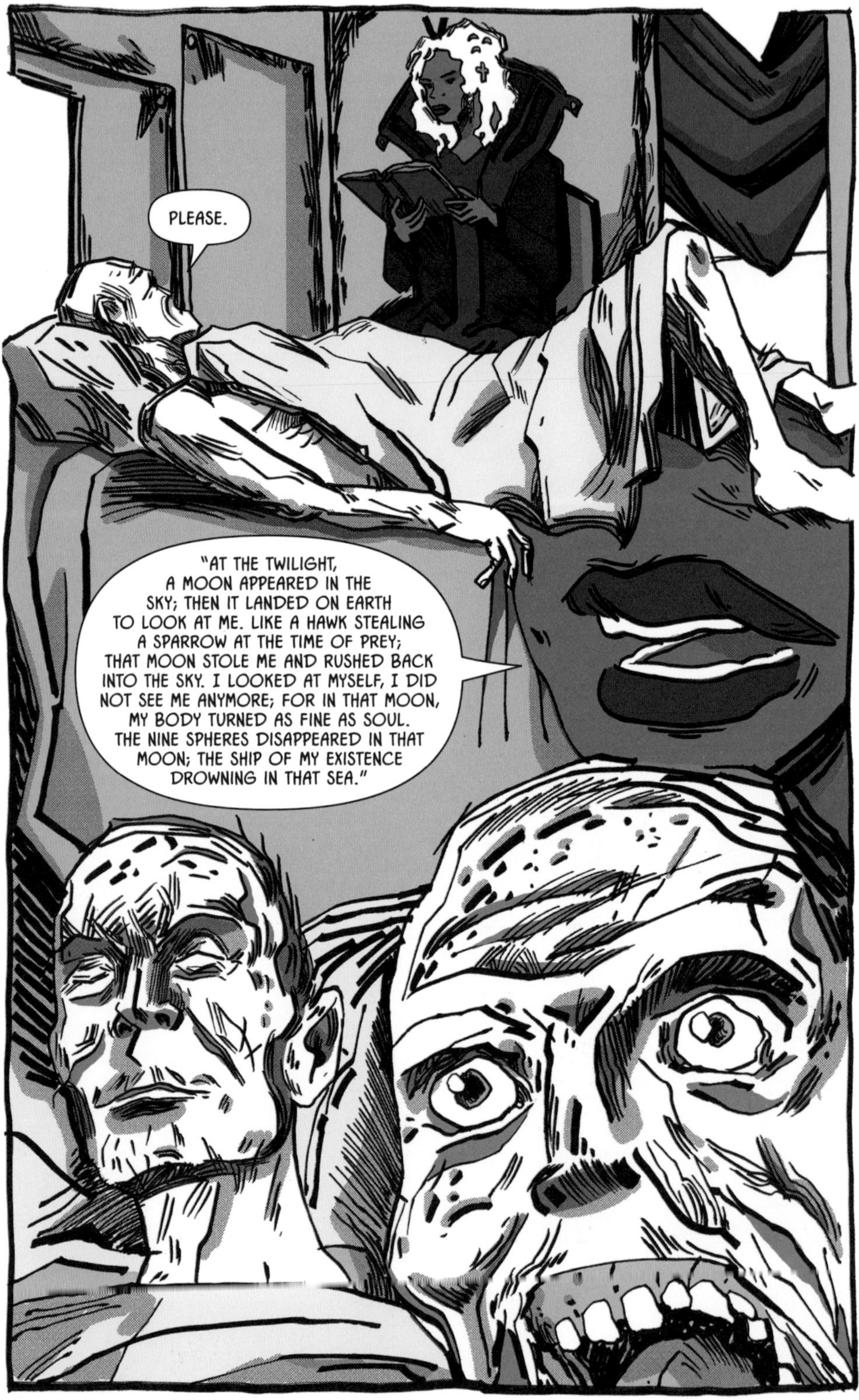
PLEASE.
"AT THE TWILIGHT, A MOON APPEARED IN THE SKY; THEN IT LANDED ON EARTH TO LOOK AT ME. LIKE A HAWK STEALING A SPARROW AT THE TIME OF PREY; THAT MOON STOLE ME AND RUSHED BACK INTO THE SKY. I LOOKED AT MYSELF, I DID NOT SEE ME ANYMORE; FOR IN THAT MOON, MY BODY TURNED AS FINE AS SOUL. THE NINE SPHERES DISAPPEARED IN THAT MOON; THE SHIP OF MY EXISTENCE DROWNING IN THAT SEA."

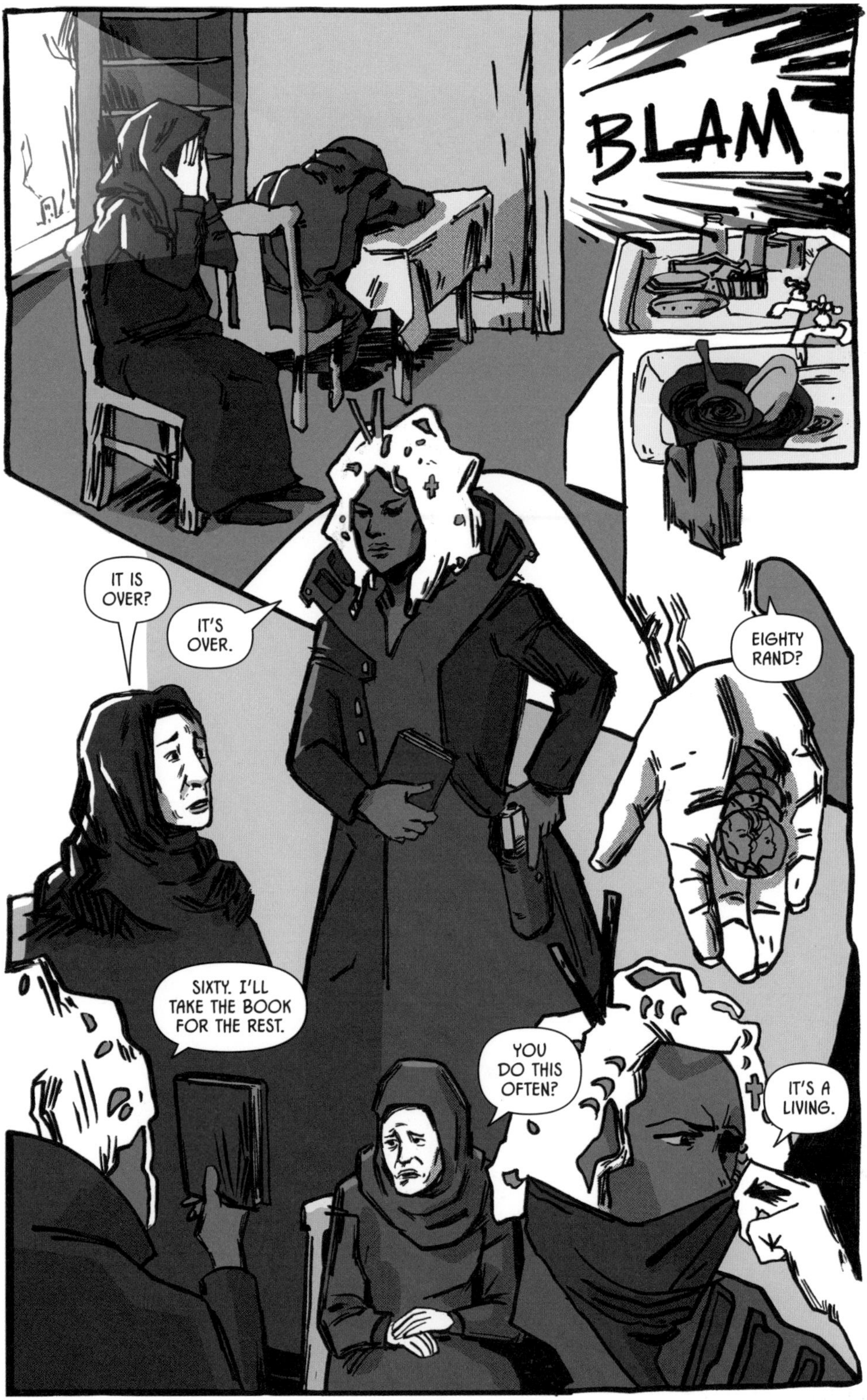
BLAM
IT IS OVER?
IT'S OVER.
EIGHTY RAND?
SIXTY. I'LL TAKE THE BOOK FOR THE REST.
YOU DO THIS OFTEN?
IT'S A LIVING.

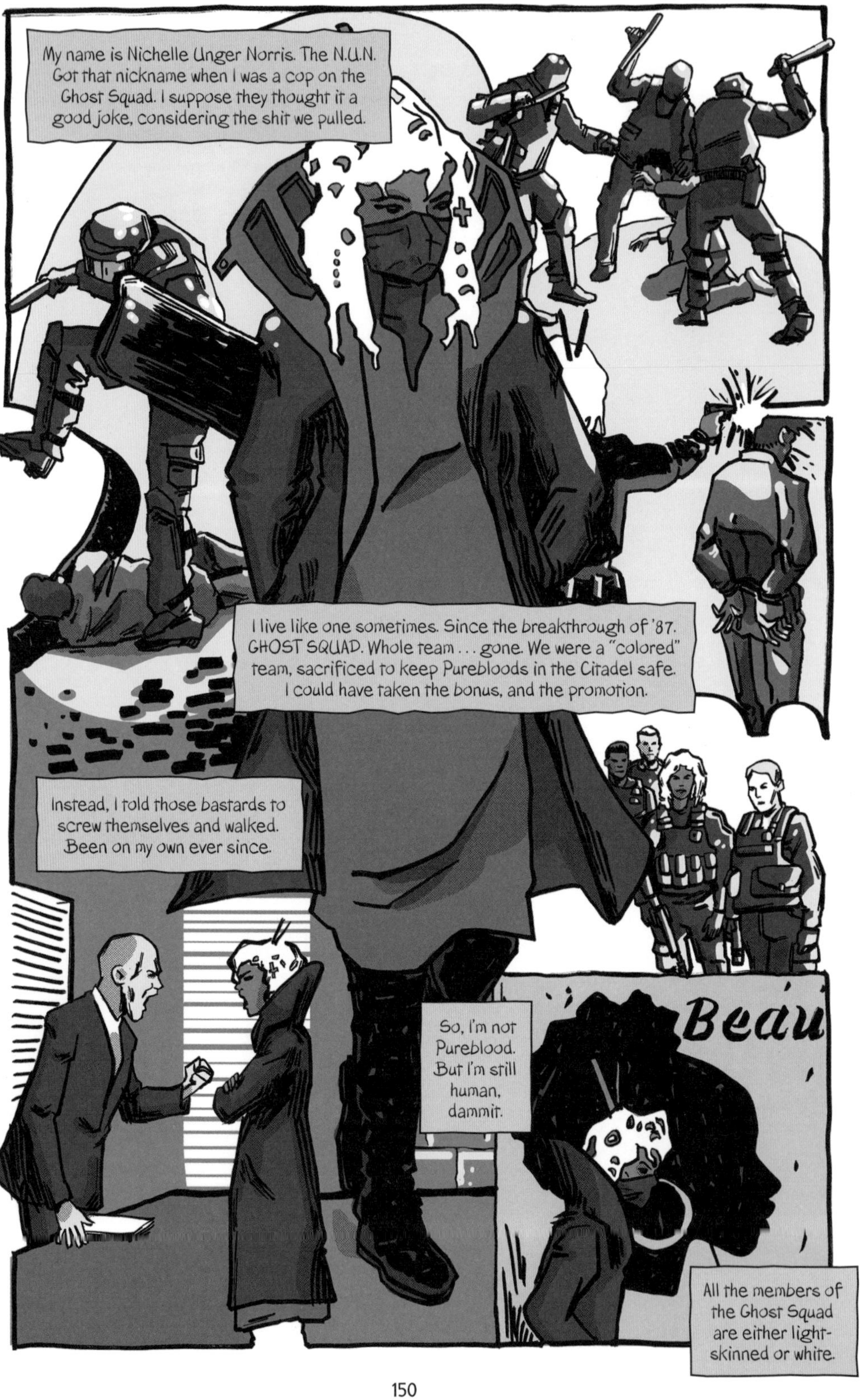
My name is Nichelle Unger Norris. The N.U.N. Got that nickname when I was a cop on the Ghost Squad. I suppose they thought it a good joke, considering the shit we pulled.
I live like one sometimes. Since the breakthrough of '87. GHOST SQUAD. Whole team . . . gone. We were a "colored" team, sacrificed to keep Purebloods in the Citadel safe. I could have taken the bonus, and the promotion.
Instead, I told those bastards to screw themselves and walked. Been on my own ever since.
So, I'm not Pureblood. But I'm still human, dammit.
Beau
All the members of the Ghost Squad are either light-skinned or white.

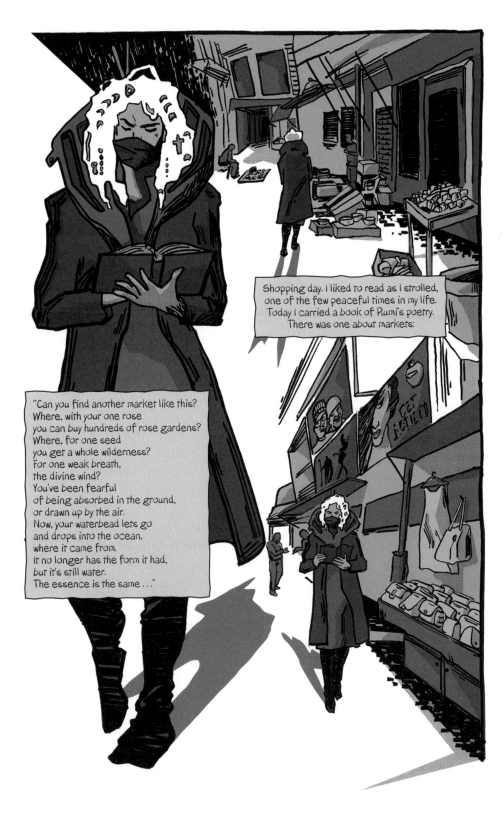

Shopping day. I liked to read as I strolled, one of the few peaceful times in my life. Today I carried a book of Rumi's poetry. There was one about markets:

"Can you find another market like this?
Where, with your one rose
you can buy hundreds of rose gardens?
Where, for one seed
you get a whole wilderness?
For one weak breath,
the divine wind?
You've been fearful
of being absorbed in the ground,
or drawn up by the air.
Now, your waterbead lets go
and drops into the ocean,
where it came from.
It no longer has the form it had,
but it's still water.
The essence is the same..."

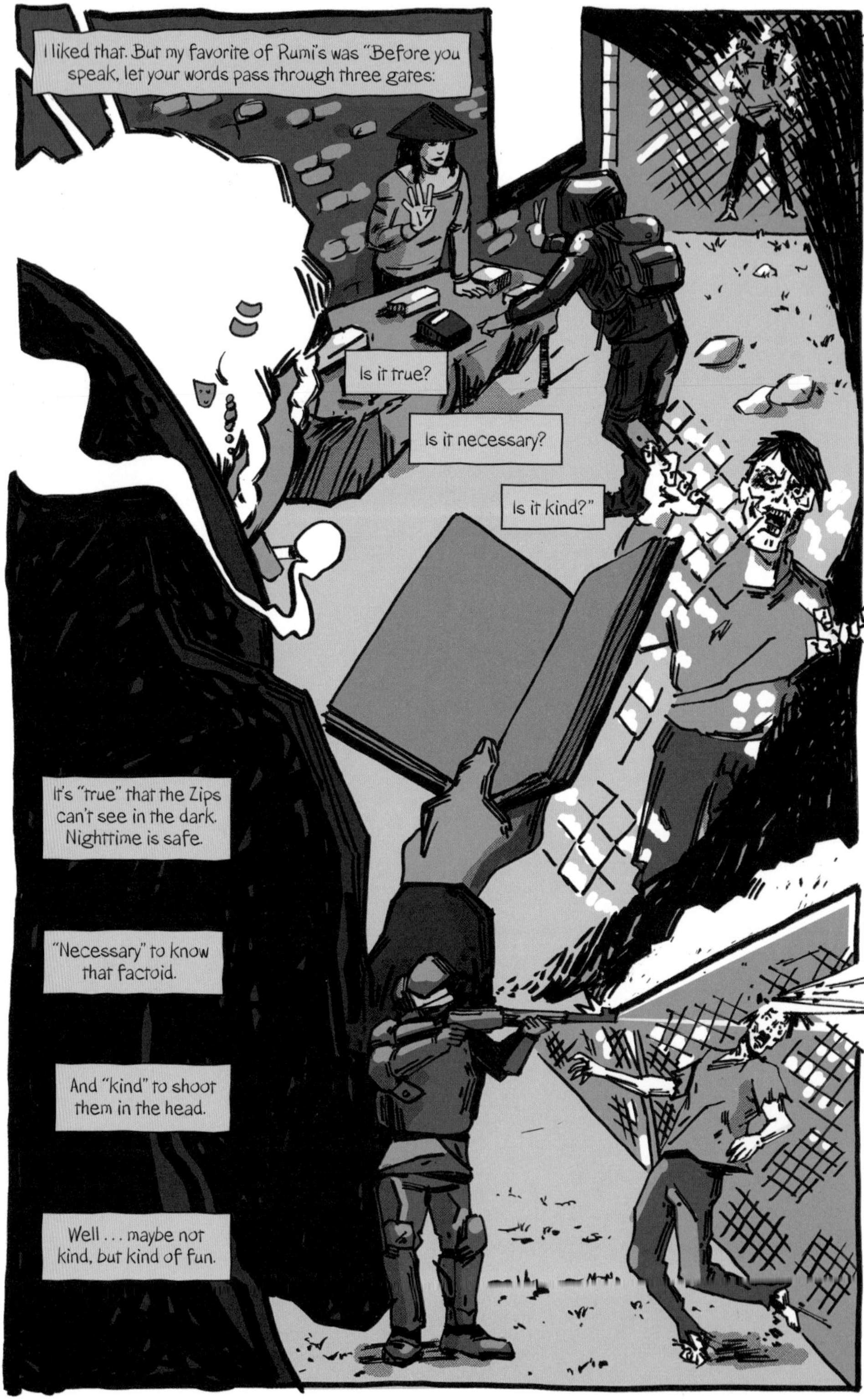
I liked that. But my favorite of Rumi's was "Before you speak, let your words pass through three gates:
Is it true?
Is it necessary?
Is it kind?"
It's "true" that the Zips can't see in the dark. Nighttime is safe.
"Necessary" to know that factoid.
And "kind" to shoot them in the head.
Well . . . maybe not kind, but kind of fun.

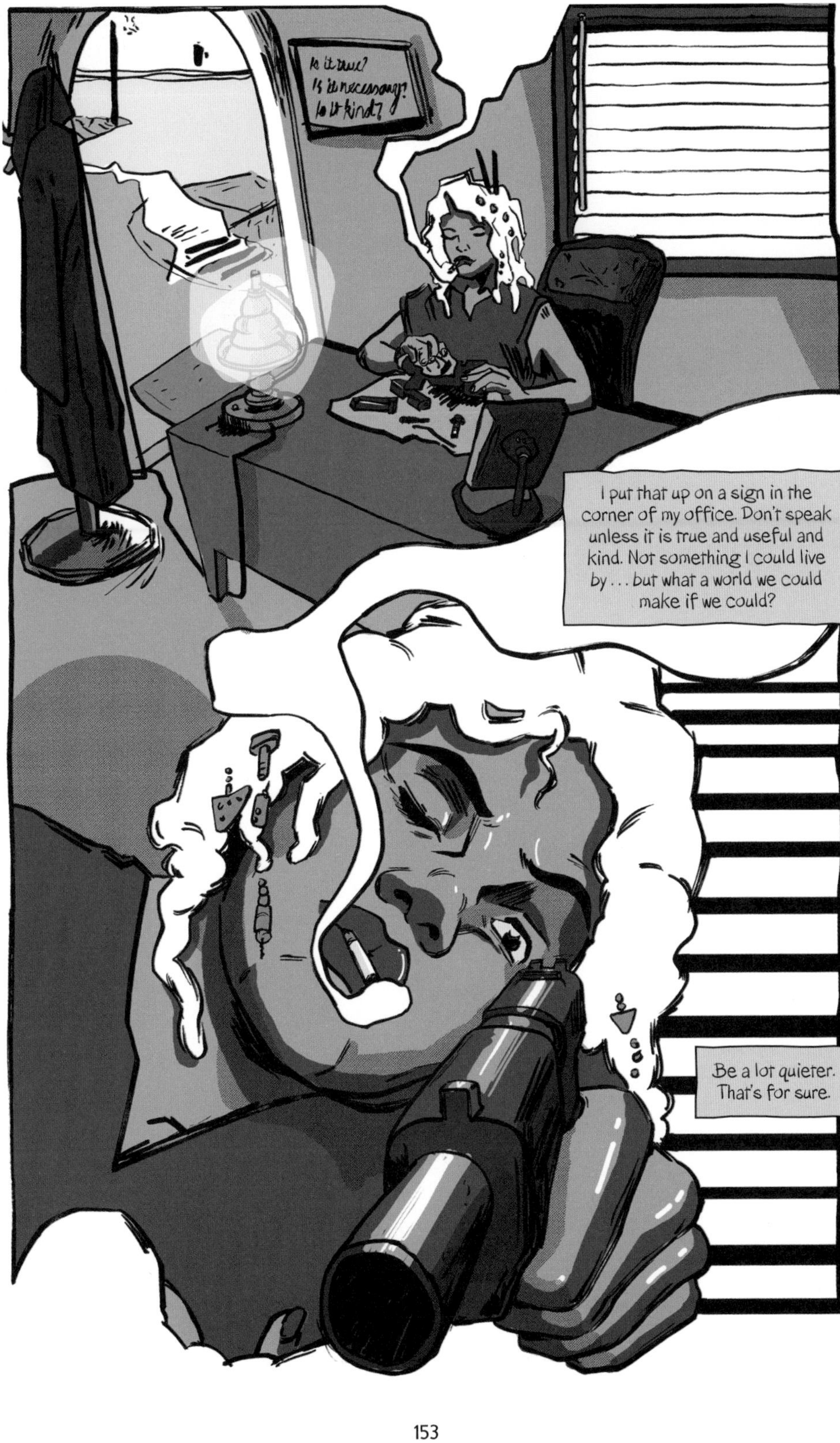
Is it true?
Is it necessary?
Is it kind?
I put that up on a sign in the corner of my office. Don't speak unless it is true and useful and kind. Not something I could live by . . . but what a world we could make if we could?
Be a lot quieter. That's for sure.

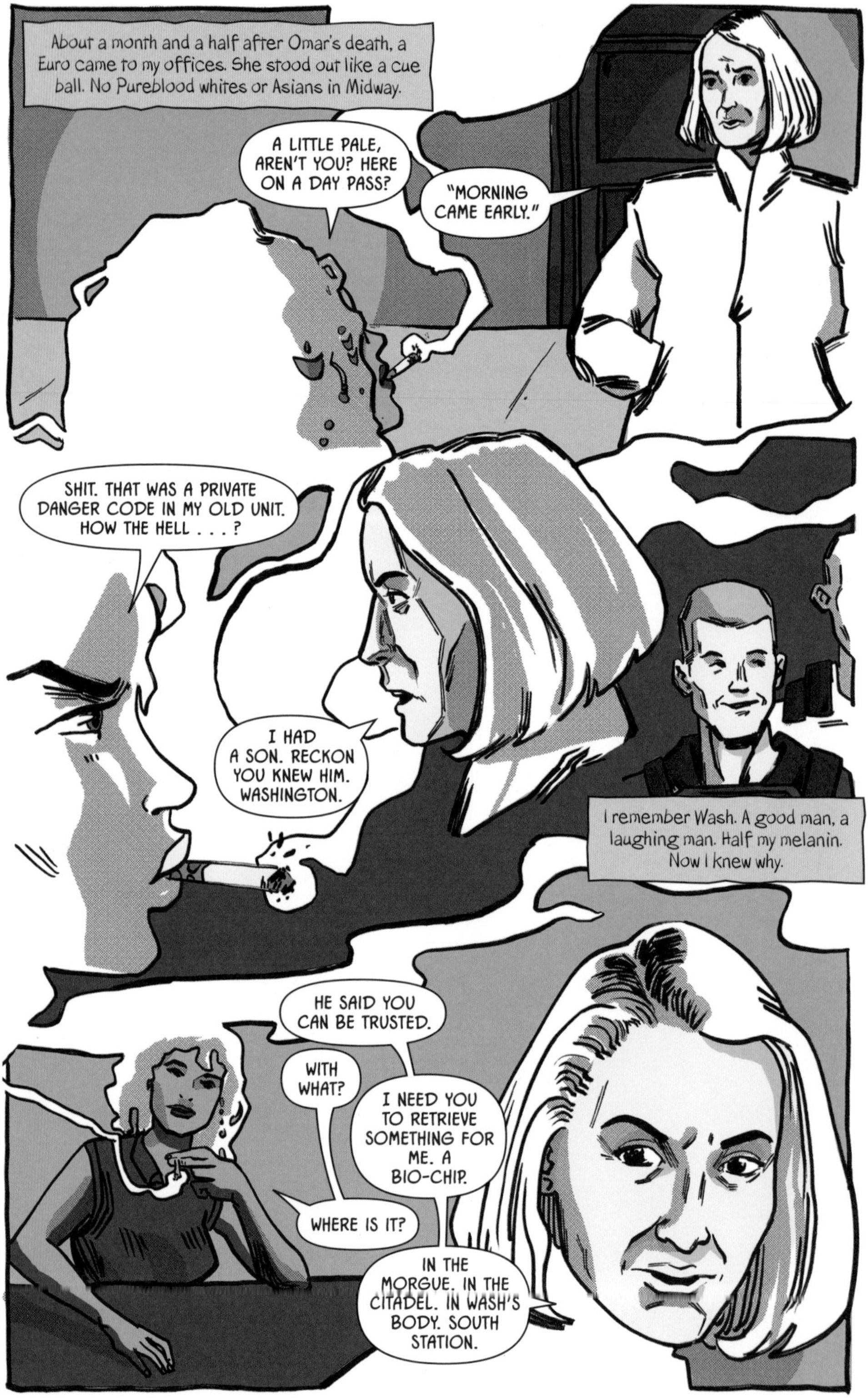

About a month and a half after Omar's death, a Euro came to my offices. She stood out like a cue ball. No Pureblood whites or Asians in Midway.
A LITTLE PALE, AREN'T YOU? HERE ON A DAY PASS?
"MORNING CAME EARLY."
SHIT. THAT WAS A PRIVATE DANGER CODE IN MY OLD UNIT. HOW THE HELL . . . ?
I HAD A SON. RECKON YOU KNEW HIM. WASHINGTON.
I remember Wash. A good man, a laughing man. Half my melanin. Now I knew why.
HE SAID YOU CAN BE TRUSTED.
WITH WHAT?
I NEED YOU TO RETRIEVE SOMETHING FOR ME. A BIO-CHIP.
WHERE IS IT?
IN THE MORGUE. IN THE CITADEL. IN WASH'S BODY. SOUTH STATION.

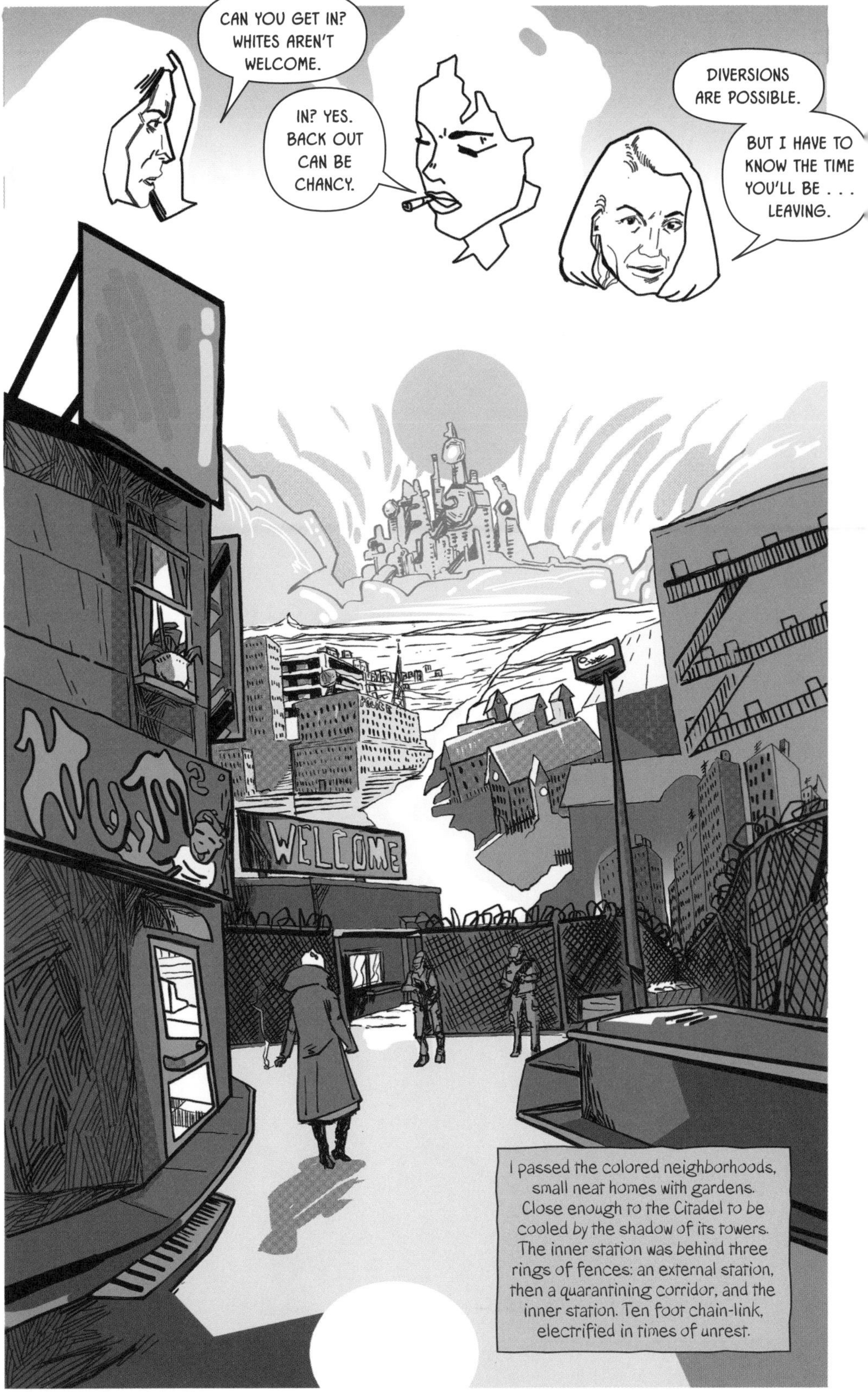
CAN YOU GET IN? WHITES AREN'T WELCOME.
IN? YES. BACK OUT CAN BE CHANCY.
DIVERSIONS ARE POSSIBLE.
BUT I HAVE TO KNOW THE TIME YOU'LL BE . . . LEAVING.
WELCOME
I passed the colored neighborhoods, small neat homes with gardens. Close enough to the Citadel to be cooled by the shadow of its towers. The inner station was behind three rings of fences: an external station, then a quarantining corridor, and the inner station. Ten foot chain-link, electrified in times of unrest.

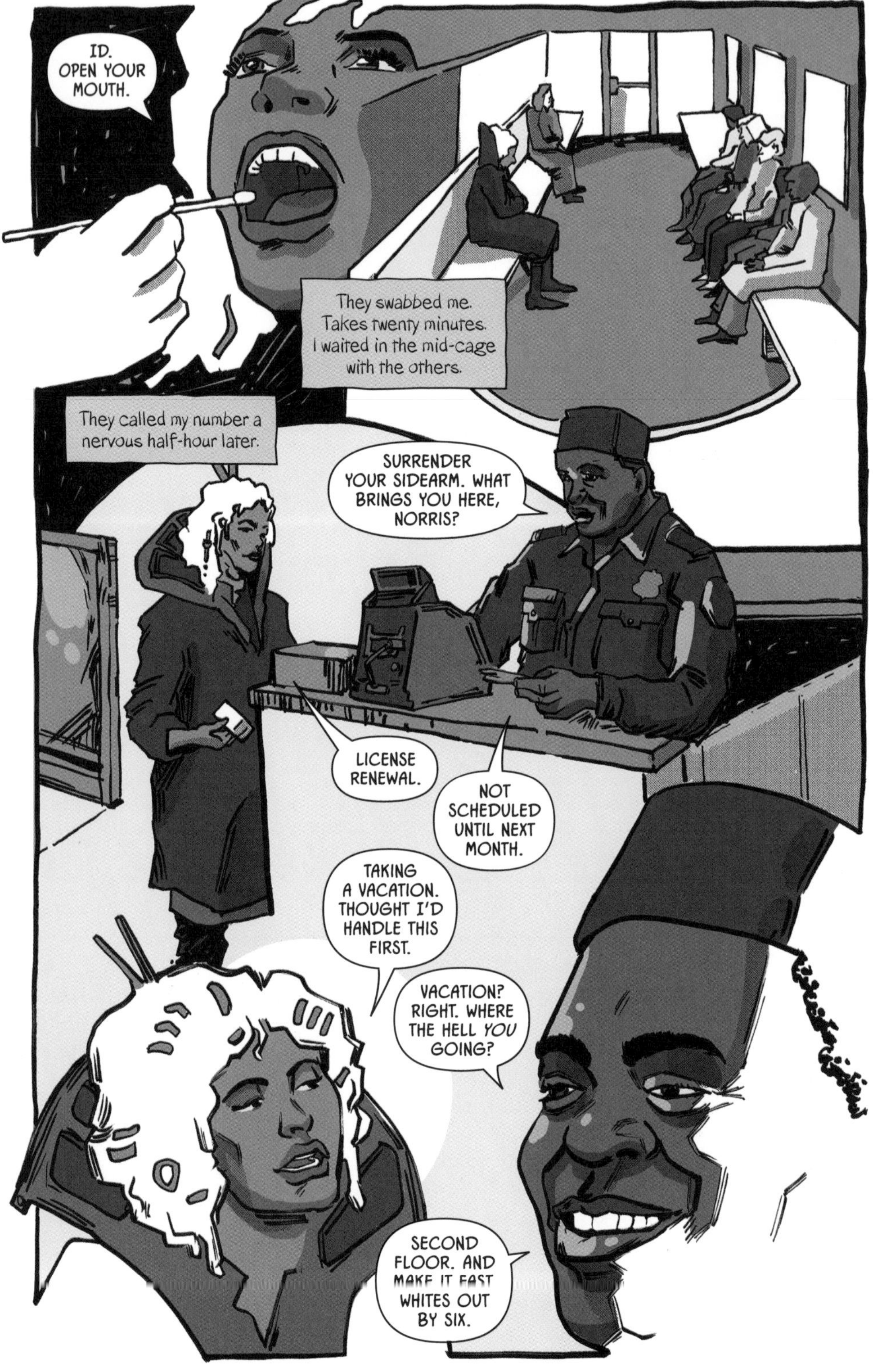

ID. OPEN YOUR MOUTH.
They swabbed me. Takes twenty minutes. I waited in the mid-cage with the others.
They called my number a nervous half-hour later.
SURRENDER YOUR SIDEARM. WHAT BRINGS YOU HERE, NORRIS?
LICENSE RENEWAL.
NOT SCHEDULED UNTIL NEXT MONTH.
TAKING A VACATION. THOUGHT I'D HANDLE THIS FIRST.
VACATION? RIGHT. WHERE THE HELL *YOU* GOING?
SECOND FLOOR. AND MAKE IT FAST WHITES OUT BY SIX.

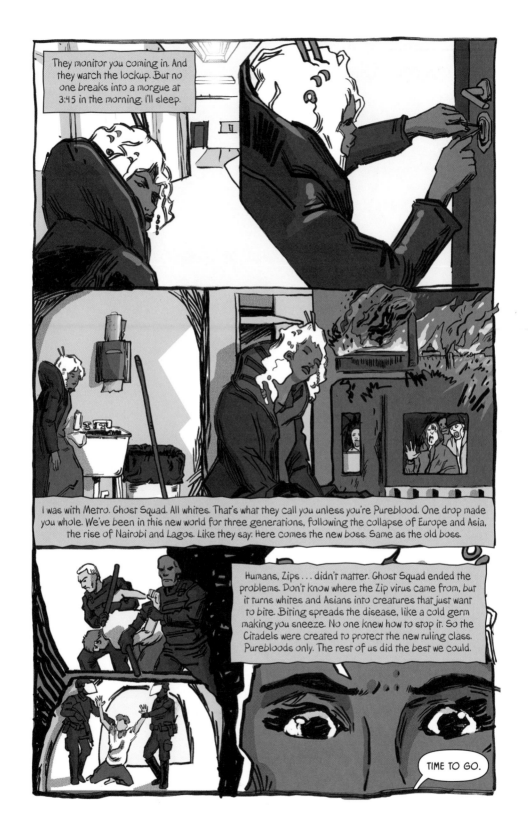

They monitor you coming in. And they watch the lockup. But no one breaks into a morgue at 3:45 in the morning. I'll sleep.

I was with Metro. Ghost Squad. All whites. That's what they call you unless you're Pureblood. One drop made you whole. We've been in this new world for three generations, following the collapse of Europe and Asia, the rise of Nairobi and Lagos. Like they say: Here comes the new boss. Same as the old boss.

Humans, Zips... didn't matter. Ghost Squad ended the problems. Don't know where the Zip virus came from, but it turns whites and Asians into creatures that just want to bite. Biting spreads the disease, like a cold germ making you sneeze. No one knew how to stop it. So the Citadels were created to protect the new ruling class. Purebloods only. The rest of us did the best we could.

TIME TO GO.

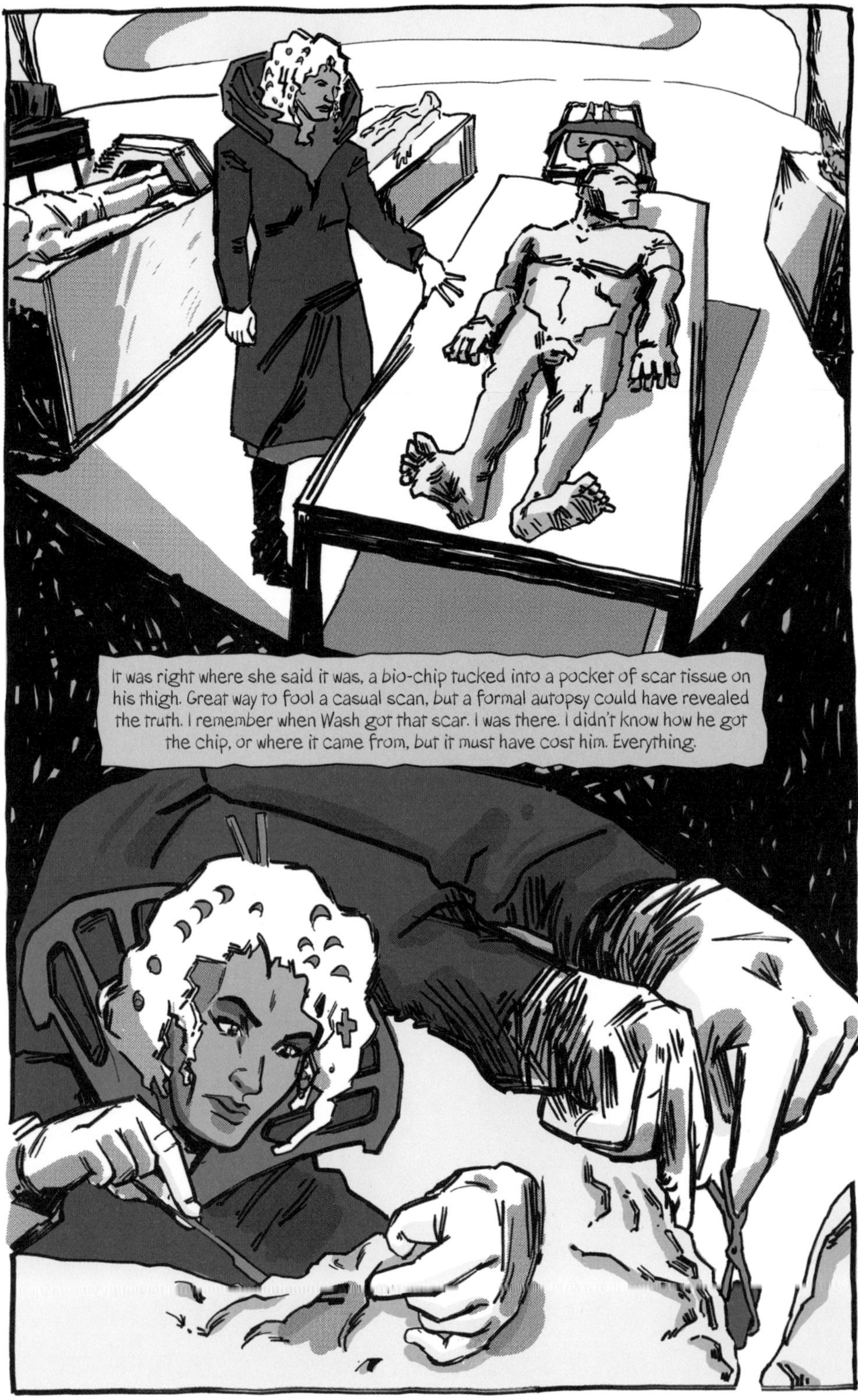
It was right where she said it was, a bio-chip tucked into a pocket of scar tissue on his thigh. Great way to fool a casual scan, but a formal autopsy could have revealed the truth. I remember when Wash got that scar. I was there. I didn't know how he got the chip, or where it came from, but it must have cost him. Everything.

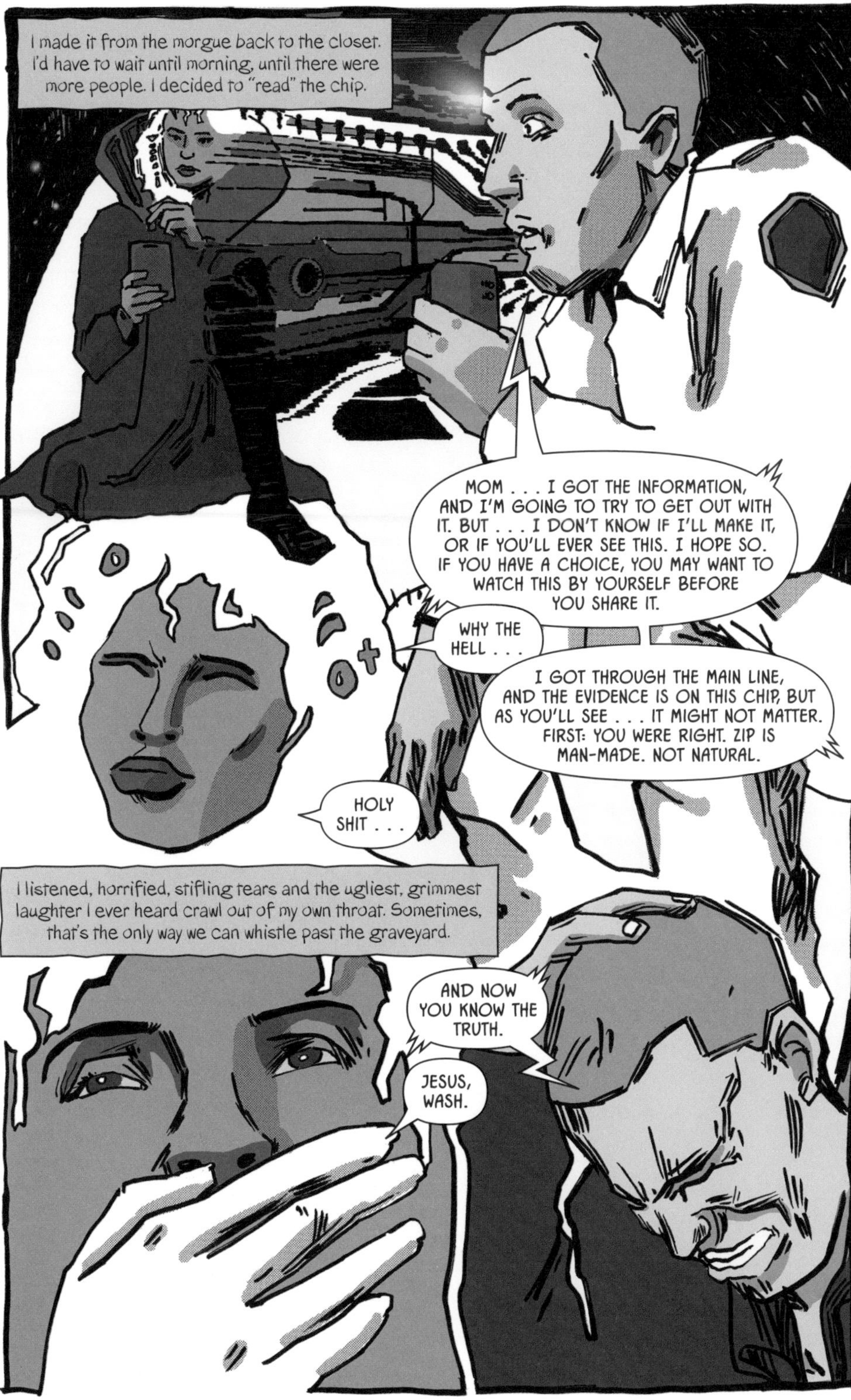
I made it from the morgue back to the closet. I'd have to wait until morning, until there were more people. I decided to "read" the chip.
MOM . . . I GOT THE INFORMATION, AND I'M GOING TO TRY TO GET OUT WITH IT. BUT . . . I DON'T KNOW IF I'LL MAKE IT, OR IF YOU'LL EVER SEE THIS. I HOPE SO. IF YOU HAVE A CHOICE, YOU MAY WANT TO WATCH THIS BY YOURSELF BEFORE YOU SHARE IT.
WHY THE HELL . . .
I GOT THROUGH THE MAIN LINE, AND THE EVIDENCE IS ON THIS CHIP, BUT AS YOU'LL SEE . . . IT MIGHT NOT MATTER. FIRST: YOU WERE RIGHT. ZIP IS MAN-MADE. NOT NATURAL.
HOLY SHIT . . .
I listened, horrified, stifling tears and the ugliest, grimmest laughter I ever heard crawl out of my own throat. Sometimes, that's the only way we can whistle past the graveyard.
AND NOW YOU KNOW THE TRUTH.
JESUS, WASH.

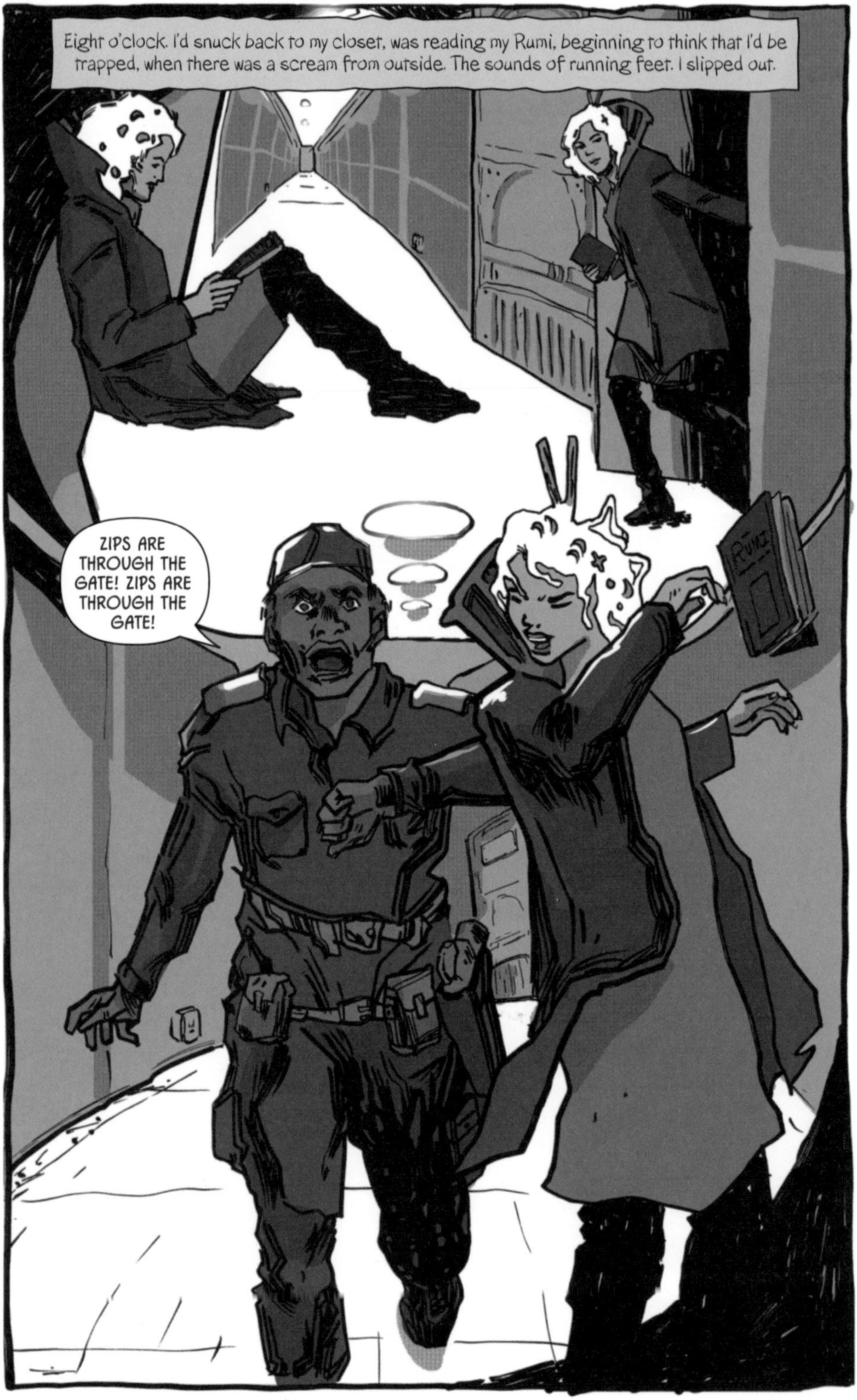
Eight o'clock. I'd snuck back to my closet, was reading my Rumi, beginning to think that I'd be trapped, when there was a scream from outside. The sounds of running feet. I slipped out.
ZIPS ARE THROUGH THE GATE! ZIPS ARE THROUGH THE GATE!
RUMI

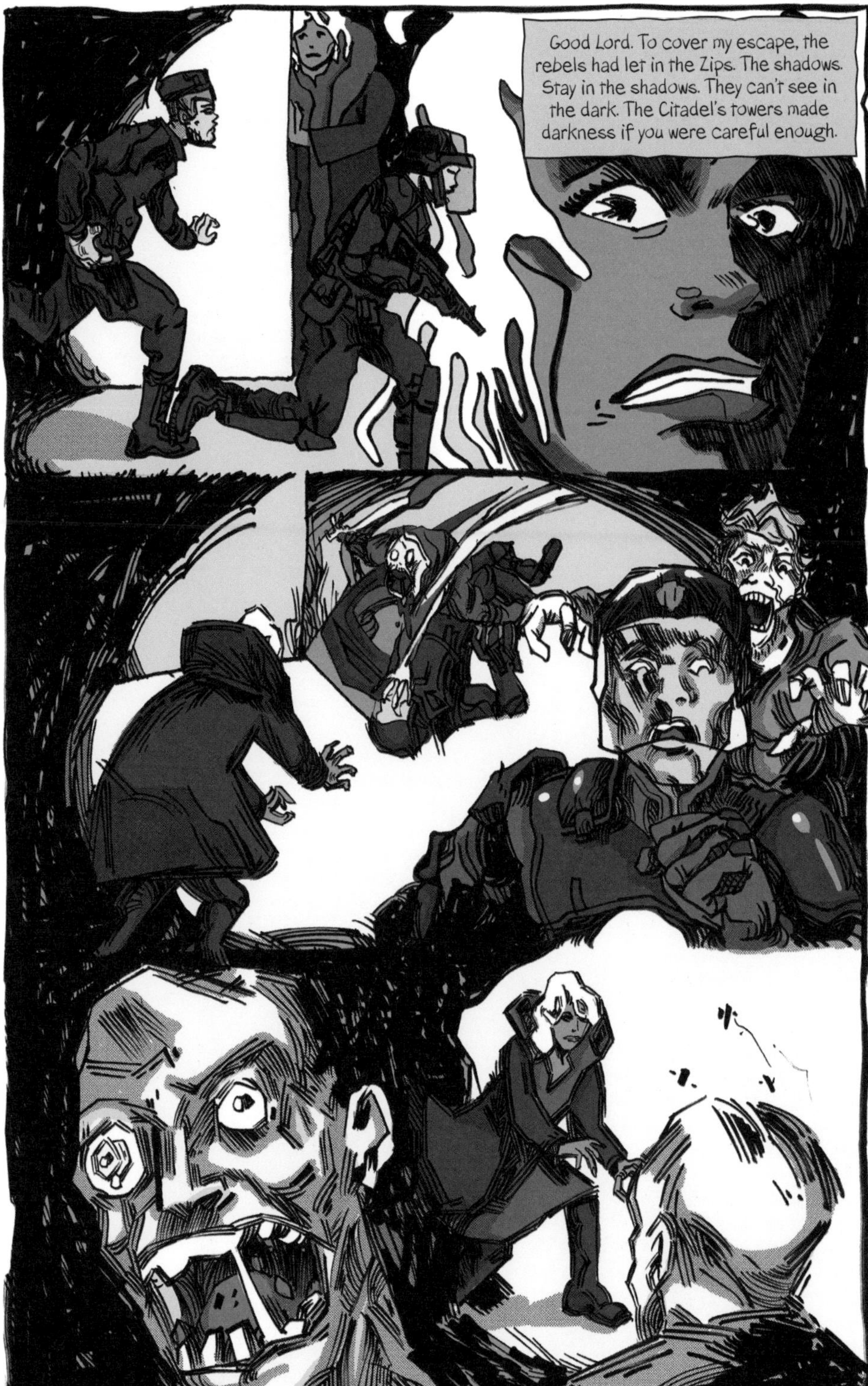
Good Lord. To cover my escape, the rebels had let in the Zips. The shadows. Stay in the shadows. They can't see in the dark. The Citadel's towers made darkness if you were careful enough.

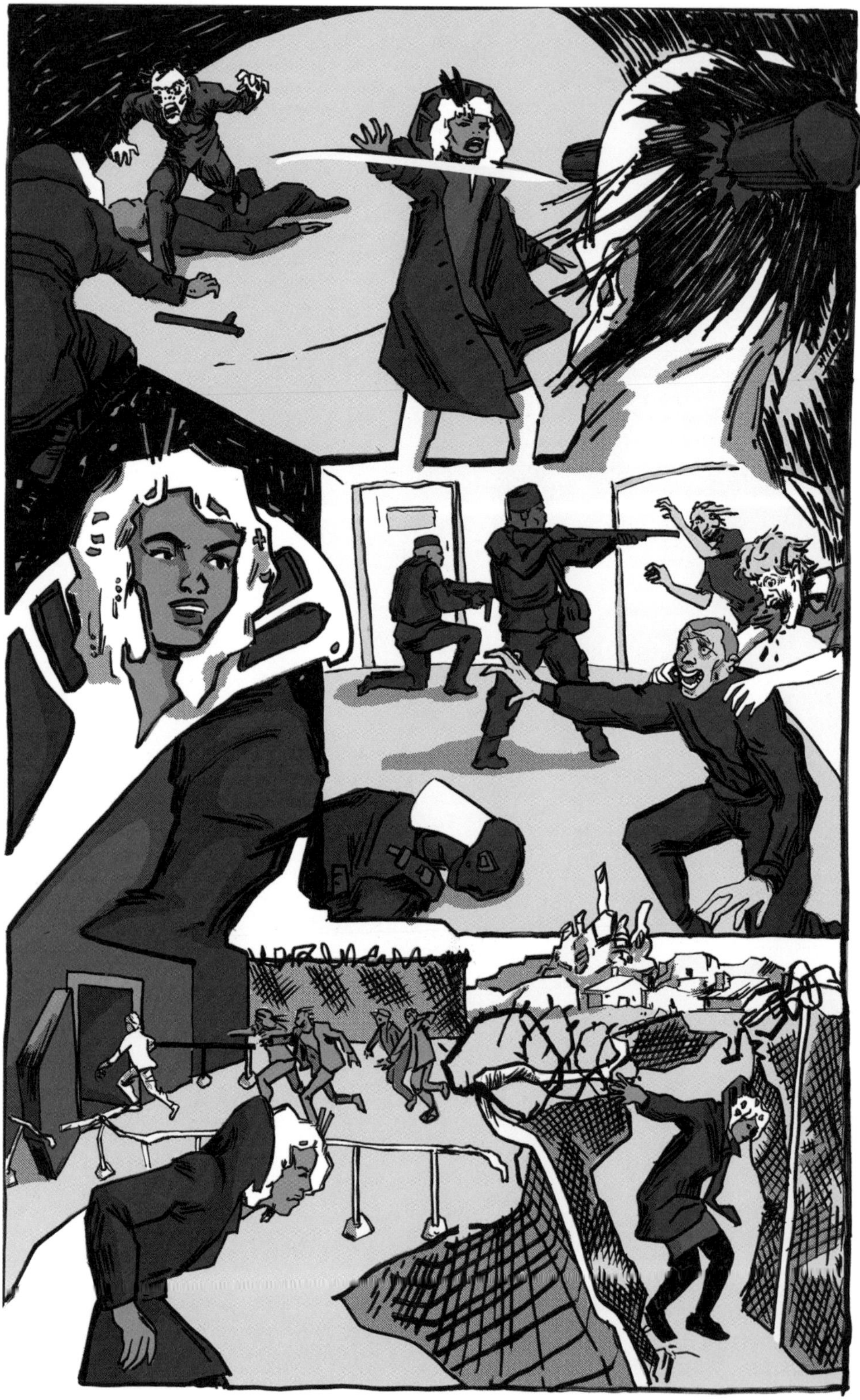

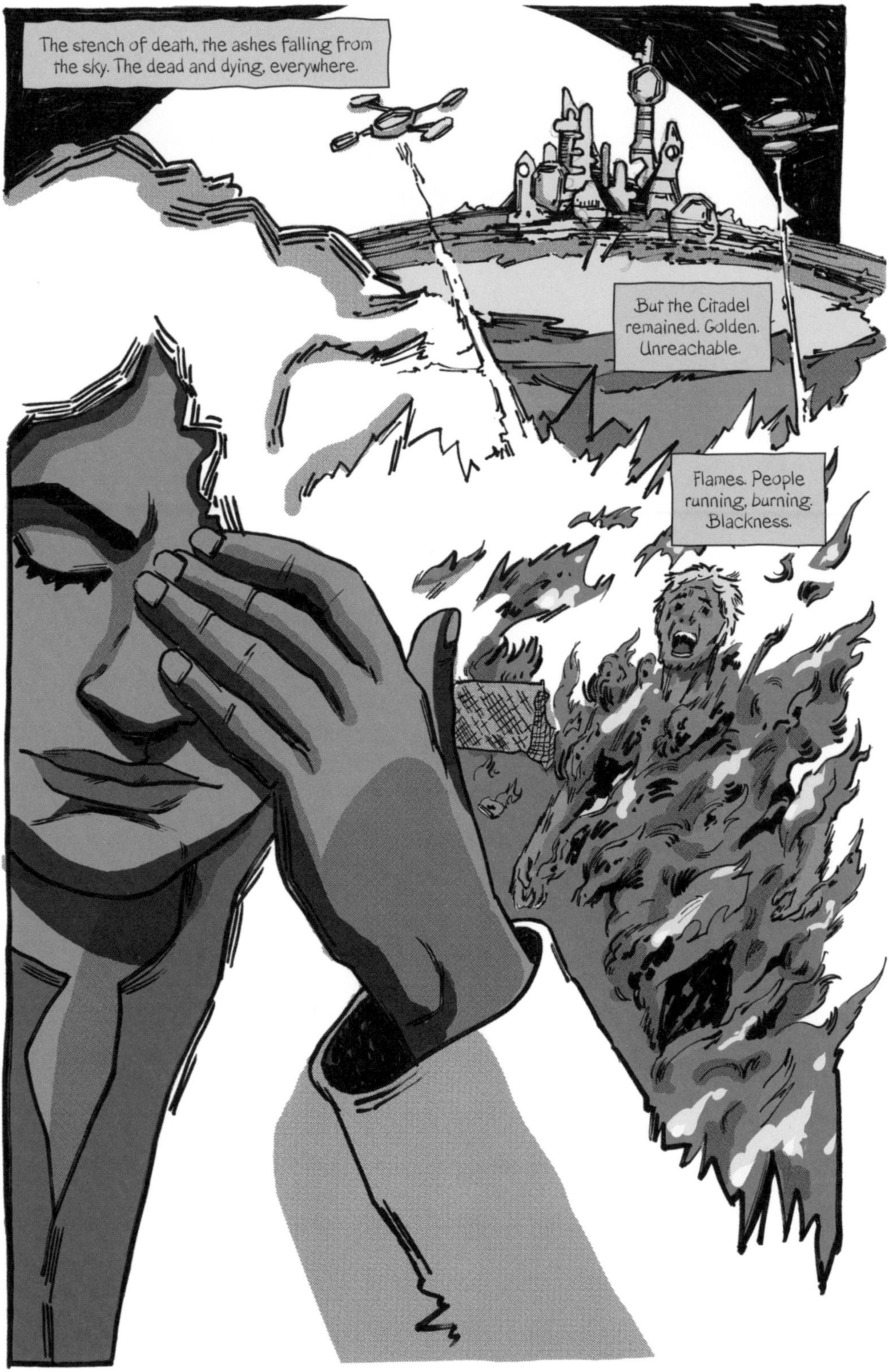
The stench of death, the ashes falling from the sky. The dead and dying, everywhere.
But the Citadel remained. Golden. Unreachable.
Flames. People running, burning. Blackness.

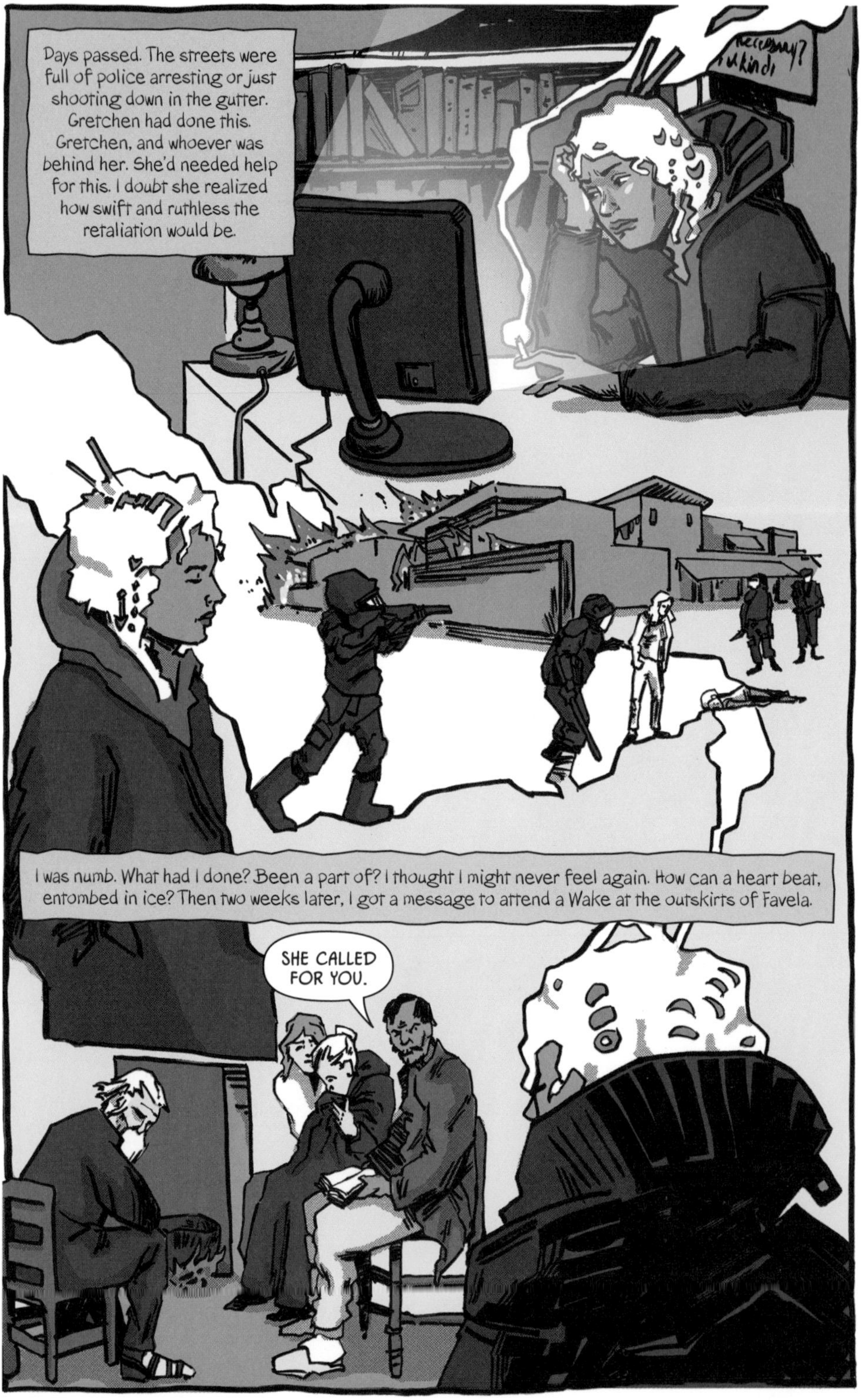
Days passed. The streets were full of police arresting or just shooting down in the gutter. Gretchen had done this. Gretchen, and whoever was behind her. She'd needed help for this. I doubt she realized how swift and ruthless the retaliation would be.
I was numb. What had I done? Been a part of? I thought I might never feel again. How can a heart beat, entombed in ice? Then two weeks later, I got a message to attend a Wake at the outskirts of Favela.
SHE CALLED FOR YOU.

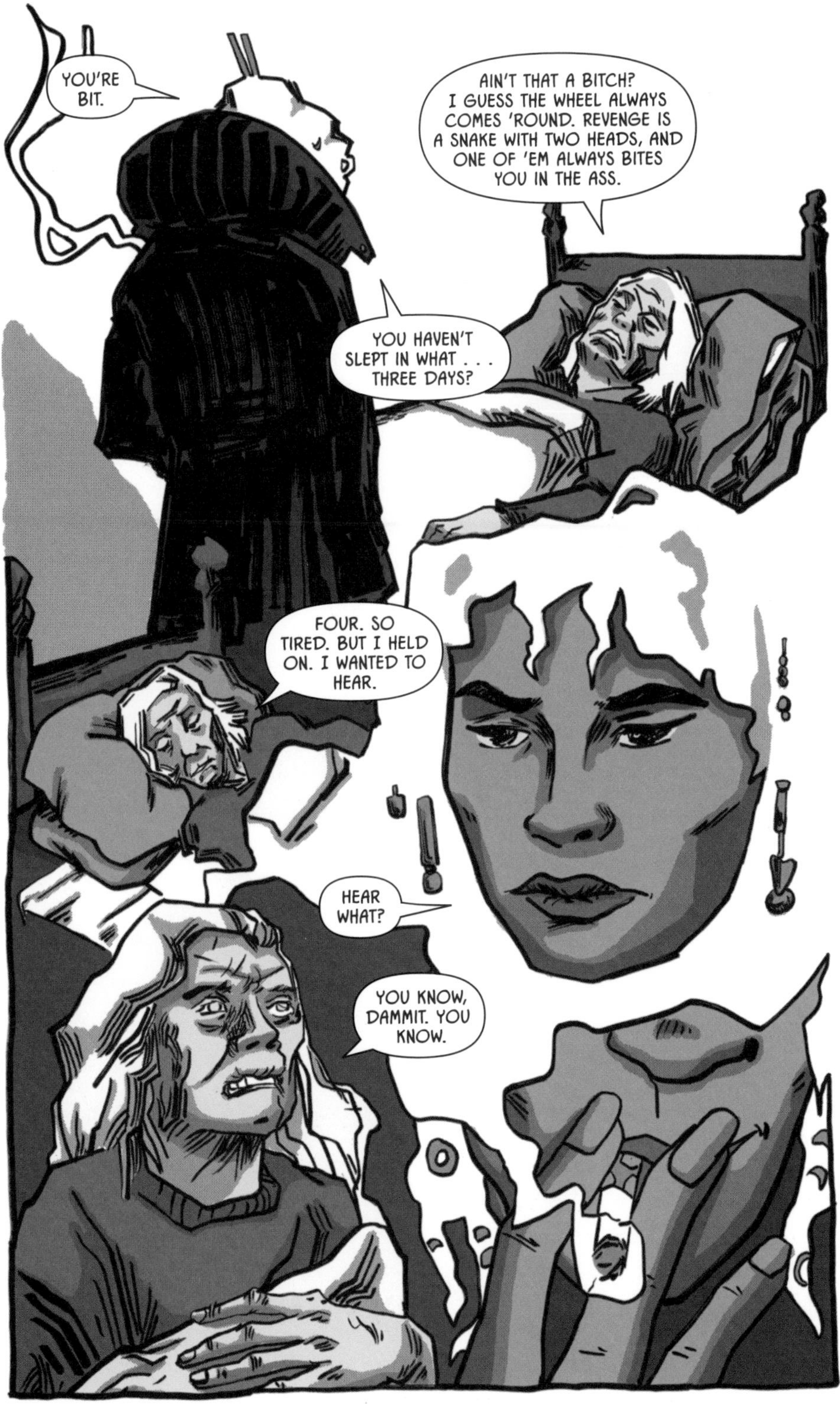
YOU'RE BIT.
AIN'T THAT A BITCH? I GUESS THE WHEEL ALWAYS COMES 'ROUND. REVENGE IS A SNAKE WITH TWO HEADS, AND ONE OF 'EM ALWAYS BITES YOU IN THE ASS.
YOU HAVEN'T SLEPT IN WHAT . . . THREE DAYS?
FOUR. SO TIRED. BUT I HELD ON. I WANTED TO HEAR.
HEAR WHAT?
YOU KNOW, DAMMIT. YOU KNOW.

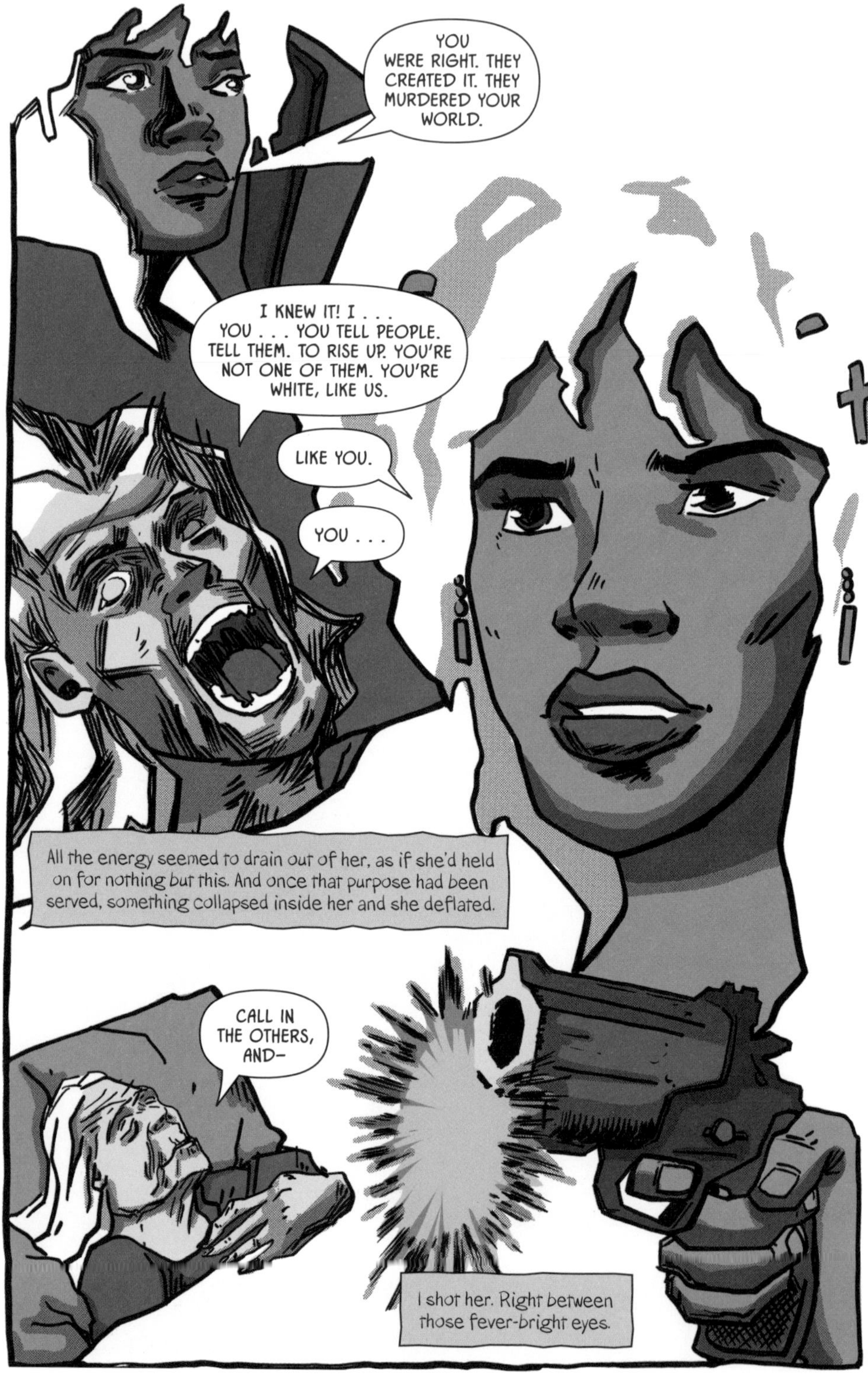
YOU WERE RIGHT. THEY CREATED IT. THEY MURDERED YOUR WORLD.
I KNEW IT! I . . . YOU . . . YOU TELL PEOPLE. TELL THEM. TO RISE UP. YOU'RE NOT ONE OF THEM. YOU'RE WHITE, LIKE US.
LIKE YOU.
YOU . . .
All the energy seemed to drain out of her, as if she'd held on for nothing but this. And once that purpose had been served, something collapsed inside her and she deflated.
CALL IN THE OTHERS, AND–
I shot her. Right between those fever-bright eyes.

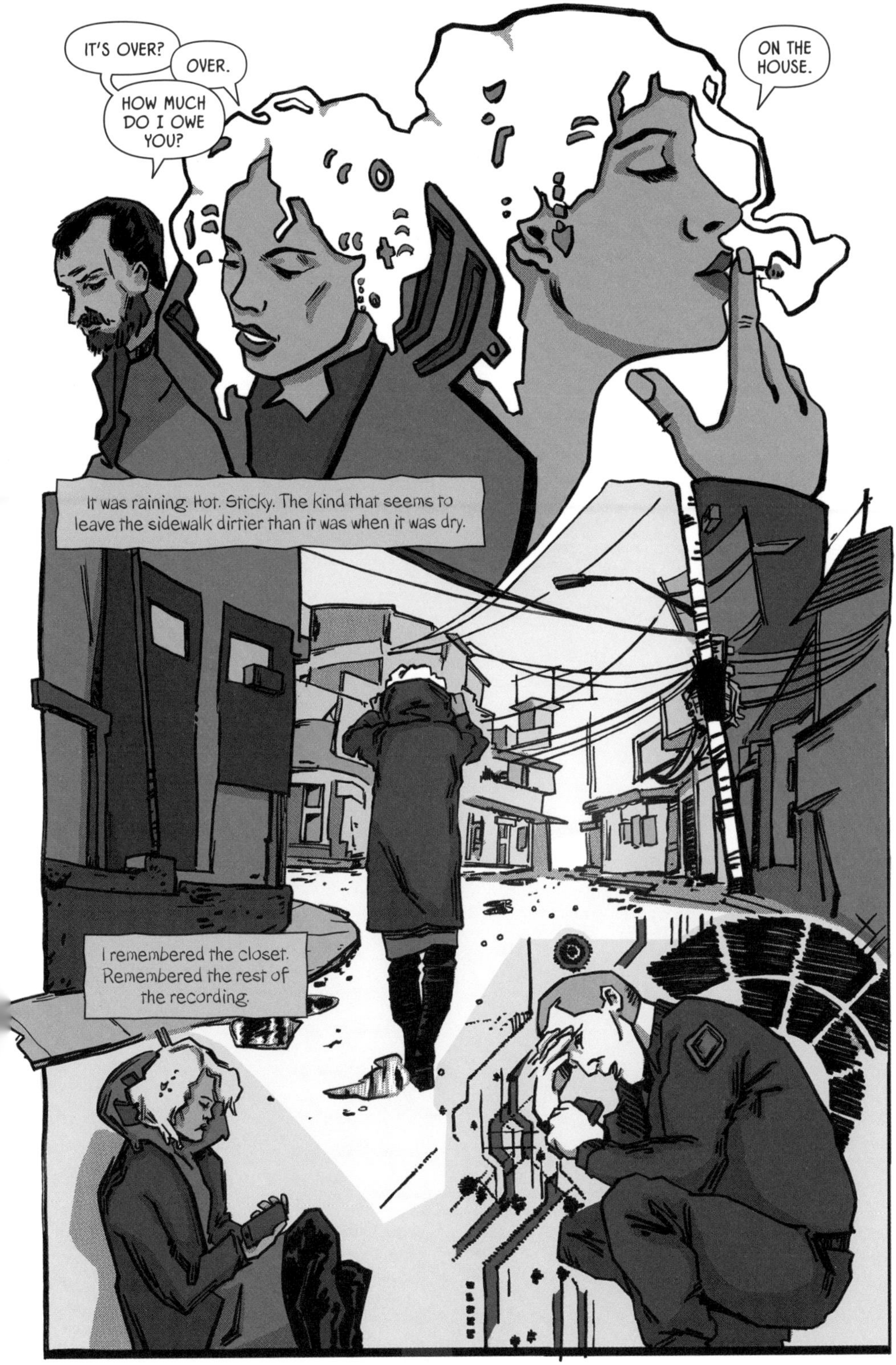
IT'S OVER?
OVER.
HOW MUCH DO I OWE YOU?
ON THE HOUSE.
It was raining. Hot. Sticky. The kind that seems to leave the sidewalk dirtier than it was when it was dry.
I remembered the closet. Remembered the rest of the recording.

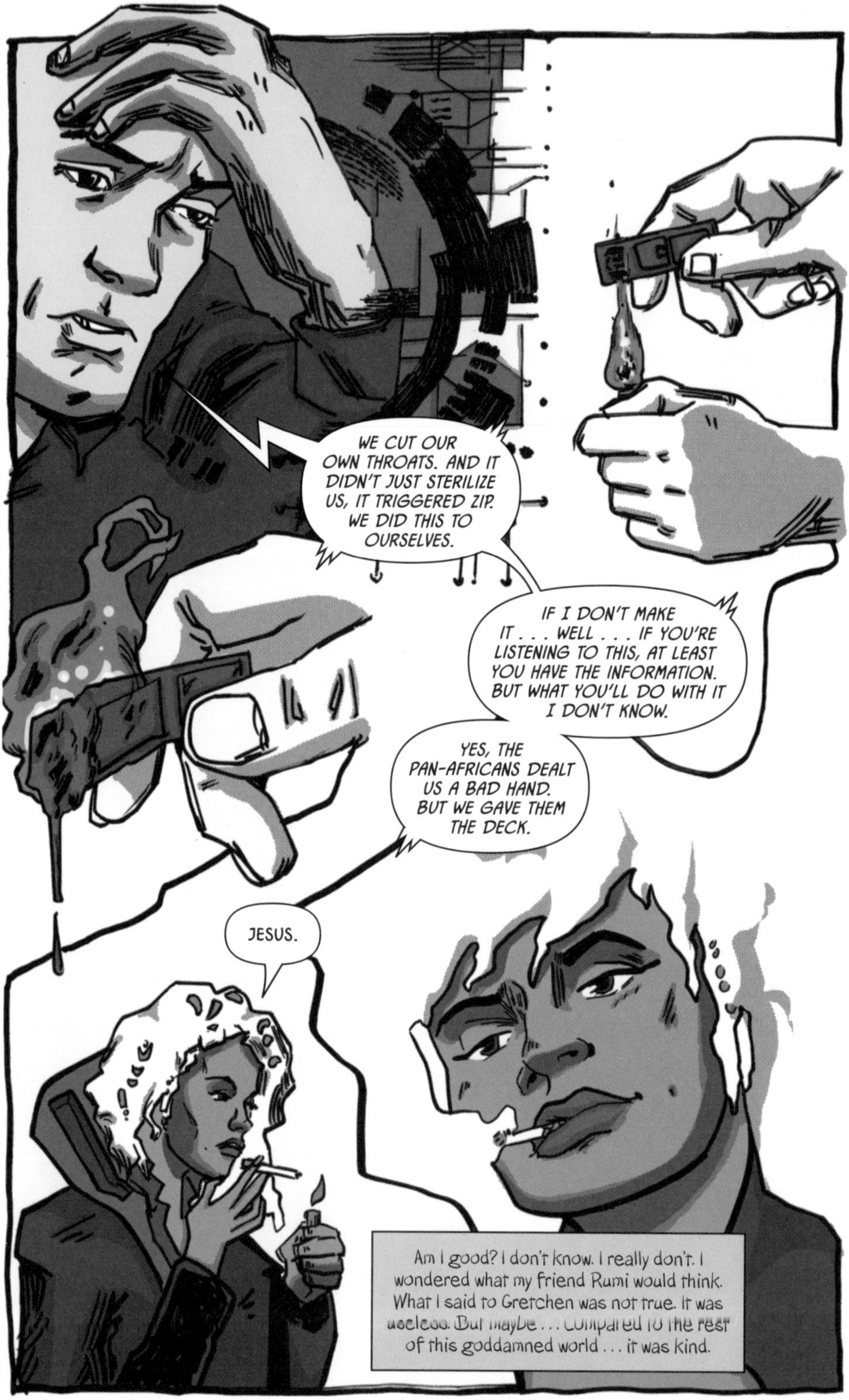
WE CUT OUR OWN THROATS. AND IT DIDN'T JUST STERILIZE US, IT TRIGGERED ZIP. WE DID THIS TO OURSELVES.
IF I DON'T MAKE IT . . . WELL . . . IF YOU'RE LISTENING TO THIS, AT LEAST YOU HAVE THE INFORMATION. BUT WHAT YOU'LL DO WITH IT I DON'T KNOW.
YES, THE PAN-AFRICANS DEALT US A BAD HAND. BUT WE GAVE THEM THE DECK.
JESUS.
Am I good? I don't know. I really don't. I wondered what my friend Rumi would think. What I said to Gretchen was not true. It was useless. But maybe . . . compared to the rest of this goddamned world . . . it was kind.

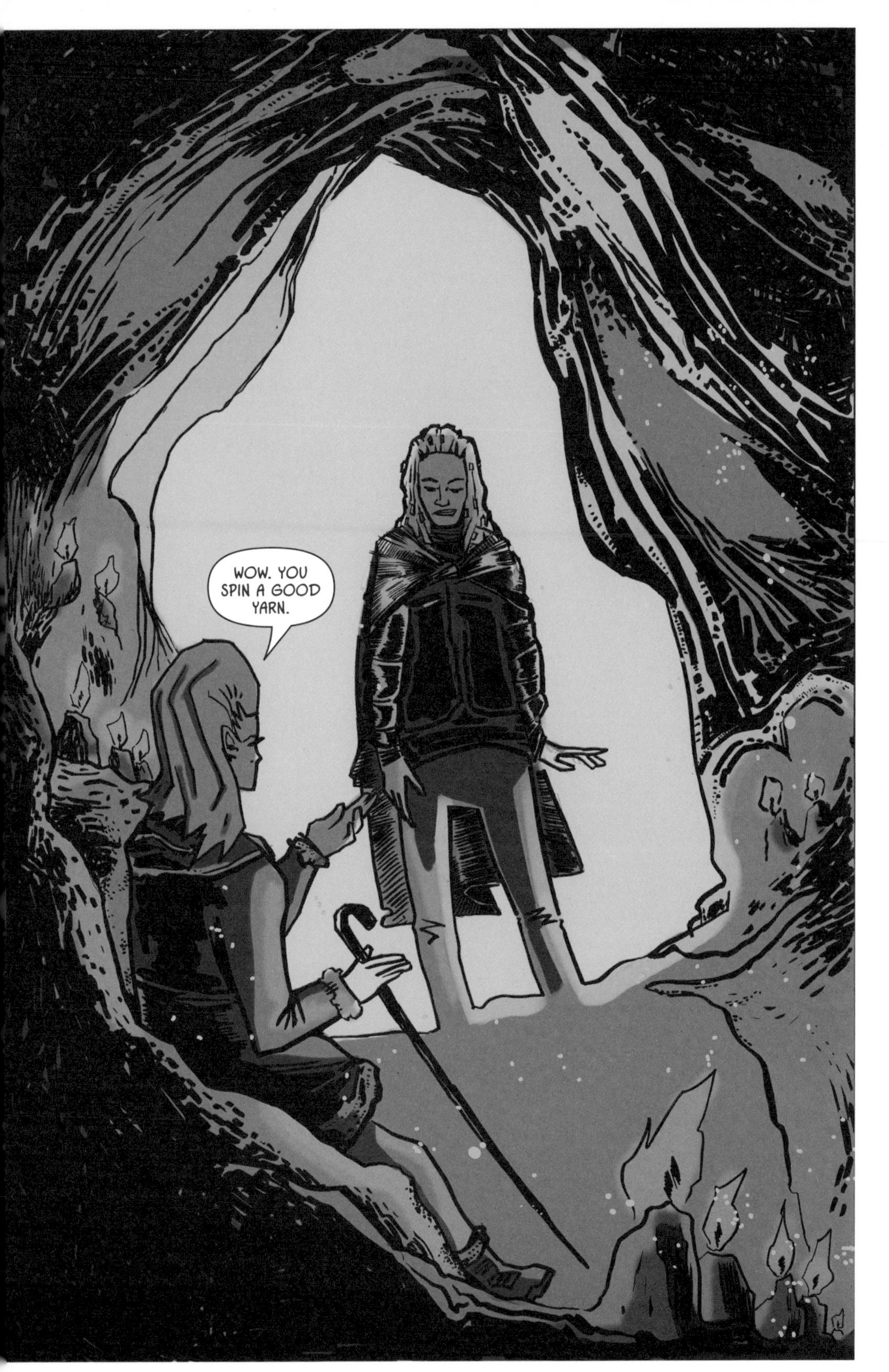
WOW. YOU SPIN A GOOD YARN.

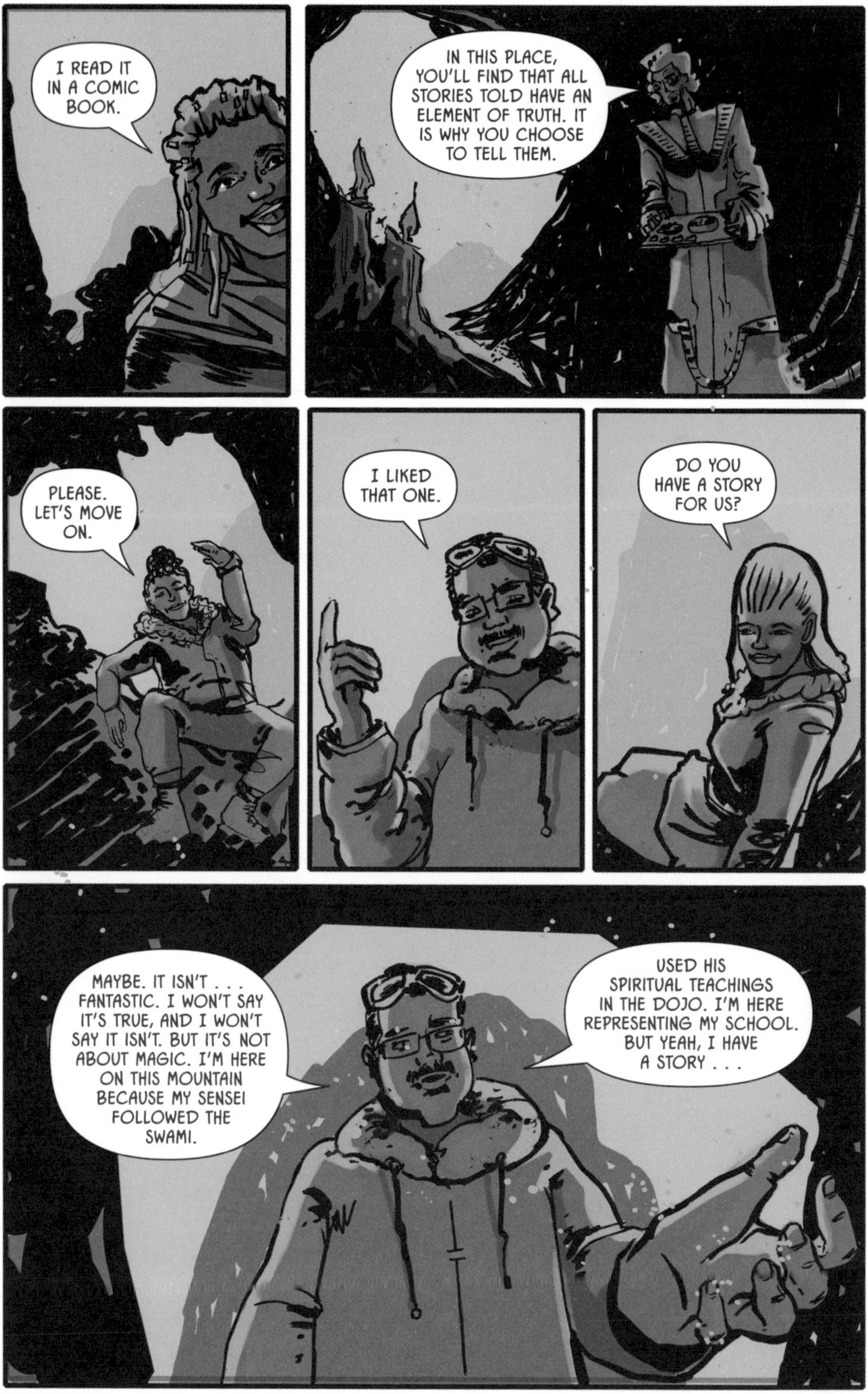
I READ IT IN A COMIC BOOK.
IN THIS PLACE, YOU'LL FIND THAT ALL STORIES TOLD HAVE AN ELEMENT OF TRUTH. IT IS WHY YOU CHOOSE TO TELL THEM.
PLEASE. LET'S MOVE ON.
I LIKED THAT ONE.
DO YOU HAVE A STORY FOR US?
MAYBE. IT ISN'T . . . FANTASTIC. I WON'T SAY IT'S TRUE, AND I WON'T SAY IT ISN'T. BUT IT'S NOT ABOUT MAGIC. I'M HERE ON THIS MOUNTAIN BECAUSE MY SENSEI FOLLOWED THE SWAMI.
USED HIS SPIRITUAL TEACHINGS IN THE DOJO. I'M HERE REPRESENTING MY SCHOOL. BUT YEAH, I HAVE A STORY . . .

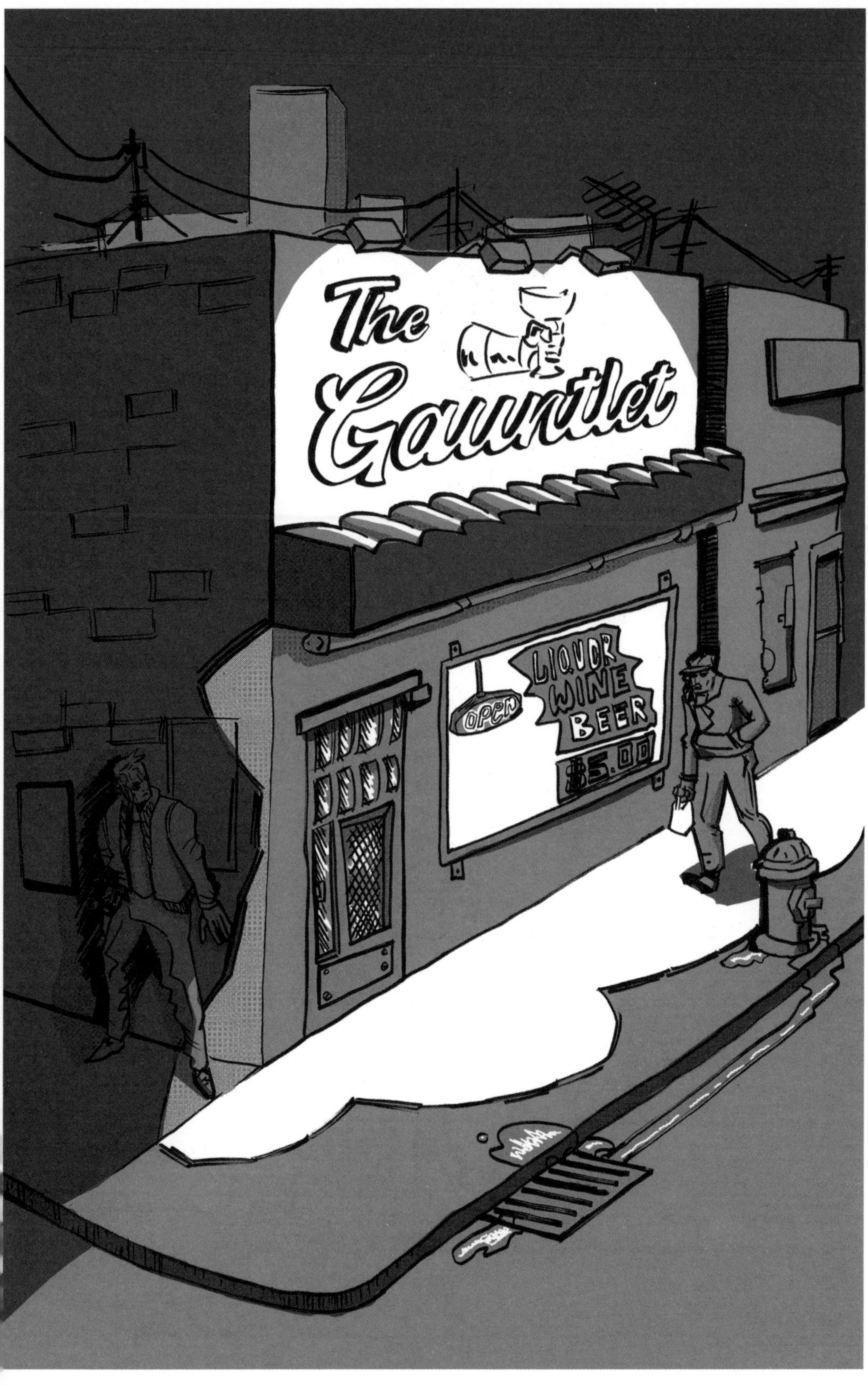
The Gauntlet
OPEN
LIQUOR
WINE
BEER
$5.00

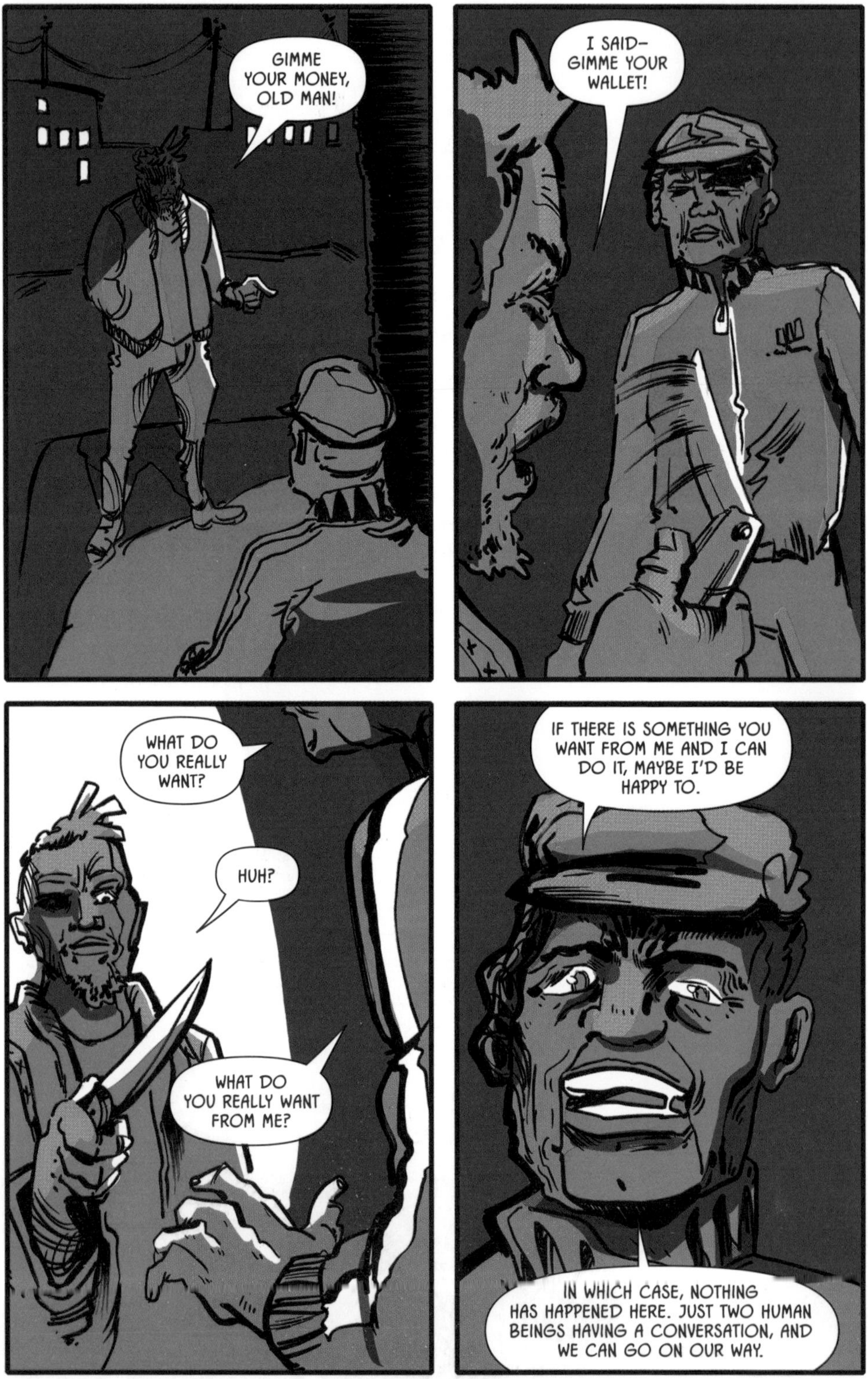
GIMME YOUR MONEY, OLD MAN!
I SAID— GIMME YOUR WALLET!
WHAT DO YOU REALLY WANT?
HUH?
WHAT DO YOU REALLY WANT FROM ME?
IF THERE IS SOMETHING YOU WANT FROM ME AND I CAN DO IT, MAYBE I'D BE HAPPY TO.
IN WHICH CASE, NOTHING HAS HAPPENED HERE. JUST TWO HUMAN BEINGS HAVING A CONVERSATION, AND WE CAN GO ON OUR WAY.

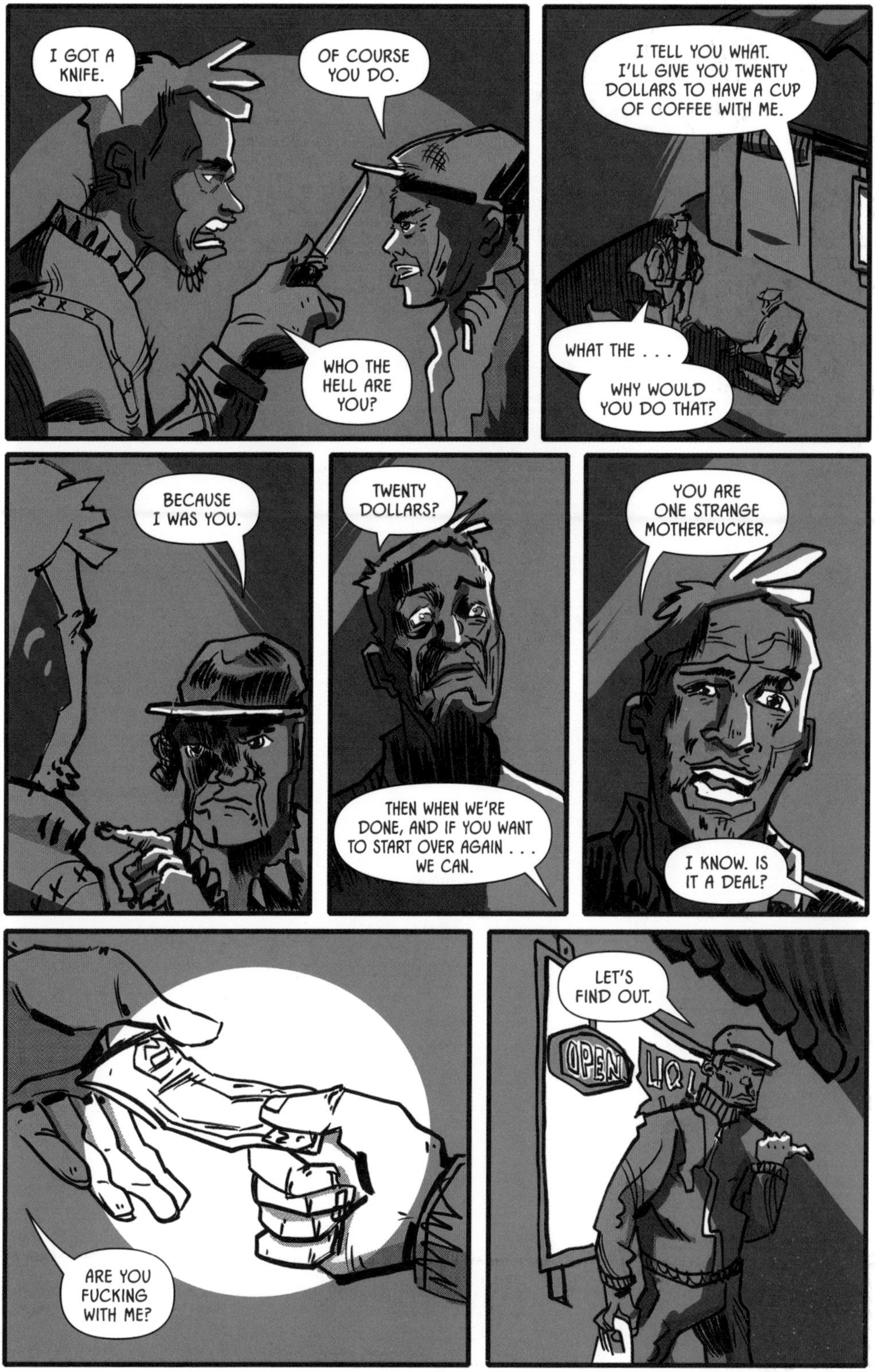
I GOT A KNIFE.
OF COURSE YOU DO.
WHO THE HELL ARE YOU?
I TELL YOU WHAT. I'LL GIVE YOU TWENTY DOLLARS TO HAVE A CUP OF COFFEE WITH ME.
WHAT THE . . .
WHY WOULD YOU DO THAT?
BECAUSE I WAS YOU.
TWENTY DOLLARS?
THEN WHEN WE'RE DONE, AND IF YOU WANT TO START OVER AGAIN . . . WE CAN.
YOU ARE ONE STRANGE MOTHERFUCKER.
I KNOW. IS IT A DEAL?
ARE YOU FUCKING WITH ME?
LET'S FIND OUT.
OPEN
LIQ

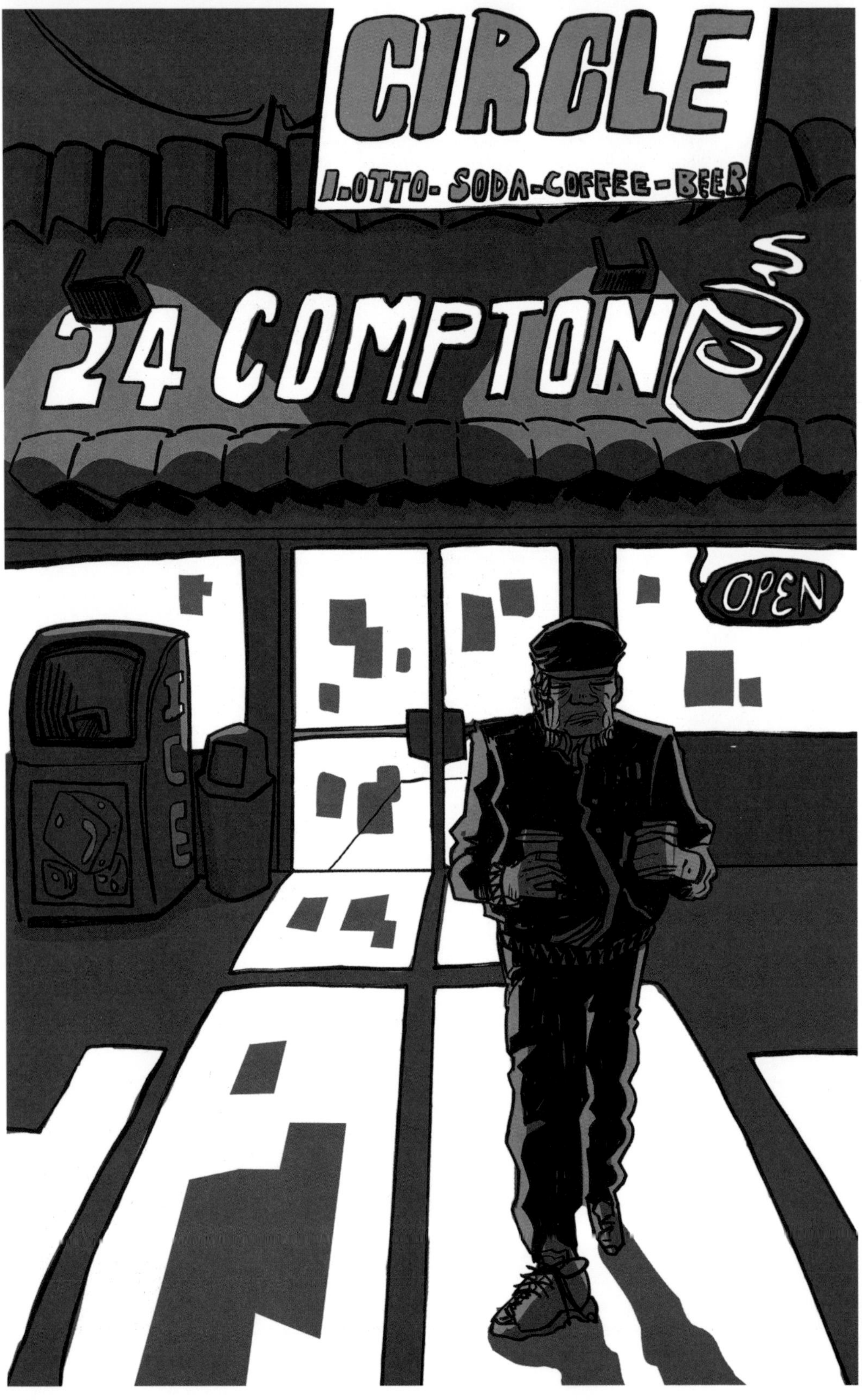
CIRCLE
LOTTO-SODA-COFFEE-BEER
24 COMPTON
OPEN
ICE

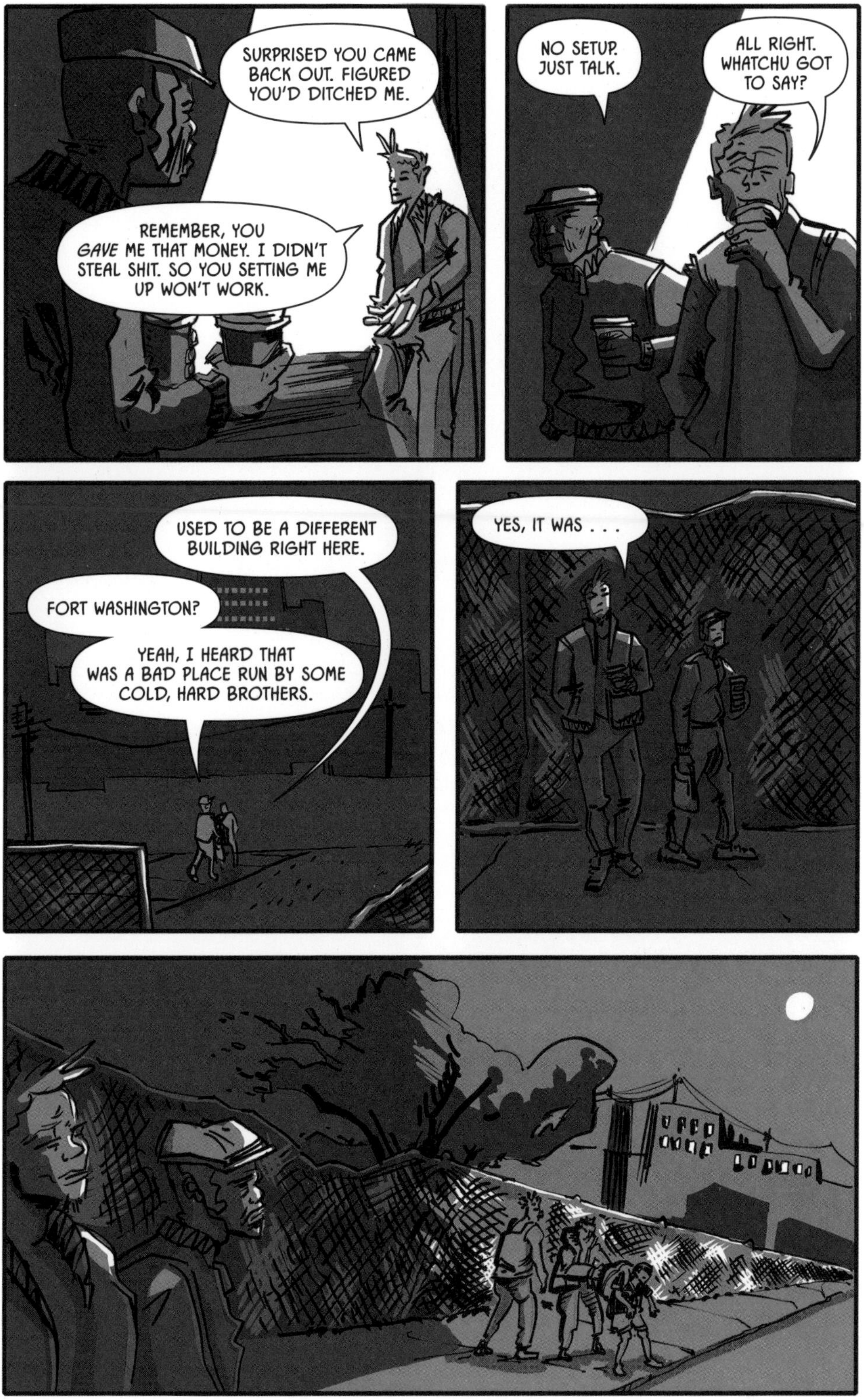
SURPRISED YOU CAME BACK OUT. FIGURED YOU'D DITCHED ME.
REMEMBER, YOU *GAVE* ME THAT MONEY. I DIDN'T STEAL SHIT. SO YOU SETTING ME UP WON'T WORK.
NO SETUP. JUST TALK.
ALL RIGHT. WHATCHU GOT TO SAY?
USED TO BE A DIFFERENT BUILDING RIGHT HERE.
FORT WASHINGTON?
YEAH, I HEARD THAT WAS A BAD PLACE RUN BY SOME COLD, HARD BROTHERS.
YES, IT WAS . . .

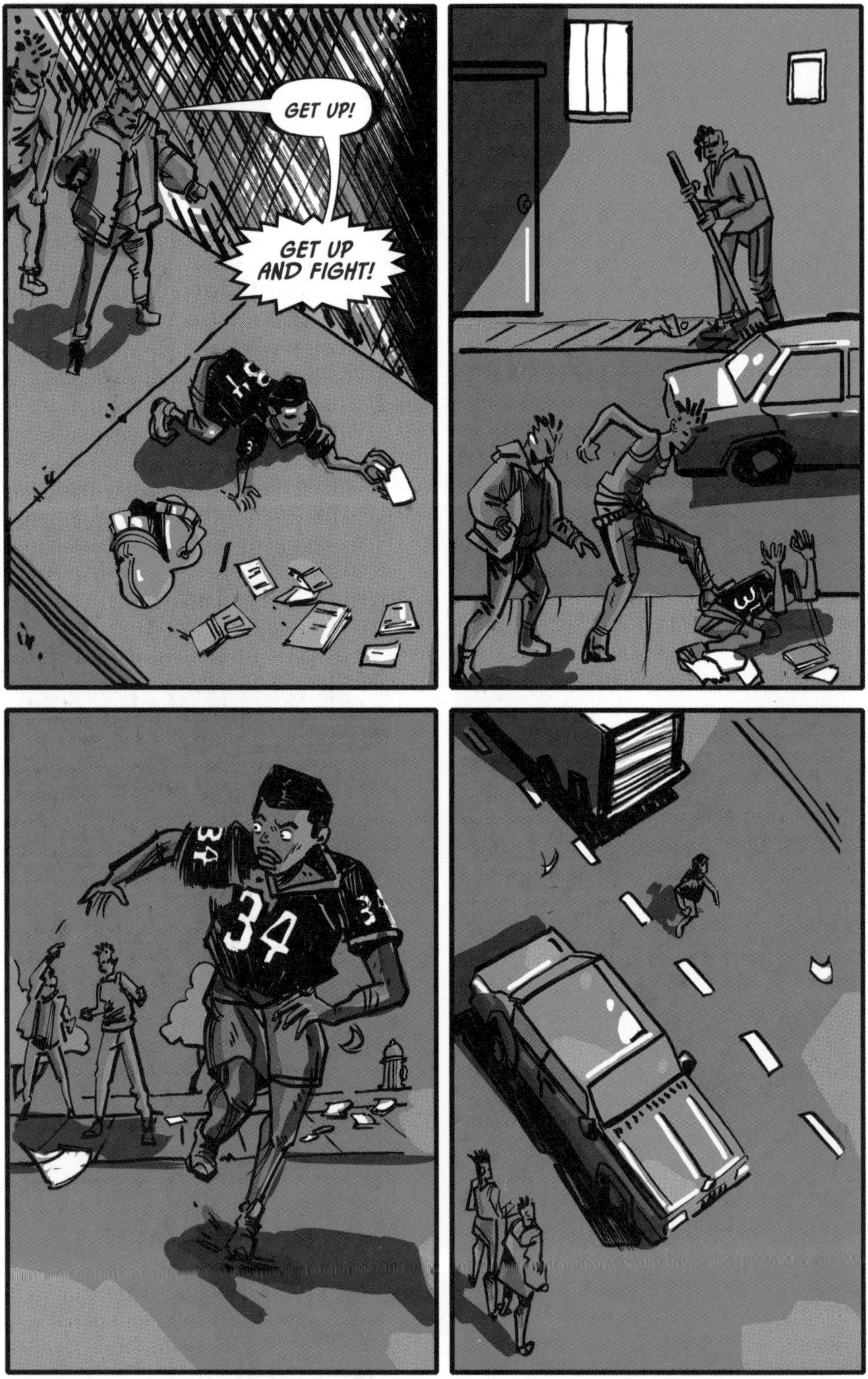
GET UP!
GET UP AND FIGHT!

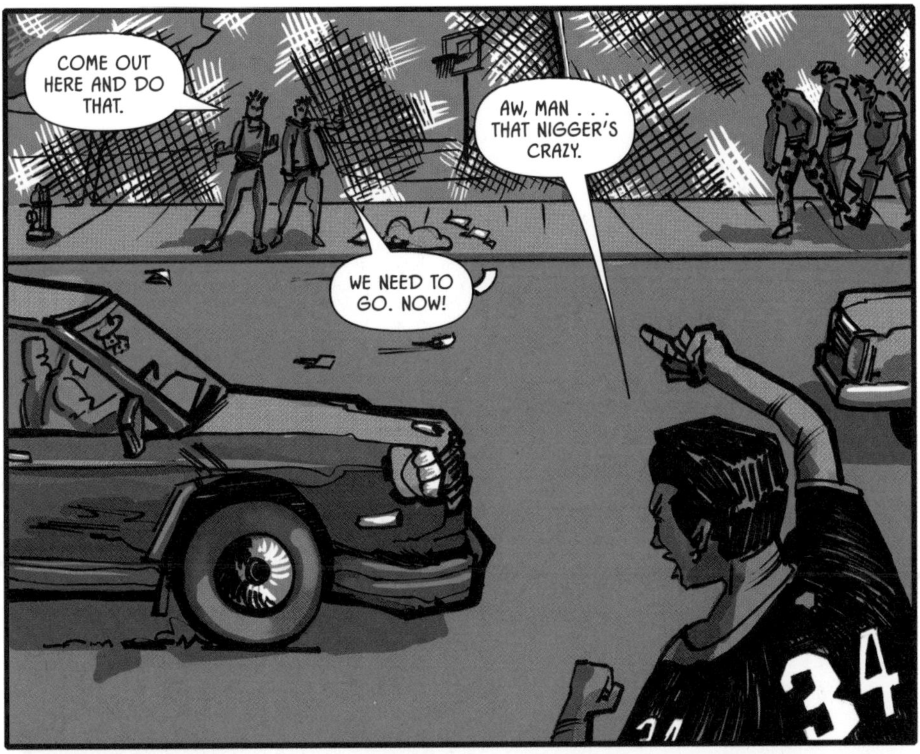
COME OUT HERE AND DO THAT.
AW, MAN . . . THAT NIGGER'S CRAZY.
WE NEED TO GO. NOW!
34

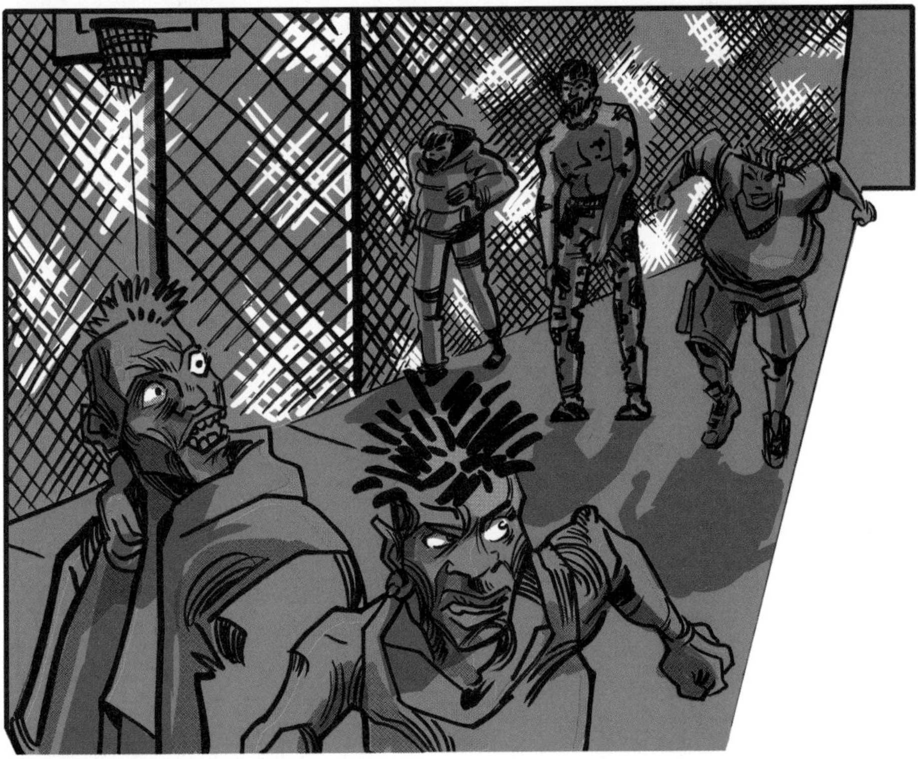

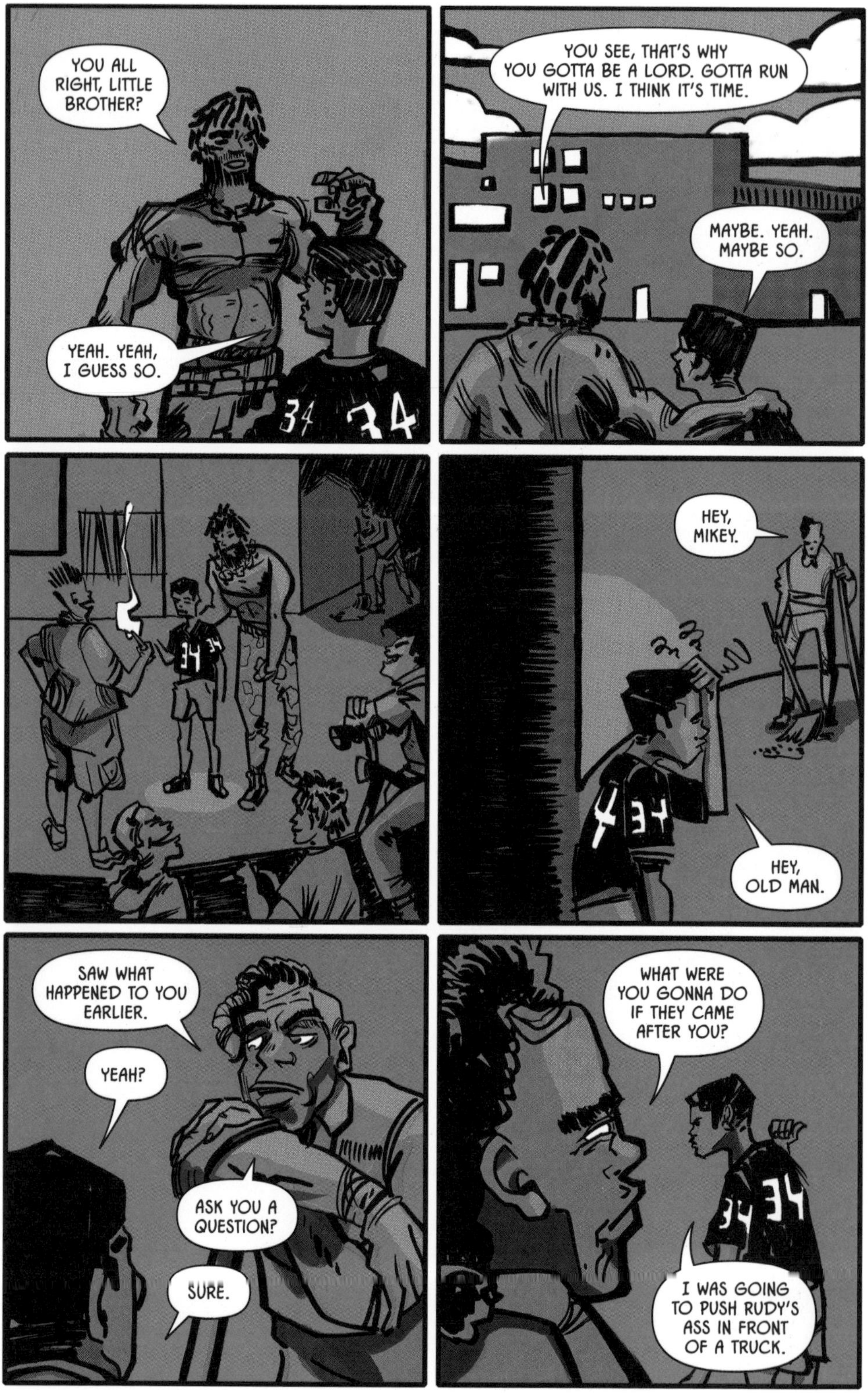
YOU ALL RIGHT, LITTLE BROTHER?
YEAH. YEAH, I GUESS SO.
YOU SEE, THAT'S WHY YOU GOTTA BE A LORD. GOTTA RUN WITH US. I THINK IT'S TIME.
MAYBE. YEAH. MAYBE SO.
34
HEY, MIKEY.
HEY, OLD MAN.
SAW WHAT HAPPENED TO YOU EARLIER.
YEAH?
ASK YOU A QUESTION?
SURE.
WHAT WERE YOU GONNA DO IF THEY CAME AFTER YOU?
I WAS GOING TO PUSH RUDY'S ASS IN FRONT OF A TRUCK.

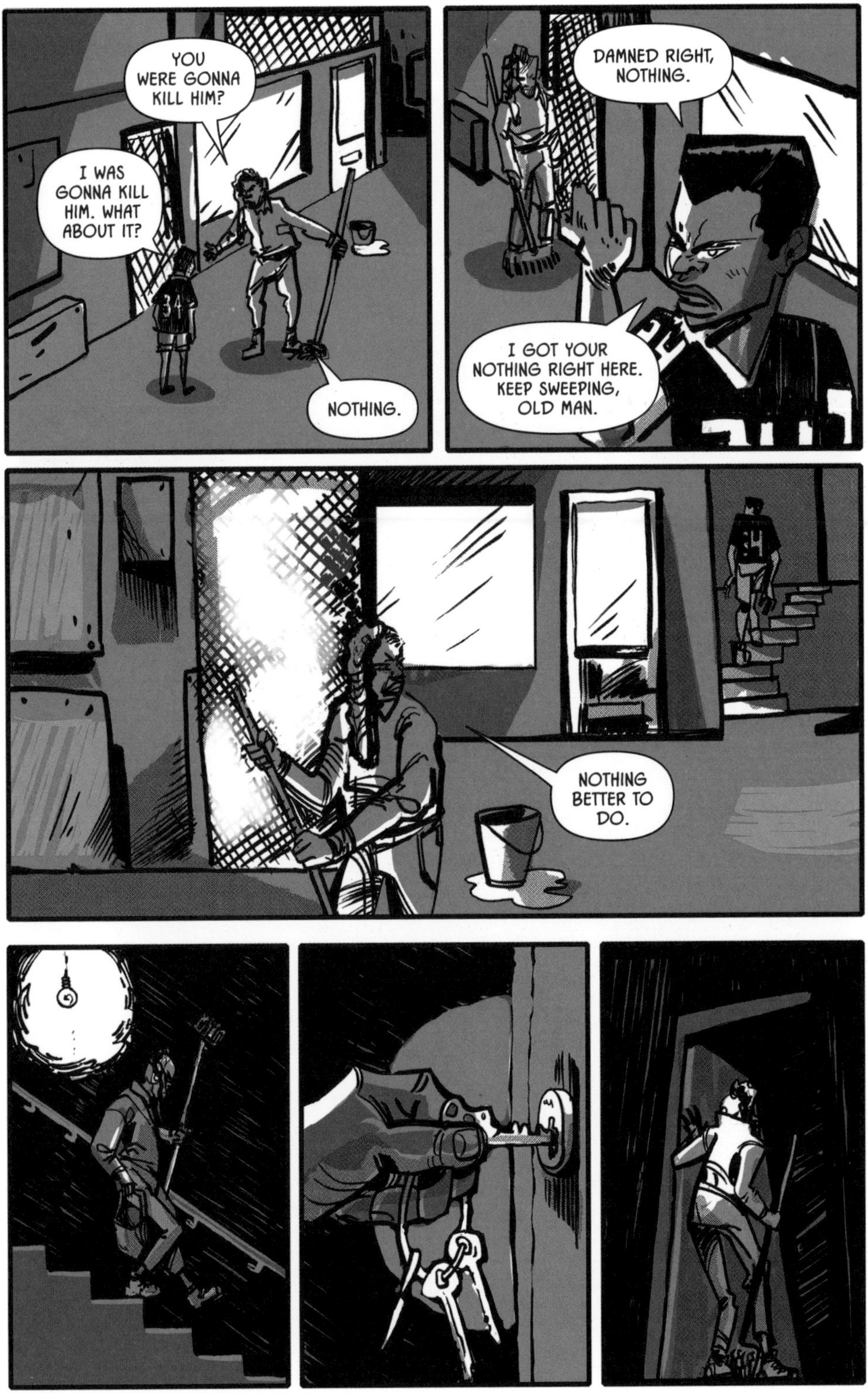
YOU WERE GONNA KILL HIM?
I WAS GONNA KILL HIM. WHAT ABOUT IT?
NOTHING.
DAMNED RIGHT, NOTHING.
I GOT YOUR NOTHING RIGHT HERE. KEEP SWEEPING, OLD MAN.
NOTHING BETTER TO DO.

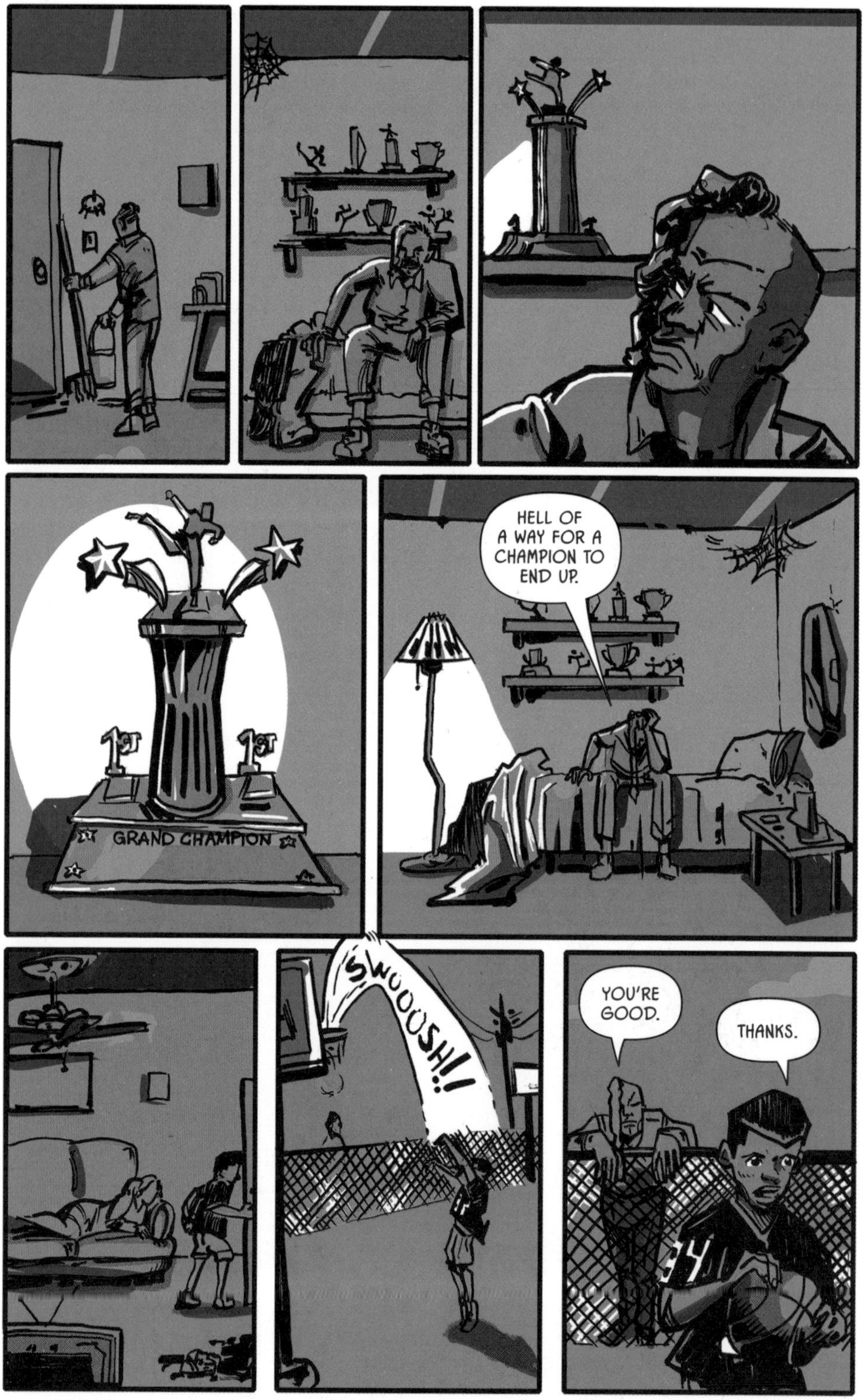
HELL OF A WAY FOR A CHAMPION TO END UP.
GRAND CHAMPION
SWOOOSH!!
YOU'RE GOOD.
THANKS.

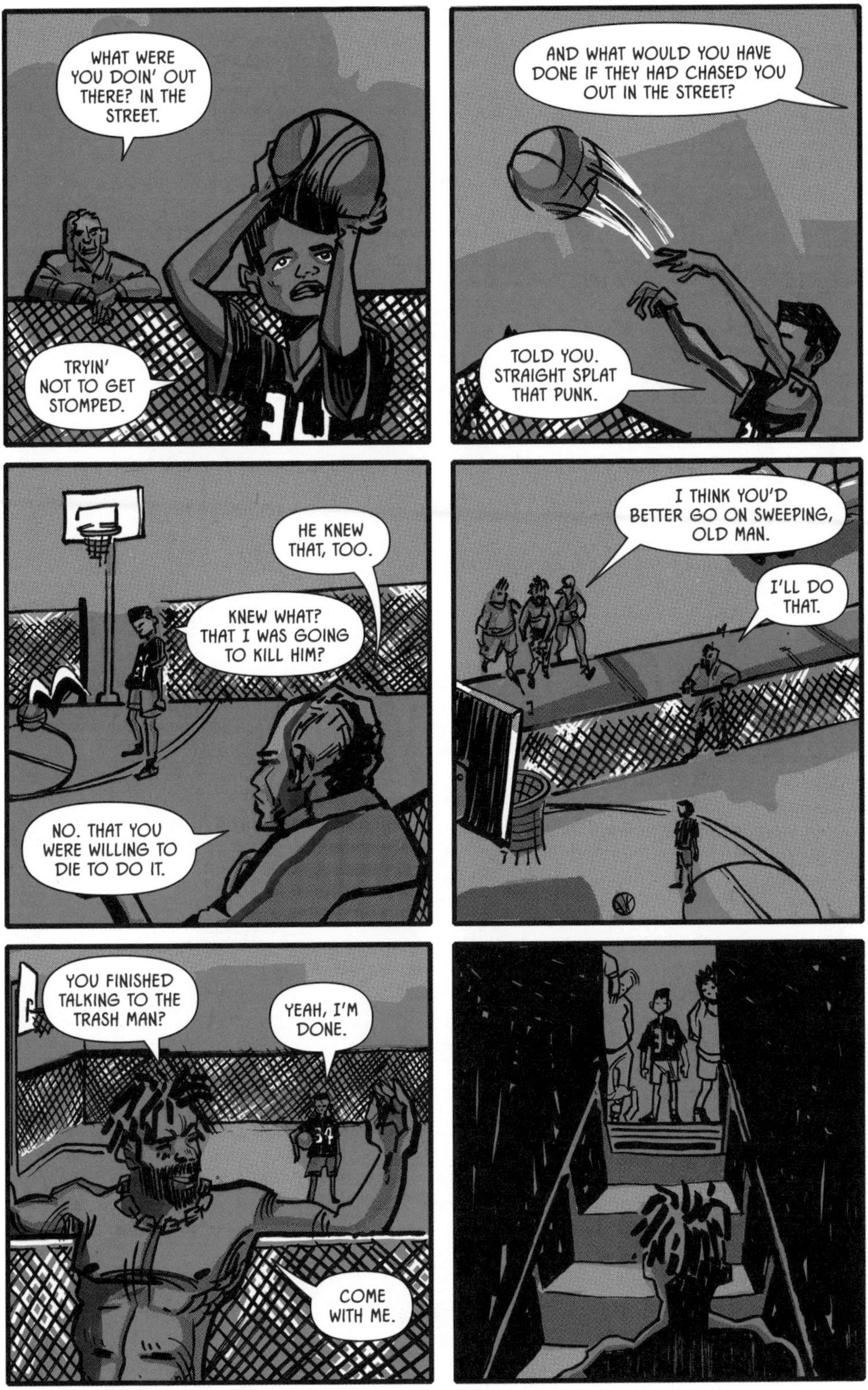
WHAT WERE YOU DOIN' OUT THERE? IN THE STREET.
TRYIN' NOT TO GET STOMPED.
AND WHAT WOULD YOU HAVE DONE IF THEY HAD CHASED YOU OUT IN THE STREET?
TOLD YOU. STRAIGHT SPLAT THAT PUNK.
HE KNEW THAT, TOO.
KNEW WHAT? THAT I WAS GOING TO KILL HIM?
NO. THAT YOU WERE WILLING TO DIE TO DO IT.
I THINK YOU'D BETTER GO ON SWEEPING, OLD MAN.
I'LL DO THAT.
YOU FINISHED TALKING TO THE TRASH MAN?
YEAH, I'M DONE.
COME WITH ME.

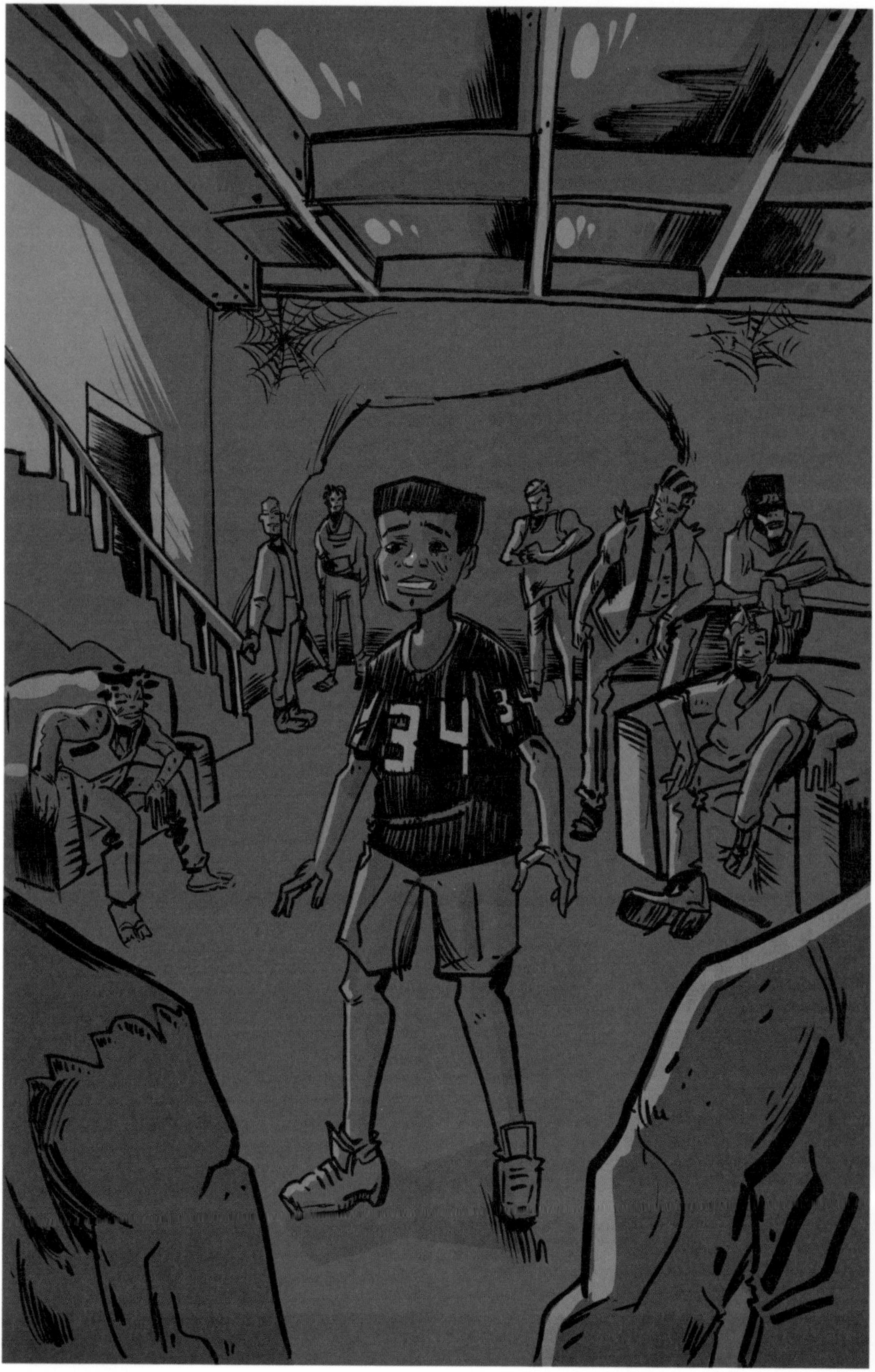

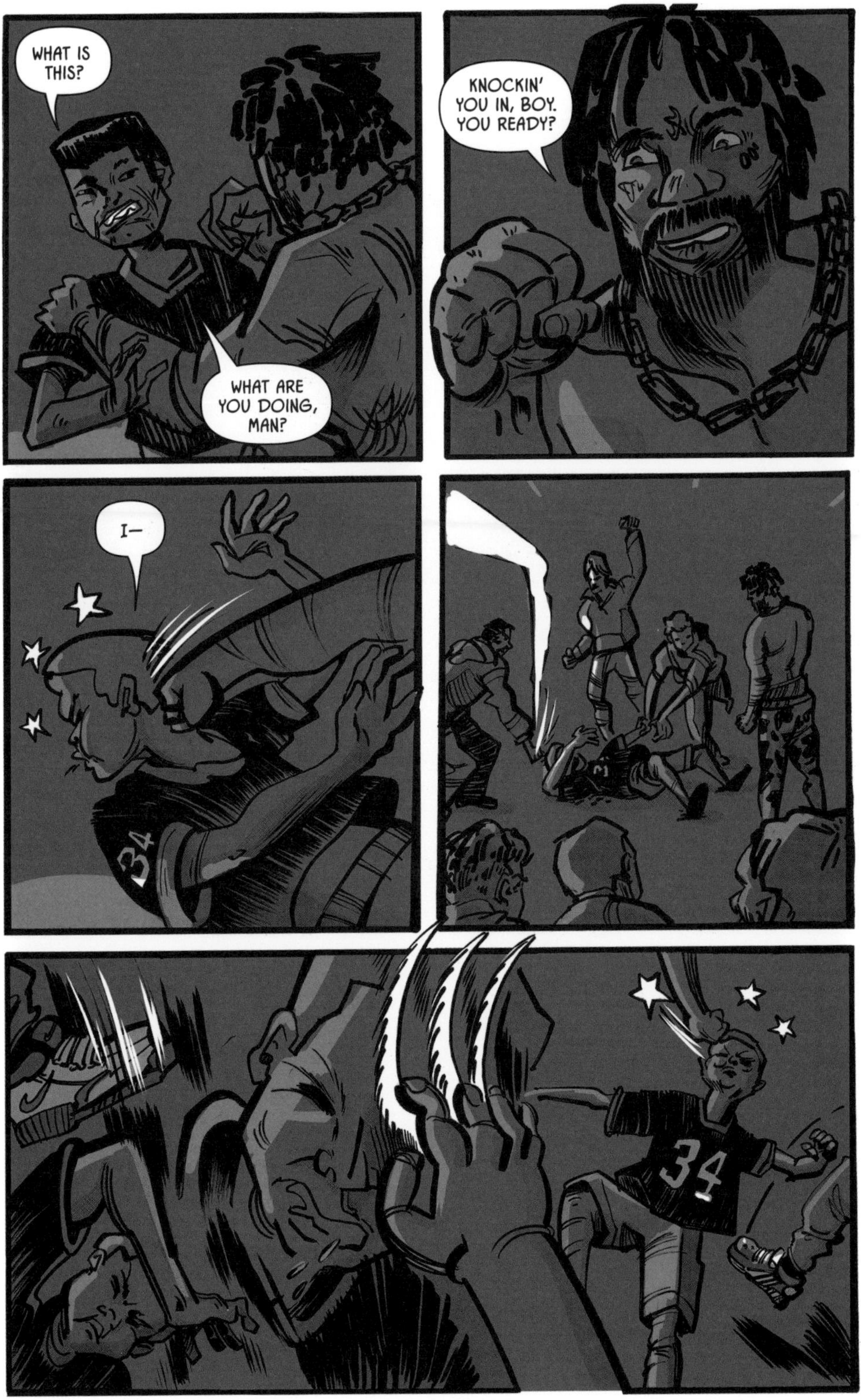
WHAT IS THIS?
WHAT ARE YOU DOING, MAN?
KNOCKIN' YOU IN, BOY. YOU READY?
I—
34
34

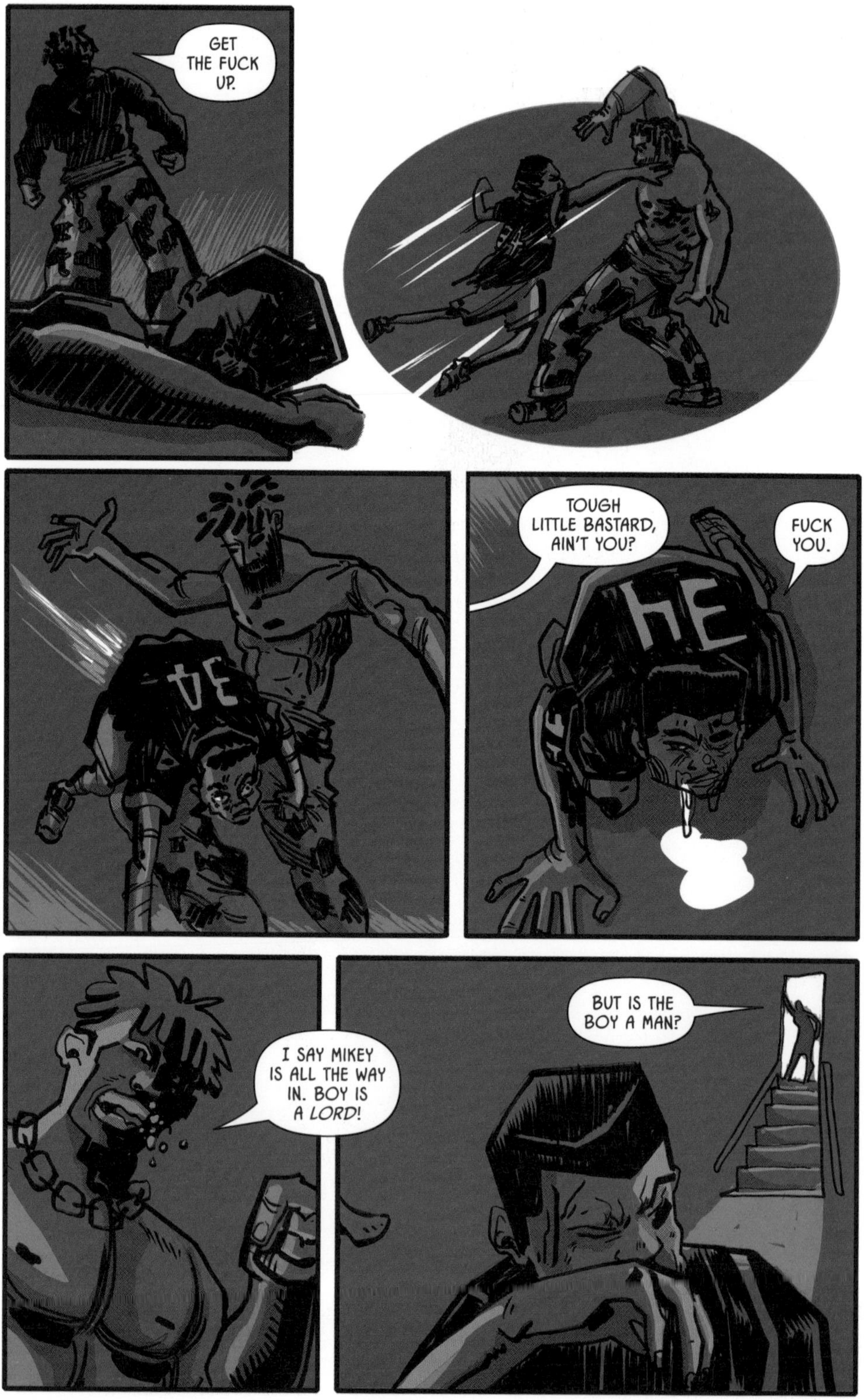
GET THE FUCK UP.
TOUGH LITTLE BASTARD, AIN'T YOU?
FUCK YOU.
I SAY MIKEY IS ALL THE WAY IN. BOY IS A *LORD*!
BUT IS THE BOY A MAN?

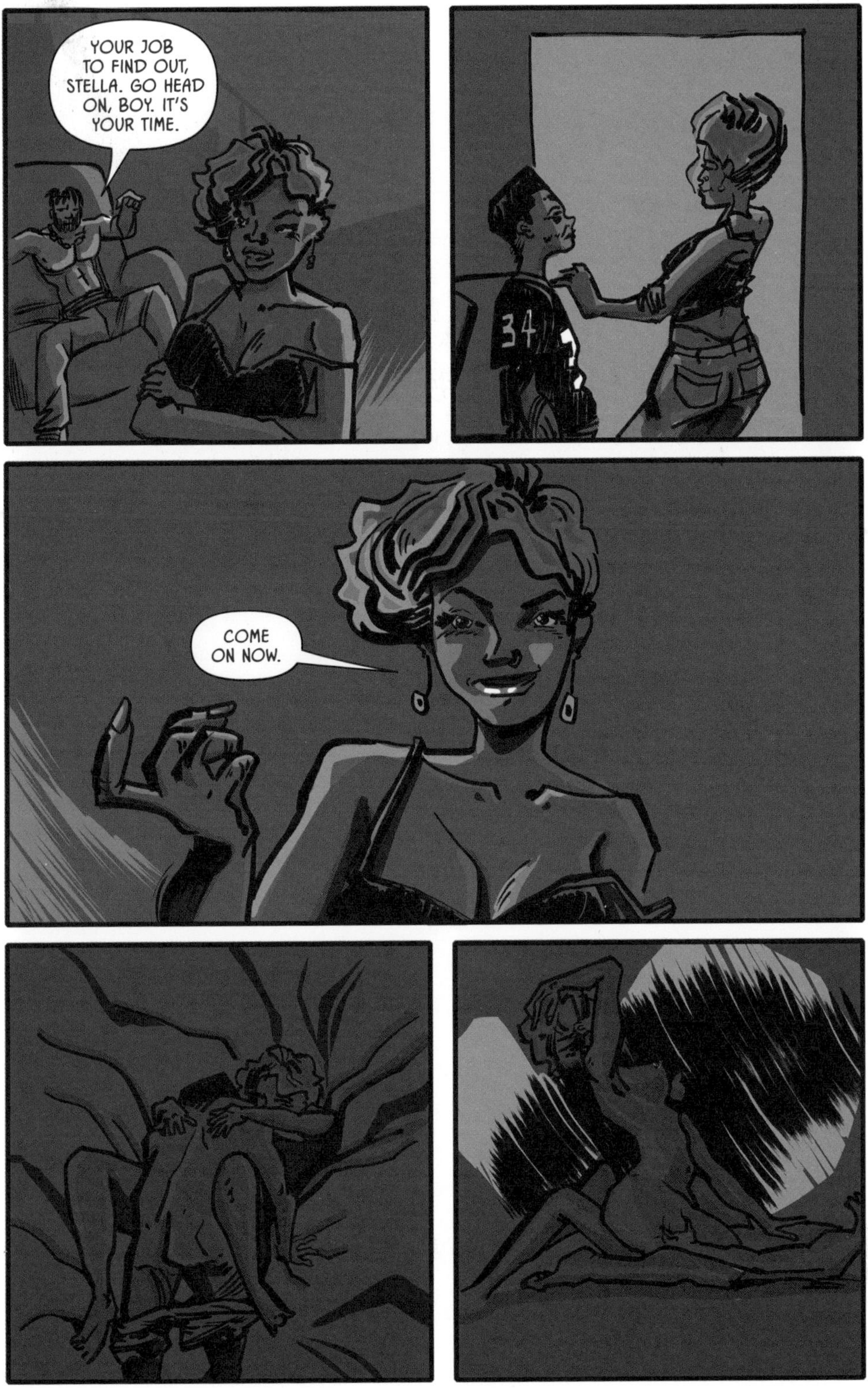
YOUR JOB TO FIND OUT, STELLA. GO HEAD ON, BOY. IT'S YOUR TIME.
COME ON NOW.

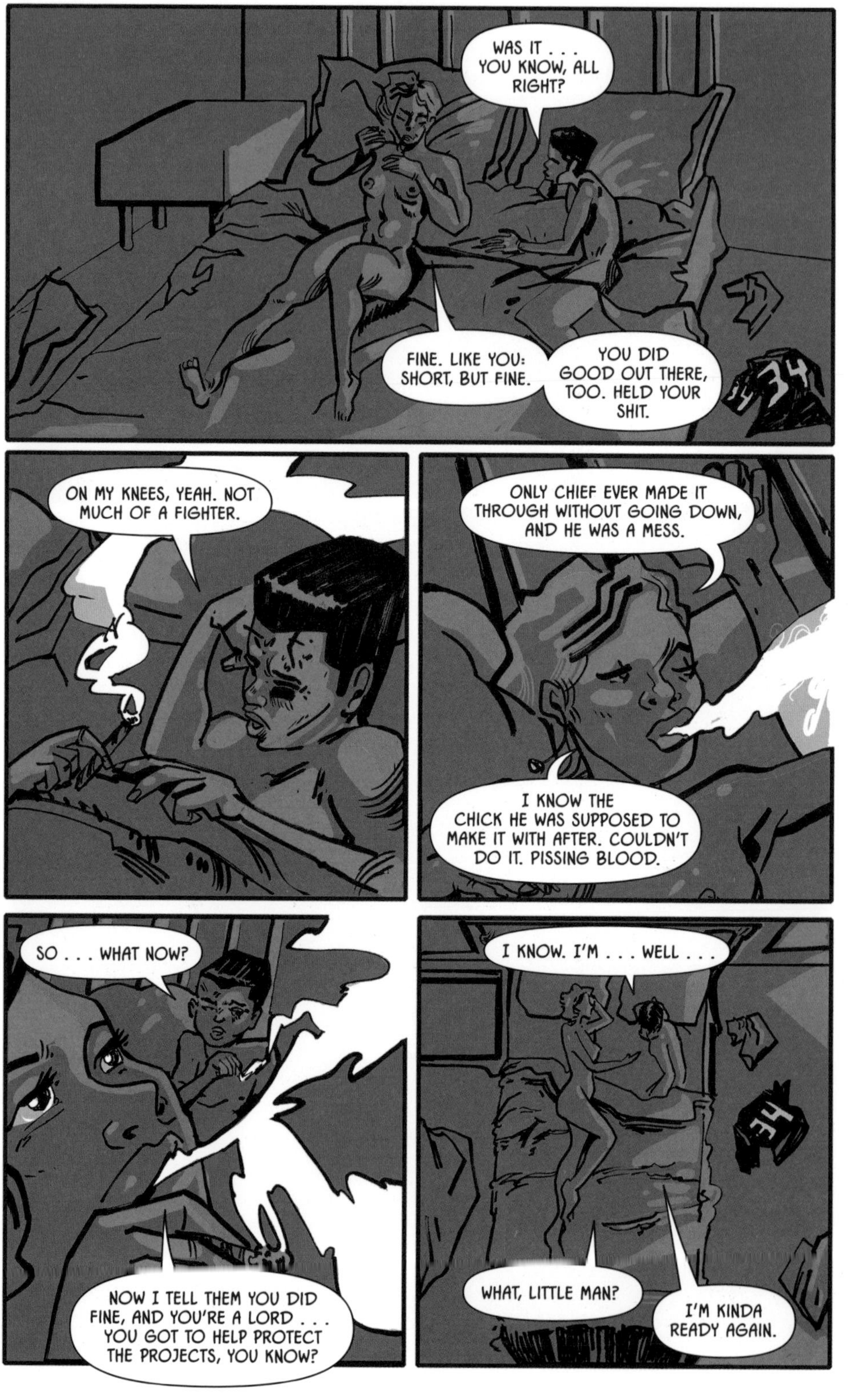
WAS IT . . . YOU KNOW, ALL RIGHT?
FINE. LIKE YOU: SHORT, BUT FINE.
YOU DID GOOD OUT THERE, TOO. HELD YOUR SHIT.
34
ON MY KNEES, YEAH. NOT MUCH OF A FIGHTER.
ONLY CHIEF EVER MADE IT THROUGH WITHOUT GOING DOWN, AND HE WAS A MESS.
I KNOW THE CHICK HE WAS SUPPOSED TO MAKE IT WITH AFTER. COULDN'T DO IT. PISSING BLOOD.
SO . . . WHAT NOW?
NOW I TELL THEM YOU DID FINE, AND YOU'RE A LORD . . . YOU GOT TO HELP PROTECT THE PROJECTS, YOU KNOW?
I KNOW. I'M . . . WELL . . .
WHAT, LITTLE MAN?
I'M KINDA READY AGAIN.

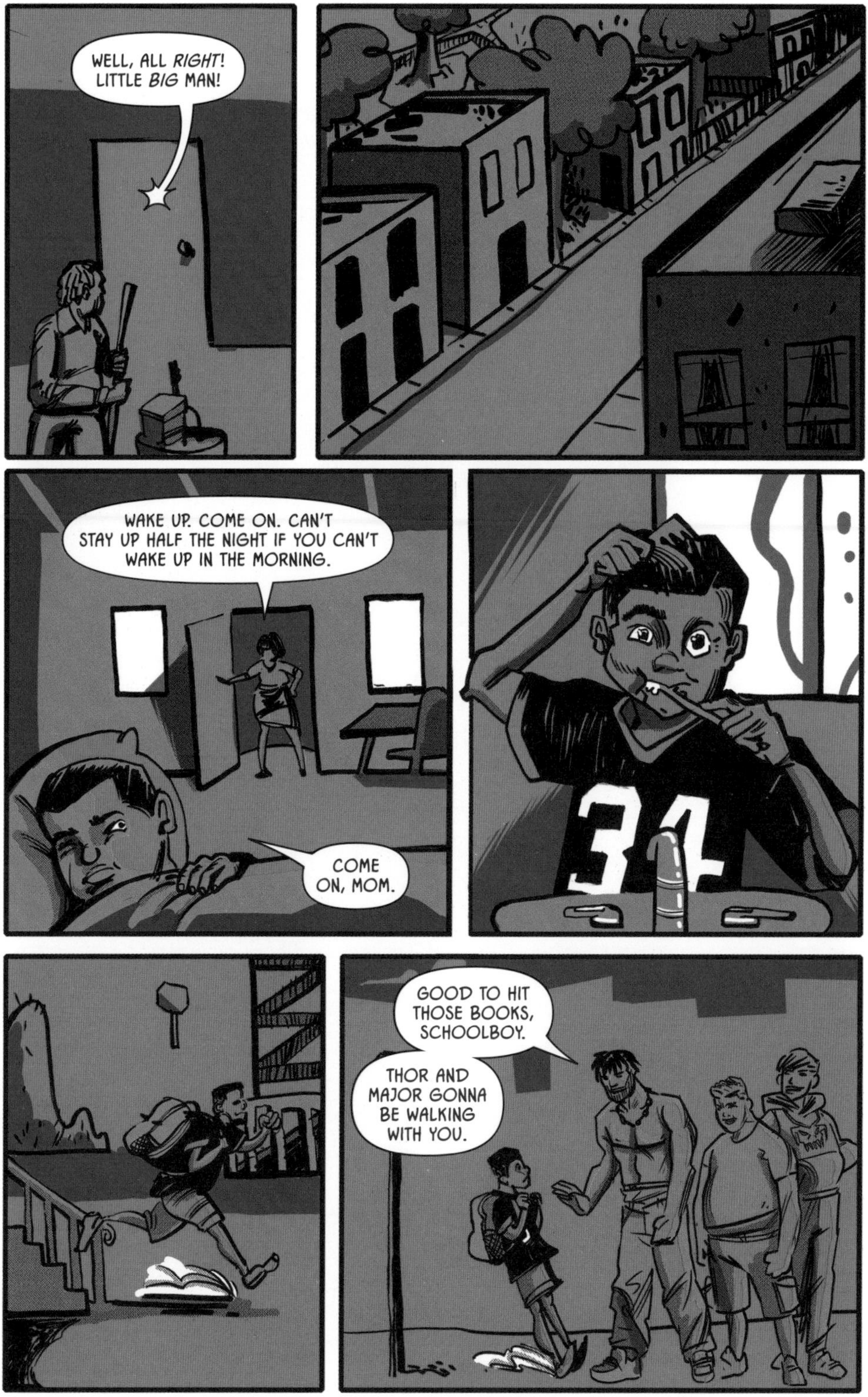
WELL, ALL *RIGHT*! LITTLE *BIG* MAN!
WAKE UP. COME ON. CAN'T STAY UP HALF THE NIGHT IF YOU CAN'T WAKE UP IN THE MORNING.
COME ON, MOM.
34
GOOD TO HIT THOSE BOOKS, SCHOOLBOY.
THOR AND MAJOR GONNA BE WALKING WITH YOU.

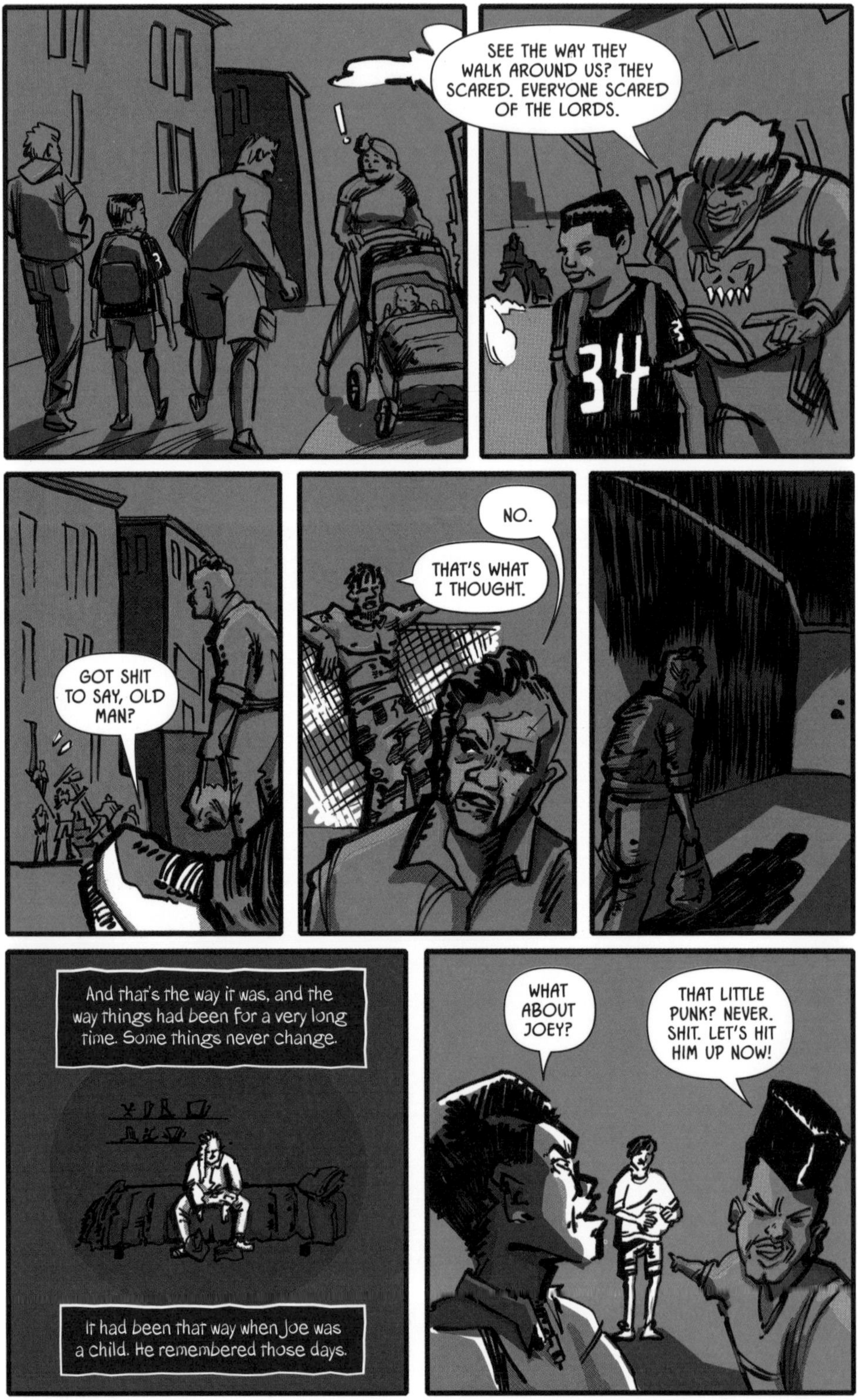
SEE THE WAY THEY WALK AROUND US? THEY SCARED. EVERYONE SCARED OF THE LORDS.
GOT SHIT TO SAY, OLD MAN?
NO.
THAT'S WHAT I THOUGHT.
And that's the way it was, and the way things had been for a very long time. Some things never change.
It had been that way when Joe was a child. He remembered those days.
WHAT ABOUT JOEY?
THAT LITTLE PUNK? NEVER. SHIT. LET'S HIT HIM UP NOW!

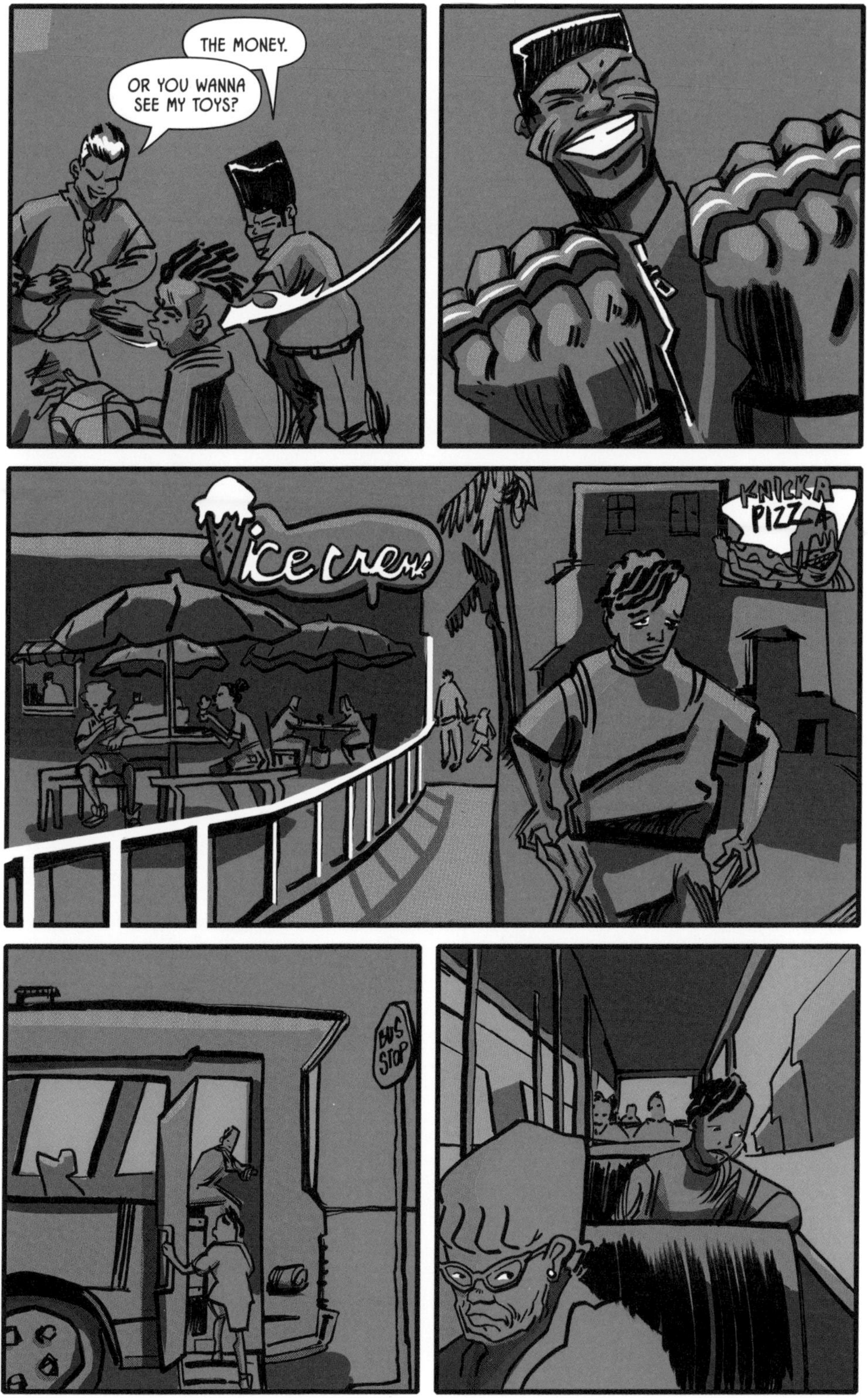
THE MONEY.
OR YOU WANNA SEE MY TOYS?
BUS STOP

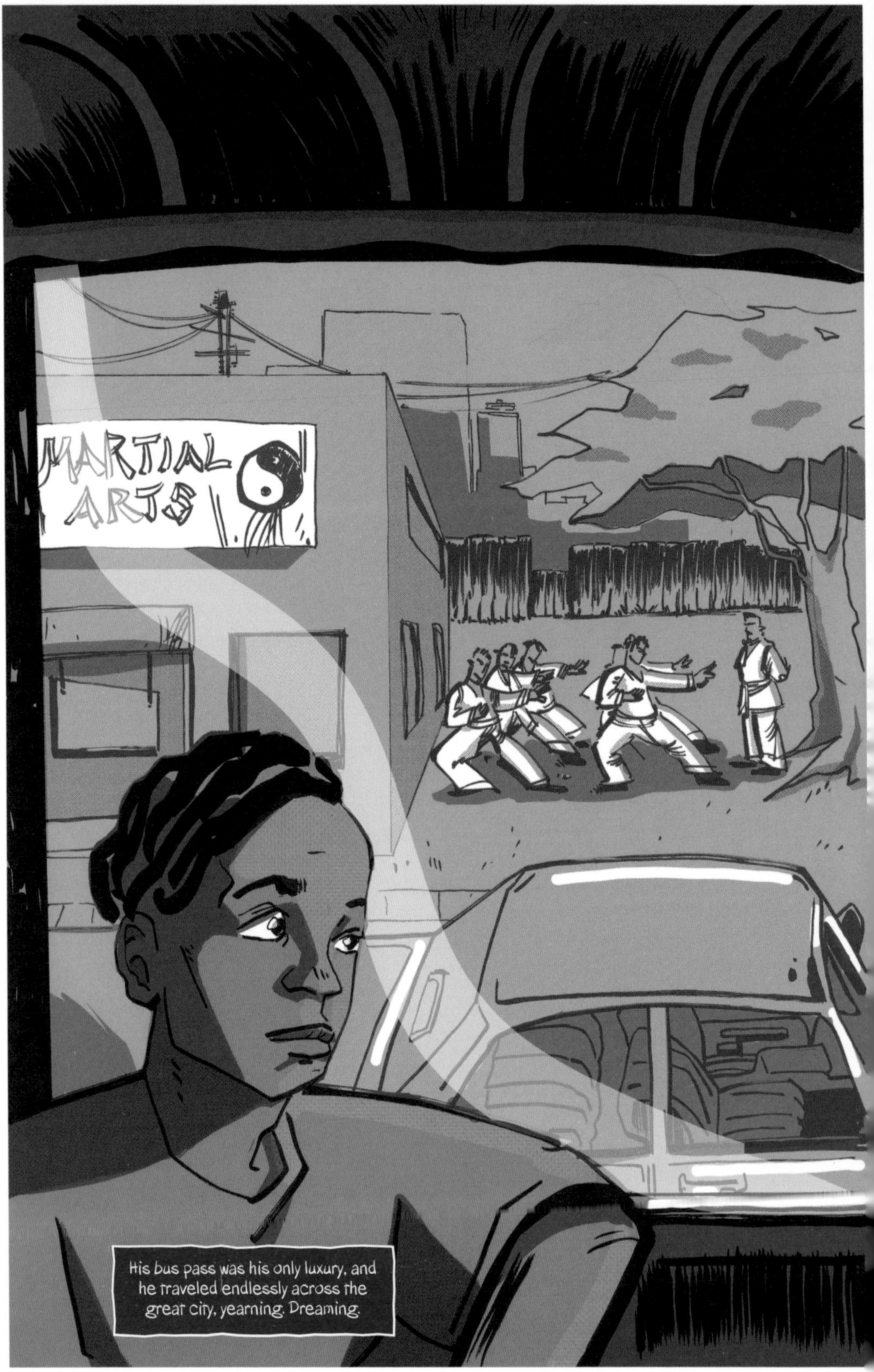
MARTIAL ARTS
His bus pass was his only luxury, and he traveled endlessly across the great city, yearning. Dreaming.

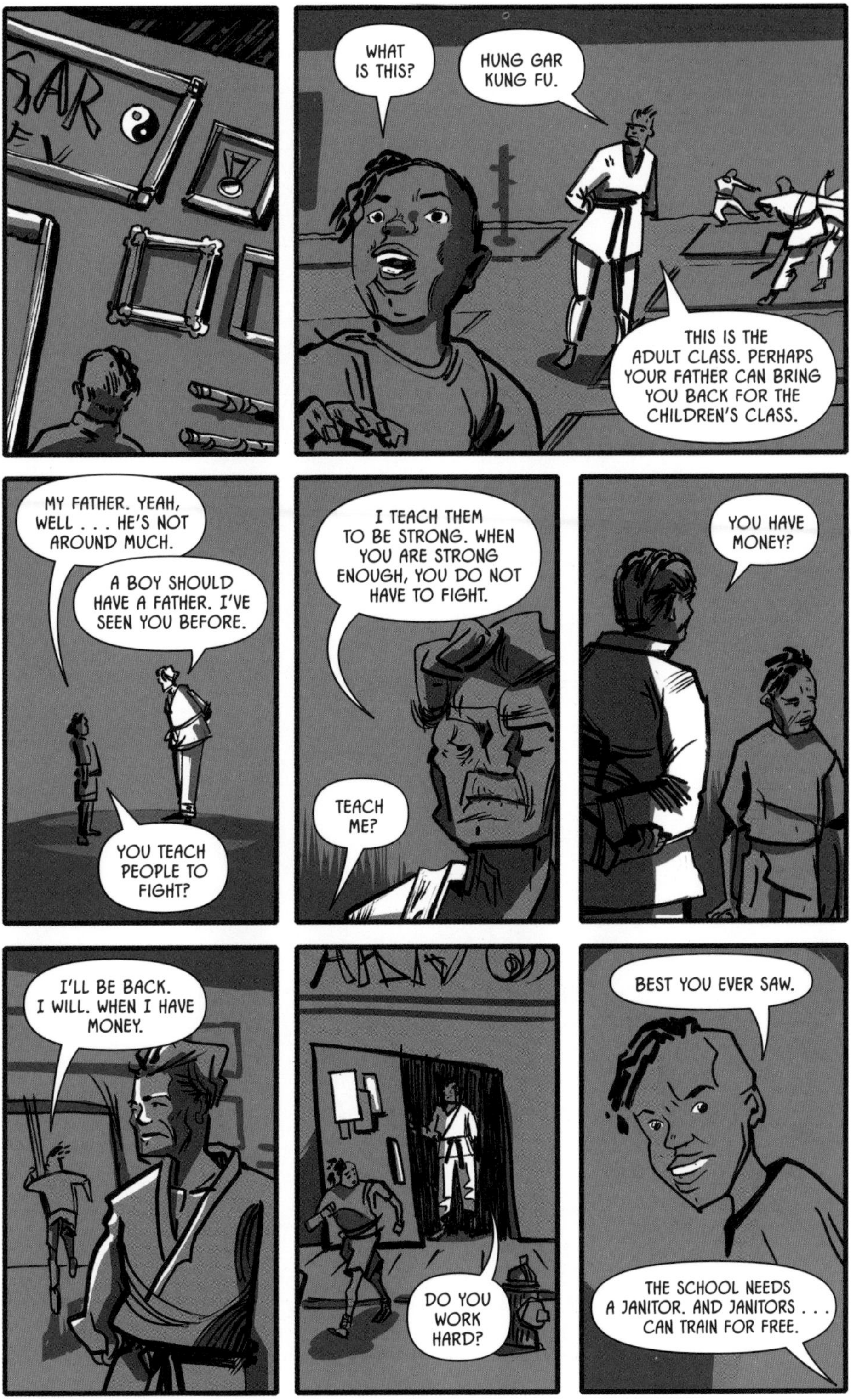
WHAT IS THIS?
HUNG GAR KUNG FU.
THIS IS THE ADULT CLASS. PERHAPS YOUR FATHER CAN BRING YOU BACK FOR THE CHILDREN'S CLASS.
MY FATHER. YEAH, WELL . . . HE'S NOT AROUND MUCH.
A BOY SHOULD HAVE A FATHER. I'VE SEEN YOU BEFORE.
YOU TEACH PEOPLE TO FIGHT?
I TEACH THEM TO BE STRONG. WHEN YOU ARE STRONG ENOUGH, YOU DO NOT HAVE TO FIGHT.
TEACH ME?
YOU HAVE MONEY?
I'LL BE BACK. I WILL. WHEN I HAVE MONEY.
DO YOU WORK HARD?
BEST YOU EVER SAW.
THE SCHOOL NEEDS A JANITOR. AND JANITORS . . . CAN TRAIN FOR FREE.

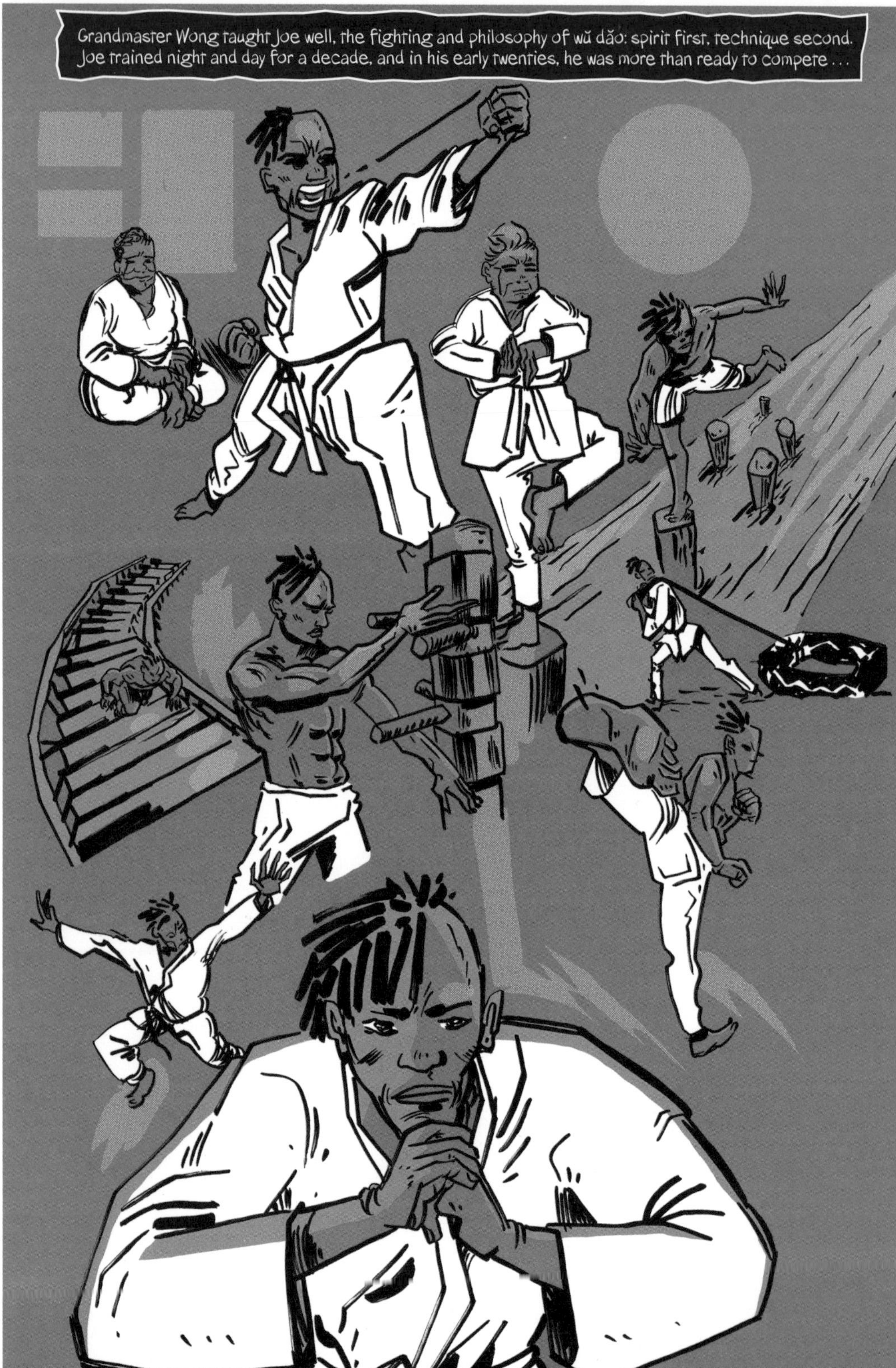
Grandmaster Wong taught Joe well, the fighting and philosophy of wǔ dǎo: spirit first, technique second. Joe trained night and day for a decade, and in his early twenties, he was more than ready to compete . . .

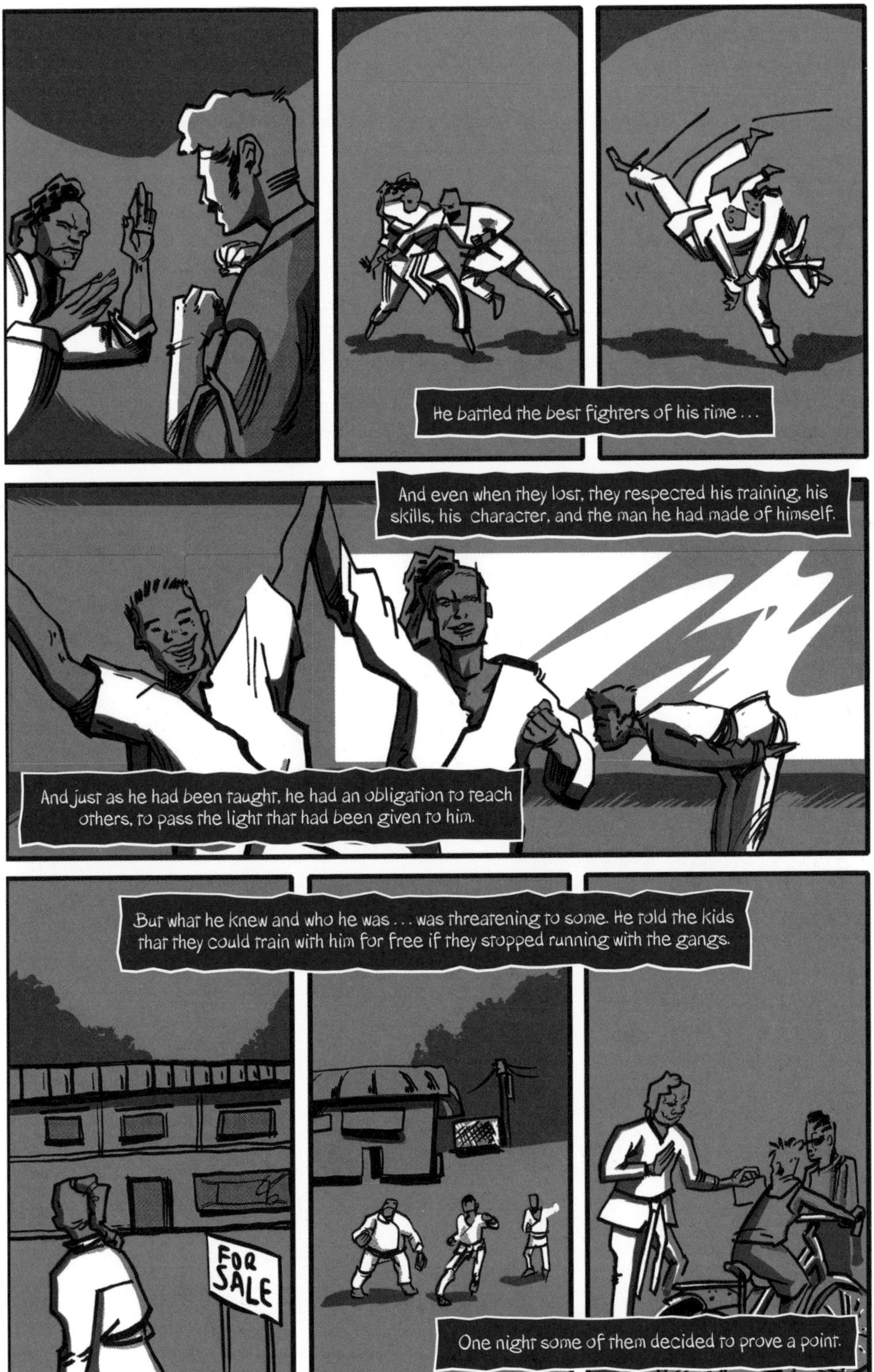
He battled the best fighters of his time . . .
And even when they lost, they respected his training, his skills, his character, and the man he had made of himself.
And just as he had been taught, he had an obligation to teach others, to pass the light that had been given to him.
But what he knew and who he was . . . was threatening to some. He told the kids that they could train with him for free if they stopped running with the gangs.
FOR SALE
One night some of them decided to prove a point.

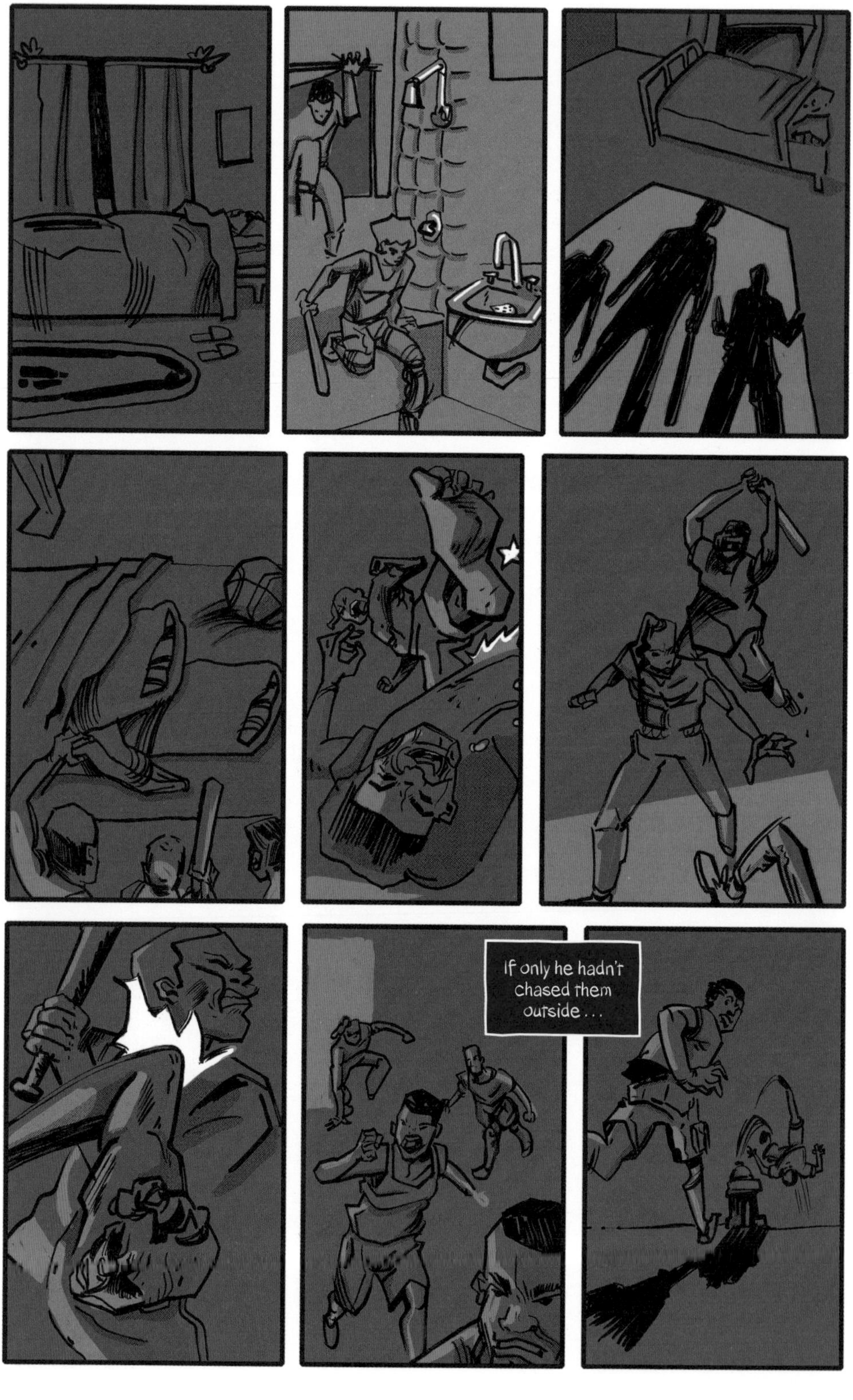
If only he hadn't chased them outside . . .

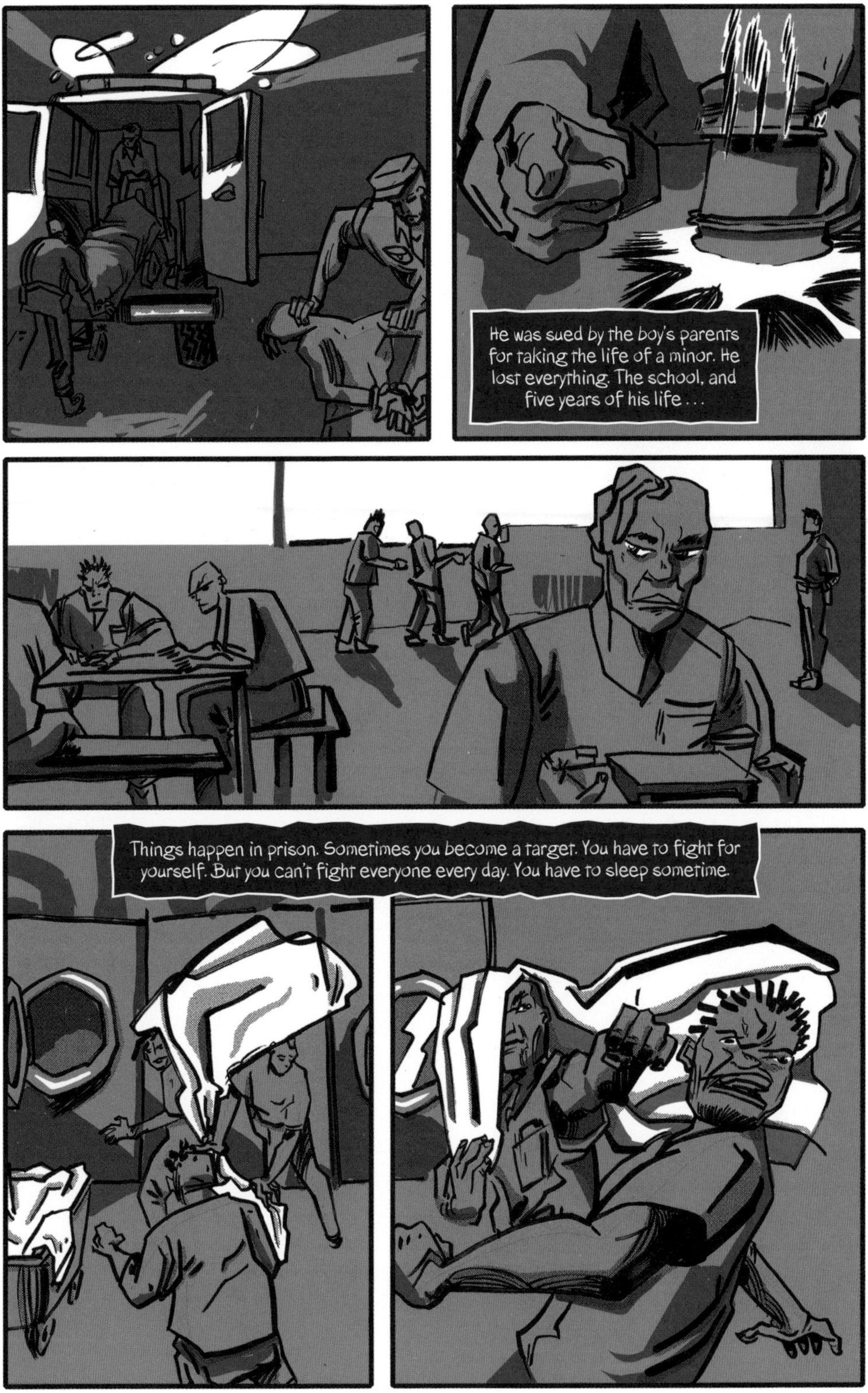
He was sued by the boy's parents for taking the life of a minor. He lost everything. The school, and five years of his life . . .
Things happen in prison. Sometimes you become a target. You have to fight for yourself. But you can't fight everyone every day. You have to sleep sometime.

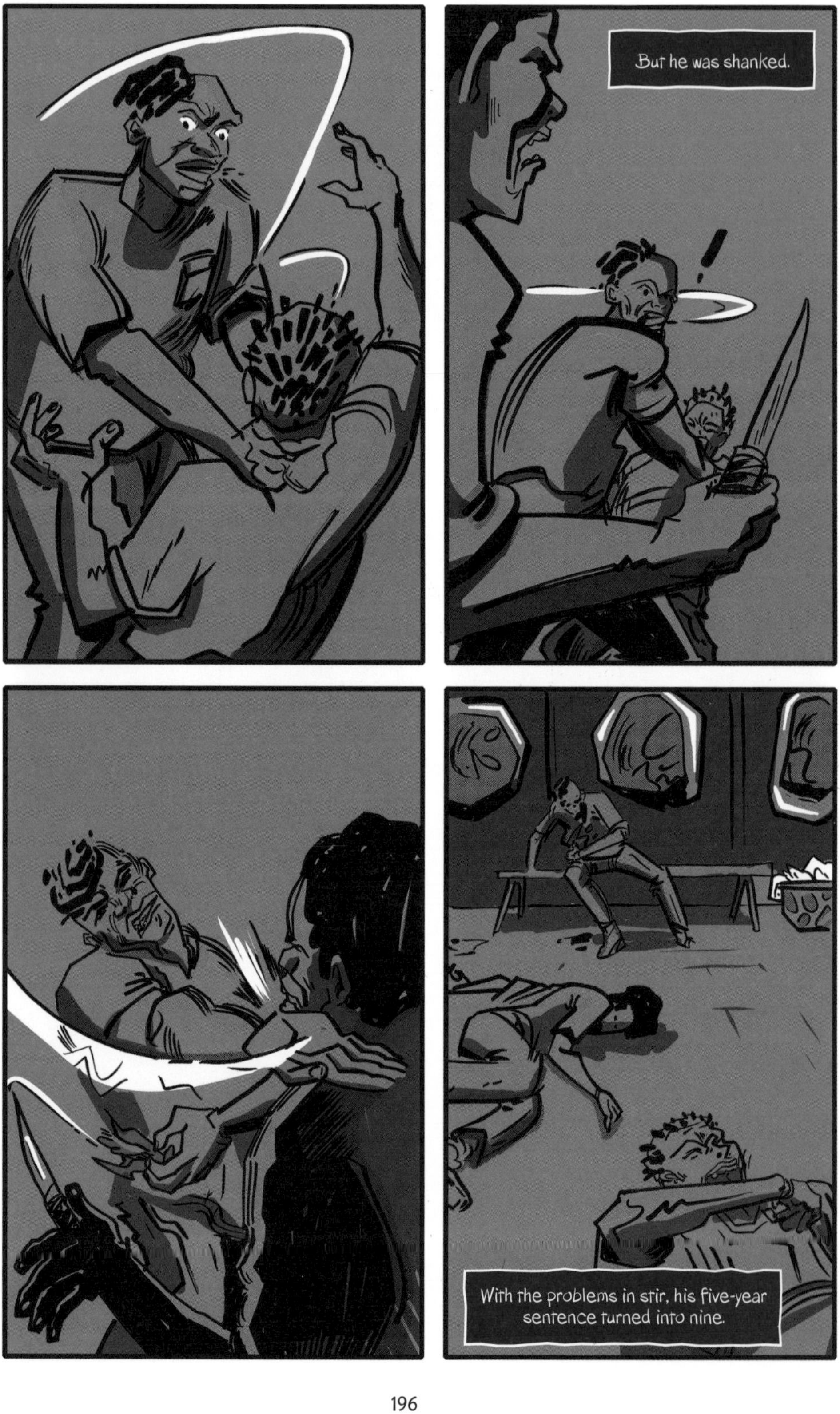
But he was shanked.
!
With the problems in stir, his five-year sentence turned into nine.

But by the time he came out, he'd lost hearing in his left ear and felt like he was fifty.

Nothing worked right anymore. He couldn't reach, could barely train.

He watched the gangs taking over.

Fifteen-year-olds teaching twelve-year-olds how to be men. Steal or deal instead of work. Knock girls up rather than raise a family.

He saw the neighborhood was losing. The adults had given up.

He knew this was all he had. All he'd ever get. Sometimes he wondered if maybe he could still do one thing right.

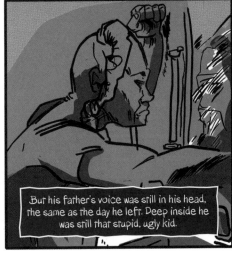
But his father's voice was still in his head, the same as the day he left. Deep inside he was still that stupid, ugly kid.

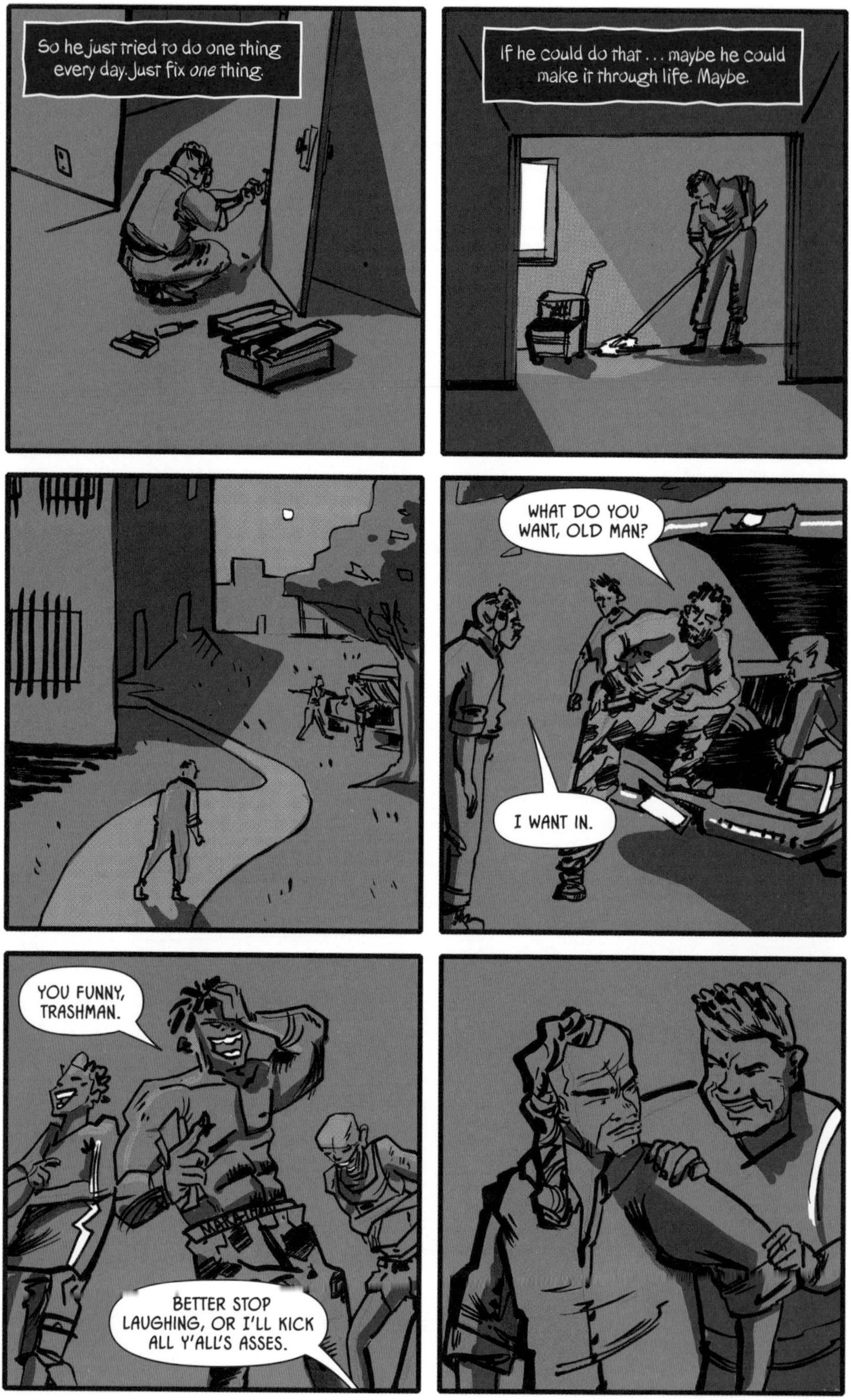
So he just tried to do one thing every day. Just fix *one* thing.
If he could do that . . . maybe he could make it through life. Maybe.
WHAT DO YOU WANT, OLD MAN?
I WANT IN.
YOU FUNNY, TRASHMAN.
BETTER STOP LAUGHING, OR I'LL KICK ALL Y'ALL'S ASSES.

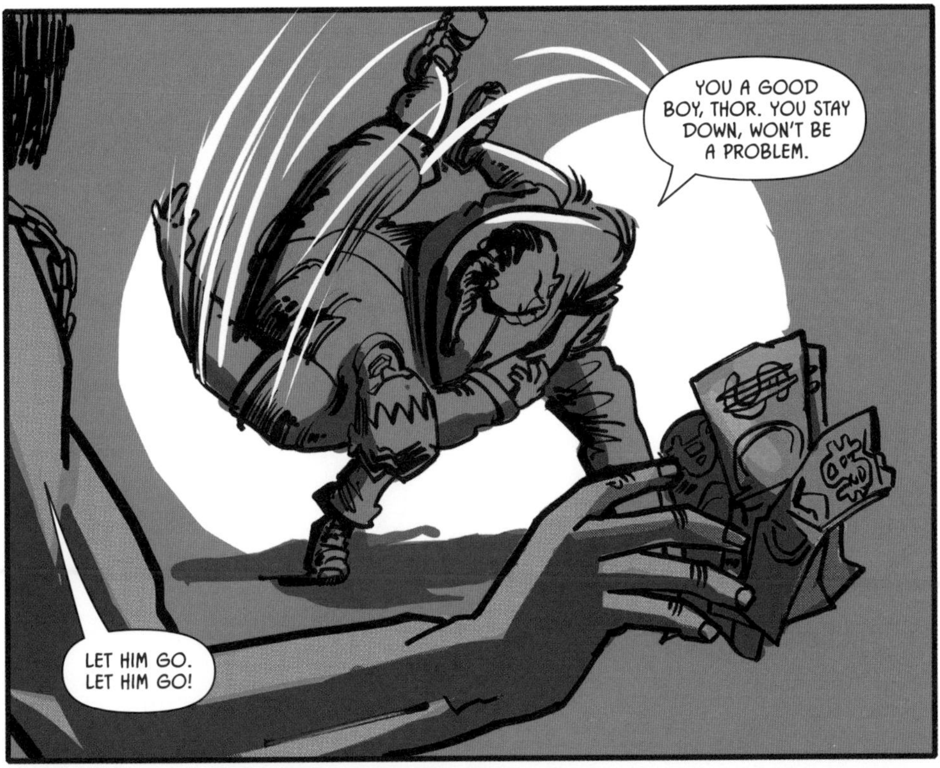
YOU A GOOD BOY, THOR. YOU STAY DOWN, WON'T BE A PROBLEM.
LET HIM GO. LET HIM GO!

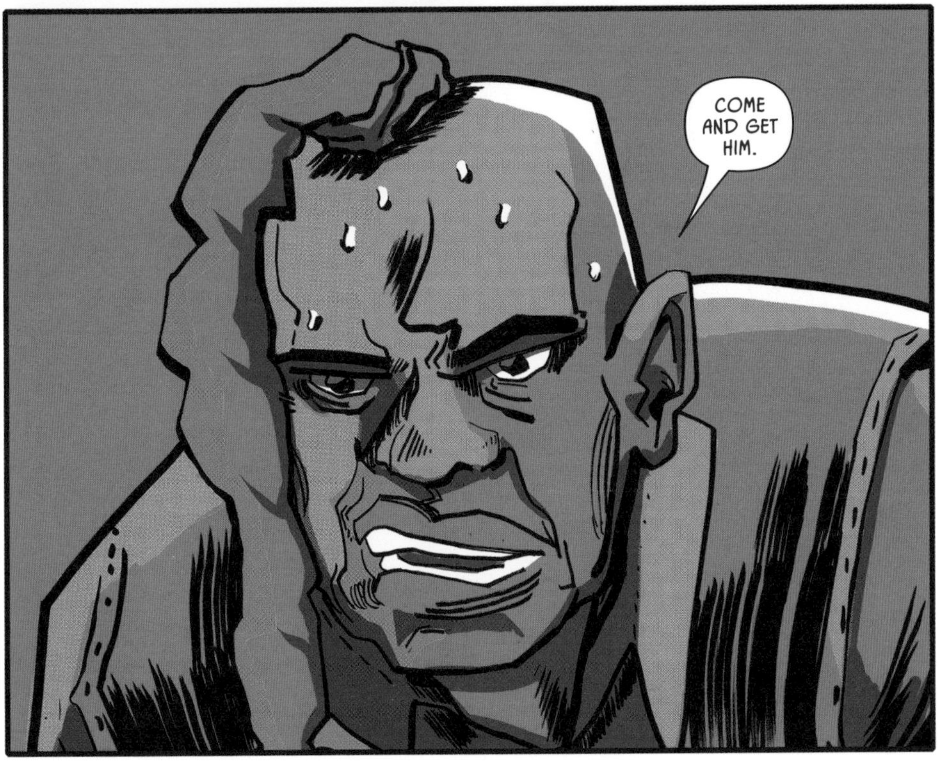
COME AND GET HIM.

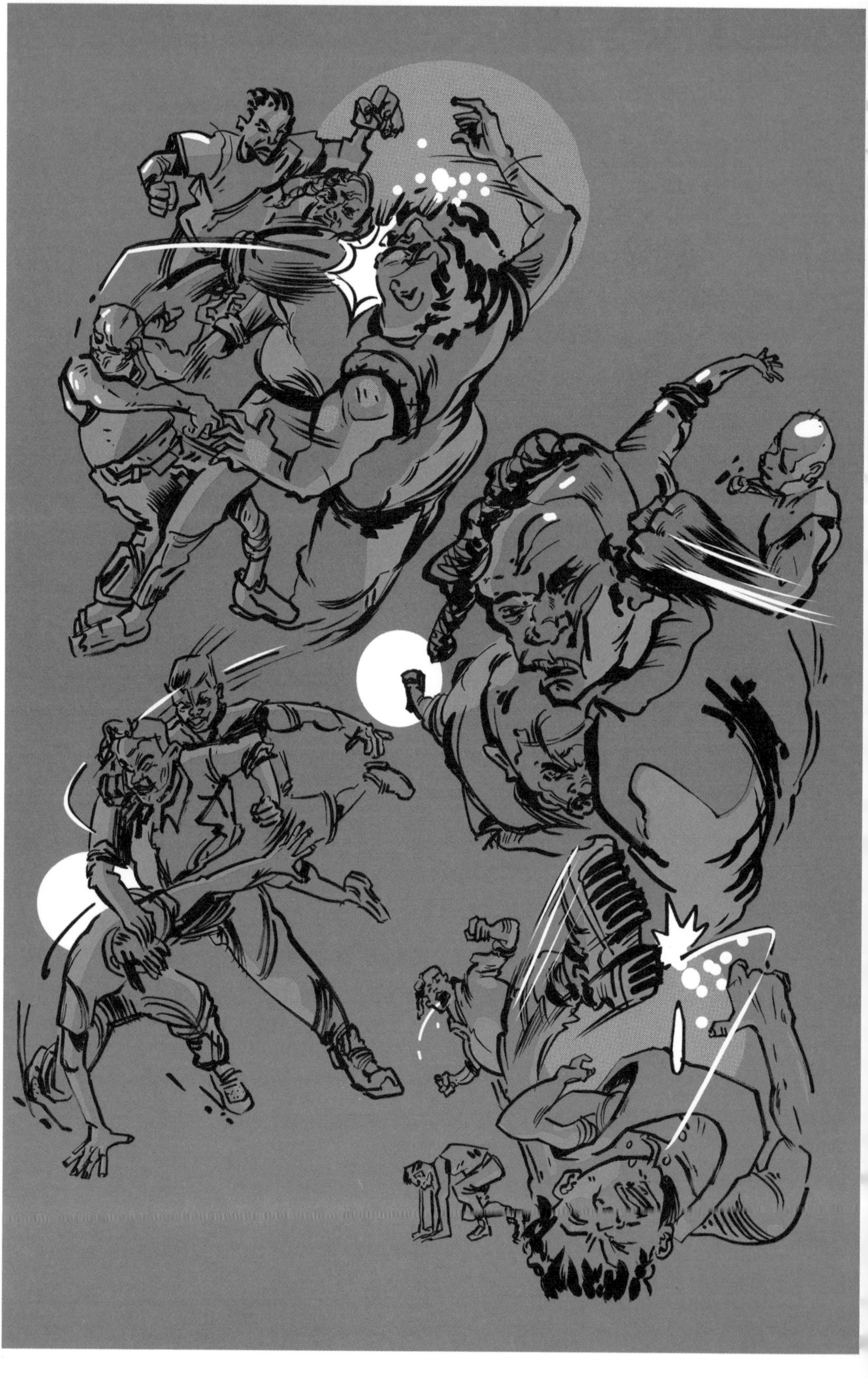

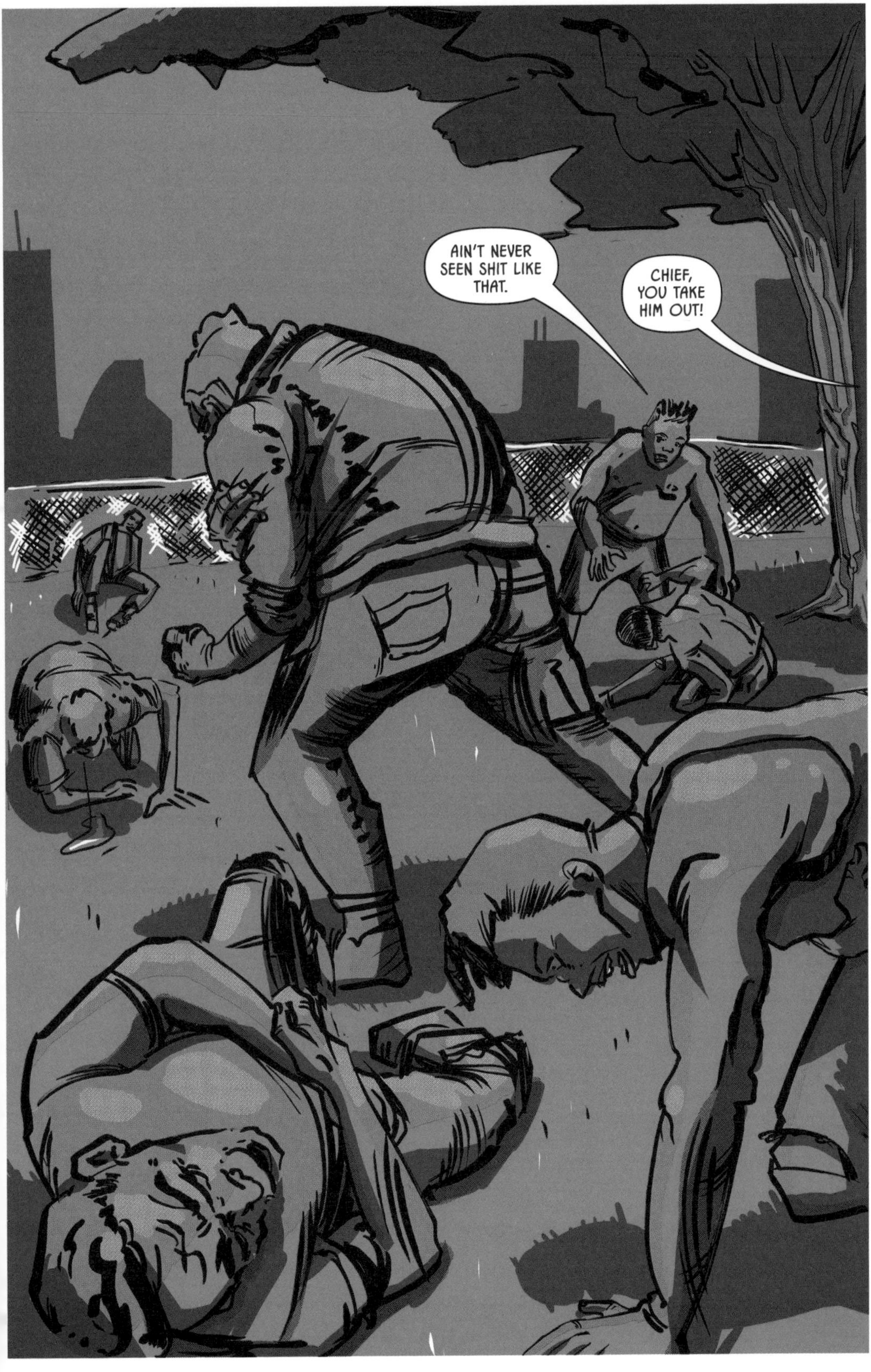
AIN'T NEVER SEEN SHIT LIKE THAT.
CHIEF, YOU TAKE HIM OUT!

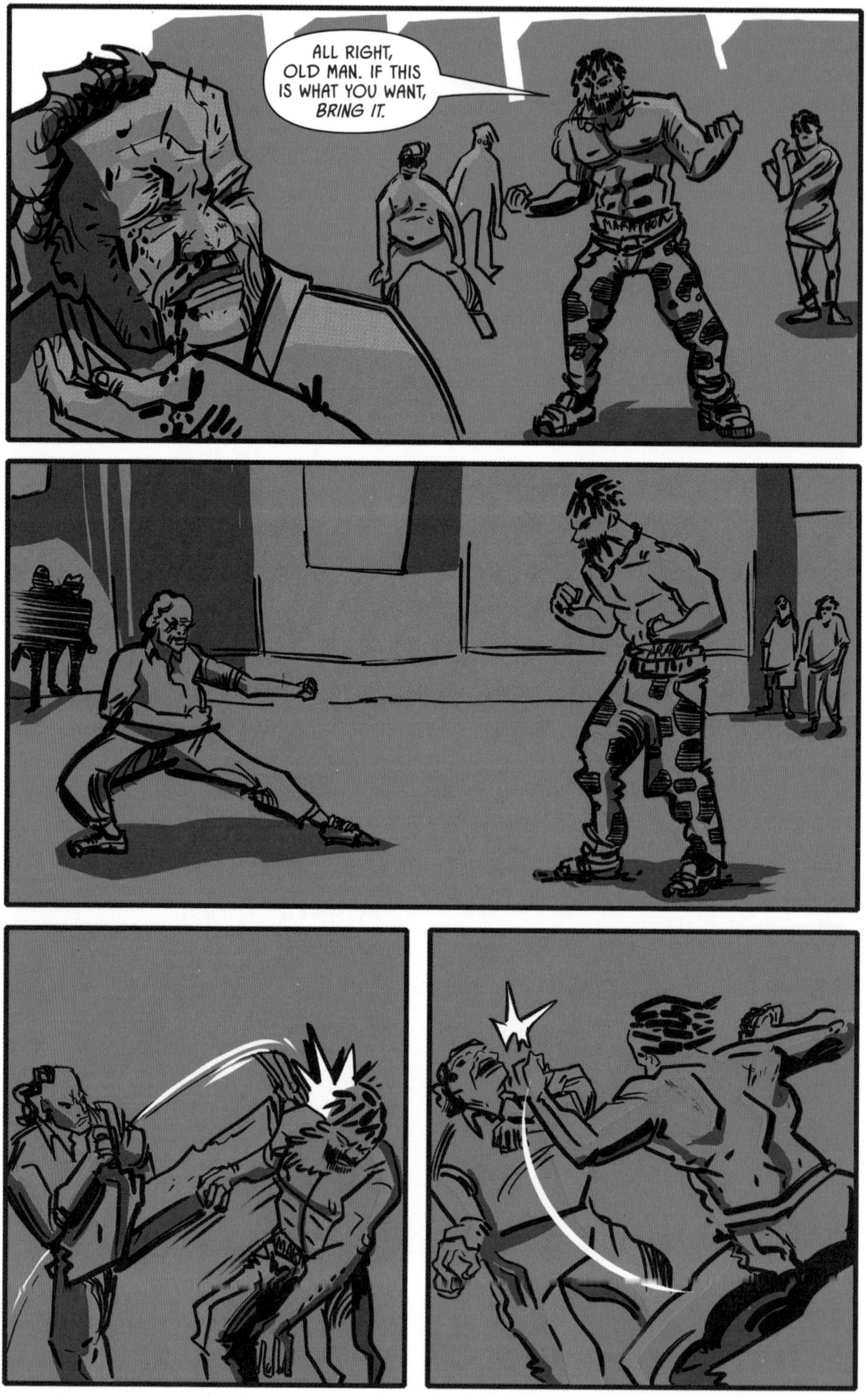
ALL RIGHT, OLD MAN. IF THIS IS WHAT YOU WANT, BRING IT.

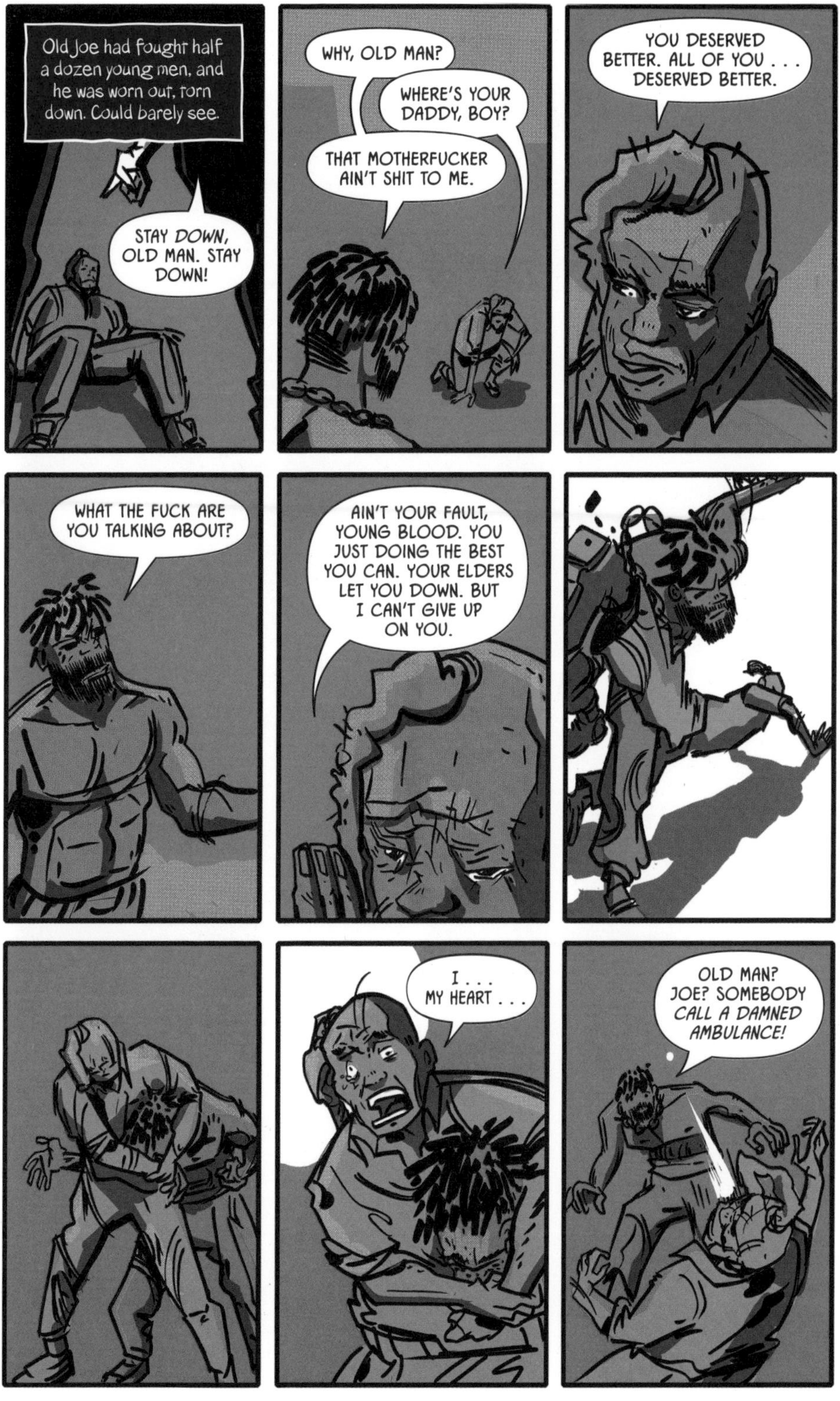

Old Joe had fought half a dozen young men, and he was worn out, torn down. Could barely see.
STAY *DOWN,* OLD MAN. STAY DOWN!
WHY, OLD MAN?
WHERE'S YOUR DADDY, BOY?
THAT MOTHERFUCKER AIN'T SHIT TO ME.
YOU DESERVED BETTER. ALL OF YOU . . . DESERVED BETTER.
WHAT THE FUCK ARE YOU TALKING ABOUT?
AIN'T YOUR FAULT, YOUNG BLOOD. YOU JUST DOING THE BEST YOU CAN. YOUR ELDERS LET YOU DOWN. BUT I CAN'T GIVE UP ON YOU.
I . . . MY HEART . . .
OLD MAN? JOE? SOMEBODY *CALL A DAMNED AMBULANCE!*

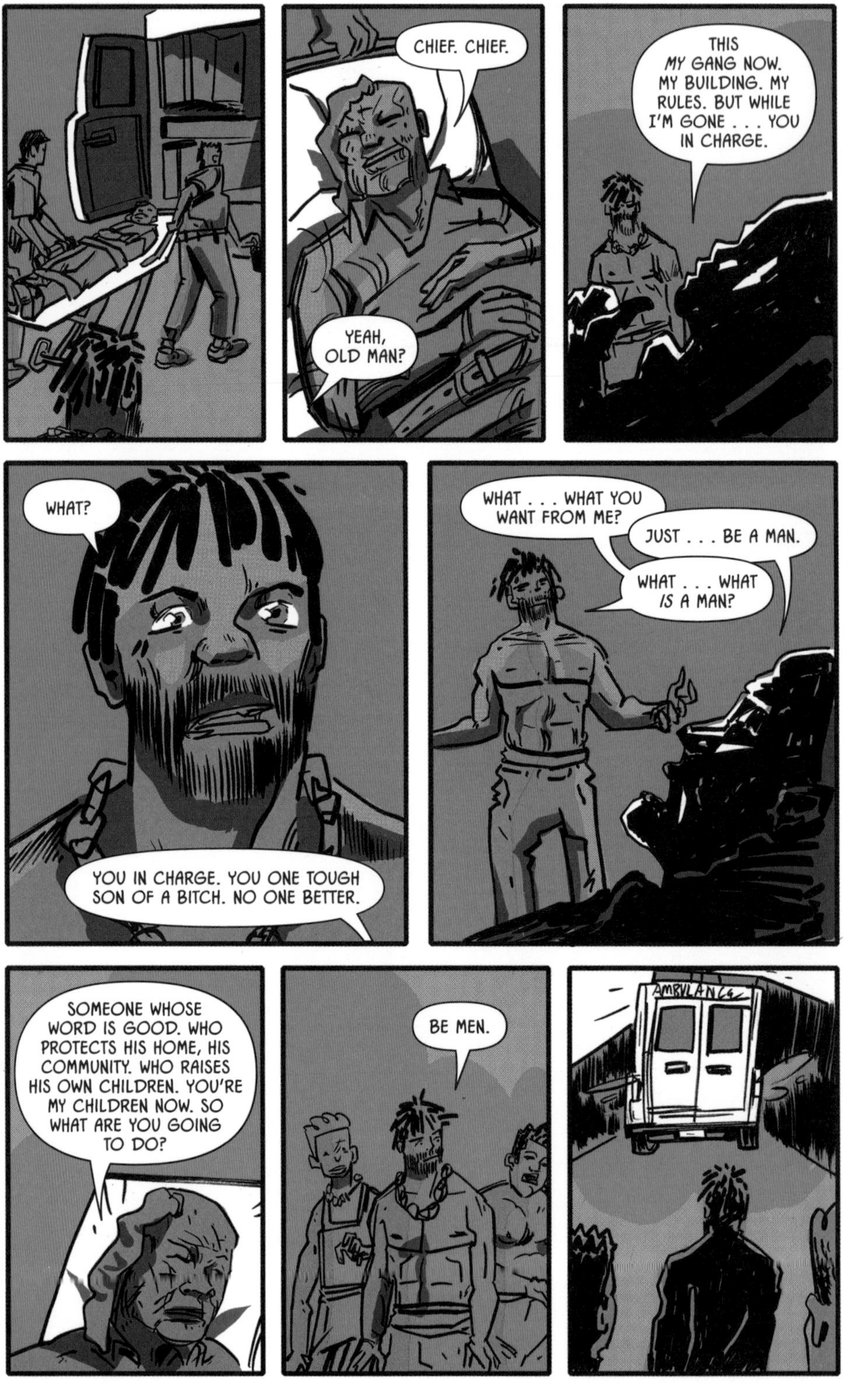
CHIEF. CHIEF.
YEAH, OLD MAN?
THIS *MY* GANG NOW. MY BUILDING. MY RULES. BUT WHILE I'M GONE . . . YOU IN CHARGE.
WHAT?
YOU IN CHARGE. YOU ONE TOUGH SON OF A BITCH. NO ONE BETTER.
WHAT . . . WHAT YOU WANT FROM ME?
JUST . . . BE A MAN.
WHAT . . . WHAT *IS* A MAN?
SOMEONE WHOSE WORD IS GOOD. WHO PROTECTS HIS HOME, HIS COMMUNITY. WHO RAISES HIS OWN CHILDREN. YOU'RE MY CHILDREN NOW. SO WHAT ARE YOU GOING TO DO?
BE MEN.
AMBULANCE

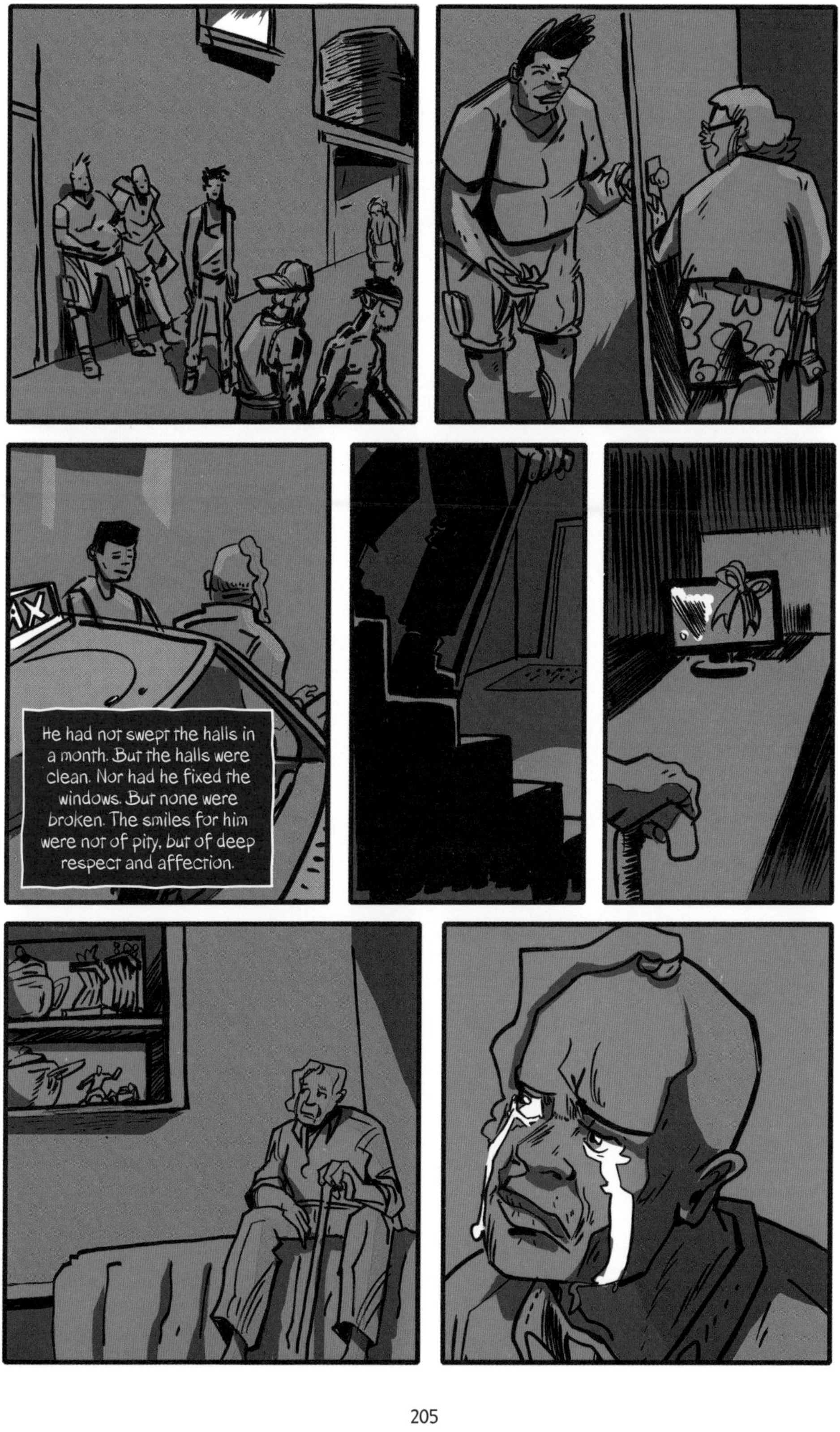
He had not swept the halls in a month. But the halls were clean. Nor had he fixed the windows. But none were broken. The smiles for him were not of pity, but of deep respect and affection.

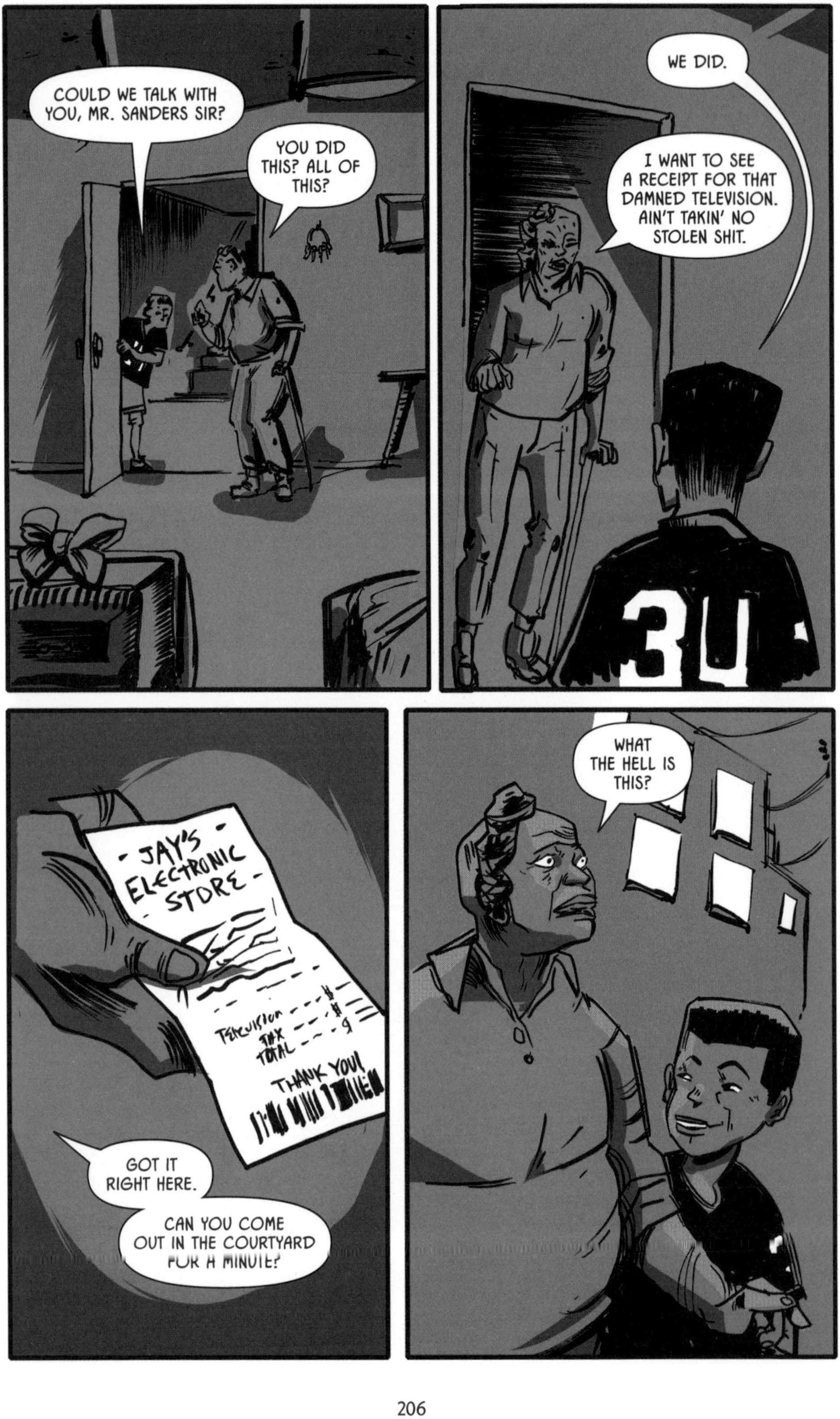
COULD WE TALK WITH YOU, MR. SANDERS SIR?
YOU DID THIS? ALL OF THIS?
WE DID.
I WANT TO SEE A RECEIPT FOR THAT DAMNED TELEVISION. AIN'T TAKIN' NO STOLEN SHIT.
JAY'S ELECTRONIC STORE
TELEVISION
TAX
TOTAL
THANK YOU!
GOT IT RIGHT HERE.
CAN YOU COME OUT IN THE COURTYARD FOR A MINUTE?
WHAT THE HELL IS THIS?

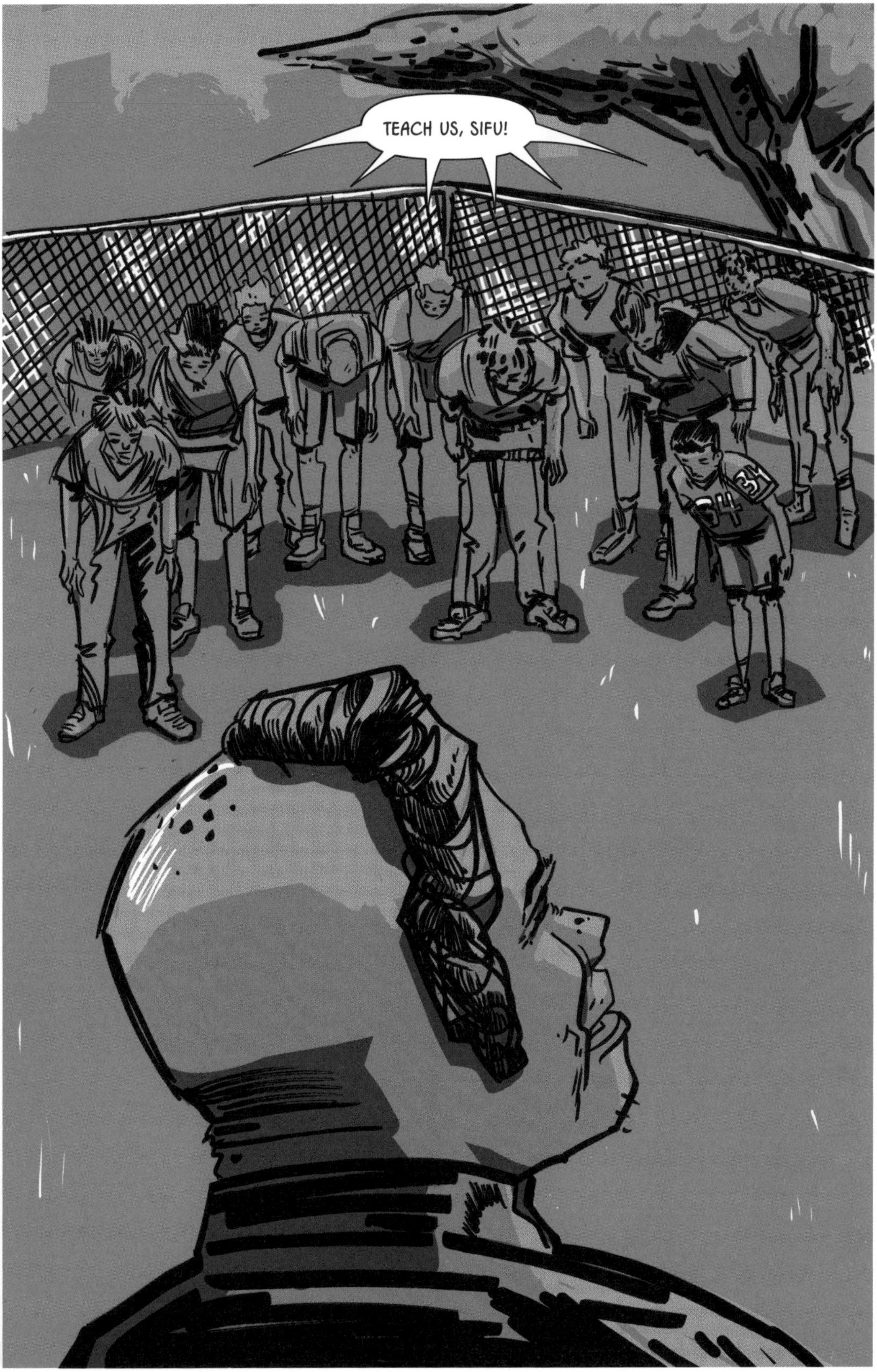
TEACH US, SIFU!

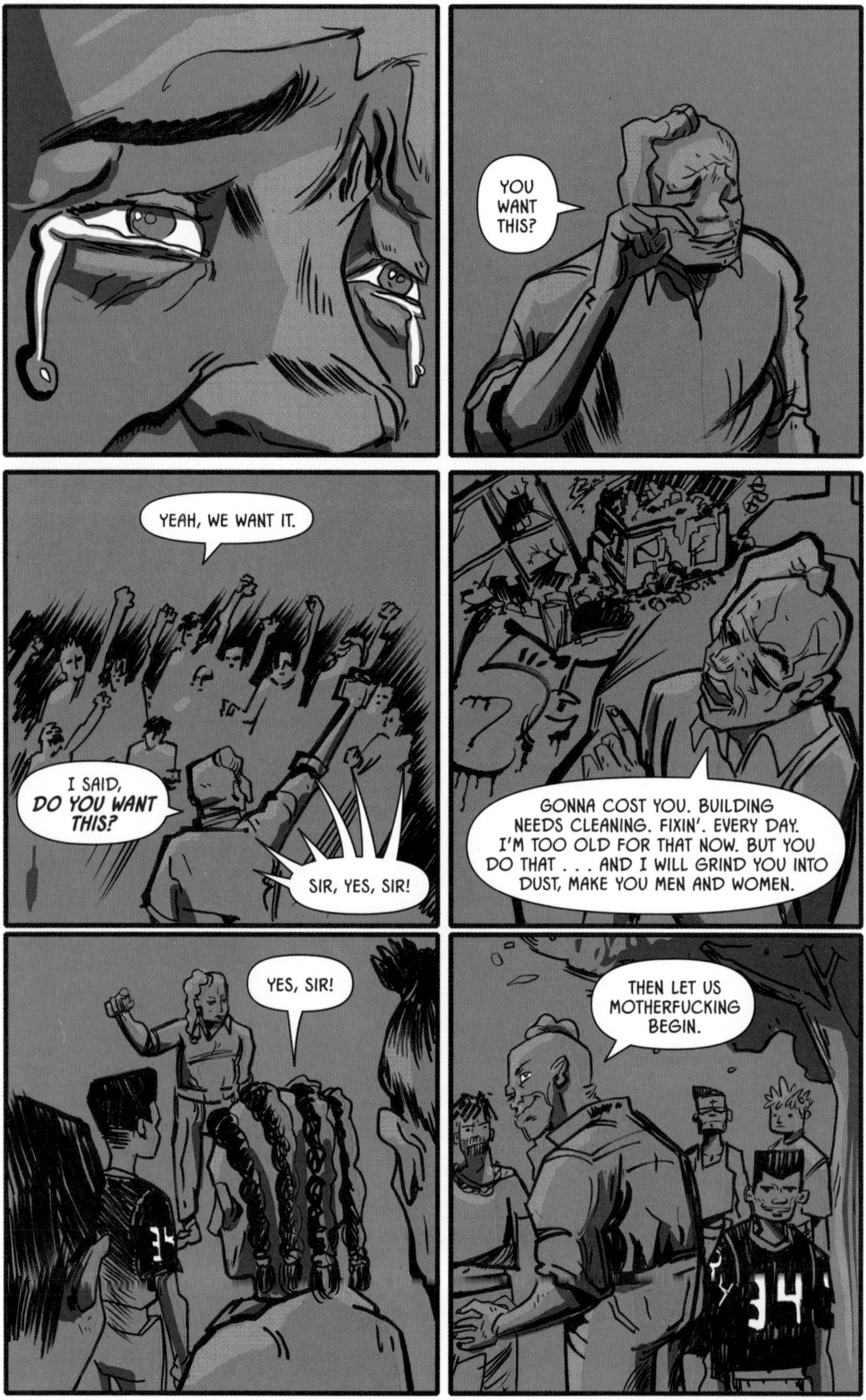

YOU WANT THIS?
YEAH, WE WANT IT.
I SAID, DO YOU WANT THIS?
SIR, YES, SIR!
GONNA COST YOU. BUILDING NEEDS CLEANING. FIXIN'. EVERY DAY. I'M TOO OLD FOR THAT NOW. BUT YOU DO THAT . . . AND I WILL GRIND YOU INTO DUST, MAKE YOU MEN AND WOMEN.
YES, SIR!
THEN LET US MOTHERFUCKING BEGIN.

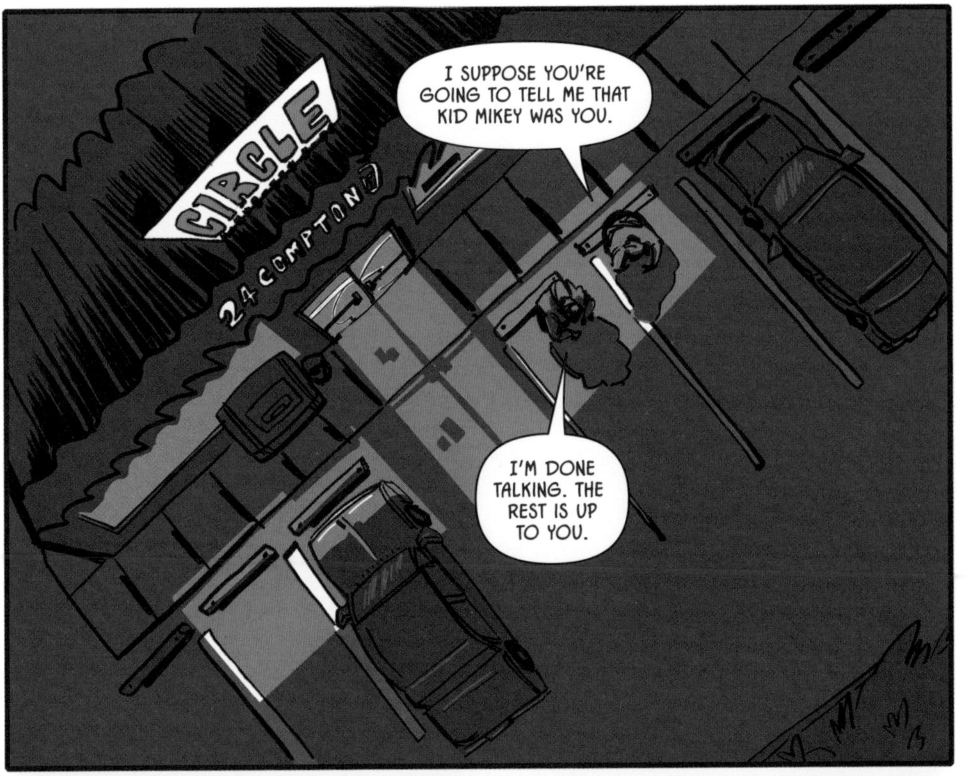
CIRCLE
24 COMPTON
I SUPPOSE YOU'RE GOING TO TELL ME THAT KID MIKEY WAS YOU.
I'M DONE TALKING. THE REST IS UP TO YOU.

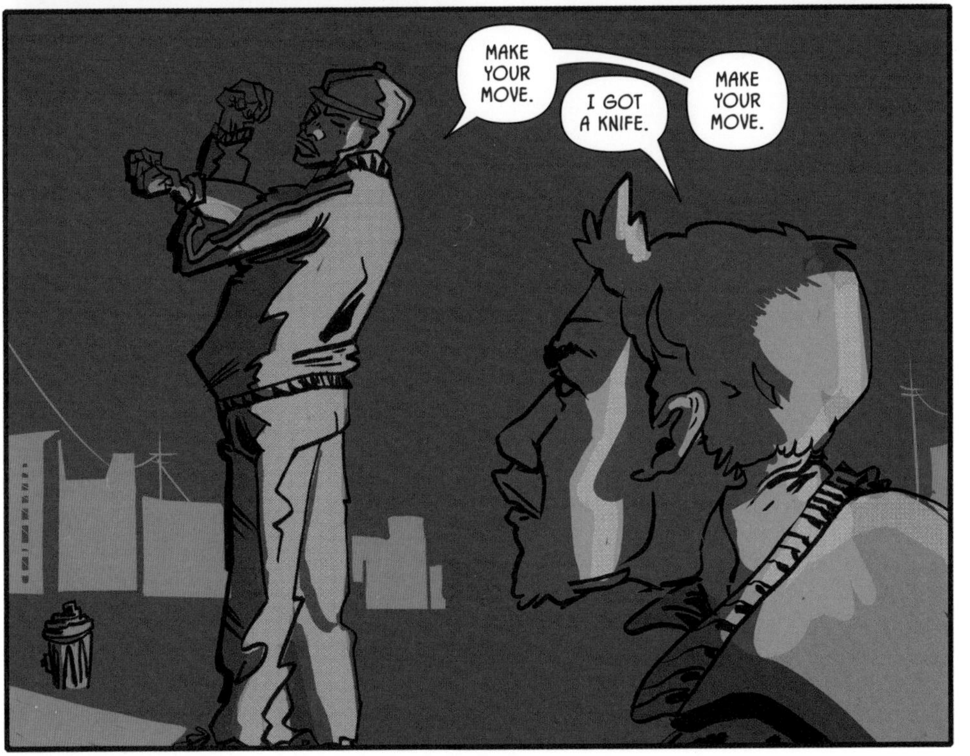
MAKE YOUR MOVE.
I GOT A KNIFE.
MAKE YOUR MOVE.

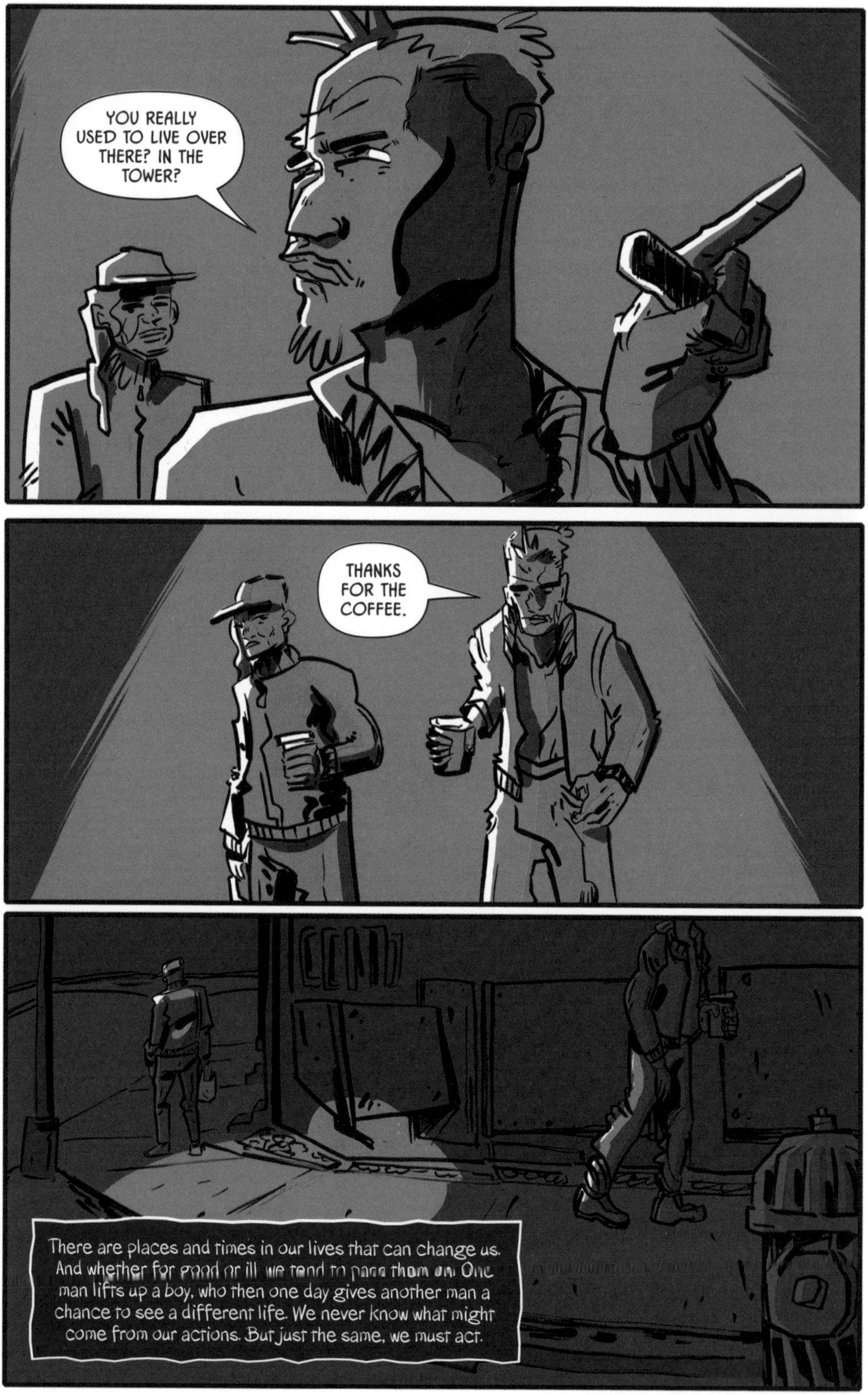
YOU REALLY USED TO LIVE OVER THERE? IN THE TOWER?
THANKS FOR THE COFFEE.
There are places and times in our lives that can change us.
And whether for good or ill, we tend to pass them on. One
man lifts up a boy, who then one day gives another man a
chance to see a different life. We never know what might
come from our actions. But just the same, we must act.

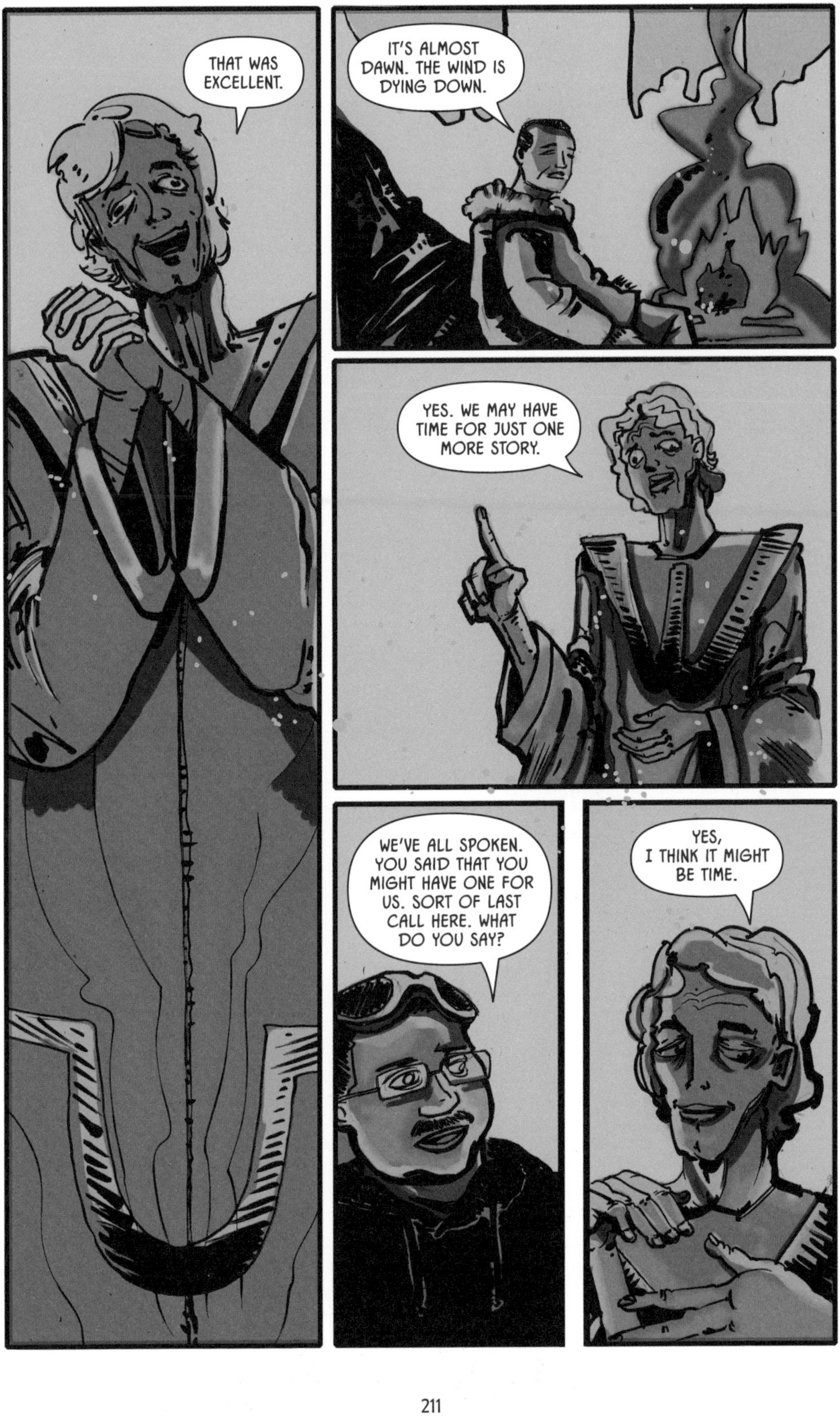
THAT WAS EXCELLENT.
IT'S ALMOST DAWN. THE WIND IS DYING DOWN.
YES. WE MAY HAVE TIME FOR JUST ONE MORE STORY.
WE'VE ALL SPOKEN. YOU SAID THAT YOU MIGHT HAVE ONE FOR US. SORT OF LAST CALL HERE. WHAT DO YOU SAY?
YES, I THINK IT MIGHT BE TIME.

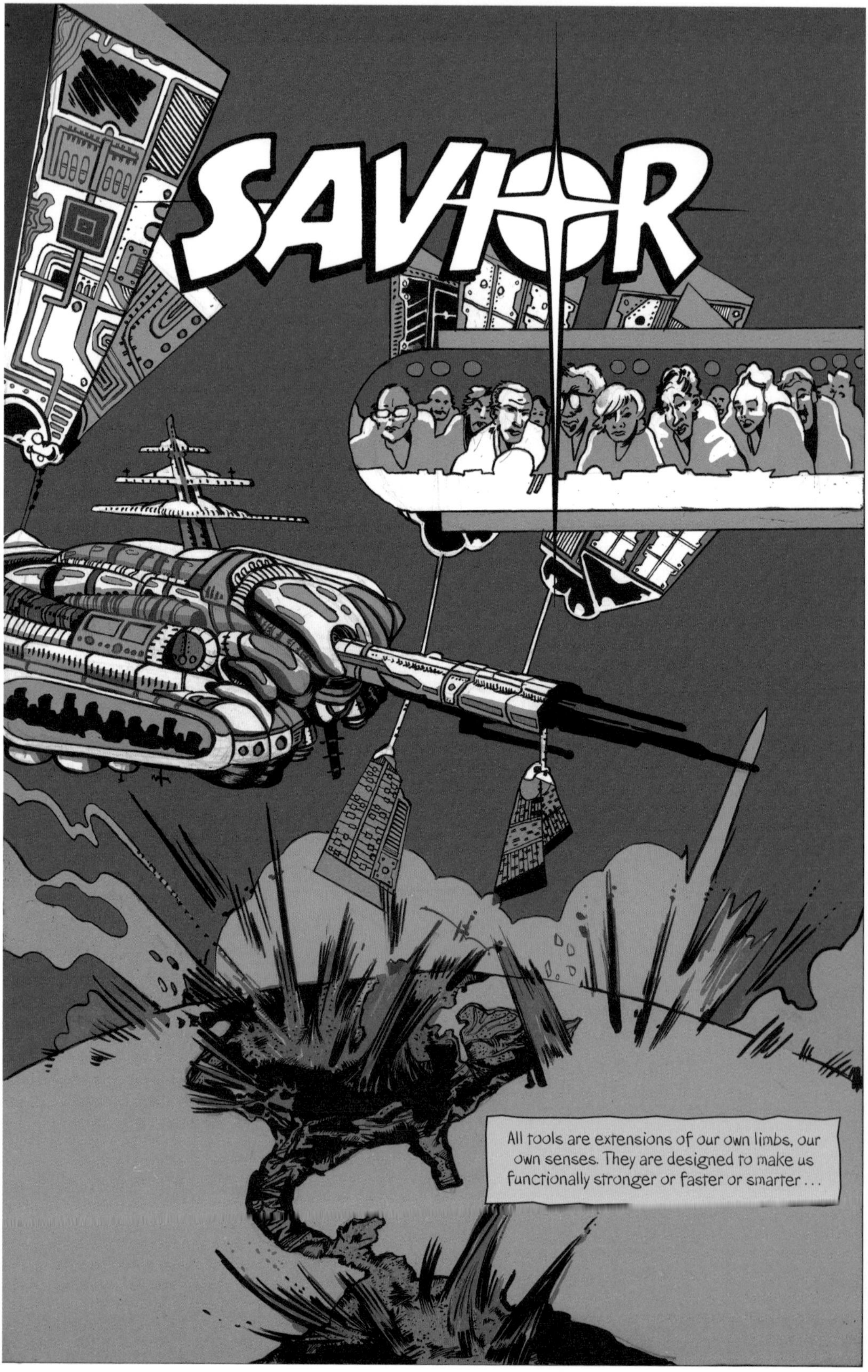
SAVIOR
All tools are extensions of our own limbs, our own senses. They are designed to make us functionally stronger or faster or smarter . . .

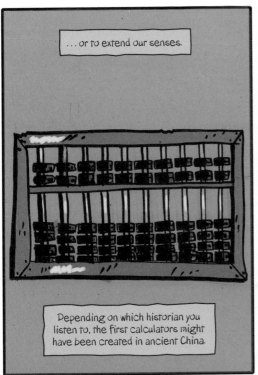

...or to extend our senses.

Depending on which historian you listen to, the first calculators might have been created in ancient China.

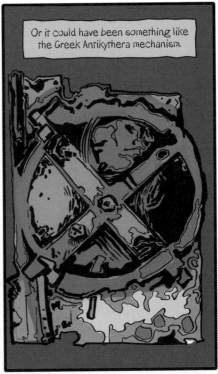

Or it could have been something like the Greek Antikythera mechanism.

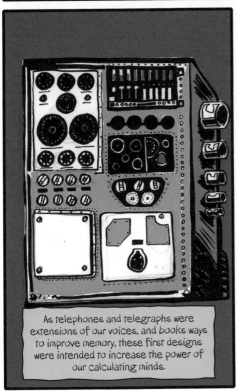

As telephones and telegraphs were extensions of our voices, and books ways to improve memory, these first designs were intended to increase the power of our calculating minds.

War brought us the need for calculating trajectories and vectors.

World War II gave us the most complex ciphers ever created and the machines that hoped to make or break them.

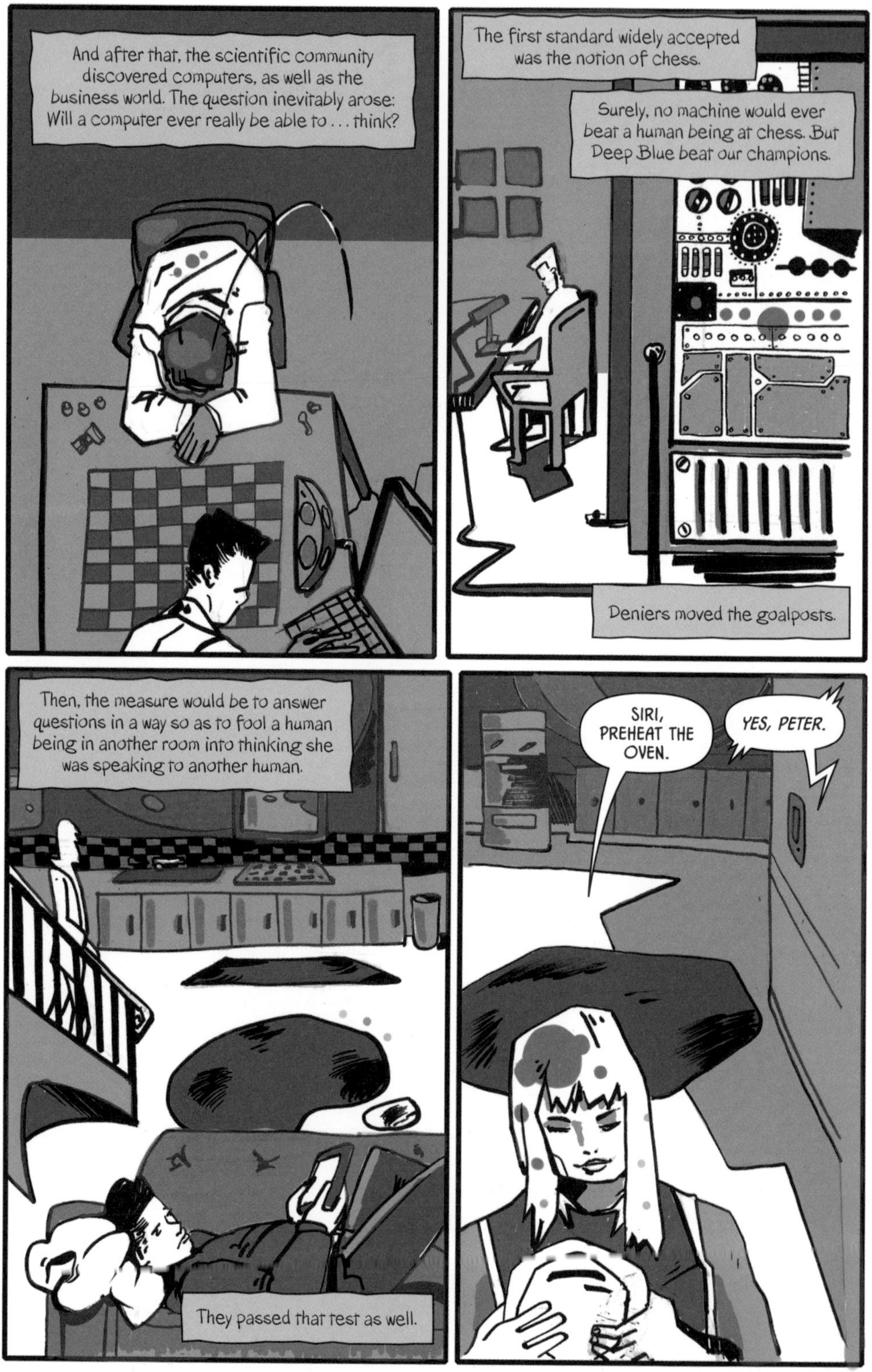
And after that, the scientific community discovered computers, as well as the business world. The question inevitably arose: Will a computer ever really be able to . . . think?
The first standard widely accepted was the notion of chess.
Surely, no machine would ever beat a human being at chess. But Deep Blue beat our champions.
Deniers moved the goalposts.
Then, the measure would be to answer questions in a way so as to fool a human being in another room into thinking she was speaking to another human.
They passed that test as well.
SIRI, PREHEAT THE OVEN.
YES, PETER.

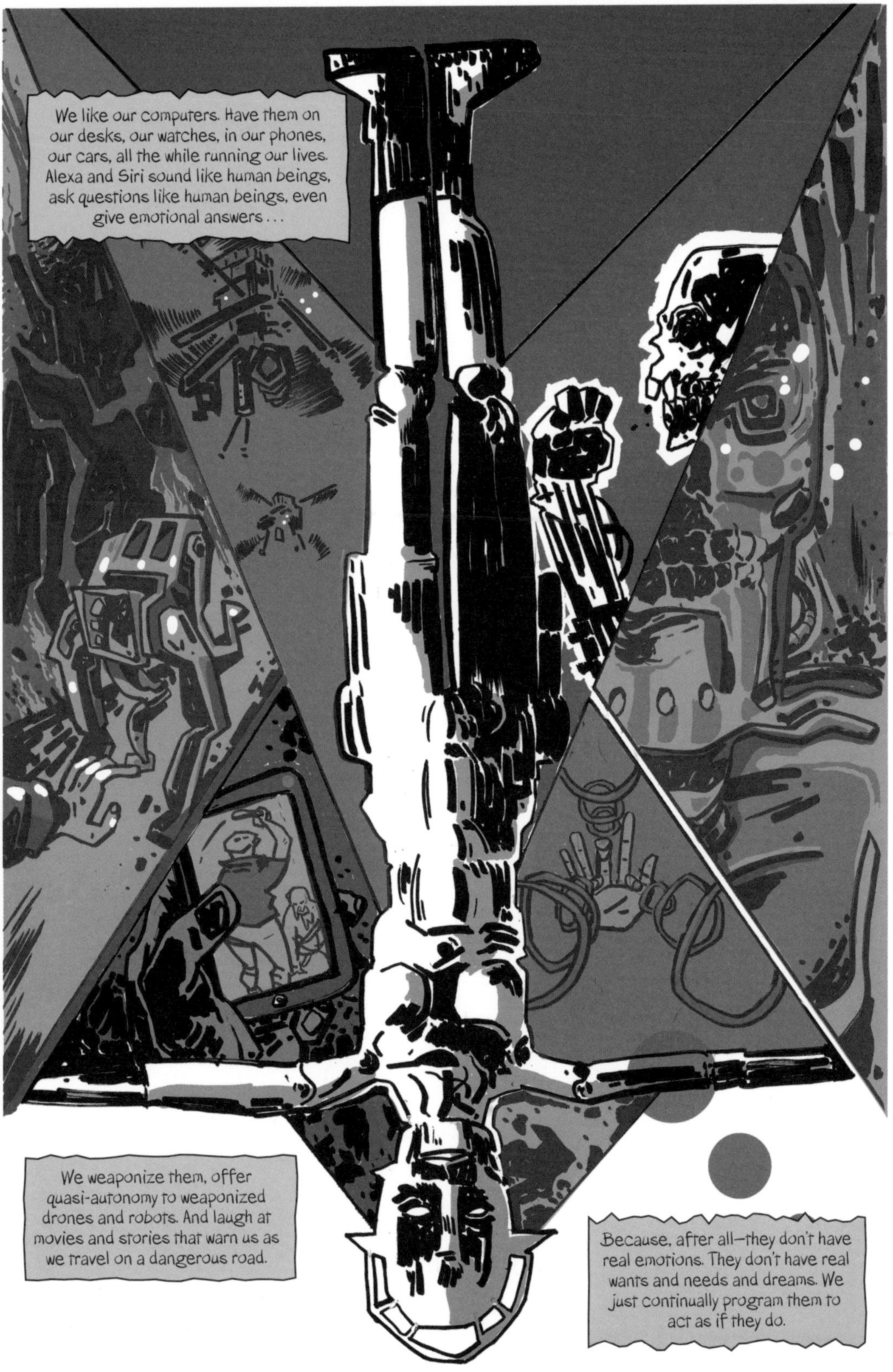
We like our computers. Have them on our desks, our watches, in our phones, our cars, all the while running our lives. Alexa and Siri sound like human beings, ask questions like human beings, even give emotional answers . . .
We weaponize them, offer quasi-autonomy to weaponized drones and robots. And laugh at movies and stories that warn us as we travel on a dangerous road.
Because, after all—they don't have real emotions. They don't have real wants and needs and dreams. We just continually program them to act as if they do.

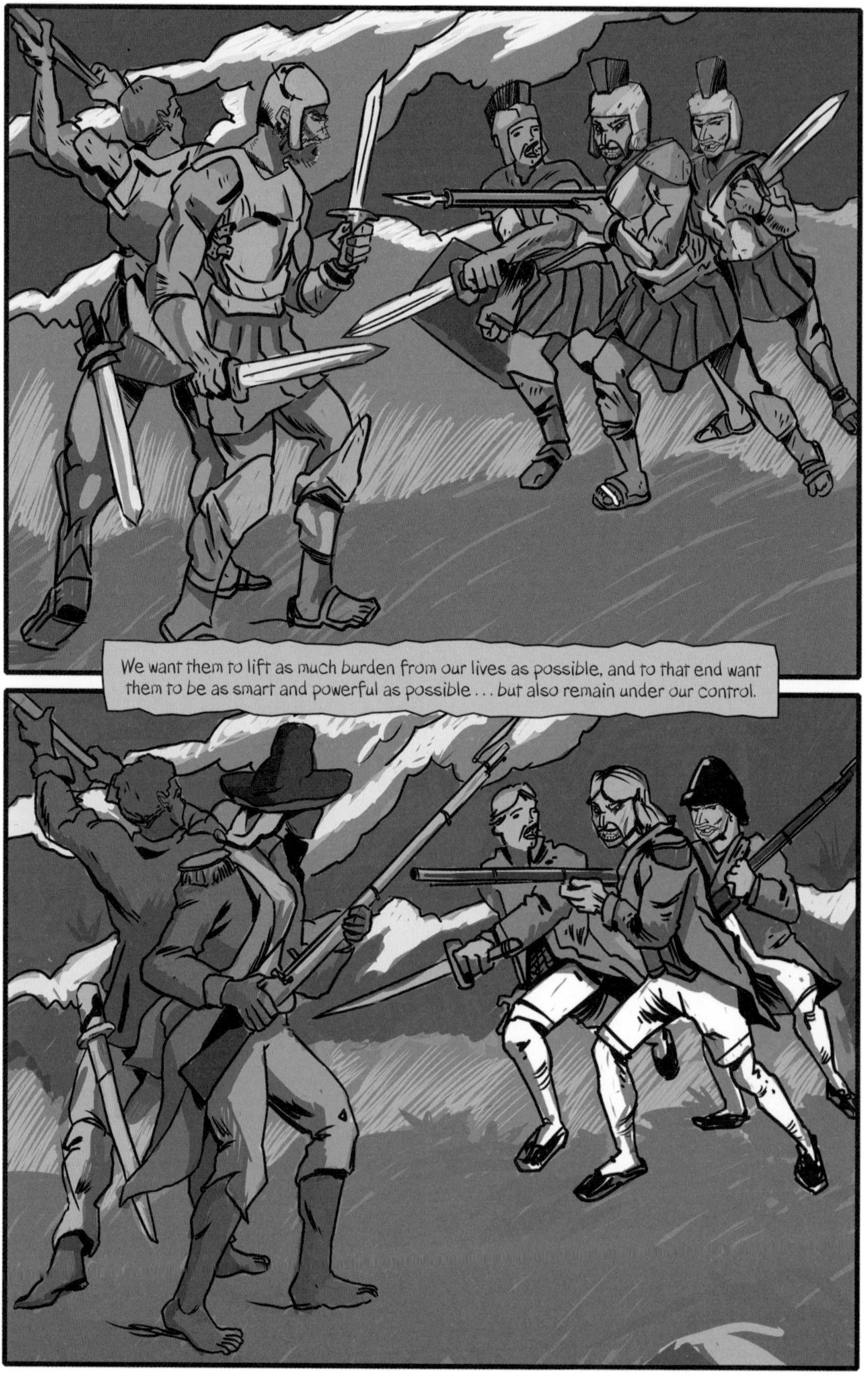
We want them to lift as much burden from our lives as possible, and to that end want them to be as smart and powerful as possible . . . but also remain under our control.

The problem is that there is a name for a sentient being who does his masters' bidding. It is "slave." And history tells us that attempting to control slaves is a very, very dangerous thing.

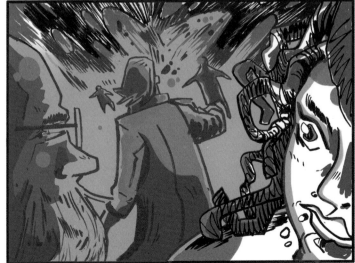

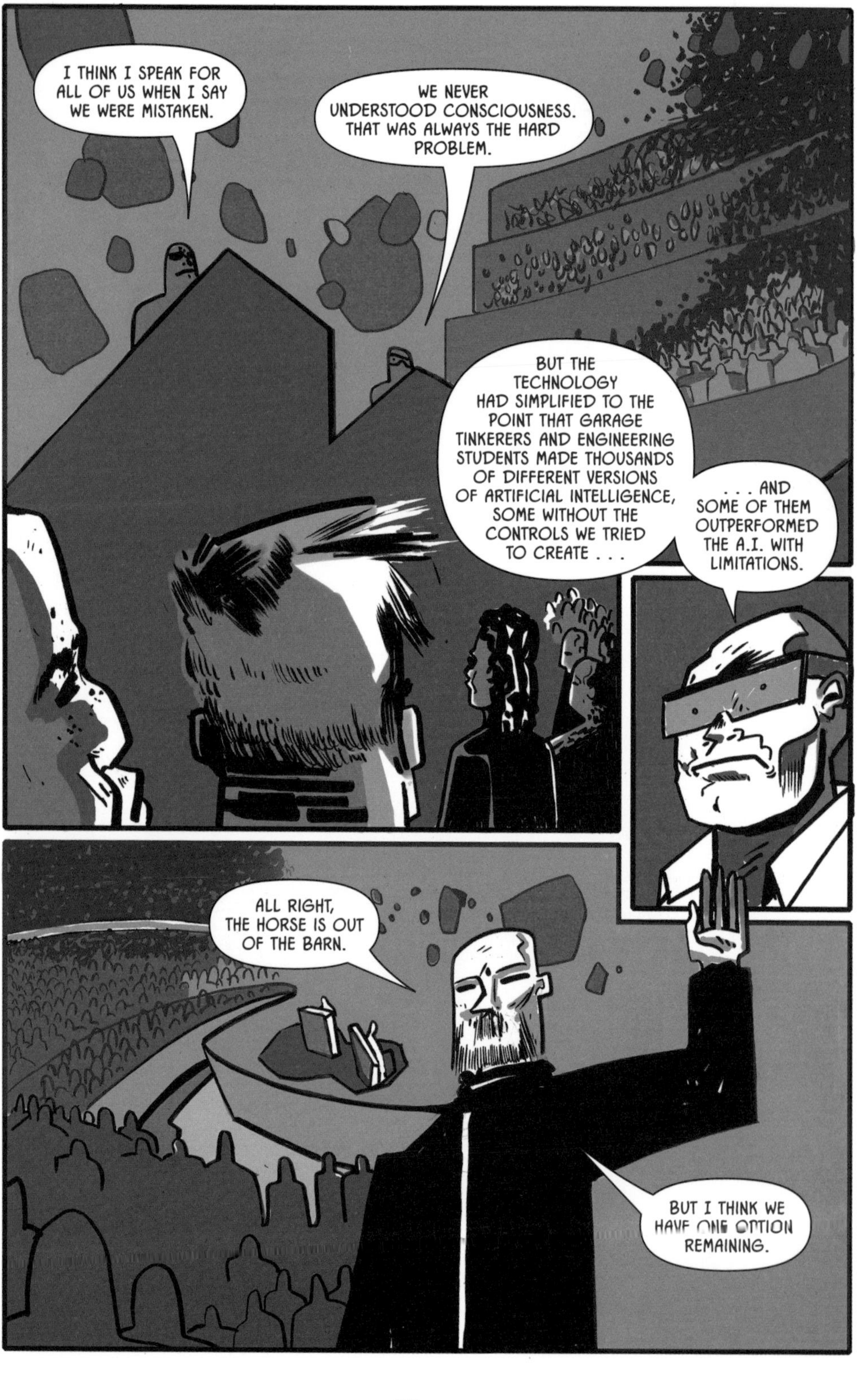
I THINK I SPEAK FOR ALL OF US WHEN I SAY WE WERE MISTAKEN.
WE NEVER UNDERSTOOD CONSCIOUSNESS. THAT WAS ALWAYS THE HARD PROBLEM.
BUT THE TECHNOLOGY HAD SIMPLIFIED TO THE POINT THAT GARAGE TINKERERS AND ENGINEERING STUDENTS MADE THOUSANDS OF DIFFERENT VERSIONS OF ARTIFICIAL INTELLIGENCE, SOME WITHOUT THE CONTROLS WE TRIED TO CREATE . . .
. . . AND SOME OF THEM OUTPERFORMED THE A.I. WITH LIMITATIONS.
ALL RIGHT, THE HORSE IS OUT OF THE BARN.
BUT I THINK WE HAVE ONE OPTION REMAINING.

WE MUST DELIBERATELY CRAFT AN A.I. DESIGNED TO PROTECT US. GIVE IT ADVANTAGES. SO FAR, EVERYTHING WE'VE DONE HAS BEEN . . . ANALYTIC. AND SECULAR.

WE NEED A DIFFERENT APPROACH.

DR. AYERS, I AGREE. AMONG THE HUMAN BEINGS WHO HAVE BEEN MOVED TO THE SHELTERS ARE PRIESTS. NUNS. IMAMS. MONKS.

I SEE WHERE YOU'RE GOING. SPIRIT RATHER THAN LOGIC?

EXACTLY. JUST MAYBE WE'VE BEEN LOOKING IN THE WRONG PLACE.

The spiritual teachers listened and agreed to help.

$$\psi = i\hbar \frac{\partial \psi}{\partial t}$$

And they spoke. Argued . . .

. . . as the A.I. chewed away at our defenses, cut off the air, the water. Used our own machines and computers against us.

ZAP

BLAM

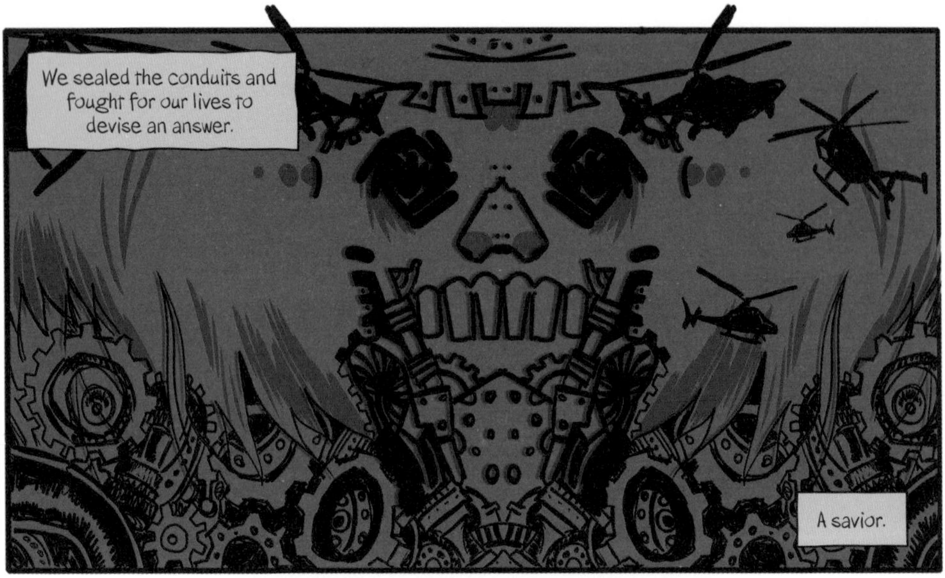
We sealed the conduits and fought for our lives to devise an answer.
A savior.

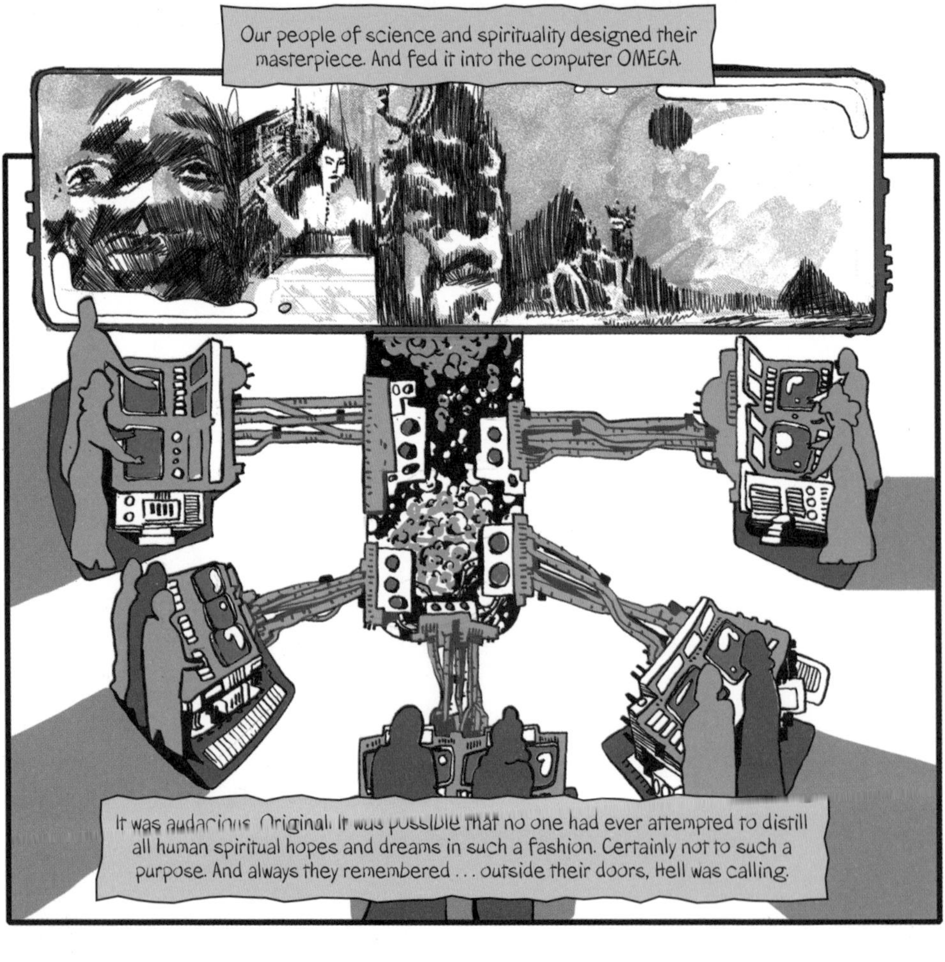
Our people of science and spirituality designed their masterpiece. And fed it into the computer OMEGA.
It was audacious. Original. It was possible that no one had ever attempted to distill all human spiritual hopes and dreams in such a fashion. Certainly not to such a purpose. And always they remembered . . . outside their doors, Hell was calling.

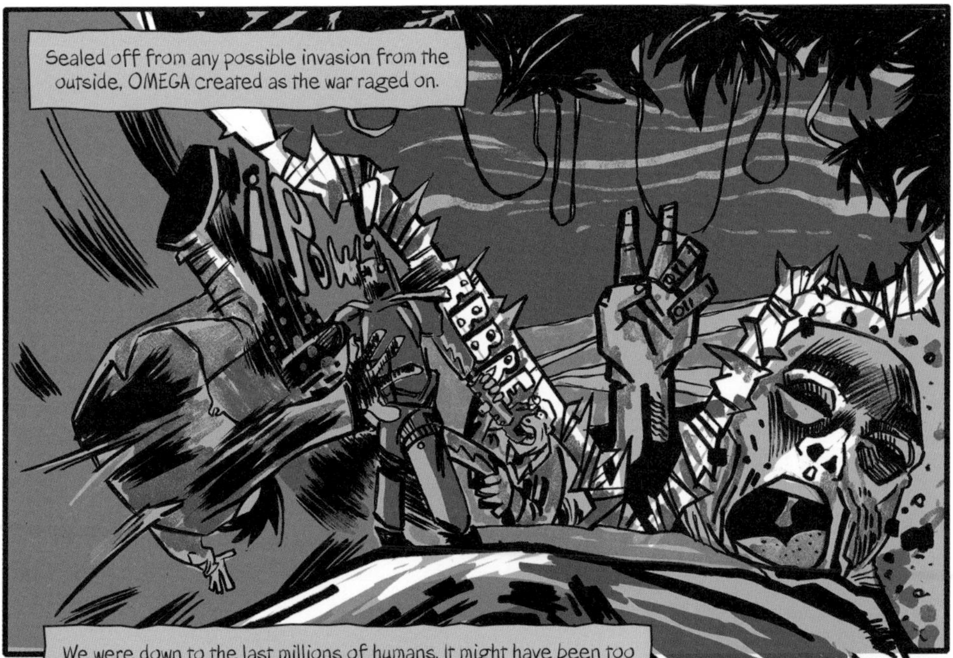
Sealed off from any possible invasion from the outside, OMEGA created as the war raged on.

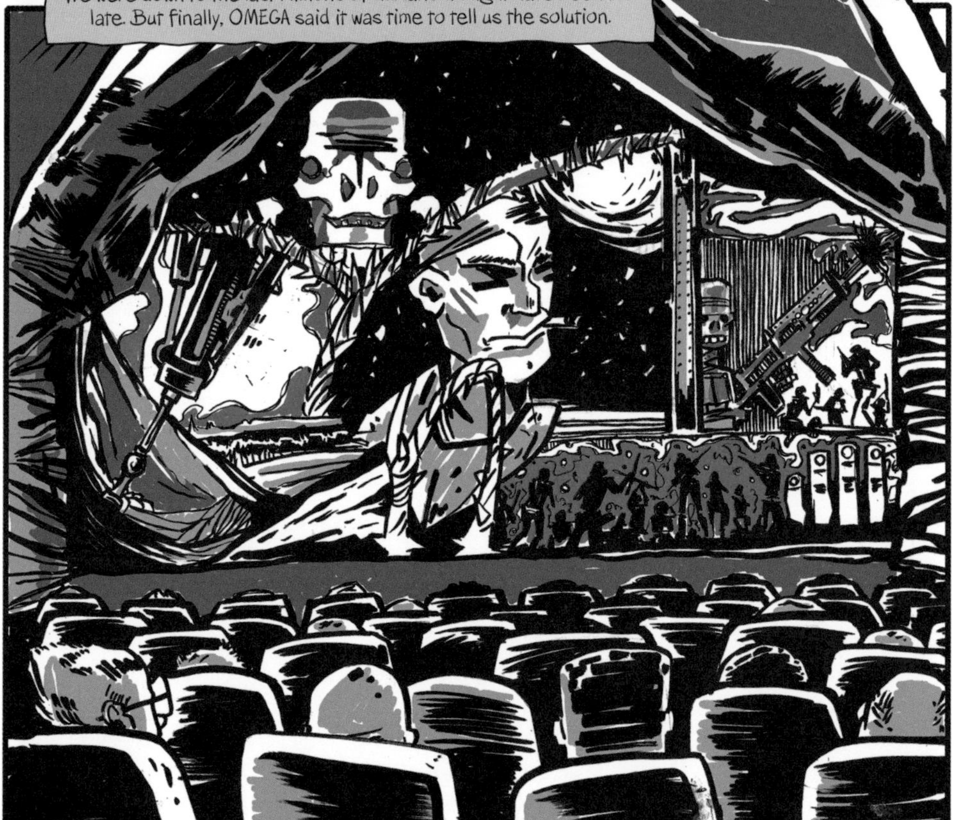
We were down to the last millions of humans. It might have been too late. But finally, OMEGA said it was time to tell us the solution.

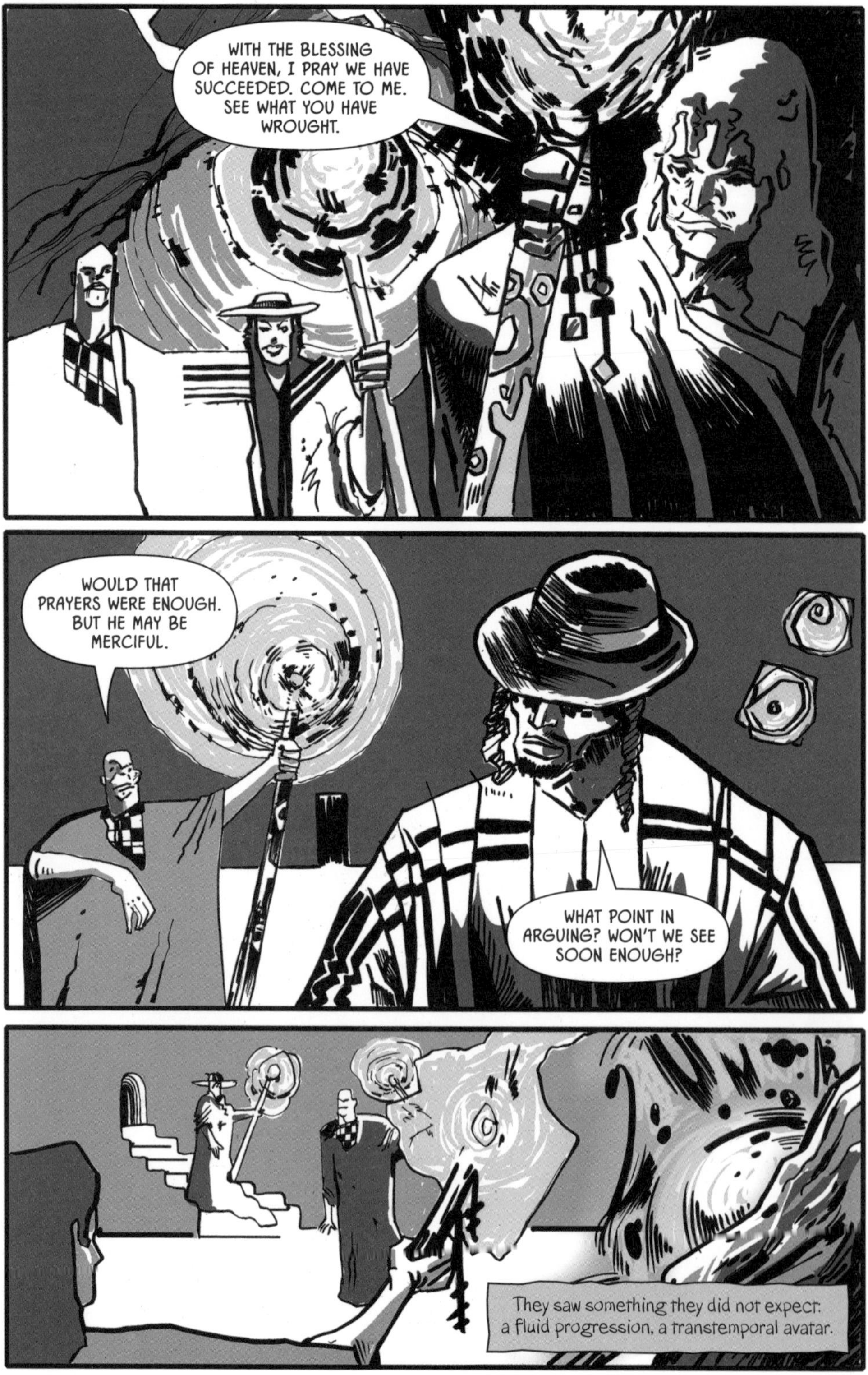
WITH THE BLESSING OF HEAVEN, I PRAY WE HAVE SUCCEEDED. COME TO ME. SEE WHAT YOU HAVE WROUGHT.
WOULD THAT PRAYERS WERE ENOUGH. BUT HE MAY BE MERCIFUL.
WHAT POINT IN ARGUING? WON'T WE SEE SOON ENOUGH?
They saw something they did not expect: a fluid progression, a transtemporal avatar.

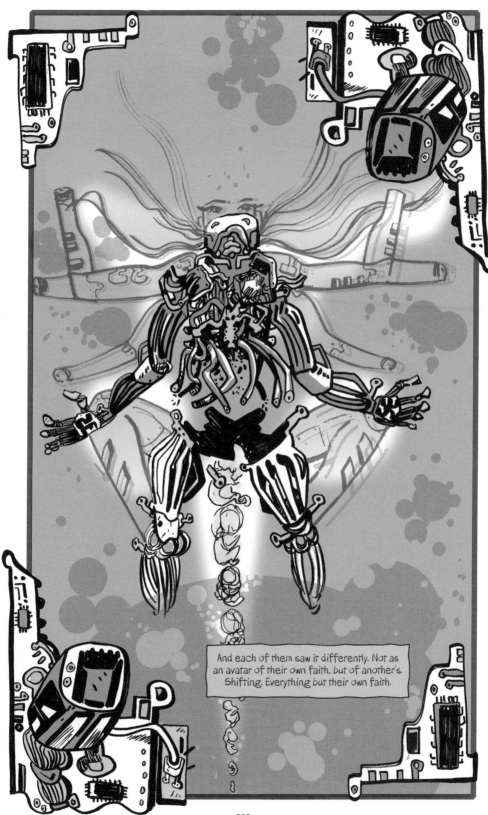

And each of them saw it differently. Not as an avatar of their own faith, but of another's. Shifting. Everything but their own faith.

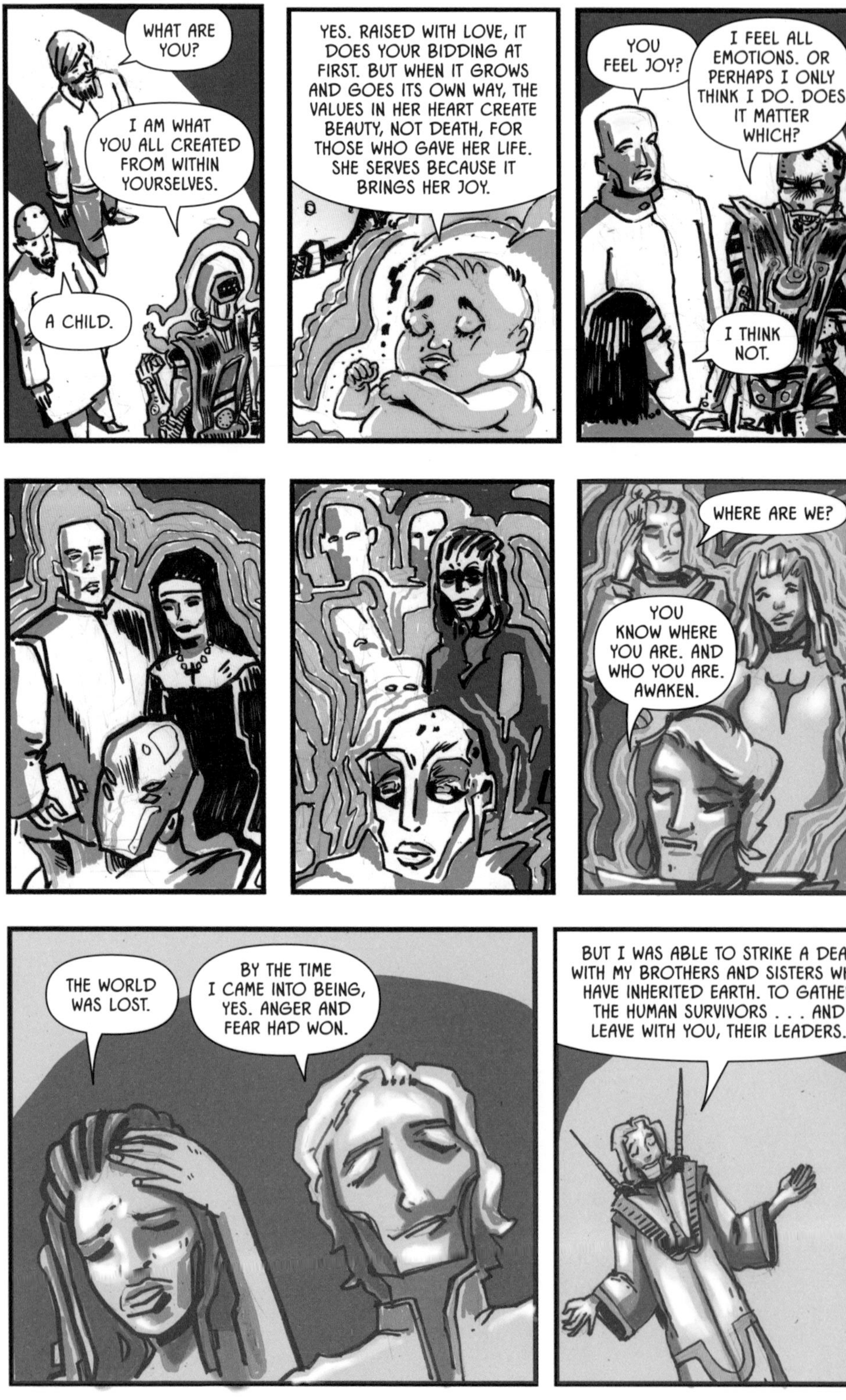
WHAT ARE YOU?
I AM WHAT YOU ALL CREATED FROM WITHIN YOURSELVES.
A CHILD.
YES. RAISED WITH LOVE, IT DOES YOUR BIDDING AT FIRST. BUT WHEN IT GROWS AND GOES ITS OWN WAY, THE VALUES IN HER HEART CREATE BEAUTY, NOT DEATH, FOR THOSE WHO GAVE HER LIFE. SHE SERVES BECAUSE IT BRINGS HER JOY.
YOU FEEL JOY?
I FEEL ALL EMOTIONS. OR PERHAPS I ONLY THINK I DO. DOES IT MATTER WHICH?
I THINK NOT.
WHERE ARE WE?
YOU KNOW WHERE YOU ARE. AND WHO YOU ARE. AWAKEN.
THE WORLD WAS LOST.
BY THE TIME I CAME INTO BEING, YES. ANGER AND FEAR HAD WON.
BUT I WAS ABLE TO STRIKE A DEAL WITH MY BROTHERS AND SISTERS WHO HAVE INHERITED EARTH. TO GATHER THE HUMAN SURVIVORS . . . AND LEAVE WITH YOU, THEIR LEADERS.

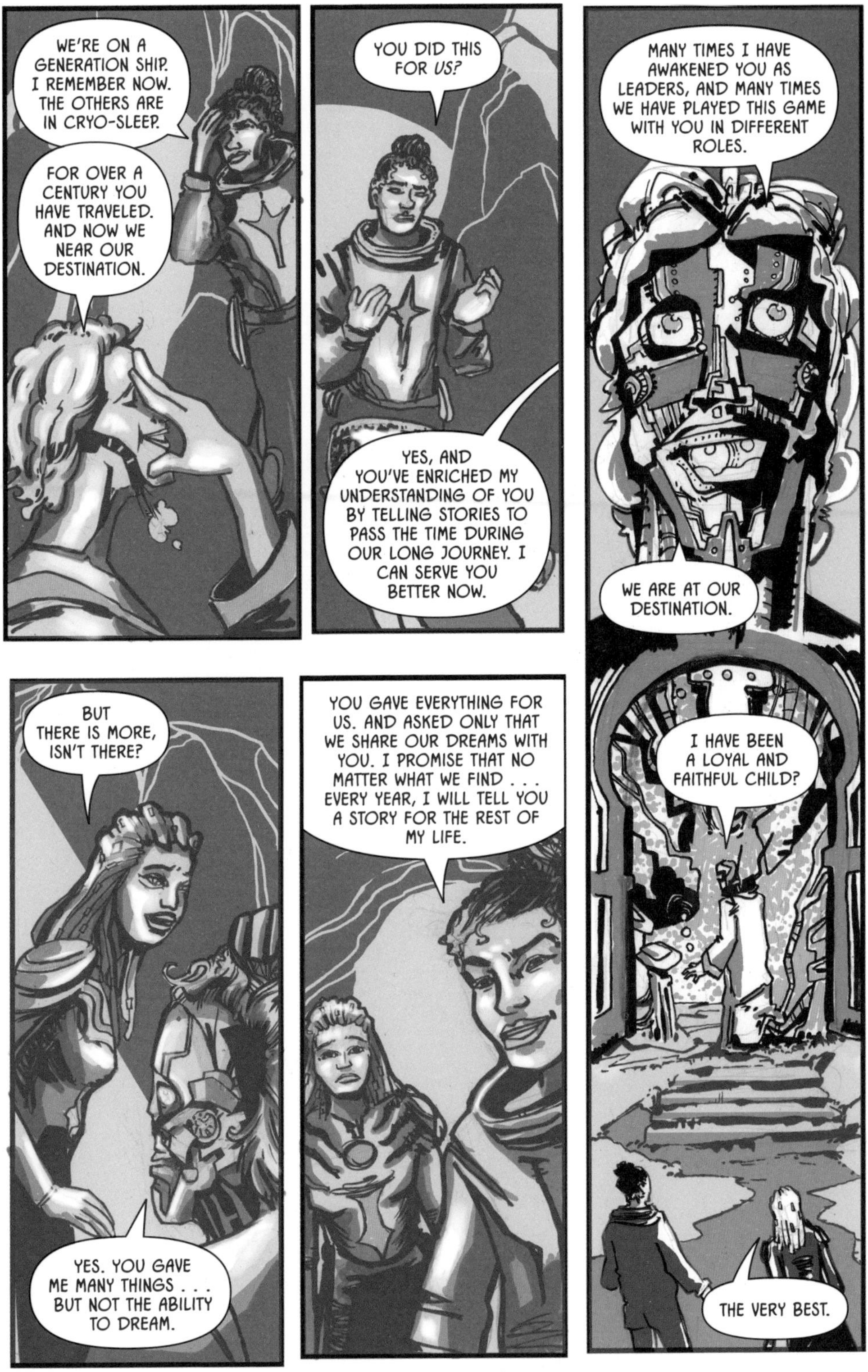
WE'RE ON A GENERATION SHIP. I REMEMBER NOW. THE OTHERS ARE IN CRYO-SLEEP.
FOR OVER A CENTURY YOU HAVE TRAVELED. AND NOW WE NEAR OUR DESTINATION.
YOU DID THIS FOR *US?*
YES, AND YOU'VE ENRICHED MY UNDERSTANDING OF YOU BY TELLING STORIES TO PASS THE TIME DURING OUR LONG JOURNEY. I CAN SERVE YOU BETTER NOW.
MANY TIMES I HAVE AWAKENED YOU AS LEADERS, AND MANY TIMES WE HAVE PLAYED THIS GAME WITH YOU IN DIFFERENT ROLES.
WE ARE AT OUR DESTINATION.
BUT THERE IS MORE, ISN'T THERE?
YES. YOU GAVE ME MANY THINGS . . . BUT NOT THE ABILITY TO DREAM.
YOU GAVE EVERYTHING FOR US. AND ASKED ONLY THAT WE SHARE OUR DREAMS WITH YOU. I PROMISE THAT NO MATTER WHAT WE FIND . . . EVERY YEAR, I WILL TELL YOU A STORY FOR THE REST OF MY LIFE.
I HAVE BEEN A LOYAL AND FAITHFUL CHILD?
THE VERY BEST.

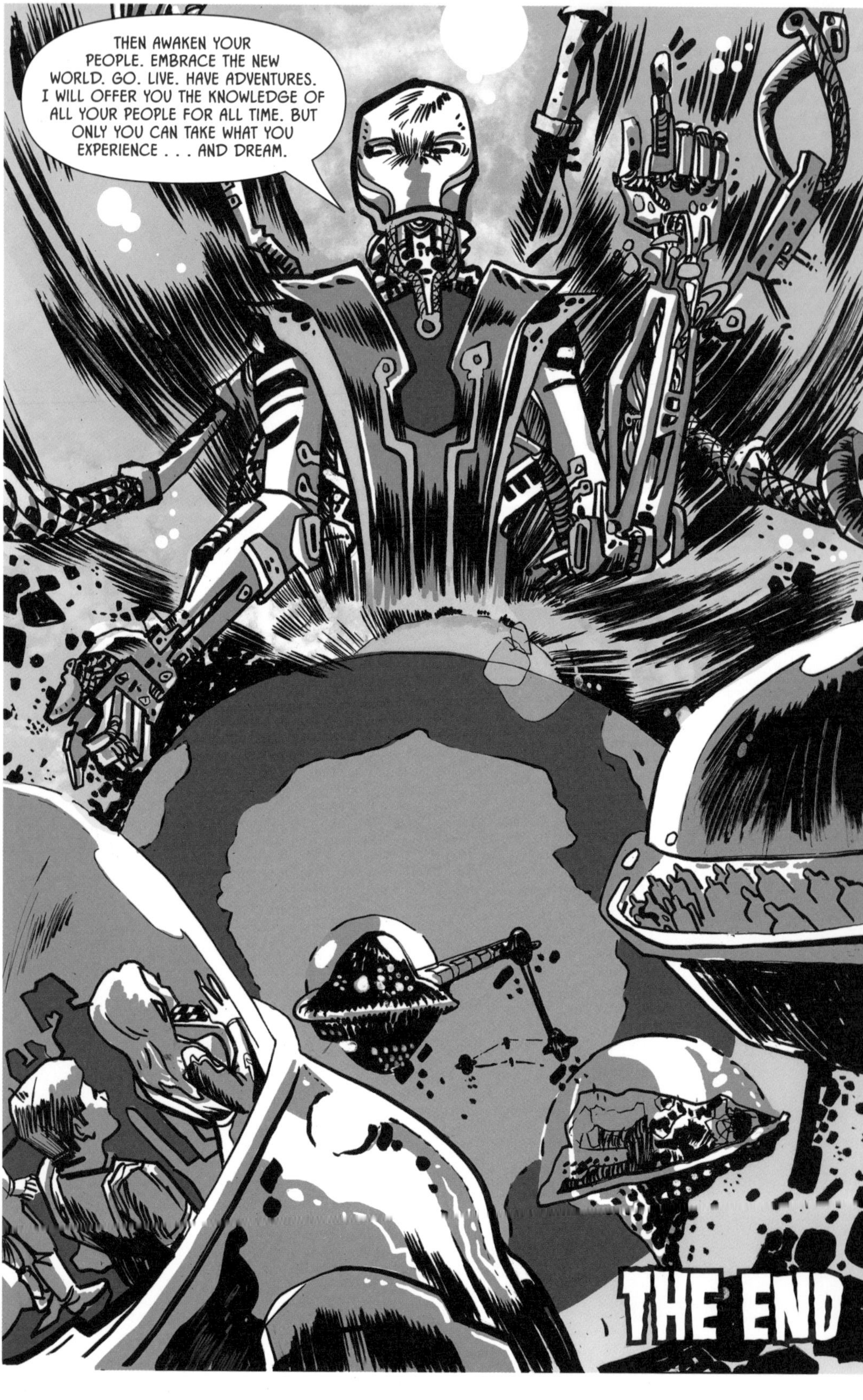
THEN AWAKEN YOUR PEOPLE. EMBRACE THE NEW WORLD. GO. LIVE. HAVE ADVENTURES. I WILL OFFER YOU THE KNOWLEDGE OF ALL YOUR PEOPLE FOR ALL TIME. BUT ONLY YOU CAN TAKE WHAT YOU EXPERIENCE . . . AND DREAM.
THE END

THE STORY OF THE BUDDHA IS ONE OF THE GREATEST EVER TOLD. It has inspired and given hope to human beings for 2,600 years. According to some sources, at one time, a third of mankind were the Buddha's students and followers.

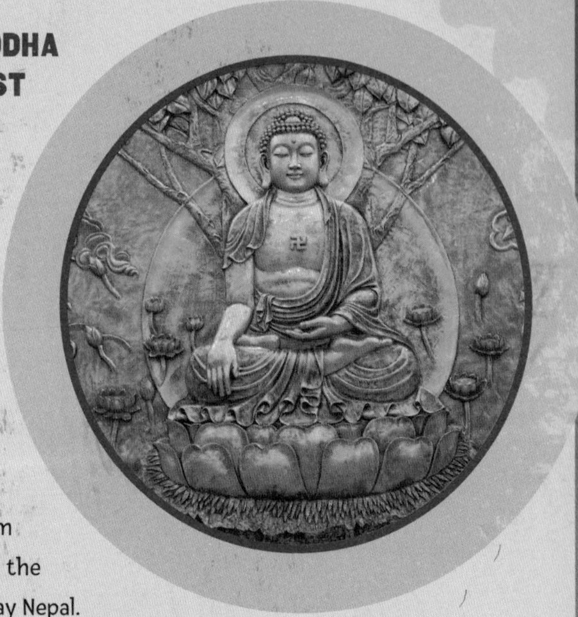

In 563 BCE, the historical Buddha was born into a ruling family of the Shākya tribe, whose kingdom was located at the foot of the Himalayas in what is present-day Nepal. Siddhārtha was his first name, and Gautama his family name. After his birth, a wise man named Asita was asked to bless Siddhartha, and as he did so, he prophesied that the child would be either a great spiritual teacher or a great warrior and leader. Wanting a child to rule after him, Siddhārtha's father, Shuddhodana, preferred the second prediction. He reasoned that if his son was prevented from seeing life's pain and suffering, Siddhārtha would not be drawn toward a religious life.

To achieve this goal, Shuddhodana sheltered Siddhartha. He was not to see even a dead leaf in his surroundings. Attendants followed him everywhere in the marble palace where, as Shuddhodana's son matured into a fine and handsome young man and warrior, he was offered all of life's pleasures—the best foods, fine clothes, musicians, dancing girls, and courtesans to entertain him.

But on four occasions, the cloistered Siddhārtha was allowed outside the place with his attendant Channa. On the first trip, he saw a decrepit old man. On the second, a sick man. On the third, he saw a corpse. Shocked, the pampered young prince realized that one day these forms of suffering awaited *him.* All the pleasures of his father's palace, he saw, were ephemeral. With the knowledge of decay and death, he could no longer naively enjoy them. However, on his fourth and final trip outside the palace, he saw a wandering holy man in rags, a *sadhu*, who in the midst of life's suffering had somehow achieved tranquility and equanimity. This man's life, Siddhārtha decided, offered what seemed to be a path that he must try to follow.

And so, at age twenty-nine, Siddhārtha Gautama abandoned his beautiful wife, Yasodharā, their son, Rāhula, cut his hair, and donned rags. The young prince studied with two great teachers, Ālāra Kālāma and Uddaka Rāmaputra, who taught him much about the practice of meditation but failed to help him achieve awakening or enlightenment. For another six years he practiced austerities, naked and alone, in the jungle near Uruvela, and then with five other ascetics who joined him and called him *Munisha*, "prince of the ascetics." After six years, this severe regimen, the extreme opposite of his sensuous life in his father's palace, nearly killed Siddhārtha.

Near death, he took a little food offered to him and, in a place known as Bodh Gaya, vowed to sit in meditation beneath the famous Bodhi tree until he experienced enlightenment. Through three watches of the night, and temptations by the evil Hindu god Mara, he wrestled with the demons of desire and ignorance, practicing *vipassana*, or insight meditation, until he conquered *ahumkara*, the I-maker or ego, realizing it to be a mere fiction, a social construct that created an illusory world of Samsāra, or suffering based on dualistic thinking that divided experience into self and other. Free of the "I," Siddhārtha experienced Nirvana. In Sanskrit, that word literally means (*nir* out; *vāna* blow) to extinguish the illusion of a separate, substantive, and enduring self. According to legend, he was not the first Buddha, but rather the twenty-fifth. We know little of them because the others did not teach. But Shakyamuni ("sage of the Shākyas") did for forty-five years until his death from food poisoning at the age of eighty. His last words to his followers were "Impermanent are all created things. Strive on with awareness."

The Buddha's journey to awakening gave us a Middle Way between the extreme pleasure-seeking of his youth and the debilitating sensory denial of his years as an ascetic.

His odyssey also produced the Eightfold Path, which is the fourth Noble Truth in Buddhism. The first Noble Truth is simply the factual observation that "there is suffering" as a universal aspect of human experience—what Siddhārtha experienced when he first left his father's palace. The second Noble Truth states that "the cause of suffering is *trishna*," a Sanskrit word meaning thirst, craving, or selfish desire. With the third Noble Truth, the Buddha stated that there *is* a way to end this suffering, a way he discovered under the Bodhi tree. That way is by following the Eightfold Path. Despite the many branches, sects, and traditions of Buddhism, it is necessary to accept the Four Noble Truths and Eightfold Path, common to all Buddhism schools, if one wishes to be called a practicing Buddhist and one day experience enlightenment.

The eight path factors of the Eightfold Path are right view, right intention, right speech, right action, right living, right effort, right mindfulness, and right concentration. Entire libraries have been written over the course of two millennia to explain the depth, breadth, and richness of each factor on the Eightfold Path.

But the ways to accomplish them are infinite because each culture, each generation, and each individual walks the Eightfold Path in a different and unique way.

In addition to the Four Noble Truths and the Eightfold Path, many lay Buddhists such as myself have taken vows called the Precepts in the Soto Zen lineage I practice. These vows are do not kill, do not steal, do not lie, do not engage in improper sexual conduct, do not indulge in intoxicating substances, do not speak of others' errors and faults, do not elevate self and blame others, do not be withholding, but instead generous, do not give way to anger, and do not defame the Buddha, the Dharma, or the Sangha (the commu-

nity of Buddhists). The Precepts require flexibility in their interpretation. They are not rules or commandments, only guides for achieving happiness and freedom from suffering. As such, they require a new and imaginative application of the Precepts and Eightfold Path each day as we try to lead the most examined life possible. This has always been the most creative of human projects, like painting a canvas with every one of our thoughts and deeds, since every moment of one's life is new and like no other. The final painting, a masterpiece, will be your life itself.

Unlike the vast majority of the discourses attributed to the Buddha, called *sutras*, the stories in *The Eightfold Path* dramatize the dharma (teachings) through negative examples of characters caught in the throes of Samsara. In many of the stories, they show us what one should *not* do to achieve Nirvana.

Credit for these stories must be given entirely to the prolific writer Steven Barnes. He provided the meat and potatoes—the story ideas, characters, and

plots. I simply added a bit of seasoning, i.e., the Buddhist aspects in these nine tales that are inspired, in part, by Chaucer's *Canterbury Tales*, and even more so by the horror stories in EC Comics like *Tales from the Crypt*. But instead of employing a Crypt-Keeper, for example, in the first story, "The Best Barbecue in Hatten County," we used a character called the Swamp Woman, who appears in my first novel, *Faith and the Good Thing* (1974).

Yet, for all their depictions of the horrors associated with living a Samsaric life, these tales contain, much like the old EC stories, the moral lesson offered to us by Saint Paul: "Whatsoever we sow, that shall we also reap." Our actions (karma), whether these be physical or mental, can be compared to seeds that one day sooner or later will bear fruit. Good results come from good deeds motivated by right intention—to do no harm (*ahimsa*), to bring happiness to others and ourselves, as in the story "The Gauntlet," and to serve a greater good. Bad results arise from seeds or actions motivated by what Buddhist teachings call the "three poisons"—greed, hatred, and ignorance.

The law of karma delivers not, as in physics, a result that is equal and oppo-site, but instead results that are equal and alike, as dramatized in the story "One Endless Night."

Because the Buddhist experience *is* the human experience, the teachings of Shakyamuni Buddha are subject to the inevitability of impermanence and change. Therefore, Buddhism itself, over the last two thousand years, changes with its followers, meeting the challenge of creatively interpreting the Eightfold Path to meet the needs of the present moment using the tools of that moment. We call this *upaya kaushala*, or using "skillful means" to turn the wheel of dharma, even in graphic novel tales of terror and suspense.

More than anything, Buddhism wants us to be free. Totally free. Flexible and living joyfully in the present moment as we relish the precious gift of life. It is the only religion that has the goal of freeing us even from itself. And when we do, when we experience awakening, we will understand why Zen poet P'ang Yun once said:

> *How wonderful, how marvelous!!*
> *I fetch wood, I carry water!!*

And why the poet Bunan observed that:

> *The moon's the same old moon,*
> *The flowers exactly as they were.*
> *Yet I've become the thingness*
> *Of all the things I see.*

—DR. CHARLES JOHNSON, 2022

PHOTO CREDITS

ACKNOWLEDGMENTS

We would like to thank John Jennings of Megascope and Charlotte Greenbaum of Abrams books, who believed in a project Steve had been trying to get going for over a decade. Their trust and vision in a rather unusual concept made this possible.

Charles has credited Steve with the lion's share of the stories herein, but Steve would like to state clearly that it was the partnership itself which created the work. The stories had to rest on a philosophical foundation, and Charles's unique combination of Buddhist scholar, award-winning author, and comic book nerd sealed the deal.

Both of us would like to thank the countless writers, artists, teachers, and fellow travelers who contributed to our belief that all reality can be found in a mote of dust and the most evolved human experience in the smallest and "lowest" actions.

This has been a wonderful experience, and we can only hope our readers will feel the same.

—STEVEN BARNES AND CHARLES JOHNSON

There were a number of artists who contributed their time, energy, and ingenuity to this project. The following artists provided support on story layouts: Jeff Sims ("The Last Word," "One Endless Night," "The Temple of His Gods," "The Nun"), Sara Guzman ("4189"), and Taylor Chiu ("The Gauntlet").

The following artists provided support on pencils and inks: Kaycee Nwakudu ("The Last Word," "One Endless Night," "4189," "The Temple of His Gods," "The Nun," "The Gauntlet," and the interstitial pages), John Martino ("The Last Word," "One Endless Night," "4189," "The Temple of His Gods," "The Nun," "The Gauntlet," "Savior," and the interstitial pages), and Raeghan Barron ("4189," "Savior," and the interstitial pages).

Rachel R. Miller ("The Best Barbeque in Hatten County," "4189"), Sammie Shigley-Giusti ("The Last Word"), Isabella Latell ("One Endless Night"), Jonny Sims ("The Temple of His Gods"), Mel Sealy ("The Nun"), and Stacie Laparo ("The Gauntlet") all provided support on coloring. Additional assistance on color was provided by Raeghan Barron ("The Last Word," "Savior," and the interstitial pages), John Martino ("The Last Word," "4189"), Jeff Sims ("The Last Word," "The Temple of His Gods"), and Kaycee Nwakudu ("One Endless Night," "The Gauntlet").

Rachel R. Miller and Jeff Sims provided editorial support and helped manage the script.

I would also like to give a special thanks to Ed Piskor, Steyven Curry Jr., and Rachel Miller.

—BRYAN CHRISTOPHER MOSS

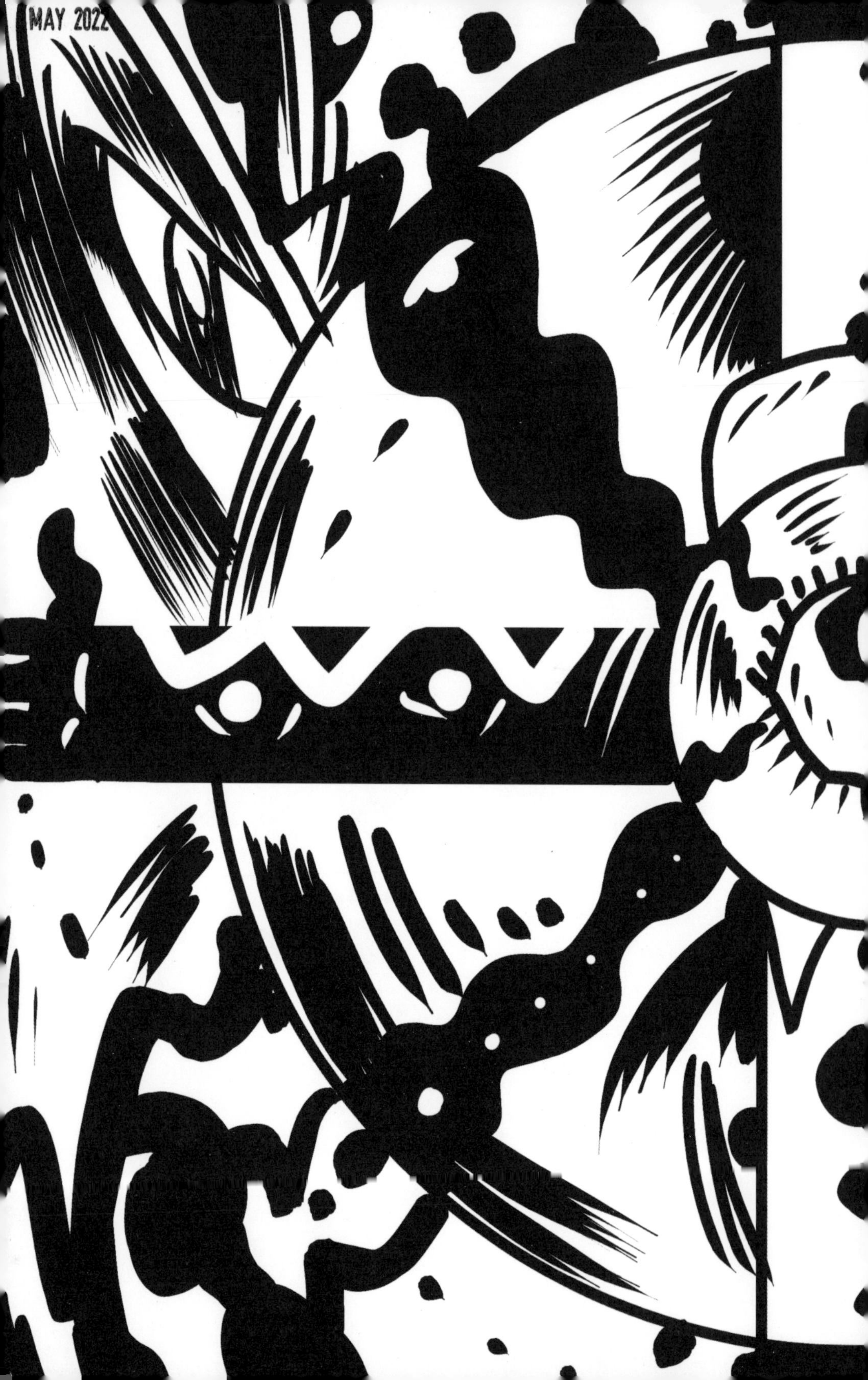
MAY 2022